The influence of pornography on behaviour

The influence of pornography on behaviour

edited by

Maurice Yaffé
Department of Psychological Medicine,
Guy's Hospital, London SE1

and

Edward C. Nelson
Department of Psychology, Institute of Psychiatry,
London SE5

1982

ACADEMIC PRESS
A Subsidiary of Harcourt Brace Jovanovich, Publishers
London New York
Paris San Diego San Francisco
São Paulo Sydney Tokyo Toronto

ACADEMIC PRESS INC. (LONDON) LTD
24/28 Oval Road, London NW1 7DX

United States Edition published by
ACADEMIC PRESS INC.
111 Fifth Avenue, New York, New York, 10003

British Library Cataloguing in Publication Data

The influence of pornography on behaviour.
1. Pornography – Social aspects
I. Yaffé, M.   II. Nelson, E.
363.4'7   HQ471

ISBN 0-12-767850-6

LCCCN 82-71234

Typeset by Oxford Verbatim Limited
and printed in Great Britain
by St Edmundsbury Press,
Bury St Edmunds, Suffolk

Contributors

Dorothy M. Dallas*
Formerly Lecturer in Education
Faculty of Education
King's College
Strand, London WC2

Antony Grey
Barrister-at-Law
Secretary of the Sexual Law
   Reform Society
90 Upland Road
London N8 9NJ

Lionel C. R. Haward
Professor of Clinical Psychology
Department of Psychology
University of Surrey
Guildford, Surrey GU2 5HX

Jonathan Miller
Theatre Director
London NW1

Edward C. Nelson†
Clinical Psychologist
Currently Visiting Research Fellow
Department of Psychology
Institute of Psychiatry
De Crespigny Park
London SE5 8AF

David Offenbach
Solicitor
29 Old Bond Street
London W1X 4JE

Christine Pickard
General Practitioner
89D Robert Street
London NW1 3QT

Sir Martin Roth
Professor of Psychiatry
Department of Psychiatry
University of Cambridge Clinical
   School
Addenbrooke's Hospital
Cambridge CB2 2QQ

Peter Webb
Senior Lecturer in Art History
Faculty of Art and Design
Middlesex Polytechnic
Cat Hill, Barnet
Hertfordshire EN4 8HT

Maurice Yaffé
Senior Clinical Psychologist
The York Clinic
Department of Psychological Medicine
Guy's Hospital
London SE1 1NP

* Deceased.
† *Formerly* at the Department of Psychiatry and Biobehavioral Sciences, University of California at Los Angeles and Harbor/UCLA Medical Center, Torrance, California, USA.

Comment is free but facts are sacred
C. P. Scott

Preface

Society's endless preoccupation with sex is matched only by its fascination with and attraction to violence. To some, these developments account for many of the ills we observe in the world today. In a short period of time we have changed from a society in which religion exerted enormous influence over man's behaviour through the propagation of Christian values to one in which those values are no longer predominantly accepted; some consider this to be good, others bad. There are those who believe that society's increasing permissiveness jeopardizes the stability of both marriage and the family, and they wish to protect their children from such influences. Pornography, in their view, is an advertisement for permissiveness. In comparison to many of the world's major problems, the debate over pornography may seem unimportant. Society after all is undergoing one of its largest upheavals in history, and order and stability are impossible to find anywhere. Everything is in a state of flux, and many real dangers exist. Thus, to many people, our continuing concern with pornography appears to be out of proportion with the actual risk that explicit sexual material poses to society. Others disagree. They see pornography as a cause, not a consequence, of our current social turmoil, and believe that their opposition to it will have an important effect upon the kind of society we have in the future.

This book contains a collection of papers written by experts who offer us a broad perspective on obscenity and pornography. Much of course has already been written about the problems in this field. Why do we need to examine it again? Have we not already made up our minds? Most of us, seeing no satisfactory resolution in sight, seem to simply agree to disagree about pornography. The nature of pornography, however, has changed dramatically within the last decade in terms of the violence it portrays. And science, as some of our authors point out, is beginning to demonstrate some harmful consequences associated with exposure to such material. Obviously, these developments justify a re-examination of the issues surrounding pornography.

The following chapters provide an unusually objective analysis of the problems in this field, and they were written for those who have a professional interest in sexually explicit materials, especially psychologists and psychiatrists, sexual educators, legal practitioners, medical practitioners, clinical social workers, social and political scientists, and both graduate and undergraduate students. Readers will undoubtedly be able to come to their own conclusions regarding the many valid arguments on both sides of this debate.

London, August 1982   *Edward C. Nelson*
                                                          Maurice Yaffé

Introduction by Edward C. Nelson

Pornography is one of those controversial social issues that drives most people to extremes of opinion. And yet, more than we care to admit, our attitudes and beliefs about sexually explicit materials are often based on little more than various subjective impressions and untested assumptions. None the less most of us adhere strongly to our own opinions in the continuing debate about pornography and it seems unlikely that factual evidence alone, however scientific, will succeed in convincing many people to alter their views. Indeed, attempts by social scientists to furnish objective information about the influence of pornography on behaviour have consistently shown that people with opposing views can each find support for their own views in the same body of evidence. Added to this, many people simply feel that "you can use studies to demonstrate whatever you want". Even among social and behavioural scientists themselves, there is some doubt about whether science can demonstrate convincingly the harmful effects attributed to viewing pornography and/or violence, or prove that there are no harmful effects. Although many people are convinced that a causal relationship exists between the availability of pornography and the decline of a society, history is also thought to provide few answers in regard to the influence of pornography on behaviour. Yet it is extremely difficult for these people to give up the belief that pornography, so often not really erotic, both directly and indirectly promotes antisocial behaviour and, in particular, aggression against women. What is unique about pornography is that it blatantly contradicts so many traditional beliefs in societies which characteristically have rejected censorship as a form of control because it infringes upon freedom of expression and choice. It is this collision of culture and control which exacerbates the issues surrounding obscenity and pornography.

Questions about the possible consequences of exposure to sexually explicit material frequently fall within the domain of psychology and psychiatry, although there are clearly other issues which involve law, religion, education and art. These issues relate to what kind of a society we want to live in and want our children to grow up in. Yet we clearly are not of one mind in this respect. Various groups within society hold different views regarding explicit sexual material. Some see it as merely a dehumanizing influence which acts to erode traditional sexual practices and moral values, and fear that other negative consequences may result from its continued availability. Many of these individuals are in favour of censorship and their reasons for this are quite clear. They fear that viewing pornography will lessen inhibitions so that individuals will be more willing to try in their own lives what they have seen on film or in magazines. Although reducing or overcoming sexual inhibitions by viewing explicit sexual material may be a worthwhile goal in therapy, such materials are not limited to therapeutic uses alone and can thus affect anyone. To opponents of pornography, that is one of the major problems. They fear that exposure to such material will negatively influence the attitudes and behaviour of those who choose to see it. The fact that much contemporary pornography portrays aggression against women as being not only justified but acceptable only heightens this fear. This has led some writers to question seriously whether repeated portrayals of sex and violence will adversely affect men to the extent that they eventually change their attitudes about the appropriateness of using force in sexual relations. Feminist writers, in particular, believe that such a reaction is likely to occur and have carried this argument forcefully into the public arena. Interest in sexual aggression against women has increased enormously as a result of their efforts. Researchers also have become increasingly interested in the effects of mass media presentations of violent sexuality upon attitudes and behaviour. This interest is strengthened by research data on observing aggression *per se* that shows viewing aggression facilitates subsequent aggression. Social scientists, however, still disagree about how dangerous viewing violence may be, and some in fact continue to maintain that it is not dangerous despite much research evidence which shows that under certain conditions viewing violence can have a powerful impact for at least a short period of time in highly aroused and angered individuals. Now that portrayals of rape and other forms of sexual aggression toward women are an accepted part of the repertoire of pornography, many people believe that this poses a serious threat to women in particular. And, as recent research evidence tends to suggest, this belief merits serious consideration.

Allegations of harm attributed to pornography have been previously investigated of course. In 1970, for example, the first large-scale evaluation of sexually explicit material was conducted in the United States by the *Commission on Obscenity and Pornography*. After two years of study the Commission concluded that there was no reliable evidence for the belief that exposure to, or use of, pornography plays a significant role in the causation of social or individual harms such as crime, delinquency, sexual or non-sexual deviancy, or severe emotional disturbances. Their report, however, was promptly rejected by the President and the American Congress. Logically, this action was not unexpected as the report provided evidence of something that the Congress did not expect to hear or wish to believe, and its judgements about the Commission's experimental procedures and resultant recommendations simply reflected the fact that its own theoretical predilections

were in marked contrast to the empirical evidence. This is not to say, however, that the Commission's findings were universally accepted within the
scientific community. They were not. But even if that had been the case, in all
probability it would not have changed anything. Indeed, there is considerable
evidence to show that people tend to interpret evidence so as to maintain their
initial beliefs – a finding which challenges the simple assumption that data
relevant to such beliefs are processed impartially. This research indicates that
judgements about the value and meaning of scientific evidence are biased by
the consistency of that evidence with the reader's attitudes, beliefs and
expectations. Through such biased assimilation, individuals tend to reject
empirical evidence that disputes their intial views and to accept and derive
satisfaction from evidence that appears consistent with their beliefs.

Research on biased assimilation and attitude polarization points out that
beliefs frequently survive the addition of non-supportive evidence because
people tend to examine it hypercritically while accepting confirming evidence
at face value. Of course this fact hardly seems surprising; indeed, anyone who
has ever argued about political, social or religious issues should be familiar
with this phenomenon. Attempts by social scientists to influence the debate
on pornography by providing objective data demonstrate this clearly and
emphasize the limitations of empirical evidence in shaping a consensus about
burning social issues. In 1972, for example, an investigation of pornography
was carried out in Britain by the Longford Committee, a pro-censorship
group. The Committee's task was to "see what means of tackling the problem
of pornography would command general support". However, in an effort to
curb any criticisms of bias, the Committee went to great lengths to see that
groups whose point of view was not represented on the Committee itself
should have every opportunity of giving evidence. An independently com-
missioned critique of the available scientific evidence regarding pornography
was therefore obtained to help in the analysis. Ironically, the Committee's
attempt to provide for an open debate that would be both objective and
rational led to this curious disclaimer of the research evidence:

> We would like to say that in our view the type of research described ... is not
> necessarily very helpful in assessing the effects of pornographic materials, since
> we do not share the belief that human beings can be usefully considered, or their
> responses measured, in clinical isolation from the many other aspects of
> experience likely to affect each individual. Nor do we feel that to use students in
> such tests is justifiable, and we cannot therefore endorse the suggestion for
> future research ... (p. 498).*

While research studies concerning pornography undoubtedly have their

* Research Survey by M. Yaffé. Appendix V in *Pornography: The Longford Report*, 1972.

limitations, rejecting all scientific contributions only emphasizes how resistant beliefs can be to the addition of non-supportive evidence. It seems likely, however, that the Committee would have been willing to acknowledge the scientific evidence if it had supported the argument that pornography is harmful.

Most of the early experimental research on pornography led many people to believe that sexual material had little, if any, effect on the behaviour and emotions of those individuals who were exposed to it; indeed, pornography was thought to be actually boring as a consequence of repeated exposure. Moreover, the absence of any definitive evidence to support the belief that exposure to pornography causes immediate or delayed antisocial behaviour among adults contributed to the idea that pornography is essentially harmless. Pornography might be offensive, distasteful and a nuisance, but it did not appear to pose a significant threat to society. Those in favour of pornography were pleased of course by this outcome and used these research findings to support their belief that pornography benefits both its users and society. Opponents of censorship were also pleased, but not all favour pornography; they simply believe that it should be allowed to exist. Yet many opponents would consider censorship if it could be proved that pornography is harmful, either to the user, or to society at large. Science, however, provided no substantial evidence of such harms which opponents of censorship *per se* might respond to. Armed with the support of science and being able to rely upon the fact that censorship is anathema to most people, those in favour of pornography found it easier to promulgate their views. And, given the existing value system of Western society, pornography's growing acceptability was virtually guaranteed. Rejecting puritanism for permissiveness during the last few decades, society has chosen to exercise less and less censorship in the pursuit of freedom of expression and individual rights. Freedom, however, is invariably restricted in all societies; we do not tolerate a person's freedom to infringe upon others' rights, for instance, and there are other situations in which we agree to give up some of our freedom for the common good. In the case of pornography, the common justification of those seeking to prohibit it is based upon a belief in its individual and social harmfulness. Unfortunately, the inherent premise of their argument is that pornography has only one set of consequences, all of which are thought to be bad. Proponents of pornography share this myopic view, only in this case the consequences are thought to be good. *Pornography, however, does not have only one set of consequences*; such a statement may be objectionable to extremists on both sides of the argument, but it is undoubtedly true none the less.

Science often finds itself embroiled in arguments about which it can provide only limited information. Such was certainly the case with regard to the 1970 debate about pornography in the United States. Thus, while acknowledging the imperfections in much of its time-limited research, the *Commission on Obscenity and Pornography* none the less concluded that explicit sexual materials are virtually harmless. This judgement seemed premature to many researchers at the time, especially while little was actually known and much more remained to be investigated. For example, the Commission lacked adequate evidence for making a judgement on the effect of pornography on young people as it was not ethically possible to use them in such studies. Many questions remained, therefore, about how pornography would affect a child's future sexual identity, attitudes, values and behaviour. Evidence was also lacking in regards to the effects of exposure to aggressive and deviant portrayals of sexual relationships; thus, instead of including assessments of interest in and arousal to depictions of rape, sex with children, and other violent and deviant themes, these early studies primarily assessed both normals' and sexual offenders' self-reported interest in and arousal to non-aggressive sexual material such as nudity, petting, intercourse and oral-genital behaviour. Of course the prevalence of violent and deviant themes in pornography is only a relatively recent phenomenon, despite the fact that sado-masochism has always been a tradition in pornographic literature. An analysis of paperback sex novels that are widely available on news-stands throughout America indicated that the number of rape scenes doubled between 1968 and 1976, and the woman almost always enjoys it (Smith, 1976). Smith describes this pornography as "basically a literature of power and domination, a literature of machismo". The attitude that is conveyed to the reader endorses aggression against women by pointing out continually that the female really does want to be subjugated; as Smith puts it, "no matter how much she says no, go ahead and do it anyway, because she'll be grateful to you afterward".

Genuine information on the issues raised here was almost entirely lacking when the Commission reached its conclusions regarding the influence of pornography on both individuals and society. Critics, of course, were quick to point out the absence of detailed knowledge about such issues, but to no avail; the harmfulness of pornography had been refuted by science. Moral absolutists across America hailed this as a "Magna Carta for pornographers". Offended by what seemed to be inevitable none the less, moralists rejected the scientific findings, less on the basis of fact and procedure than on the assumption that pornography is simply evil and inherently liable to cause harm. Unfortunately, in reaching a conclusion which at best was provisional, science found itself locked into a political argument, not a scientific one, over whether pornography is a good or bad thing. Science appeared to be endorsing the value of pornography without reservation, despite acknowledging the limitations of its research findings. Proponents of pornography took advantage of this opportunity by advertising that studies had shown pornography to be good for you. Opponents, of course, felt differently; they believed that the battle within society to define the moral structure within which man shall live had been dealt a severe blow. Obviously, given the existing value system of each side, the scientific evidence was unlikely to win over many adherents of the moral majority.

Science's interest in pornography has increased enormously over the past decade; prompted both by criticism of the Commission's research and by arguments that the new sex and violence trend may affect negatively both attitudes and behaviour toward women and, in particular, may cause and/or perpetuate undesirable perceptions of rape and aggressive behaviour generally, recent studies have focused upon investigating the hypothesized link between sex and aggression. So far the evidence suggests that certain forms of pornography, those which foster the association of violence and sexuality, may exert an appreciable influence upon the way we both perceive and deal with aggression. Exposure to violent pornography, for example, appears to increase males' acceptance of interpersonal violence toward women and facilitate, under certain conditions, subsequent aggression by them. A re-examination of pornography is of particular importance now for this reason, and because these research findings are likely to be used by opponents of pornography to request new restrictions upon it. Attempts to regulate pornography, of course, inevitably raise the issue of censorship and how we wish to live in society.

Pornography is an area in which there are few certainties and little evidence to support arguments on either side of the controversy. What is neeeded most at this time is open discussion that is objective, rational and wide-ranging. In attempting to meet this need we have brought together the work of experts in the fields of psychology, psychiatry, law, education, medicine, art and the theatre.

Sir Martin Roth begins our re-examination of pornography by placing it into historical and cross-cultural perspective. The explicit representation of sexual love is to be found in all ages and epochs with some fluctuations between restraint and freedom in expression. He finds, however, that to an increasing extent the explicit materials of the last decade have been concerned with novel themes; today portrayals of sadism, violence and humiliation of women have largely replaced the more tender and caring representations of sexual love that previously characterized pornography. Posing questions about the causes for the steep escalation in its availability, Roth feels that to blame society for it all is unhelpful and unilluminating; it is more likely that the central idea of violent domination in the sexual act has caught on and spread partly because it has a certain psychological appeal. This appeal is linked to the belief that aggressiveness and power are inseparably entwined with sexual desirability and success in the male. Its transmission down the ages partly reflects the contagiousness, power and durability of certain concepts and ideas, yet Roth believes that the coupling of human aggression and male sexuality undoubtedly has some biological substrate, although it is not pre-destined by heredity. The view that pornography merely reflects the inborn constitutional predisposition to sexually violent behaviour conflicts with several lines of evidence. Patterns of behaviour are not completely determined during the first years of life; a certain measure of plasticity remains until adolescence and even later. Roth claims that it is untenable for science to argue that pornography may prove beneficial in the treatment of sexual disabilities and to assert at the same time that sexual conduct cannot be influenced so as to make it overtly aggressive and violent, particularly when some predisposition for such behaviour is already present. Contemporary pornography which fosters the association of violence and hatred with the sexual act may exert effects of fateful importance, he fears, upon the way we love and the manner in which we deal with our aggressive tendencies.

The issues surrounding censorship and total freedom of expression are discussed by our next two authors. Jonathan Miller, in his philosophical discourse on censorship, provides us with a fascinating account of how people justify their desire to suppress pornography. In attempting to distinguish and clarify the lines which separate the principles upon which exponents of censorship draw their arguments, Miller points out how easily those who oppose pornography change principles in midstream or else justify their adherence to a principle in one class, with concealed reference to the self-evidence of that in another. Examining the alleged harmful effects of pornography, he concludes that society's ability to evaluate risk is seriously in question when it judges the harms of pornography to be greater than say the well-established risks of smoking; harm is now so clearly established that "if prophylactic legislation against cigarettes were a serious intention of the law one might expect to see something more than a statutory warning on the side – on the side mind you! – of the packet." Miller's thesis is that, whereas there are dangers inherent in say the physical pollution of the environment, the anxiety over pornography and sexual misconduct is disproportionate to the risk involved; society must identify the genuine risks and exorcize the phantoms.

Another view of censorship is offered by Antony Grey. He contends that all censorship is harmful because it diminishes human freedom and interferes with the spontaneity of communication. Grey dispels the belief that opposition to censorship is based upon the assumption that all pornography is harmless; such opposition rests in fact upon the contention that the operation of censorship is at least as harmful to society as the ready availability of pornography. Censorship, he feels, is a habit of mind which, once it gains a foothold, spreads like a cancer. Whatever its starting point, the end of the censor's road is likely to be the same: repression of "dangerous" ideas, not only about sex but about morals, politics, art and life. In the end, Grey feels that the crucial questions are not whether pornography is harmful or whether it should be banned, but to what extent individuals in society should carry moral responsibility for themselves.

Dorothy Dallas is unique among our contributors in having had professional experience with sex education. Her historical account of the development and use of sexually explicit visual materials to transmit factual information about sex is more than a description of a technological advance; it is also an account of the ambivalence sex educators have had about teaching sex. Teachers, for example, have been accused of using visual materials such as films as a cloak of darkness for their own embarrassment about sex education. Ironically, Dallas points out that many films, while successful with teachers, failed to reach their intended audiences – average pupils of late adolescence – because little research had been conducted to assess their *attitudes* about the subject matter; producers simply assumed that all audiences possessed a certain set of norms in this regard. Communication through visual materials improved significantly as a result of recognizing such problems; in the past visuals tended to distort reality, to moralize, and to actually frighten audiences. Indeed, Dallas mentions that one television programme on sexually transmitted diseases, available on film, was generally thought to be too stark for schools, until one adviser showed it to a group of parents who thought it was not frightening enough. Generally, however, visual materials are intended to generate meaningful discussion about sexual issues. Pornography, in contrast to such materials, provides very poor norms with respect to both sexual attitudes and behaviour; moreover it distorts the truth when it ignores all constraints, because there is no society in which all sexuality has been given completely free rein to express itself at random. Today, Dallas indicates the use of visual materials in sex education is declining; what is taking its place now is the use of education through the emotions, whether by book or film. The use of simulation exercises and role playing enables students to become directly involved with this process which emphasizes dealing with youngsters' feelings and attitudes about sex, as well as understanding human relationships.

Shifting to different ground now, Peter Webb takes a look at erotic art and pornography. Webb's thesis is that there is a clear dividing line between the two although images of erotic art have often been sexually explicit to the point where they could be confused with pornography by those who consider only subject matter. Pornography, he feels, is created *only* for the purpose of stimulating sexual appetite and arousal, and to cater for sexual fantasies. Erotic art, on the other hand, can induce a very high level of aesthetic awareness in the viewer; it will have also, in the long run, a more lasting appeal and a more tangible value than pornography. Using illustrations to support his thesis, Webb contends that erotic art can afford a very satisfying and also a very disturbing experience of genuine value, which often leads to great insight and enlightenment. Although erotic art can have a deliberate sexual appeal, it can provide at the same time a very useful historical perspective to the true value that sex can have as a mutual activity; indeed, Webb argues that whereas pornography can lead to exploitation, erotic art presents a true celebration of love.

Pornography appears always to have been designed by men for men. Sir Martin Roth remarks on this obvious one-sidedness in the opening chapter, and feels that it must be taken into account in any attempt to understand and interpret pornography; in part he thinks the maleness of pornography is rooted in certain biological Achilles heels, peculiar to male members of the human species.* Christine Pickard, in contrast, thinks this phenomenon is less biological than cultural. In her chapter she examines the contention that women are less sexual than men, and that their minimal interest in viewing explicit sexual materials results from this. Males, of course, do report much more exposure to, interest in, and reaction to erotic material than do females on sex surveys. Research studies show, however, that women do not have a lesser capacity to become sexually aroused by erotic material. Pickard believes that differential socialization experiences account for women's lower reported interest in sexual material; females, for example, generally have more negative experiences with sexual material while growing up. Thus, when they are asked about or shown pictures of sexual activity, they are more likely to react negatively; in comparison, males do not receive this defensive conditioning. She argues that females' expressions of *disinterest* in sexually explicit material, despite their ability to respond to it, are best reflected by the poor sales figures of explicit erotica to women. In contrast, romance continues to sell very well among women. Pickard points out how some novelists are now taking advantage of the traditionally acceptable romantic format to market the traditionally unacceptable erotic one; packaging romance a bit differently, these novelists combine it with erotica in a way which capitalizes on the selling power of pure romance plus the arousing power of erotica – and the sales figures are extremely impressive. More women are willing to buy this form of stimulation which appears to be just as arousing as straight erotica and its social content is much more acceptable. Pickard feels that these findings again suggest that social desirability accounts for much of the discrepancy between women's inherent capability to respond to sexual material and their basic disinterest in acquiring what is normally seen as pornography.

* See Roth, this volume, for a more extensive discussion of this.

Most people base their views about pornography on whether or not they believe it to be harmful, not on whether they believe it to be beneficial. Maurice Yaffé draws attention to this fact in his review of the benefits that many people derive from sexually explicit material. Distinguishing between material deliberately designed for sex education or therapy purposes and "pornography" sold in the market place, Yaffé points out that such materials have demonstrated their value in situations where deficits or misinformation about sex prevails; indeed, sex education programmes using sexually explicit material have a generally positive effect on those who are exposed to them. Sexual materials are also of particular value in the treatment of sexual dysfunction, and for the assessment and treatment of sexual deviations. Some indications for the therapeutic use of sexually explicit materials include: couples with communication difficulties; inability to discuss sexual matters using specific terms due to inhibition; sexual naivety and ignorance; and anxiety about sexual behaviour. Yaffé believes that these materials have a definite place as an adjunct to a wide variety of procedures in both sex education and therapy, and he suggests that they may play an increasingly valuable role in the future in the prevention of sexual disorders. Unfortunately, those who oppose the availability of sexually explicit materials are also opposed to sex education, despite the lack of evidence to indicate that the latter promotes promiscuity or other undesirable consequences.

One of the primary reasons pornography is an issue today is because of the legal restrictions surrounding it. Such prohibitions have not always existed of course; pornography merely coloured the cultural scene at one time. Reflecting on this in his historical account of the origins of censorship in Britain, Lionel Haward attributes the growth of legislative attempts to contain and control pornography to the introduction of widespread printing in the eighteenth century and the growth of literacy in the nineteenth century. George III set the anti-pornography wagon on its way, and by 1857 Parliament had passed the first of the *Obscene Publications Acts* to curb the publication of pornography. Today, the law in Britain dealing with obscenity is based upon the 1959 *Obscene Publications Act*. Part of this Act reflected a change in public attitudes towards sex in that it recognized that sexually explicit material could have some merit which redeemed it in the eyes of the law; under this "public good" category, psychologists were allowed to be brought into court as expert witnesses in obscenity trials. Haward examines the role of forensic psychologists called to give expert testimony in court, and describes the sources of information upon which they base their evidence about obscene materials. Regarding obscenity, he maintains that the existing legislation is unsatisfactory in many ways; it is comparable to having a law prohibiting speeding on the highway, but which gives no speed limits for reference, relying instead on only what a prejudiced pedestrian regards as too fast.

In the opening chapter Sir Martin Roth raises a number of concerns about the influence of violent pornography upon the way we love and the manner in which we deal with our aggressive tendencies. My chapter entitled "Pornography and Sexual Aggression" evaluates Roth's concerns in a review of the recent research evidence linking sexually explicit material to harmful sexual and aggressive attitudes and behaviours. The evidence is limited, of course, but none the less it lends credibility to the belief that viewing violent sexuality negatively affects males' attitudes and behaviour toward women. This is not to say that it is the most important contributor to sexual aggression, because other influences also affect the way in which we deal interpersonally with our aggressive feelings; for example, various personality characteristics, traits, and attitudes help determine the probability of aggression. Non-aggressive erotic depictions, in contrast to aggressive ones, appear to be relatively benign and innocent forms of sexual expression, although social concern about the effects of long-term exposure to this material still exists because of the possibility of conditioning arousal to sexual objects or situations that are not part of normative arousal-activity patterns.

Society is not of one mind in regards to the possession, use or display of sexually explicit materials and it is never likely to be. And certainly the belief that the criminal process can, in its present form, be relied upon to make appropriate judgements on the obscenity of a book, magazine, film or play does not seem warranted. David Offenbach discusses the problems inherent in a legal solution to obscenity in our final chapter, and argues that if there are going to be any criminal prohibitions against the publication of "obscene" material, then it is clearly important to make the definition of obscenity more objective. Creating a law to do this in a clear, consistent and above all workable manner appears to be *our* mission impossible.

References

Smith, D. D. The social content of pornography. *Journal of Communication*, 1976, **26**, 16–23.
Yaffé, M. Research survey. In Lord Longford (Ed.) *Pornography: The Longford Report*. London: Coronet, 1972.

To Min

Contents

1

Pornography and society: a psychiatric view*

Martin Roth

Pornography Past and Present

The literal meaning of pornography is the delineation of the life of prostitutes. But in current usage it denotes literary or graphic representations of sexual conduct whose deliberate intention is to arouse sexual desire and to facilitate its expression. Pornography is judged by this contrived design to be sharply distinct from works of art which may engender sexual excitement but are removed from the realm of the pornographic by their embodiment of a new personal vision or insight, the artistic stamp of creation. While a valid distinction may be conceded, sharply drawn demarcation lines between the two worlds would entail arbitrary judgements and circular arguments. For not only have creations, judged as pornographic yesterday, repeatedly gained acceptance as art – and often the inspired revolutionary and original art of today – but many examples of this process in reverse can be cited.

In 1863, Manet exhibited a painting which portrayed the artist and his friends taking lunch in a state of harmonious communion with each other and their surroundings, engaged in pleasures delicate and civilized, which are liable nowadays to engender feelings of nostalgia. There was, however, a naked woman among the handsome, fully clad young men. The painting immediately aroused scandal and outrage, and was rejected by the jury for the French Royal Academy. Yet in a few decades Manet and his fellow Impressionists were to transfigure the vision of the most gifted and influential painters of that period, and to change the manner in which ordinary people perceived the world around them. Now the crowds who indignantly

* This chapter is based on the Fifth Goodman Lecture, delivered by the author at the Royal Society, London on 24 May, 1977.

brandished their fists, sticks and umbrellas at *Luncheon on the Grass* and later at *Olympia* could not have been aware that an art form, which had dealt in a far more free and explicit manner with sexual love, had flourished in Japan for centuries and remained active at the time in question. To our eyes, these prints capture the essence of deep and tender feelings by their spontaneity and movement, their natural balance of vigour and restraint; but the openly erotic examples used to be quietly excluded from scholarly works and were judged coarse and vulgar by cultivated Japanese of the period. For they were pornographic in the strict sense of the term, having dealt almost entirely with the life of courtesans.

Examples of the opposite tendency, rejection or relegation of the erotic art of one era to the limbo of the pornographic in the subsequent one, are also readily found. The pillow books given to newly-married Chinese couples and the *Kama Sutra* were originally written as instruction manuals, but would be classed as pornography in many countries at the present time. One has to give a special gratuity to be allowed access to certain frescoes in Pompeii, and ladies are liable to be looked at askance. Scholarly works containing a comprehensive account of the arts of classical Greece which dealt in bold and uninhibited ways with heterosexual and homosexual love are locked away in great libraries; special permission is required to gain access to them.

So it has been in the past. Whether this mutual exchange between art and pornography down the generations and the ready assimilation of one into the other will or should continue remains an open question. For the emphasis and exaggeration of certain old themes and the entry of a number of new ones in modern pornography call for a reappraisal of its psychological and social effects in the contemporary world. This chapter is therefore largely devoted to the implications of that change in contemporary erotica which has gradually substituted sadism, violence and the humiliation of women for the ordinary or tender representation of sexual love that was the central feature of the pornography of the past.

Some Lessons from the Past

An examination of the pornography of previous ages has certain lessons to teach. First, erotic art and pornography have been produced in abundance in every historic epoch and culture. Secondly, erotica and pornographic art appear always to have been produced in the main by males for the consumption of males. This one-sidedness is consistent and obvious, but it appears to have received relatively little attention. As it is rooted in certain biological Achilles heels, peculiar to male members of the human species, it has to be taken into account in any attempt to understand and interpret pornography. The third inference may have a bearing on the possible influence of pornography upon human behaviour. There is a wide range of variation in the pattern of sexual relationships depicted by the erotica that have survived from different cultures throughout the ages.

The explicit representation of sexual intercourse and the patterns of behaviour closely bound up with it provides some clear threads of continuity. For the erotic art handed down by Chinese, Hindu,Greek and Roman civilizations, the Renaissance engravings of Giulio Romano, the bawdy verses of Pietro Aretino and a large body of contemporary art and pornography are separated for the large part by differences of emphasis alone. And as the infliction of some measure of pain is a frequent concomitant of intercourse, it is not surprising to find a hint of sadism occasionally in unexpected places. In many beautiful St Sebastians painted at the time of the Renaissance, the pale naked body of the youthful tenderly drawn saint is pierced with arrows and blood streams from the wounds. Sado-masochistic as well as homosexual elements are present, but restrained and kept in control and proportion in the greatest paintings by deep religious feeling and a broader aesthetic vision. Flagellation becomes a prominent theme in the illicit pornography of the Victorian era, but it was not new and it does not follow that it was more widely practised in nineteenth century England than in earlier epochs. Homosexual behaviour has been found in the great majority of cultures that have been thoroughly investigated (Ford and Beach, 1951), but there were some exceptions. It is of interest that in the large body of erotic art created by the Incas of Peru, homosexuality appears entirely absent although an astonishing variety of sexual acts is depicted (Hoyle, 1965).

The new facts that have recently come to light about Ancient Greece carry these suggestions a stage further. Dover's (1978) studies have provided a picture of the sexual life of the Greeks in classical times which is more detailed and comprehensive than the accounts available about any other civilization of the Ancient World. The Homeric poems contain no allusion to homosexual relationships which are first represented in Greek vase paintings in the sixth century B.C. The pattern of sexual love as regards roles assumed by the older and younger man, the practices adopted in sexual intercourse, and the character of the relationship between them was far removed from anything with which we are familiar. And there is no record of the form of exclusive homosexuality that is found at a prevalence of about 5% or more within many societies in the modern world. Hence both the patterns of sexual conduct manifest in different civilizations and the erotica produced by them have varied between relatively wide limits. These variations have occurred within intervals of time too short for evolution by natural selection to have played an appreciable part in fashioning them. There is some measure of corroboration from these sources that sexual behaviour in man is not wholly pre-set by inborn factors, but may be shaped and conditioned or conjoined with patterns of conduct that have no necessary connection with it. Social influences comprising political, economic, and religious factors interacting with hereditary predisposition were probably the main agents of change. But the influence of ideas, fashions and their manner of representation in art cannot be ignored as independent agents of change in sexual behaviour.

This leads naturally to the fourth and last inference which may be drawn from historical records. The explicit representation of sexual love is to be found in all ages and epochs with some fluctuations between restraint and freedom in expression. But to an increasing extent the explicit materials of the last decade have been concerned with *novel* themes; with the subjugation, humiliation, and torture rather than the love of women and, to a lesser extent, of men. This chapter is therefore mainly concerned with these aspects of pornography, themes of sex and violence about which the past has little in the way of lessons to offer.

The Maleness of Pornography

The sado-masochistic themes which figure so prominently in contemporary written and visual pornography reflect deviations that are almost entirely confined to men, and the material is intended and purchased mainly by them. We may take the example of the masochistic theme of bondage, which accounts for a high proportion of space in pornographic publications, and seemingly appeals to a large clientèle. *Either* sex may be depicted as harnessed, bound or enslaved by ruthless tormentors. But it is *men* who are generally depicted as manacled by the hands or feet, encased in tight-fitting suits of latex rubber, helmeted, gagged, suspended from horizontal bars by leather thongs which end as a tight collar round the neck and can cause asphyxiation at the slightest movement. The private enactment of these fantasies in real life sometimes has a fatal end, through failure of the elaborate chain of precautions needed to protect against the risk of self-hanging or death by other means; and it is such a point, dangerously near asphyxiation, that many such individuals aim to reach in order to achieve sexual orgasm. The verdict of suicide that may be pronounced following the inquest is incorrect. For it is accidental death that has usually occurred in the course of a bizarre form of displacement of sexual desire from its normal channel of expression in a relationship with another human being. It is possible that such films and pictures, as well as the paraphernalia of chains, leather thongs and flagellators on sale in "porn" shops, are employed mainly for stimulating fantasy or for play and titillation. But there is too little evidence for such assumptions to be justified or safe, and the burden of proof rests on those who make them.

In the past, the male monopoly of pornography has been explained in terms of masculine dominance. In recent years, however, the women's liberation movement has begun to redress the imbalance. Unfortunately, a price has had to be paid for such emancipation, in the form of increased susceptibility to disorders to which women had formerly been relatively immune. These include a rise in the prevalence of alcoholism, smoking and maladies associated with them, as well as a higher rate of crime and consummated suicide; but these do not approach near the rates found among men (Litman, 1975). A parallel development has been the proliferation of lesbian pornography and literature. It is noteworthy that in much of the pornography with lesbian themes, the central female character often evinces contempt for, or revulsion from her own sex; this is a long way removed from Hall's (1928) erotic lesbian novel *The Well of Loneliness*. The women often dominate or deal brutally with their partners, and their aspirations to the male gender role are manifest in their behaviour in sexual intercourse, and in the attitude they adopt in their relationships to both men and women. In the role enacted by the male in much contemporary pornography, we seem to have travelled a very long way from the Casanovas and Don Juans who for all their vainglorious boasting, their conquests, and their scalp-hunting, loved women in their own fashion. They did not asphyxiate them by painting them over in gold, nor did they project missiles at their victims with cigarettes – a touch which incidentally Freud would have appreciated.

Some Origins of the Contemporary Change in Emphasis

When did the upsurge in violent pornography begin? Opinions vary. As far as crime fiction is concerned, George Orwell (1945) detected a turning point in *No Orchids for Miss Blandish* by James Hadley Chase, which enjoyed great popularity during the Battle of Britain. Orwell contrasted it with previous crime stories and those in particular in which Raffles, the gentleman burglar, figured as hero–villain.

Miss Blandish, the daughter of a millionaire, is kidnapped by some gangsters, who are killed off by a larger and better-organized gang. They hold her to ransom in order to extract half a million dollars from her father. Amongst the gang is a young man named Slim, whose pleasures in life involve driving knives into people's bellies, and cutting up animals with pairs of rusty scissors. Slim is sexually impotent, but takes a kind of fancy to Miss Blandish. Now Slim's mother, who is the real brain behind the gang, sees this as a chance of curing her son's sexual problems and tries to keep Miss Blandish in custody until Slim should have succeeded in raping her. After many efforts and much persuasion, including the flogging of Miss Blandish, the rape is achieved. Meanwhile, Miss Blandish's father has hired a private detective and by means of bribery and torture, he and the police manage to round up and exterminate the whole gang. Slim escapes with Miss Blandish, and is killed after a final rape. The detective prepares to restore Miss Blandish to her family. By this time, however, she has developed such a taste for Slim's caresses that, unable to live without him, she jumps out of the window of a skyscraper.

There are so many perceptive insights that one is led to wonder whether the book was not written by a psychiatric gangster using a *nom de plume*. The cure of Slim achieved with the collusion of the dominant mother who has an emotional strangle-hold on her son carries strong homosexual overtones. And the brutal beating into submission of Miss Blandish, whose superior intelligence and social status would in a normal encounter have rendered Slim impotent, has a compelling authenticity.

The book has eight murders, numerous killings and woundings, an exhumation with a description of the stench, the flogging of Miss Blandish, the torture of another woman with red-hot cigarette ends, a strip-tease act and a third degree scene. There is one episode in which a gangster has an orgasm while being knifed. Orwell's conclusions are of interest. Comparing the schoolboy atmosphere of Raffles' books with the cruelty and corruption of *No Orchids* he reflects, "One is driven to feel that snobbishness, like hypocrisy, is a check upon behaviour whose value from a social point of view has been under-rated."

Pornography – "Hard" and "Soft"

It is not unusual to make a distinction between "soft" pornography, whose declared purpose is to stimulate commonplace erotic ideas and fantasies, and what has come to be classed as "hard" pornography, in which all the constraints of reality are removed and the standards of the prevalent culture violated. Some evidence does exist to suggest that normally-adjusted individuals tend to reject certain kinds of hard pornography. Yet *No Orchids* had been read by half a million people in 1945 when Orwell was writing, and many contemporary novels, whose content does not essentially differ from that of hard pornography, achieve larger sales.

A recent work, for example, by a distinguished author of science fiction, written in a fast-moving, sparse and brilliant prose, uses the motor car as a sacrificial altar for bleeding and dismembered characters who find, in mutilation and death among the jagged masses of twisted steel, an inevitable climax for their passionless acrobatic and polymorphous sexual acts. Ordinary erotic magazines whose total readership must run into millions are interspersed with images of torture and submission. The hard pornography of yesterday is liable to evolve by gradual stages into the soft pornography of tomorrow. The pictures shown to witnesses at the Linda Lovelace trial might graduate and qualify for public consumption by the same process. In one, a female in chains was seen tied up by a naked man pointing a sword at the woman's genitals. In another, a man with a cat o' nine tails was striking a woman on her vulva. Yet another – a girl with distress on her face and her arms manacled – is cut; a man with a bayonet is inflicting the cuts. All these were described by expert medical witnesses as beneficial because of their value in promoting masturbation.

The last two or three decades have seen the proliferation of pictures of wardresses, inflicting tortures in concentration camps, and vivisection experiments on women performed by Swastika-laden Nazis. Teenage girls are flogged, tortured and sexually assaulted. Scantily-clad jack-booted Nazi women are shown branding their victims. There is nothing comparable with this material in the pornography of the past. It is a world apart from the nursery regressions of Victorian flagellation. In the proportion of the material devoted to sadistic themes, the extent to which cruelty and subjection displace and submerge sexual love, and the character of the psychopathology to which it gives expression, contemporary violent pornography reflects a qualitative change in the historical development of erotica. If we pose questions about the causes for the steep escalation in its availability and consumption, clear answers elude us but some appear more insubstantial than others. To blame "society" for it all is unhelpful and unilluminating. It is more likely that the central idea of violent domination in the sexual act has caught on and spread partly because, like other ideas that have gained wide currency, it appeals powerfully to the emotions. For reasons discussed in the next section, it is liable to be adopted at the least in play or fantasy by men in particular. Such ideas are disseminated by a far stronger motive force than are fashions in clothes, popular songs and forms of expression in art, all of which sometimes spread for indefinable reasons.

Male and Female Sexuality

The much-flaunted virility of the male proves to have a feeble biological foundation. It is he who is liable to incapacity in the sexual act through guilt or anxiety, whereas the woman, whether or not she is aroused, remains sexually competent in the majority of cases. And with a measure of skill she can act as if she were fully competent, if not superiorly endowed. It is the male sex which is the impotent one with sexual organs less well innervated than are those of the female. As Slater (1973) has pointed out, whereas the vagina and clitoris are richly innervated the phallus in comparison is relatively anaesthetic and all too often paralytic.

This contrast between the sexes has biological, social and physiological aspects. The woman has a far greater investment in the sexual act. The consequences for her in pregnancy and childbirth and the rearing of children extend over the years. Nature has, therefore, taken great care to ensure her sexual competence and has, in addition, provided her with a special bonus; for the sexual orgasm which she experiences at the culmination of the act is a uniquely human phenomenon not found among other higher animals. In comparison, for the male, the risk of death or other adversity from sexual intercourse is negligible. His investment in the sexual act is much smaller, and it must be for this reason that he has been provided by natural selection with more fragile sexual equipment. Skill and effectiveness in sexual behaviour are less easy to acquire for the male, more liable to disorder and disruption, and the disabilities that develop through deprivation or deficiency in the formative years have proved much more difficult to surmount in males than females (Harlow and Harlow, 1965). Moreover, Nature's predisposition is to produce females. In the absence of certain hormonal substances (androgens) the developing infant with a male hereditary constitution will have the outward appearance of the female, but the converse is not true. If the ovaries are absent and the hormones which they secrete are lacking, normal female internal and external organs will develop, although such an individual will, of course, be infertile.

Nature, in fact, appears to have treated the male as if he were altogether more dispensable that his female partner. He has a higher mortality rate at all stages of the life span, and with few exceptions has a greater susceptibility to illnesses and a greater liability to die from them. From birth onwards he is less capable than the female of responding with antibodies to certain infections. Through the possession of a second X chromosome females are provided with protective isoalleles or paired genes that enable them to escape a whole range of hereditary diseases which are found in full-blown form almost entirely in the male sex. They therefore remain largely immune from haemophilia, nephrogenic diabetes insipidus, some drug-induced anaemias and deficiency of the para-thyroid glands. They are the exempt carriers of diseases for which men have an almost exclusive monopoly; and with a substantially longer life-span they have a far better chance of an uneventful passage through middle life into old age.

In describing the female as a castrated male with a strong unconscious motivation to compensate for this deficiency, Freud (1910) ignored evidence that points in another direction. Women may have a higher prevalence of neurosis, but alcoholism, drug dependence, murder, violent crime, consummated suicide, dangerous driving, as well as sexual deviations of every kind are all more characteristic of the male of the species. He may be the greater warrior and hero and more often a musical or mathematical genius. Perhaps he has greater need to sublimate. Be this as it may, both in regard to physical and psycho-sexual robustness, it is the male that is the weaker sex. Blessed are those with two X chromosomes, for they shall inherit the earth. One difference between the sexes has probably contributed to this asymmetry. Over many thousands of generations, and until about a century ago, childbirth carried an appreciable mortality. Women must therefore have been exposed to a much more fierce pressure from natural selection. This may have been partly responsible for their lesser mortality, greater longevity, and perhaps their greater robustness and stability as sexual beings.

Pornography and Psychopathological Aspects of Sexual Deviation

Hard pornography depicts forms of sexual adaptation that have to be regarded as morbid and it panders to others that have, in their fully-fledged and exclusive form, to be viewed similarly. Deviant forms of sexual behaviour have proved to be substantially more common among the males of the human species in every culture investigated; this holds for sadism, masochism, exhibitionism, transvestism, trans-sexuality, fetishism, bestiality, necrophilia and homosexuality, both of the exclusive and the bivalent kind.

The predicament of the male has some of its origins in emotional conflicts which constitute an ineluctable part of the human condition, for it is to be found anywhere. The paradise of sexual bliss — sex without fear, guilt or shame — is largely mythical. It follows that hard pornography falsifies the truth when it ignores all constraints, because there is no culture in which all sexuality has been given completely free rein to express itself at random. The taboo on parent–child incest is universal, and this entails inhibition in circumstances where the emotional bond is strong, although as Freud and others have taught, there are often powerful undercurrents of sexual desire to be curbed and rechannelled. Moreover, society's attitudes are ambiguously poised. Chastity is approved, virility is admired, promiscuity is frowned upon, though envied, impotence ridiculed. Such contradictions could not have been better contrived if one were setting out deliberately to engender conflict and neurosis. The situation was *not* essentially different in Ancient Greece as Dover (1978) has pointed out. For if we are to judge from art and literature, the young man when wooed was expected to assume the role of modest virgin. If he displayed or described actual pleasure in the sexual act, he was criticized or reviled.

This provides some insight into the reasons why the male deviates in his sexual behaviour in ways that provide the central themes of pornography. The sexual act and the human relationship it celebrates demand highly developed emotional qualities, psychological attributes, and physical skills which have to be learned by the man in particular. As the activity is conflict-laden, some anxiety is inevitable. But it is the male who is most liable to suffer failure and humiliation in the stages of adolescent exploration when he is seeking to define his needs and identity. A fear-laden aversion may be surmounted in some but well-learned in others, so that neurosis and deviation become firmly ingrained. So it is that other channels, less hedged with taboos and offering less resistance may be chosen. The psychogenesis of the commoner forms of deviation can then be described as follows.

(In place of an emotional relationship with a real woman, the fetishist will find outlets in her furs, her high-heeled shoes, her hair, or her underclothes; or, guilt may be subdued in masochistic submission which may, in runaway fashion, reach extremes of self-abasement and humiliation such as flagellation and torture, surrender to menial tasks, the licking of shoes, or the cleaning of lavatories; or, the feared object is overpowered and mastered by exposing her to humiliation and violence as in sadism. The transvestite assumes women's outer identity.)Thus attired, he may be sexually competent. In exclusive male homosexuality, the man seeks a partner of his own sex for similar reasons. Lesbian homosexuality may be viewed in a similar manner, but its exclusive form is far more rare than in males. And the trans-sexualist's displacement presses him towards more radical solutions: he wants a surgeon to remove his hated genitalia and transform him into a glamorous female seductively attractive to men. Contemporary pornography panders to all this. Whether we deal with hard pornography, or with *No Orchids for Miss Blandish*, or with displays available in most large cities of the Western World, peering beneath the thin camouflage, it is fear, envy, hatred, and the desire for the humiliation of women, rather than the love of women, that we often find.

Attempts have recently been made to exclude *all* forms of sexual deviation from the realm of disorder or disease, partly on the grounds that the spurious label of medical pathology is responsible for much of the intolerance and the suffering. This is not in keeping with the findings of psychoanalysis and clinical psychiatry. Freud, who helped to bring compassion and objectivity into the treatment and study of sexual deviation, attributed the exclusive forms to arrested development:

> If perversion instead of merely appearing alongside the normal sexual aim and object, and only when circumstances are unfavourable to them and favourable to it – if instead of this it ousts them completely and takes their place in all circumstances – if in short perversion has the characteristics of exclusiveness and fixation, then we shall usually be justified in regarding it as a pathological symptom (Freud, 1910).

Here, clinical observation supports psychoanalytic theory in that those with extreme forms of deviation, such as sadism and masochism of an exclusive or predominant kind, are usually found to exhibit some distinctive traits and abnormalities of character beyond the domain of their sexual propensities. If this is the case, then any influence exerted by deviant pornography in reinforcing or initiating such tendencies will not be confined to private sexual acts. They will be liable to affect conduct in wider spheres than the sexual ones and consequently exert generally adverse effects upon social adaptation and social welfare.

Aggression and Sexuality in Biological and Historical Perspective

The relationship between aggressiveness and sexuality has been extensively discussed by biologists and behavioural scientists in recent years. The strength of the correlation between them would be expected to determine the extent to which pornography might shape the fantasies and actual behaviour of ordinary people. The sexual and aggressive instincts, according to psychoanalytical theory, direct the course and outcome of personality development, and erotic and destructive urges are regarded as being inseparably entwined at each stage. However, as a result of the condemnation of frank aggression by social forces that operate through institutions and culture, aggressive tendencies may be displaced and expressed in symbolic form.

Psychiatric and psychoanalytic observation cannot of course at the present time offer precise evidence regarding the strength of the contribution made within any one society by hereditary factors on the one hand, and environmental influences prevalent during the early formative stages of development on the other. But many biologists would endorse the view which postulates a close relationship between sexuality and aggression. For aggression may be expected to confer advantages in mating, and it will also favour the dissemination of the genes of individuals strongly endowed with aggressive traits through the dispersal of populations (Wynne-Edwards, 1962), and the fostering of social stability in hierarchies. Indeed, Lorenz (1963) has suggested that aggressiveness is an essential precondition for establishing lasting bonds of love and friendship. There are, however, reasons for calling in question the view which regards the link between male aggressiveness and sexuality as a biological constant, shaped by genetic factors in the course of evolution and camouflaged but not essentially changed by social circumstances. As Hinde (1974) has pointed out, the link between aggressiveness and sexual reproduction is subject to the law of diminishing returns; for it may interfere with mating rather than assist it.

The old antithesis of nature *vs* nurture is misleading since neither can operate alone. And, in general, the tendency to aggressive and violent conduct has to be conceived as arising from a whole range of factors at different levels – genetic, familial and social. Yet, one body of empirical observations in relation to human behaviour has to be given considerable weight in such a discussion. Over a wide range of personality disorders that manifest themselves in consistently aggressive–impulsive, anti-social, suicidal and sexually sadistic behaviour, the familial evidence from personal historical records is unequivocal. It is not necessary to invoke such explanations as "original sin", or wholly genetic causes to explain these phenomena. Such individuals are almost invariably found to have been submitted to extreme and repeated forms of emotional deprivation and often violent abuse in the formative years.

Specific *familial* influences stand out as the most conspicuous agents in the shaping of such personalities; indeed, the behaviour patterns of these individuals show a marked tendency to overlap. Adverse familial circumstances *cannot* have been merely expressions of a genetical predisposition common to the parents and their disturbed offspring, for there is independent evidence in relation to persistent conduct disorders of childhood (Rutter, 1978) that the environmental factors are of major importance in their own right. But, although these seem to be necessary in the majority of cases, they are not sufficient as causes. Some of those exposed to trauma and deprivation in childhood mature with personalities intact. In the case of exclusive male homosexuality, genetical factors and hormonal influences probably contribute to a limited extent. But a large and consistent body of evidence suggests that both homosexual and trans-sexual individuals have been reared in families in which the father is either absent, or the female parent's influence predominates for other reasons (Bieber *et al.*, 1962; Roth and Ball, 1964; West, 1968). The family setting has to be regarded as a necessary though not sufficient factor in causation.

The changes in attitude of trans-sexuals, who have sought to alter their gender in increasing numbers, resulted from the research of Hamburger *et al.* (1953) who first described the details of such an operation. A clear distinction was initially thought to exist between those with trans-sexualism and those with the exclusive forms of male homosexuality; the latter were believed to be unlikely to become candidates for an operation that would deprive them of the organs whereby they achieved gratification. This prediction was soon refuted by the rising numbers of male homosexuals who came to request the operation that would enable them to change to a female gender role. The operation proves a failure in a relatively high proportion of such cases and some plead to have the effects reversed. This confirms the clinical impression that the glamour and drama attached to "sex change" procedures by the media, through the massive and sensational publicity devoted to this topic, played a significant role in changing a form of sexual behaviour in basic and irreversible ways. Reference has already been made to Dover's (1978) study of homosexual life in Ancient Greece which showed that social attitudes towards the behaviour of the passive partner were far removed from our own. A whole array of social attitudes and conventions regulating sexual conduct had evolved and been disseminated within a relatively short period of biological time. An extensive body of vase paintings and other visual art and literature depicts sexual courtship and intercourse, prescribing some roles and forbidding others. It is likely to have played a part, in association with other influences, in moulding behaviour.

Male Aggressiveness and Sexuality – The Spread and Transmission of an Idea

The belief that aggressiveness and power are inseperably entwined with sexual desirability and success in the male has been handed down through the ages in many, but not all, cultures and is fostered and reinforced from many sources. The traditional hero is an adventurous, intrepid explorer or violent conqueror (Roth, 1968), and in contemporary literature often ruthless, destructive and affectless in his sexual and personal relationships. The behaviour of kings and rulers in history reinforces this image. Military glory and political power appear entwined with expansive sexual behaviour in the lives of kings and rulers from the earliest days of recorded history. The mythical gods and heroes of Ancient Greece and the Emperors of Rome illustrate this theme. The behaviour of despotic rulers has repeatedly displayed a combination of sexual greed, cruelty and murder of women. Henry VIII, Jan Bockelson the leader of the millenial revolution in Münster in the sixteenth century (Cohn, 1962), and in our own times Idi Amin, are some of the names that come to hand. The Napoleonic legend which echoed down the nineteenth century and remains influential to the present day was compounded by women vanquished as well as armies conquered. The remark, "Power is the supreme aphrodisiac" was attributed to Henry Kissinger. It may have been apocryphal but it has a stamp of authenticity, and came to be widely attributed to him.

The relationship between military and political power and sexual behaviour awaits an authoritative historian. The coupling of human aggression and male sexuality undoubtedly has some biological substrate. But there is enough variation (Mead, 1949) to make it plain that it is neither as wholly pre-destined by heredity nor as immutable as might appear. The image so repeatedly reinforced during history has selected one of many possible human identities. Its transmission down the ages partly reflects the contagiousness, power, and durability of certain concepts and ideas.

This is well exemplified by rape, a relatively uncommon offence during periods of peace and social tranquility, but liable to escalate in times of war and social disorganization. It has been regarded with revulsion by most cultures. But, as Szent-Györgi (1963) has pointed out, this did not prevent the rape of the Sabine Women from being depicted as one of the glories of Ancient Rome. It is, then, merely one among other forms of violence inflicted upon nations forced into subjection by soldiers of victorious armies. Dover quotes anthropological data (Vangaard, 1972) which testify to the fact that human societies have often subjected strangers and trespassers to homosexual assault to bring their subordinate status home to them. "Vulgar idiom" in many languages, including four letter words in our own, gives clear expression to these connotations of the sexual act (Dover, 1978). There is other evidence that elements of hostility and revenge and humiliation are integral parts of sexual assault. During periods of social disturbance, when inhibitions and restraints are loosened, both violent anti-social acts and sexual crimes are liable to escalate. There can hardly be any doubt that we are living through such a period. Hence, in evaluating the possible effects of an influence, such as sadistic pornography, that might diminish constraints, trends in non-sexual and violent crime have to be examined together with those for sexual crimes. Evidence for the overlap between them has already been cited.

Dawkins' (1976) discussion of the manner in which ideas that have psychological appeal may spread is germane here. His book, *The Selfish Gene*, is mainly devoted to the thesis that we are temporary and disposable repositories for the genes to carry. But the final chapter is devoted to an exposition of the view that arresting fashions, new ideas, and also whole systems of belief may be propagated from person to person and from the brain of one man to that of his neighbour. A novel idea or belief which proves psychologically attractive and therefore successful may endure to be transmitted down the generations in a manner which is analogous to the transmission of traits by genes. It is such "memes", from the Greek *mimemes* for imitation, that have become the new agents in human evolution. They spread with a rapidity far beyond the capacity of genes to rival. The analogy with genetic transmission is close and significant for whole systems of belief commencing in the minds of one or a small group of men. Their propagation may occur with greater rapidity and place a more indelible stamp upon the thought and conduct of beings than the traits determined by the genetic endowment of the originators. So it is that the contributions of Socrates, Shakespeare, Haydn, Milton, Michaelangelo, Bach, Plato, Beethoven and Karl Marx are still with us, though the genes for which they were temporary repositories have long since vanished into the gene pool of humanity.

In the case of the coupling of male virility with violence, as in many other traits, culture and environment may have merely reinforced one genetic predisposition rather than others. But a different outcome might have been envisaged. Huxley (1958) has described a range of qualities unique to man: speech, tradition, tools, conceptual thought, mathematics, music and art, romantic love, an unprecedented range of individual variability, all-year-round fertility, humour, science and religion. To these may be added yet another trait which might be selected by cultural emphasis alongside certain qualities in Huxley's list to fashion a different image.

> Corporate forms of aggression as enacted in all their variety for thousands of years would not have been possible without man's capacity for self-sacrifice and social co-operation (Roth, 1972).

Some Implications for Pornography

It would be unrealistic for the reasons outlined above, to regard sexually violent pornography as the representation of a set of disagreeable actions that merely mirror the preformed fantasies or behaviour of a tiny minority of abnormal and damaged individuals; because such actions relate to widely prevalent sexual conflicts that are vicariously acted out, they may exert some effects upon a relatively wide range of individuals. They may be employed, of course, merely in play, fantasy, or the promotion of masturbation, but the possibility that they can also displace other attitudes and shape sexual behaviour to some degree should not be dismissed.

To disentangle the effect of any one influence, such as pornography, from a multitude of others which influence current crime rates is difficult enough. The problem is further compounded by the fact that violence and cruelty in sexual behaviour passes by diffusion from under-the-counter pornography in novels and men's magazines into the communication of everyday media; themes of bondage, fetishism and violence enter in subtle or suggestive ways, or as open and dominant themes. Hitchcock's *Psycho* which froze the blood of audiences many years ago is demoted to black comedy. *Playboy*, *Mayfair* and *Men Only* vie with one another in the varying amount of sadism and masochism interfused. It seems inevitable that it should escalate. Now the sadistic element in pornography reflects emotions of resentment, hatred, domination, revenge and also envy. It is envy of a partner who is free from the deficiencies that are liable to reduce the male to a state of helplessness. In the place where he has invested his greatest pride, he finds himself poorly endowed. It is the inner uncertainty and fear of humiliation by the better endowed female partner that makes the male sex the jealous sex. The forms of jealousy that culminate in murder and commonly present in courts of law are almost exclusively confined to the male of the species.

Pornography and Sexual Behaviour

The factual evidence bearing on the relationship between pornography and sexual behaviour is scanty and conflicting. In such a situation, inferences drawn from any one body of observations are likely to prove misleading. Hard evidence is difficult to obtain in this field and caution has to be exercised in forming judgements, particularly where they are likely to form the basis of social policies. Goldstein *et al.* (1973) concluded from their enquiries that explorations with a partner of the same sex had begun in most homosexuals before they had been exposed to any explicit representation of homosexual acts. However, retrospective memory is notoriously fallible when a year or more has elapsed since the events in question, even where those under investigation can be safely assumed to be impartial witnesses. It appears highly improbable that the development of exclusive homosexuality would be influenced by explicit materials. It is a more open question whether they would affect the liability to give overt expression to the much more widely prevalent tendency to facultative homosexuality.

Some observers have claimed that although pornographic material does promote sexual arousal, its effects are limited by a filtering process that causes the observer to reject those forms of a sexual behaviour which conflict with pre-established standards and values. For example, Goldstein *et al.* described adolescents as having reacted with revulsion to pornographic material which incorporated aggression and humiliation of others. The finding is of some interest, but the *form* of the immediate response provides no information regarding possible influences on subsequent behaviour. There is a tendency to regard the basic patterns of sexual response as having been irrevocably laid down before maturity. The adult is judged to be immune to exposure to pornographic materials, and to patterns of sexual conduct with which he has not previously been familiar. Sexual arousal along pre-formed patterns may occur, but Goldstein *et al.* have concluded that unfamiliar forms of sexual behaviour are not imitated. However, the evidence is too slender to justify firm conclusions. It is known that the quest for a change in gender role may begin in the thirties, forties or even later in individuals in whom such tendencies have not found overt expression and have co-existed in some cases with a heterosexual life including marriage, reproduction and the rearing of children.

It has been claimed that sex offenders do not differ significantly from non-sex offenders, or non-offenders in the extent of their exposure and preoccupation with erotic material. But not all the evidence points in this direction, and the effects of retrospective distortion are impossible to eliminate. The results could stem from an attempt to substantiate a claim to

normality, or from a desire to direct blame onto influences promoting sexually aggressive behaviour that were outside the individual's control.

Sexual crimes that represent a risk to the lives of others are relatively rare
and attempts to establish any correlation in their prevalence and the availability of pornographic material are bound to entail a large margin of error.
In this situation, however, clinical evidence should not go unheeded, particularly when it comes from many sources. The clinical picture of one type of
sadistic murderer has been defined by various investigators (e.g. Brittain,
1968). The individuals in question are always male, rather quiet and intro-
verted. They indulge in sadistic sexual fantasies which reflect their interest in
neo-Nazism, torture and black magic. An armory of guns and weapons of
torture and a collection of pornography featuring the sado-masochistic
theme of bondage and the infliction of sadistic torture on others is commonly
found among their possessions, although they may be carefully concealed.
Those who exhibit the syndrome are recognized by forensic psychiatrists in
many countries as constituting a considerable social risk; the Moors
murderer, Ian Brady, and the Cambridge rapist both exemplified the
phenomenon.

It is impossible to assess the contribution made by pornographic material
to the behaviour exhibited by such persons. The view that they merely reflect
the inborn constitutional predisposition to sexually violent behaviour conflicts with several lines of evidence. And the belief that sexual, neurotic, or
other patterns of behaviour are completely determined and pre-set during the
first years of life does not accord with the evidence drawn from observations
on human psychological development. A measure of plasticity remains until
adolescence and even later. Sexual responses can be conditioned within
certain limits, and linked with other responses; an analogue for fetishism for
boots has in fact been created by conditioning procedures (Rachman, 1966).
Moreover, films, photographs, and similar materials with explicit themes
have been employed in the treatment and shaping of sexual responses. It
cannot be claimed that pornography may prove beneficial in the treatment of
sexual disabilities and asserted at the same time that sexual conduct cannot
be shaped so as to make it overtly aggressive and violent, particularly when
some predisposition for such behaviour is already present.

The view which considers the *entire* repertoire of sexual behaviours exhibited by adult sexual offenders to be present in their constitution is at
variance with the observations of Frisbie (1969) who found that, among
those who had been violent during sexual offences, 21% had used more
serious violence in subsequent offences. Her conclusion was that: "We dare
not under-estimate the dangerousness of the sex offender who employs
aggression in dealing with his victim."

The findings recorded in the course of self-report studies are marked by many inconsistencies. It is claimed that sex offenders use pornography for arousal and masturbation, but also that their response is marked by guilt and revulsion (Goldstein *et al.*, 1973); their study reported that sex offenders, including rapists and paedophiles, had less exposure to sexually explicit materials than control subjects, but the work has been criticized on the grounds of the size and bias of the sample (Eysenck and Nias, 1978). It is difficult to reconcile these results with the findings of Davis and Braucht (1973). In a retrospective study of 365 subjects, drawn from a wide range of social groups including jail inmates and deviants (rapists, voyeurs and transvestites), the amount of exposure to pornography proved to be negatively correlated with indices of moral character; it was positively correlated with sexual deviance and deviant practices, as also heterosexual experience and homosexuality. Kercher and Walker (1973) report exposure to sexual themes as having been found unpleasant by rapists, although physiological measures showed arousal. But the findings of Abel *et al.* (1977) were rather different; rapists responded with erection more often than other offenders to scenes of rape. The most frequent responders were found among those who had offended often, injured victims or attacked children. Non-sexual, violent material evoked *similar* effects in a proportion of cases. It is clear that little reliance can be placed on subjective reports which prove highly inconsistent. The objective indices are more telling.

Having regard to the fact that pornographic materials are liable to engender rapid satiety and boredom, the theory that they provide a means of catharsis for violent offenders rests on a feeble foundation. There is nothing in the published evidence to give solid support to the cathartic theory. Rape is a premeditated act and its victims are, in most instances, not merely forced to have sexual intercourse, but threatened, physically assaulted, and defiled by urine and faeces. These are acts of hostility and revenge (West, 1978), and it appears improbable that photographs or films can provide alternative means of expression that will sidetrack rapists into the safer channels of private fantasy and masturbation.

Pornography and Trends in Sexual Crimes in Denmark

Controversy regarding the significance of trends in sexual crimes following the increased dissemination of pornography in Denmark has proved of value in clarifying certain issues. Kutchinsky (1971, 1973, 1978) has reported that following the increased availability of pornographic materials in the middle of the 1960s there was a significant decline in several forms of sexual offence. He considered that the reduction in the number of acts of physical indecency towards women may have been due to lower reporting rates and that the decline in voyeurism and exhibitionism may have arisen from changed attitudes towards reporting by the police. He concluded, however, that the reduction of indecent assault on children could not be so explained, and he related this to the greater availability of hard core pornography in Denmark. This claim has been contested by Court (1974, 1975, 1976, 1977) who has adduced evidence which points in an opposite direction. He found that those countries in which explicit sexual materials had been made freely available exhibited a parallel increase in the prevalence of sexual crimes. In contrast, other countries where constraints have been imposed have shown no such increase. Kutchinsky rejects the possibility of a causal relationship between such parallel trends. He claims a special evidential status for the absence of a concomitant rise in sexual crimes when pornography is made increasingly available: "On the other hand, to disprove that pornography is the cause of sexual offences is a lot easier under certain circumstances, namely in the event that a high or increased availability of pornography is not accompanied by a high or increased incidence of sexual offence." But Kutchinsky appears to be arguing that when a reduction in the number of certain kinds of sexual crime is observed instead of an increase as in the case of Denmark, this is ". . . most probably the very direct cause" of the change, in this case, a substantial decrease in child molestation.

Kutchinsky's (1973) argument is difficult to follow. Court's claim that there is probably a causal relationship between a parallel increase in the rate of sex crime and pornography had been judged invalid by this author. But the objections apply with equal force when a causal explanation is imputed to negatively correlated trends. Although an attempt was made to eliminate the possible effects of concomitant changes in public attitude and the behaviour of the police, the evidence is too indirect and weak to validate any causal association between such imprecisely defined and complicated social phenomena. A gradual decline in the prevalence of sexual crimes had already begun prior to 1964. Moreover, the men who assault children sexually nearly always suffer from disorders of personality of a serious nature. The claims that films and photographs can provide an adequate substitute for the behaviour of living victims strains clinical credulity.

No distinction was made in the enquiries into Danish trends between erotica and other material. Recent evidence, however, has emphasized the importance of this line of demarcation. Studies by Feshbach and Malamuth (1978), for example, have led them to conclude that men who view erotica representing sado-masochistic encounters ". . . tend to be more stimulated than others by the idea of rape and less sympathetic to the victims". Such themes have figured with growing prominence in recent years in the entertainment offered by the media and the cinema; in the film *Charlotte*, made by Roger Vadim, a woman is strangled by a man during sexual intercourse*. A

* See Note Added in Proof (p. 25).

further point is that in evaluating the possible effects of sado-masochistic pornography on social behaviour, the prevalence of violent offences of a non-sexual kind cannot be omitted from consideration. For sexual offenders who are re-convicted are just as likely to be found guilty of a non-sexual as of a sexual offence (Radzinowitz, 1957). No line of evidence in this field is clear, consistent and compelling. The polarity between censorship and unfettered freedom of expression presents society with difficult dilemmas, but little weight can be attached to the inherently unreliable data drawn from trends in sex crimes in attempts to resolve them.

Immediate Tasks

The first need is to strip the subject clean of its encrustations of self-deception and myth and face the problems with fresh understanding. The knowledge that has been acquired about the causes of sexual misery and frustration, the personality damage with which they are often associated, and their vicarious forms of expression in deviant forms of sexual behaviour, particularly those with a component of violence, needs to be made more widely known. The public at large and those concerned with the media should be better informed about the psychopathological aspects of pornography.

Some of the lesser known works of celebrated artists are often quoted as validation by historical precedent, of the materials which are achieving increasing circulation at the present time. There is little substance in these comparisons. The bawdy cartoons of Rowlandson in the last century were playful, affectionate, and innocuous in comparison with the materials shown at the Linda Lovelace trial to which reference has already been made. The same statement can be made of the more distant, cold and introspective erotic paintings of Fuseli in the previous century.

Escalation in the cruelty and violence of content is clearly in evidence. It is reinforced by competition for the glittering prizes in a potentially vast market. The misconception that such materials appeal to a small minority of warped and stunted individuals has to be dispelled. Masters and Johnson (1979), for example, have shown that sado-masochistic fantasies are in some measure widely prevalent among normal individuals and not confined to those with deviant forms of sexual behaviour. Clinical observation also shows that sexual excitement and climax are not infrequently generated by scenes of violence, and evidence of some effects in reverse has already been cited. It is *essential* to distinguish between the candid representation of sexual love on the one hand, and explicit material which normalize sadism and humiliation on the other. If a definition of corruption is needed, the task might well commence with the display of young children submitted to flagellation and oral intercourse.

Until quite recently, little attention has been paid by the police and forensic experts to the possible relevance of pornographic materials to sexual or violent crimes. The searches conducted for such materials, liable to be hidden, have neither been consistent nor systematic. The frequency with which pornographic materials have been reported in the possession of those who have committed sexual offences cannot therefore be given very much weight. More importance has to be attached to the possible effects of violent pornography on ordinary people than the small minorities specifically pre-disposed to behaving in real life in the manner depicted. Unfortunately, as a result of continuing escalation, sadistic erotica are likely to achieve acceptance through the mere fact that they are so widely available. In this way, there is a danger that sexual violence will numb the sensibility which enables ordinary people to respond with compassion to suffering and humiliation; at the worst, such portrayals may condition enjoyment and perhaps the infliction of pain by individuals in whom such propensities might otherwise have remained dormant.

The potentiality of the human species may be developed in many directions according to the social and psychological environment in which its members live and develop. It must not be forgotten that only a few decades ago, large numbers of people from some of the most civilized countries in the world were rapidly conditioned to carry out acts of unspeakable cruelty. It is an indispensable pre-condition for any balanced consideration of the problem of control that the facts should be made available, so that they can appeal to the sense of responsibility of those concerned with communication through the media. Public attitudes may then be re-shaped from their present apathy, dissociation, and resignation to some more positive stance. Objections are often voiced against the description of such materials in terms that reflect value judgements. Terms that express irritation and distaste are judged to be preferable to "obscenity". But if it is solely on the strength of the subjective annoyance and embarrassment of the majority that such materials are rejected, certain implications follow. Those who wish to have violent pornography disseminated without restriction in all the media are then justified in regarding themselves as an oppressed minority, constrained by the arbitrary tastes of a majority whose influences happen to predominate in contemporary culture. A different situation may then confront society in a few decades. The minority that wishes to have sado-masochistic pornography freely available may have graduated so as to have become the majority; those who react to such material with repugnance may have dwindled into a dissenting and deviant minority expected to visit segregated shops to purchase the articles only they regard as inoffensive.

This chapter has been mainly devoted to the psychological and biological origins of the themes with which modern pornography deals. It has examined also some of the hazards which may be run should the trends which are evident at the present continue unabated. A balanced, liberal and constructive policy rooted in psychological insight is needed, and it can evolve only from greater enlightenment and wide-ranging public debate.

It has been recognized for centuries that a control on freedom of expression presents difficult social, moral and ethical issues. The noble and eloquent words of Milton (1644), used in *Areopagitica* in defence of unfettered freedom of printing, are often quoted in this context. He had no doubt, dangers notwithstanding, that unrestrained freedom in the publication of books represented the lesser evil.

> Why should we then affect a rigor contrary to the manner of God and of nature, by abridging or scanting those means which books freely permitted are, both to the trial of virtue and to the exercise of truth? It would be better done, to learn that the law needs to be frivolous, which goes to restrain things, uncertainly, and yet equally working to good and to evil.

However, the punitive measures he was prepared to take against those writings proved after publication to have been blasphemous or harmful have to be added, unacceptable as they may be to us. He was of the opinion that the State and Commonwealth should ". . . have a vigilant eye how books demean themselves as well as man, and thereafter to confine, imprison, and to do sharpest justice on them as malefactors." The purpose of this quotation is to make the point that Milton's utterances on the subject were made from within a moral order assumed to have compelling and unassailable authority. This order has been largely eroded in the centuries that have followed. But if censorship of any form is ultimately judged undesirable, or if any measures of control introduced should prove impossible to implement, this should *not* be allowed to obfuscate the issues. It will not mean that pornography is harmless.

Concluding Remarks

Certain consequences that might follow if the runaway trends are not halted require to be considered. If extreme aggressiveness as depicted in pornography and the penumbra of more widely circulating materials comes to be accepted as an essential trait of the sexually successful male, young men will compete more and more with one another. They will try to prove themselves by feats of violence and daring in schools and football grounds, and in aggressive and anti-social acts towards others. There are bound to be victors and vanquished, each with their fears and hatreds.

Finally, if the stereotype of the aggressive predatory male has emerged somehow as a fashion or a cult at some point in history, we have to take thought as to how new fashions that displace the traditional ones might be generated. This is not inherently impossible. For example, in Japan, after some centuries of development in which Ukiyo-e prints depicted sexual love with naturalism and tenderness, there was an abrupt change. Towards the middle of the nineteenth century blood and violence were inter-fused and there was an increasing brutality in the treatment of erotic prints. Public displays of women having sexual intercourse with animals are described; as such themes had previously been absent, Western influences had very likely contributed. A fashion had emerged and spread, which then waned and all but vanished.

It would be desirable to have this progression replicated in our own culture. For although the evidence summarized in this chapter is not conclusive, it is consistent with the belief that those forms of contemporary pornography which foster the association of violence and hatred with the sexual act may exert effects of fateful importance upon the way we love and the manner in which we deal with our aggressive tendencies.

References

Abel, G. G., Barlow, D. H., Blanchard, E. B. and Guild, D. The components of rapist's sexual arousal. *Archives of General Psychiatry*, 1977, **34**, 895–908.

Bieber, L., Dain, H. J., Dince, P. R., Drellich, M. G., Grand, H. G., Gundlach, R. H., Kremer, M. W., Rifkin, A. H., Wilbur, C. B. and Bieber, T. B. *Homosexuality: A Psychoanalytical Study*. New York: Basic Books, 1962.

Brittain, R. P. In F. E. Camps (Ed.). *Gradwohl's Legal Medicine*. Bristol: Wright, 1968.

Cohn, N. *The Pursuit of the Millenium: Revolutionary Messianism in Medieval and Reformation Europe and its Bearing on Modern Totaliterian Concepts*. London: Mercury, 1962.

Court, J. H. Pornography – personal and social effects. In N. McConaghy (Ed.). *Liberation Movements and Psychiatry*. Sydney: Geigy, Psychiatric Symposium, 1974.

Court, J. H. *Law, Light and Liberty*. Adelaide: Lutheran Publishing House, 1975.

Court, J. H. Pornography and sex-crimes: A re-evaluation in the light of recent trends around the world. *International Journal of Criminology and Penology*, 1976, **5**, 129–157.

Davis, K. E. and Braucht, G. N. Exposure to pornography, character and sexual deviance: A retrospective survey, *Journal of Social Issues*, 1973, **29**, 183–196.

Dawkins, R. *The Selfish Gene*. Oxford: Oxford University Press, 1976.

Dover, K. J. *Greek Homosexuality*. London: Duckworth, 1978.

Eysenck, H. J. and Nias, D. K. B. *Sex, Violence and the Media*. London: Maurice Temple Smith, 1978.

Feshbach, S. and Malamuth, N. Sex and aggression: Providing the link. *Psychology Today, 1978*, **12**, (6), 111–122.

Ford, C. S. and Beach, F. A. *Patterns of Sexual Behaviour*. New York: Harper, 1951.

Freud, S. *Three Contributions to the Theory of Sex*. New York: Nervous and Mental Disease Publishing Co., 1910.

Frisbie, L. V. *Another Look at Sex Offenders in California*. California Mental Health Research Monograph No. 12, 1969.

Goldstein, M. J., Kant, H. S. with Hartman, J. J. *Pornography and Sexual Deviance*. Los Angeles: University of California Press, 1973.

Hall, R. *The Well of Loneliness* (1928). Reprinted London: Corgi Books, 1968.

Hamburger, C., Stürüp, C. K. and Dahl-Iversen, E. Transvestism: Hormonal, psychiatric and surgical treatment. *Journal of the American Medical Association*, 1953, **152**, 391–394.

Harlow, H. F. and Harlow, M. K. The affectional systems. In A. M. Schrier, M. K. Harlow and F. Stollnitz (Eds). *Behaviour in Non-human Primates* (Vol. 2), pp. 287–334. New York and London: Academic Press, 1965.

Hinde, R. A. *Biological Bases of Human Social Behaviour*. New York: McGraw-Hill, 1974.

Hoyle, R. L. *Essay on Erotic Elements in Peruvian Art*. Geneva: Nagel, 1965.

Huxley, J. Cultural process and evolution. In A. Roe and G. G. Simpson (Eds). *Behaviour and Evolution*, pp. 437–454. New Haven: Yale University Press, 1958.

Kercher, G. A. and Walker, C. E. Reactions of convicted rapists to sexually explicit stimuli. *Journal of Abnormal Psychology*, 1973, **81**, 46–50.

Kutchinsky, B. Towards an explanation of the decrease in registered sex crimes in Copenhagen. *Technical Reports of the Commission on Obscenity and Pornography* (Vol. 7). Washington D.C.: U.S. Government Printing Office, 1971.

Kutchinsky, B. Eroticism without censorship. *International Journal of Criminology and Penology*, 1973, **1**, 217–225.

Kutchinsky, B. Pornography in Denmark – A general summary. In R. Dhavan and C. Davies (Eds). *Censorship and Obscenity*. London: Martin Robertson, 1978.

Litman, G. Women and alcohol. *New Behaviour*, 1975, July, 126.

Lorenz, K. *On Aggression*. London: Methuen, 1963.

Masters, W. H. and Johnson, V. E. *Homosexuality in Perspective*. Boston: Little, Brown, 1979.

Mead, M. *Male and Female*. Harmonsworth: Penguin, 1949.

Milton, J. *Areopagitica* (1644). Reprinted Cambridge: Deighton-Bell, 1973.

Orwell, G. Raffles and Miss Blandish. In *Decline of the English Murder*. Harmondsworth: Penguin, 1945.

Rachman, S. Sexual fetishism: An experimental analogue. *Psychological Record*, 1966, **16**, 293–296.

Radzinowicz, L. *English Studies in Criminal Offences* (Vol. 9). London: Macmillan, 1957.

Roth, M. Personal view. *British Medical Journal*, 1968, **2**, 309.

Roth, M. Human violence as viewed from the psychiatric clinic. *Americal Journal of Psychiatry*, 1972, **9**, 33–46.

Roth, M. and Ball, J. R. B. Psychiatric aspects of intersexuality. In C. N. Armstrong and A. J. Marshall (Eds). *Intersexuality in Vertebrates and Man*. London and New York: Academic Press, 1964.

Rutter, M. Family, area and school influences in the genesis of conduct disorders. In L. Hersov, M. Berger and D. Shaffer (Eds). *Aggression and Anti-social Behaviour in Childhood and Adolescence*. Oxford: Pergamon Press, 1978.

Slater, E. *Biological Differences and Social Justice*. The Geoffrey Vickers Lecture of the Mental Health Trust and Research Fund delivered at Middlesex Hospital, 1973. (Published in the New Statesman.)

Szent-Györgyi, A. The promise of medical science. In G. Wolstenholme (Ed.). *Man and His Future*. London: J. and A. Churchill, 1963.
Vanggaard, T. *Phallos* (English translation). London, 1972.
West, D. J. *Homosexuality*. Harmondsworth: Penguin, 1968.
West, D. J. Rape as revenge. *New Society*, 1978, **45**, 684–686.
Wynne-Edwards, V. C. *Animal Dispersion in Relation to Social Behaviour*. London: Oliver and Boyd, 1962.

Note Added in Proof

The period that has elapsed since this chapter was prepared, has seen the introduction of video cassettes in which the murder and dismemberment of women during sexual intercourse is enacted. At the time of writing, these cassettes are freely available for purchase and viewing in private.

2

Censorship and the limits of permission*

Jonathan Miller

Of all the prohibitions which we lay upon ourselves, sexual censorship is perhaps the most peculiar, for it lays a ban not upon *acts* so much as upon *experiences*, or at least upon such acts which acquire their risky significance by becoming experiences for those who witness them. A substantial proportion of these forbidden scenes do not even consist of representations of acts which are in themselves forbidden; there is no embargo upon the representation of murder, theft, or the breaking of contracts upon the stage. A peculiar notion of risk attaches itself therefore to the violation of certain boundaries that society seems to uphold between private and public activity. So deeply ingrained is this sense of risk that much popular anxiety is expressed whenever the lines that express it are blurred or are in danger of being blurred; an anxiety which resembles, in ways which I hope to reveal later, the fervour which was expressed on behalf of the law against unlimited immigration, anxiety about our entry into Europe, and similar too in some ways to the opposition which is somewhere voiced against the introduction of comprehensive education.

We should note in passing that in addition to the call for prohibition against the spectacle and description of the private parts and their various activities, there is a widespread requirement that we also forbear the use of certain special words which mention these activities or features of the human physique, but whilst terms such as "private parts" and so on are just admissible in this assembly there are terms which I cannot even utter here at the risk of causing a riot or my own arrest – being endowed with a peculiar power to

* This chapter was originally published in 1972 as the Sixth Annual Lecture under the 'Thank-Offering to Britain Fund', and was delivered at the British Academy, London, on 20 October, 1971.

endanger or offend those who might hear them. I will enlarge on this later when I go into the whole question of the origins of our feelings of insult, offence, and abuse.

Let me say in passing that while such words are, or seem to be, endowed with a special power to endanger or corrupt, their endowment varies peculiarly with the social situation in which they are uttered: it is hard for example for me to utter them here. It is hard to utter them in mixed companies of men and women, and they have a peculiar resonance when used in front of children. I would like to suggest that they acquire part of their risky power in this respect more by the social classes which they thereby outline than by any intrinsic actual capacity to pollute or harm.

Whatever pornography is or is not, it is quite clear that the public display of nudity, the widespread representation of sexual activity and the free use of "polluting words" has increased quite markedly in the last few years. But perhaps more important than that there has been a widespread outcry against it all and a feeling that it is getting out of control. There have been a series of requests that the law pay attention to it: prosecutions have been mounted and festivals of light have been convened. And as one might expect in debates over large-scale matters of public concern, both sides refer to principles which each hold to be axiomatic and binding. These axioms, however, are inconsistently applied and each side takes much pleasure in pointing out the way in which their opponents suspend allegiance to their favoured principle when other issues conflict with them. The opponents of censorship, for example, frequently resort to the axiom that it is wrong for any authority to assume that it has a privileged access to the knowledge of the best interests of the community: the exponents of censorship, however, are quick to point out that this axiom against paternalism can be conveniently relaxed in order to allow legislation against racial propaganda. Conversely, those who object to breathalysers, seat belts and speed limits on the grounds that they thereby infringe personal liberty, are open to the accusation that they are being quite inconsistent in their simultaneous appeal for sexual censorship. And in the same way, those who ask for legislation against the indiscriminate architectural assault on the visual environment seem sometimes impervious to the claims of those who rest their appeal for censorship on some of the same broad principles.

Now I am pointing out these inconsistencies not in an effort to discredit either side but simply to show that slogans and axioms enjoy at best a provisional status in the sphere of conflicting moral interests, and that they are referred to partly in proportion to the way in which they seem to sponsor or underwrite these interests. This is not because human beings are incorrigibly hypocritical but because ethical principles are open to the use of discretion. It is not in the nature of moral discourse to expand steadily towards a fixed circumference of axiomatic certainty. As Professor Emmett has pointed out,

> moral judgements remain problematical and it is indeed possible that skill in making moral judgements can only grow through facing the fact that they *are* problematical. To face them responsibly is to approach them as moral problems where the answer is not always provided by looking up the local book of rules.

This hardly means, however, that principles play no part in our moral negotiations: indeed, it is part of what we mean by a moral decision that reference to general principle is necessary in arriving at it. This does not mean, however, that discretion need not apply in the use of a principle, and the fact that in any given instance to which a principle A nominally applies an exception is made, merely shows us something further about the way in which we use principles, namely that there may be other principles or policies which conflict; in which case, reference to a higher principle still will be made in deciding which of the conflicting pair should prevail. In fact as Professor Dworkin points out, it is an integral part of the concept of principle that it makes sense to ask how important it is. The inconsistent application of a principle therefore need not imply – though it may of course – that hypocrisy is at work, but simply that the priority of competing principles has been acknowledged. Nor does it invalidate or cancel the future relevance of the overridden principle.

The point is that it is often hard to identify those axioms which assign weight to competing principles, thereby making it *look* as if advertised principles are adhered to only so long as they yield convenient decisions for those who uphold them. When for instance the exponents of the principle of free expression suspend their allegiance to it in order to allow legislation against racial propaganda, it would be foolish to identify this simply as an example of expedient equivocation. All that has happened is that the exception to one favoured principle has been justified, at least in the eyes of those who recognize its authority, by a supposedly higher principle: namely that it is wrong, harmful, or offensive to advertise the racial inequalities of men.

Controversy arises then largely over the acceptability of such axioms which assign and distribute importance among lower competing principles, and also over the precise wisdom which can be extracted from any given principle with regard to the case in hand.

It is I think a mistake to visualize the system of moral judgements as a series of principles hung from a central axiom, like a chandelier; as if when confidence was withdrawn from that single source of authority, the whole structure falls with a crash. We construct our moral positions instead rather like the Forth Bridge, out of competing principles which bear against one another in a subtle system of cantilevers which carry the weight of conflicting interests across the span of relevant concern. And it is important to understand that there are concealed structural elements in this bridgework which inconspicuously distribute the weight amongst the various principles along lines which are not strictly speaking rational. I believe for instance that those who insist on the self-evident right of a society to protect itself against moral decay often do so out of a heavy emotional investment in what they imagine to be the *status quo*. Conversely, those who appeal to the self-evident sanctity of free expression frequently do so out of the peculiar irrational emphasis which they put upon the redeeming power of sexual release.

This does not mean that I wish to see personal preference ousted from controversy: indeed it is hard to imagine how it could be. I think, however, that we must try, wherever possible, to visualize the motives which finally distribute weight amongst all the conflicting principles which we bring to bear.

Now broadly speaking, there are three classes of principle from which the exponents of censorship draw their arguments: first and most simply is the *moral* justification, which asserts that pornography, and indulgence in it, is wrong; that it is the task of the law to prosecute it as one of the forms of vice. Secondly, there is the *prudential* principle which claims that pornography is in some way socially *harmful*, and lastly there is the argument which insists that even if pornography were neither immoral nor harmful it is at least *offensive* and that the public has a right to be protected against insult, abuse, and nuisance.

Now I have artificially distinguished and clarified the lines which separate these three classes of justification: they blur off into one another and as one examines the controversy closely one can see that those who wish to see pornography controlled will often change principles in midstream or else justify their adherence to a principle in one class, with concealed reference to the self-evidence of that in another. In the face, for instance, of growing empirical evidence against the notion of *harm* in pornography – exponents of control will revert to principles bearing upon the *immorality* of pornography. For example, when challenged about the reasons why pornography is held to be *offensive*, reference will then be made to its intrinsic *harmfulness* and vice versa. I tend myself to believe that any argument in favour of control should rest firmly on the principle of freedom from offence simply because I believe that the ambiguities and contradictions which are associated with the other two are so great that no clear principle emerges from them to take self-evident precedence over the advantages associated with free expression.

The distinctions are further blurred by the fact that there is argument over the nature of moral controversy anyway and it is never quite clear how we can identify a truly *moral* dispute when it is taking place. Arguments about social harm, for instance, are not merely controversial on account of the contradictory facts available but because it is hard to agree about the criteria which determine the moral value placed upon these facts. With the exception of certain crude biological consequences, it is hard to agree as to what would count as an instance of harm, and even in the case of physical injury it is often felt that these are outweighed by other harms which arise from measures designed to offset them. Large numbers of Americans for instance agree that ill-health *is* a harm but suspect the risk of greater spiritual and moral harm arising from undue dependence upon socialized medicine. Nevertheless, it is convenient for the sake of discussion to artificially distinguish the three notions respectively of vice, harm, and offence so long as we understand that allegiance to principles drawn from one of any of these three is often cantilevered by concealed reference to the other two.

Vice then to start with. The most stringent expression of this, although not explicitly aimed at pornography, is contained in James Fitzjames Stephen's (1874) reply to John Stuart Mill: it was, Stephen claimed, the proper task of the law to persecute the principal forms of vice and to promote virtue wherever possible. Stephen then went on to assert that certain activities – presumably sexual ones – are unquestionably evil and wicked. The problem then arises, as to the criteria by which the unquestionable viciousness of certain conduct is to be recognized. In a uniformly Christian community most of the sexual vices can be identified as the closed series of activities mentioned as such in the Scriptures. And in a different area: for Jews, there is a fixed menu of food prohibitions hereby defining dietary vice by index. So long as the authority of these prescriptions is acknowledged there is no problem about identification of vice. Stephen goes on to assert, however, that these prescriptions must square with popular intuition and that it would be improper to try and implement prohibitions which did not match public feeling. However, not only does Stephen regard the essence of popular revulsion as a reason for withholding the hand of the law on occasions, it is evident that he thinks that its actual presence will be a positive inspiration as to when and how heavily the law should act. He thereby credits public intuition with a special power for identifying viciousness, on the assumption presumably, though he never openly says so, that this faculty will, even in the absence of explicit allegiance to the Scriptures which list such vices, reproduce the prescriptions embodied in natural law. Now in Stephen's case one is immediately led to inquire why popular opinion on these matters was given such a privileged status, in view of the fact that in his subsequent chapter on equality he demonstrated that he felt no such thing. Stephen acknowledges "the triumphant progress of popular franchise", for instance, admitting at the same time however that he is "altogether at a loss to understand how it can rouse enthusiastic admiration in anyone whatsoever". Now one immediately wants to ask how a man can view the concrete implements of public feeling with such suspicion and at the same time credit that very feeling with a special capacity for identifying vice and rationing its punishment.

Quite apart from the inconsistencies in Stephen's own position, a problem arises anyway as to the moral credentials of indignation as such. For if public hatred of its activity is to be a leading criterion for the identification of its viciousness, and if this sense of indignation need only rise to an agreed threshold of vehemence and unanimity, one might be tempted to imagine that it was only necessary to poll a representative sample of opinion, add up the individual quanta and call upon the law whenever the sum exceeded a certain agreed value. Now quite apart from the practical problems of canvassing opinions on the Clapham omnibus, how can one be sure that the samples of indignation thus obtained represent truly *moral* instances? Revulsion and indignation can arise from many sources, not all of which fulfil the stipulated requirements of *moral* hatred – whatever these may be.

Stephen, however, seems unmoved by such doubts and is content to allow a vehement call for revenge to prompt the law's action. This, however, holds the law to the ransom of any extreme popular sentiment. The law can be recruited on behalf of almost any extreme feeling on the part of the public as long as this meets the required standards of intensity and unanimity. As Professor Hart (1969) has pointed out, though, the spine-chilling principle of emotional populism was almost explicitly recognized by the Nazi morality statutes of 1935. (A society, incidentally, which put peculiar emphasis upon cleanliness and fear of filth, and which applied the notions of filth very widely beyond obscenity to certain racial groups and also to certain categories of modern art. This is a point to which I hope to return later.)

Nevertheless, in a democracy one cannot ride roughshod over public opinion and those who initiate reforming legislation ahead of public sentiment must expect to have the tables turned on them at the next election. Fortunately, on the other hand, it has often been shown that the *fait accompli* of reform is frequently followed by a somewhat more realistic view of the offences which once excited such irrational indignation. In this sense the law may, far from enforcing morals, help to recreate in the public imagination, a new conception as to what will henceforth count as morals. Stephen himself once claimed that the crime of murder was held to be heinous partly because men were hanged for it. True enough: since the abolition of this peculiarly interesting ritual, murder has lost its aura of sacred dread and popular opinion now sees most examples of the crime in a somewhat more realistic light, freed as it is from the melodramatic shadows of the execution shed. In much the same way sexual spectacle loses part of its horror when the prohibitions enshrined in restrictive law are relaxed. Of course the opponents of permission claim that this is precisely the effect which they fear, that the growing indifference of the public to the inherent immorality of spectacles now overlooked by the law is precisely what the retention of a repressive law is meant to avoid. But this argument leads to an absurd circularity; for if popular indignation against certain acts can subside when the law chooses to ignore them, such a sentiment is hardly the most reliable criterion to judge whether or not the law should have authority over them in the first place.

In recent years a more sophisticated version of the morality principle has been formulated, most distinctly by Lord Devlin in his Maccabaean lecture in 1954, and in his book *The Enforcement of Morals* (1965). Now according to this formula, the immorality of certain acts is a necessary but not a sufficient justification for the law's action against it. The threshold requirement is provided by the recognition that the spread of the activity would threaten the shared morality of society at large. His argument then goes as follows: since society is held together by the restraints of its shared morality, the extensive spread of practices that violate that morality would allow the community to fall apart. In this case, according to Devlin, the state has as much right to use the law against such practices as it does against treason.

Now there is a weak and a strong way to interpret this proposal, both of which are open to objections. In the weak sense the immoral tendency of certain conduct, say the sale of and indulgence in pornography, is purely arithmetical. That is to say with each successive person who falls prey to its charms, society has lost a quota of its previous virtue. The immorality of the society is then co-extensive with the arithmetical sum of those who indulge in pornography. In this weak sense there are no causal consequences imputed to the act of indulgence – to indulge is to *be* immoral; so that in a society of X members, N of whose numbers indulge, the simple coefficient of pornographic immorality is N over X. Presumably Lord Devlin does not identify the immoral tendency of an act in this weak arithmetical sense, but in a stronger more causal fashion, to the effect that each new recruit to the vice in question thereby renders himself susceptible to further acts which when performed by the majority would have consequences beyond the loss of grace occasioned by the single act of indulgence itself. And in this way the aggregate of immoral consequences might be larger than the sum of the individual indulgences taken separately. Now in both the weak and in the strong sense the immorality of the act in question is at least a necessary condition of its being a subject of legal concern, but this throws us back to the unsettled question of how we recognize the necessary minimum of immorality. As a Christian, Lord Devlin would presumably have no difficulty whatsoever because religious intuition would supply the answer. However, he realistically acknowledges that a large part of the population is no longer Christian, so that like Stephen he is forced to fall back on popular feeling, as if in some way this were an anamnestic residue of the original piety. We have already seen though how unreliable this source of authority is.

Lord Devlin is, however, on firmer ground with the stronger version of his doctrine, since the suggestion that the spread of certain immoralities, so-called, might lead to *harm* is at least open to investigation and takes us some way into the next class of the two mentioned earlier, i.e. the area of *harms*.

There are, however, two fundamental problems which lie upstream on the empirical issue of whether or not harmful effects flow from the use of pornography. These problems are associated with the way in which we visualize the so-called shared morality of the community. In the first case, as Professor Hart asks, is it actually true to claim that society has a shared morality, a seamless structure, and how do we recognize it? Might we take a census of avowed ideals, or like ethnologists, merely try to infer these ideals from broadly observed consistencies of behaviour? It is my belief that whichever approach we take we will almost certainly discover that society is amazingly plural: social classes vary between one another and even within classes you will find an astounding scatter of practices and ideals. This I think is what Professor Hart means when he accuses Lord Devlin of hovering above the terra firma of contemporary social reality.

There is, however, a slightly more awkward problem associated with Lord Devlin's claim that morality is what holds society together, for expressed in this way it visualizes morality as an independent system of restrictions which holds in place a structure that would otherwise disintegrate. Such a view springs I believe from a Hobbesian fiction of the state of nature wherein human beings, unrestrained, fall upon one another and consume themselves in lust and greed. As far as I can see we have no more reason for accepting this view of man than that of Rousseau, which conceived the state of nature to be a sublime harmony of good humour. The rules, principles, policies, and ideals by which we live are as much *constitutive* as they are *regulative*, that is to say they exist not simply to prevent a ferocity which we otherwise dread, but partly to define the identity of the community which might otherwise be unrecognizable both to itself and to outsiders who look at it. The laws of cricket, for instance, largely exist in order to render the game visibly distinct from any other game which might be played with ball and stumps: if we alter the rule about "overs" for instance, and allow sixty balls to be delivered from each end there is a trivial sense in which one might say that the game of cricket has disappeared. It is more accurate, however, to say that it has altered its constitution. When the rules of football were relaxed in order to allow players to handle the ball, there was not an outcry against the possibility that a Hobbesian version of the familiar sport would now ensue, but simply a slow formal recognition that an alternative constitution had created a new game. It would be foolish of course to pretend that all rules are of this constitutive sort – there are well-known *restrictive* rules, against fouling for instance, which were introduced in order to restrain strong tendencies amongst the players to have their way in spite of the constitution. No doubt some of our so-called moral principles are of this type, but I would claim that in this stage of our sociological knowledge we have not successfully distinguished amongst them all. And I would maintain, if only for the sake of heuristic argument, that the rules about pornography fall very largely within the constitutive class and that by relaxing them we will simply change the constitution of public life. Whether this will be for the worse or not is hard to predict – I am not even certain of the criteria by which we would tell. There is no clear argument as to what would count one way or the other. Meanwhile it seems unwise, improper, and unjust to use the law to enforce the maintenance of a constitution on the much disputed assumption that we now have the best of all possible worlds.

It is fair to admit, however, that causal consequences generally agreed to be *harmful* might issue from the widespread use of pornography.

We have passed therefore into the area of *harm* and before trying to sketch a plan of the harms which we envisage we should I think remind ourselves at least of three considerations which decide how or when action should be taken to offset them. First there is the question of the *probability* that harm will arise from the use of pornography. Secondly, we must estimate the *gravity* of the harm produced, and finally we must know and accept the *price* of such measures that we take to offset it. With these three variables in the back of our mind let us draw a map of possible harms that might arise from the uncontrolled supply and consumption of sexual spectacle.

The crudest hypothesis asserts that pornography somehow raises the level of sexual excitement in the consumer and that to some extent he finds this pleasurable. Under the heading of vice this in itself would be enough, but under the heading of *harm* we must take the issue several stages further. In other words what possible harms might result from increased sexual excitement? *(a)* It might lead the excited consumer to perform acts that were unacceptably harmful to himself, *(b)* it might lead him to perform acts that were unacceptably harmful to others, *(c)* it might produce excitement that leads him either to the unsuccessful pursuit of satisfaction or else to no activity at all, but in either case leaving him in a condition of frustrated excitement which might in turn be *(a)* unacceptably harmful to himself, *(b)* lead him to *indirect* satisfactions that were unacceptably harmful to others, i.e. which made him dangerously aggressive or socially unreliable in other ways.

It is very hard to obtain reliable figures on all these variables, but from the investigations published in the President's Report in the United States it seems that the excitement produced by pornography is short-lived anyhow, and whatever satisfactions are sought in that short term are either acceptable to the law as it now stands or else so subtle in their long-term effects that we simply cannot make them out. The most immediate consequence is either an increase in masturbation, or an increased resort to satisfaction through the cooperation of available partners. Now while it is true to say that the law does not, nor do most people wish it to exert sanctions against either self-abuse or fornication, one could only make a case for the aggregate harm arising from widespread fornication on the grounds that the extensive and intensive negotiations necessary for obtaining lawful satisfaction will be more harmful than the sum of any supposed harm arising from any individual acts between consenting adults. This sort of view of harm is close to the public lawn argument so beloved of moral philosophers, namely that the deterioration of an important public commodity, like a lawn, increases with each successive violation which in and of itself, produces only a subliminal effect.

Two points arise here, one empirical and one normative. Is there any evidence to show that pornography leads to increased fornication on a long-lasting and widespread scale? Secondly, are the secondary effects of this overall change in conduct sufficiently harmful to merit the task of imposing restrictions upon such stimuli that supposedly give rise to them? Once again it is extremely hard to answer these questions. Let us take the empirical one first. There is I think no clearcut evidence to the effect that fornication has increased very markedly since the introduction of freely available pornography. Of course to be fair it is hard to know how one would ever know, since unlike rape, fornication is not a reportable incident. Indirect evidence from the rise of venereal disease may or may not indicate a rise of such activity. I imagine it does, but there is no evidence to show that pornography has played a significant part: rather it shows that sexual conduct all round is now much freer and that public indulgence in pornography is part and parcel of a large-scale trend that has its origins elsewhere. Anyway, from what we know about the mind it seems very unlikely that mere spectacle or description can excite to the point where long-lasting changes of social conduct ensue. The mind is not a passive receptacle that can be tuned like an electric accumulator. Such a crude physical model assumes a view of human nature that ought to shame its exponent. Sexual satisfaction is sought for a thousand different reasons, and our motives both for seeking it and abstaining from it are too complex for pornography to play anything more than a marginal role in shaping its overall expression in society.

So that the second question of what it would be like if we became a nation of fornicators is almost meaningless. You have to interfere with the physical substance of the brain before sexual activity becomes noticeably out of control. Pornography is a complex experience, one that encounters a personality elaborately structured with tastes, scruples, compunctions, affections, loyalties and ambitions.

Are there, on the other hand, any classes of person at special risk from the exciting effects of sexual literature or spectacle? Common sense suggests that there might be, especially the immature and the unhealthy. Take the unhealthy first: one might expect that those whose sense of other people's presence was deficient in some way might be more than usually susceptible to sexual stimulation. The facts on the other hand are equivocal. Sexual criminals are sometimes found in possession of pornographic literature but it is hard to say whether this is even a contributing cause of their crime. It could represent – and I believe it does – a futile effort to obtain harmless satisfaction. Conversely in a large series of sexual criminals investigated in America it was shown that they had if anything been under-exposed to pornographic material. One way or the other, the group at risk is so small and the probability of harmful influence so minute that it hardly seems worth the complex administrative and social costs of protecting the community from them by prohibiting the overall sale of pornography.

What about the immature? It seems improbable that children can be swayed one way or the other by witnessing or reading about the varieties of sexual activity. There may of course be other effects and these we shall come to in a moment, but in terms of *excitement* I believe that the sources of erratic behaviour in children are notably those which involve personal relationships between peers and parents and that these exert an overriding effect which makes obscenity and pornography a relatively small influence. This does not mean however that I believe that there are no artificial sexual excitements for young people, but simply that they do not coincide with the pornography which we dread. A profound sexual excitement is clearly associated in young people with the performance of popular music and not simply with those performances which fall within the category of the obscene. Pop idols, notably the Beatles in the early 1960s, whose performances were models of propriety, can become the subjects of sexual hysteria. It would however be extremely hard to set up criteria for censoring them. Our willingness to prohibit spectacles that are overtly obscene, it seems to me, reverts to justifications based on our belief that the spectacles are *vicious*, over and above any *harms* which we might impute to them.

Finally, in regard to the stimulating effects of pornography, one might add that whatever capacity pornography might or might not have in this direction, partly arises from the fact that it is prohibited and that once we have become habituated to it, the sexual activity excited will revert to a normal level anyway. This is evident from the fall-off in the commercial success of blue films in America.

What other effects then apart from increases in the sheer quantity of sexual excitement could ensue from the unrestricted consumption of pornography? I can conceive three further classes of possible influence. The first is what I call the *imprinting* effect, the next the *exemplary*, and finally the *impoverishment* effect. The *imprinting* effect might work as follows: it is theoretically possible that by offering a variety of sexual representations to the public at large one might thereby pervert the normal sexual appetites and crystallize desire around inappropriate and therefore harmful objects. I call this the imprinting effect by analogy with the phenomenon reported by the ethnologists who show that animals can, if exposed at susceptible moments in their life, be fixated upon inappropriate sexual objects. If this became widespread one might have reasons for feeling anxiety, if only for the future existence of the race. However, the origin of human sexual preference is much more obscure than this anxiety suggests. To start with, the factors which determine preference are actual rather than representational, that is to say that they have to do with concrete life situations in which the subject is a protagonist as opposed to a spectator of scenes; and it is hard anyway to know which particular situations exert the prime effect in this regard. Apart from which the main lines of preference are almost certainly set up by the time exposure to pornography is even likely; and whatever exposure is provided during this phase will almost certainly pass unnoticed except by adults who are aghast for other reasons altogether at the thought of a child witnessing representations of the sexual act in all its variety. However, it is possible that while the main lines of sexual preference are established in the first seven years of life, there could be a latent leeway for subsequent modification and that pornography might exert its effects at this point, say in early adolescence. The evidence here however is quite equivocal and although there are some figures to show that exposure to pornography at an early stage is associated with a high incidence of promiscuity and perversion, it is hard to say that one is the cause of the other. Addiction to pornography at an early age might be a concomitant feature of personalities that were inclined to promiscuity and deviation anyway. Anyway the harms arising from these consequences are both ambiguous in nature and marginal in frequency, as compared say to the well-established risks of smoking, which are both larger in quantity and in my view at least, socially and morally destructive – much more so than either promiscuity or perversion. The loss of man hours, the injury to families, the loss of heads of families and of mothers and the personal hardship that arises from smoking in the shape of chronic bronchitis and narrowed heart arteries are now so clearly established that if prophylactic legislation against harm really were a serious intention of the law one might expect to see something more than a statutory warning on the side – on the side mind you! – of the packet.

The same goes for the immoderate intake of fats and sweets and confections, most of which have an indifferent utility, all of which however shorten life and impair the quality of that part which precedes death. I point this out simply to indicate that our peculiar immediate interest at this moment in the harmful effects of pornography must on the evidence of our comparative indifference to more clearly established sources of harm spring from other, less prudential reasons, and that we pile up whatever empirical evidence we can in order to provide a utilitarian justification for a standpoint that actually has its origins elsewhere. For want of a better term I would call this an example of moral materialism, parallel to what William James recognized as medical materialism in the matter of food taboos. I will enlarge on this later.

Meanwhile let us move to the supposed *exemplary* effects of pornography. What I mean by this is that the representation of sexual activity on well accredited channels of public communication might seem to lend official approval to conduct whose effects were socially harmful. This assumes however *(a)* that there is a widespread state of sexual readiness, only requiring an authoritative example in its favour to produce a concerted output of such behaviour, *(b)* that the authority of such an example was uniformly recognized, enough to override all the other various and widely distributed scruples which bear upon the matter, *(c)* that the conduct thus released is socially harmful enough to require the attention of the law. Now while I admit that sex is an urgent appetite it is not by any means uniformly pressing. The assumption that morality and law are laid over an ancient state of primeval promiscuity is a fiction long since abandoned by serious anthropologists. Whatever permissive example is offered by the authorized publication of sexual spectacle works upon a plural population of sexual motives, which are in turn heavily modulated by the individual personal contexts wherein sex has its place. We are not spring-guns of lust, ready to fire at the first blundering footstep of unwary example. Secondly, not everyone recognizes the authority of those who promulgate such examples; and it is my firm conviction anyway that society can readily accommodate itself to such conduct that might be released by the threshold stimulus of such accredited example.

There is however another more subtle exemplary effect of sexual spectacle which one might reasonably deplore without necessarily wishing to see the law invoked to prevent it. This effect I think is associated more with art and with advertising than with hard pornography. It involves the idea that a peculiarly valuable form of personal fulfilment can actually be obtained through sex. Promoted through well accredited channels and expounded by admired public figures, this dogma – which has some of its origin in writers like D.H. Lawrence – suggests a peculiar sexual route for obtaining personal satisfaction and fulfilment. Now, human variety being what it is, large numbers of people thus encouraged will fall short of the advertised satisfaction and may henceforth feel ashamed of having failed to realize an ideal that is currently held in high, and I think unrealistic, esteem by some well recognized authorities in the community. Offered the lure of self-fulfilment through sex, many people, the young in particular, might be induced to experiment before they were emotionally prepared for it and in the face of the almost inevitable disappointment, not forswear sex forever exactly, but fall into a premature pessimism about human relationships in general which might obstruct subsequent sexual adjustment. On the other hand, the sexual ignorance of the young has to be set against this and it is useful to bear in mind that pornography undoubtedly provides the first useful introduction to the possible varieties of sexual experience – not altogether a bad thing. Anyway, there are many other forms of misleading literature which might do harm perhaps by virtue of authoritative example – films, plays, and books which advertise an ill-founded social optimism could equally lead to the harm of sharp awakening, yet no one calls for censorship of *The Sound of Music* for instance or for restrictions upon works that advertise the pleasures of wealth and fame.

Finally, we come to the well-established theory that pornography offers an impoverished version of human life. The David Holbrook theory. Certainly an exclusive diet of pornography is thin fare and as an exclusive image of human fulfilment it presents a dismal spectacle. But then so is a diet of cookery books and reports of wine tasting. There is a very sound reason for this: one which was first elucidated by the neurologist Sherrington when he divided animal activity – and human activity too – into two compartments, the appetitive and the *consummatory*. Briefly, consummatory behaviour comprises all those elementary reactions which bring certain chains of pursuit to a conclusion – food entering the mouth reaches a certain point at which a highly stereotyped irreversible event takes over, and the food is swallowed. Immediately before that the food may be chewed and savoured and as one moves back from the act of eating itself, behaviour becomes progressively more varied and optional, intelligent and interesting with regard to the food pursued. We feel hungry, assess the priority of this feeling in the context of all our other desires and obligations, and then if the time is ripe choose a restaurant, and then look at a menu: finally we converge upon the stereotyped consummatory act of swallowing. All that is most characteristically human though occurs during the long preliminary appetitive phase. The nearer we approach consummation the more stereotyped we become and the less we can be distinguished from one another. So also with sex – our humanity expresses itself in those infinitely various ways wherein we negotiate with one another for eventual satisfaction. Gewndolen Harleth and Cleopatra differ from one another not by virtue of their performances in bed but in the subtle programmes of encouragement and procrastination that lead to the final relatively monotonous conclusion.

One of the reasons I am sure why pornography tries so hard to multiply the varieties of performance is that it knows implicitly that it is dealing with a phase of behaviour penultimate to a stereotyped outcome. No novel, for example, ever finds it necessary to advertise the 180 postures of friendship. Pornography achieves its characteristic poverty because it is set aside from an area where variety and individuality can be expressed. I have always felt that the most convincing image of hell is that of Dante in which one would be condemned to repeat the stereotyped manoeuvres of sexual pleasures forever; one in which the punishment comprises no more and no less than the need to perform, in eternity, the very sin for which the punishment was inflicted in the first place. For this reason alone I cannot fear the harmful effects of pornography, since anyone normal who has been exposed to pornography, hard or soft, far from falling under the sway of its pornotopian spell loses interest after a while and returns with pleasure and gusto to the varieties of experience of the world at large. Those who become addicted to its characteristic impoverishments are in a mental state close to that of an obsessional neurotic who will actually seek its stereotype in order to enact a symbolic representation of their personal mastery over life. We know for instance that patients with organic brain damage will actually seek an environment whose ritualized monotony falls within their capacity to control it; so with pornography. Far from impoverishing people it offers for those who for some reason or other *are* impoverished a secure annex of controllable fantasy within which their limited emotional versatility will not show up. For the rest it is a holiday where they are free for a moment to indulge their fantasies and furnish themselves with new images; for fantasy after all plays a vital and nourishing part in maintaining the health and versatility of the imagination. Like dreams, we need fantasies in order to play with emotional conjectures; and a mind unstocked with the variety of alternative conjectures is not equipped to meet the challenges of reality.

Another objection to pornography runs as follows: that it advertises a view of the world where people use each other as objects. The answer is, it may or may not. He who extracts from pornography an endorsement of his tendency to exploit another as if he had no feelings, is already crippled by some early failure in psychological manufacture and he will exploit his sexual partners just as he does his family or his colleagues in business. At a time in history when our institutions make promiscuous objective use of human beings anyway it seems inappropriate to focus on pornography as a special source of this tendency.

Anyway, I am convinced that the asphyxiated poverty of much pornography arises from the fact that sex and its representation have been quarantined for so long that pornography has fallen into an invalid condition, thereby acquiring the contagious features which we dread. Re-established as part of all the other things which we consume, it will revert to its normal complexion and proportion.

Meanwhile, however, it continues to give *offence* and there seems to be no good reason for inflicting mental distress upon those who fear its appearance. I feel that plays and films should advertise their sexual content so that those who wish to enter can do so and those who are likely to be offended can abstain. Shops which sell hard-core pornography should conceal their wares from the street. Television is a harder problem since the instrument invades the home and people should feel as free from insult arising from this source as they rightly expect from the general post. Nevertheless people are free to turn off the instrument and although this may seem to infringe their right to use the full resources of a public commodity, they can freely switch channels and often do so to avoid subjects which merely bore them without asserting that they are thereby deprived of a quota of their licence worth.

But let me for a moment subtract insult from injury and ask why certain spectacles and words *should* be offensive. Is it because those who fear them suspect its capacity to injure? If so, they must infer it by intuition since, as we have already shown, the evidence one way or the other is hard to obtain and not even available to the people who hold such vehement opinions on the matter. Or do they find it offensive because it is inherently vicious? In which case by what criteria, apart from the fact that it is felt to be offensive, do we tell whether it is vicious or not? I believe myself that no empirical evidence against the supposed harm of pornography will ever convince those who are opposed to it. It is hard to imagine a more exhaustive report than the President's Commission and yet when confronted by it the President himself rejected its conclusions out of hand. What I believe is going on is as follows: sexual acts and their representation in public are deemed to be both immoral and offensive for reasons which are undisclosed, and that prudential justifications for this opinion are then imported to satisfy the demands of a society which is widely committed to utilitarian principles. This I have already called moral materialism and as an illustration of what I mean I'd like to refer to a parallel form of materialism which is used to underwrite the value of the kosher food laws. For this analysis I am indebted to Mary Douglas and her book *Purity and Danger*, published in 1966.

For orthodox Jews it is immoral to consume certain foods and offensive to witness such consumption. Certain prudential reasons have been imported to justify these practices, to the effect for example that shellfish and pork are unhygienic. Now it seems unlikely that either pork or shellfish *are* intrinsically more harmful than mutton or trout, and whatever risks *are* associated with them could hardly have been inferred by the authorities who first prohibited them. Besides if you examine all the other abominations of Leviticus you will find that they include prohibitions that could not be explained by any stretch of the medical imagination. Professor Douglas suggests that such a system of prohibitions can only be understood *as a*

ystem and that the community by observing it, actually registers its recogniz-
ble apartness from races all round. In other words, very briefly, systems of
prohibition frequently exist in order to enshrine a symbolic model of the
social order and indeed of orderliness in general. Lines are then drawn not so
much to fence off an otherwise prevailing savagery but to represent the
valuable assurances of pattern and predictability.

The notion of pollution and filth then attaches itself not so much to any
intrinsic property of what is feared, but to the fact that what is feared violates
some boundary which has been established for symbolic reasons.

We tend, therefore, to abhor objects, persons, or incidents which somehow
violate reassuringly distinct classifications of the world. Not because any of
these things displays properties that are intrinsically dangerous, but because
they have features which upset our notion of what is what. The notion of filth,
horror, and pollution becomes associated therefore with whatever defies the
common categories or classification. Broadly speaking, they fall into the
following groups:

A. *Dubious animals*

Those mentioned in Leviticus, for example. Also spiders and insects which
display anomalous forms of locomotion.

B. *Marginal elements of the human body*

Excreta, nail clippings, hair, saliva, and semen. Substances which are not
quite part of the body, but which are not truly constituents of the outside
world either. In this category one can include the abhorrence of certain
misuses of bodily parts – the wrong thing in the wrong place, e.g. buggery,
fellatio, and cunnilingus. In other words, practices which violate the accepted
classification of the human sphincters and their function.

C. *Persons who do not fit any of the convenient social slots*

Ghosts, vampires, and werewolves.
Tramps, hippies, and homosexuals.
Jews, gypsies, and bastards.

D. *Certain unclassifiable substances*

Substances that present anomalous physical properties such as stickiness or
sliminess.

Substances that cause alterations of consciousness half way between
cooperative alertness and complete unconsciousness.

E. *Unfamiliar artifices which defy familiar classifications*
Modern art and modern music. The commonest form of abuse levelled
at these manifestations at their first appearance is filth, mess, and noise.
Immediately the audience understands, however, the new classification into
which these forms fall, indignation tends to disappear altogether.

F. *Deviations from accepted social practices*
Bad table manners, breaches of courtesy, and all those forms of conduct
which fall outside the ordinary rules or standards.

G. *Obscenity and pornography*
Strictly speaking, these do not belong in a class on their own and the horror
which they arouse is caused by the ways in which they coincide with one or
another of the groups mentioned above.

Clearly it would be foolish to try and explain our horror of public obscenity
on the basis of this explanation alone. The origin of sexual modesty is very
complicated and varies in form from culture to culture. Nevertheless, I think
it is possible to explain *some* of the rules, and the horror which is aroused by
breaking them, on a purely constitutive basis. For instance, we are anxious
about children witnessing the sexual act, not necessarily because there is a
substantial danger in their doing so, but because the rule *preventing* them
from doing so helps to define what we mean by a child. In an advanced
technological society it becomes more and more important to segregate the
immature so that they can be trained in the elaborate skills which will allow
them to prosper and be useful. In order to train someone like this, however,
they must be labelled and marked off as socially distinct from all those that we
exempt from pedagogical pressure. In other words, we impose or manufacture the innocence of children, thereby creating a class of individuals who
are recognizably "in statu pupillari"; or as Ivan Illich says, "Defining
children as full-time pupils permits the teacher to exercise a kind of power
over their persons."

The same principle applies to women and to the way in which we carefully
protect them from obscene spectacle or foul language. Our culture requires a
class of person to raise children, and in order to visualize this regiment of
nursemaids we confer upon them the privilege of chastity and thereby render
them socially visible and politically manageable.

But why should the present outcry be so shrill? The obvious answer would
be that there is more obscenity than hitherto, and that anyone in his right
mind would be disturbed. Now, although there is some truth in this reply, it
oversimplifies the case by isolating one anxiety and ignoring related worries
about pollution in general. Just as it's hard to account for the dietary abomi-

nations of Leviticus by a piecemeal material analysis of the individual abominations concerned, it is futile to try and explain the growing anxiety about
moral corruption without taking into consideration the concurrent fuss over
other forms of pollution – racial, social, and chemical.

What I believe is happening is this. Our collective picture of both the
physical and social world is undergoing one of the largest upheavals in
history. Atomic physics has disturbed the familiar distinction between matter
and energy. Biology has dissolved the boundaries between animals and men;
psychology has helped to blur the line between responsibility and determination and all around the social scene has become distressingly fluid. Individuals
can be reconstructed from their separate organs. Living cells can be assembled from their living molecules. Social classes are no longer separated from
one another and yet, whilst merit is subsidized in order to allow a rapid
upward mobility, countervailing moves are afoot to mitigate the unprecedented inequalities to which these initiatives give rise. Everything is in a
state of flux. Small wonder then that symbolic representations of order and
stability, such as are reflected for example in the various systems of etiquette
and decorum, are reasserted with fresh enthusiasm, and their violation condemned with a shrillness which is quite out of proportion to the danger
involved. Of course there *are* dangers associated with the physical pollution
of the environment. Poisoned air and foul rivers represent a genuine hazard
for human survival. Similarly, incoherent sexual misconduct on a wide scale
could seriously endanger the integrity of the social fabric; but the anxiety is
disproportionate to the risk and represents an irrational response to the
alteration of order in general. We have seen such manifestations several
times in recent history. During the political confusion of Weimar, people
became unreasonably anxious about moral and artistic corruption and also
about racial pollution. Not because there were any substantial hazards
involved, but because these symbols of pollution represented a vivid symbol
image of an order in jeopardy. The American historian Richard Hofstadter
has strikingly christened this response as a "paranoid style" and along with
sociologists like Daniel Bell, has shown how it constitutes an irrational and
finally destructive answer to the threats posed by modern life. In fact, modern life
is dangerous and uncertain; our collective destiny unprecedently confused. It
behoves us therefore to discriminate all the more carefully amongst various
hazards involved. We must identify the *genuine* risks and exorcize the
phantoms. Our current concern with obscenity and pornography merely
delays constructive social action and presents a spectator from another planet
with an image as absurd as that of someone trying to adjust their dress before
jumping from a burning building.

References

Devlin, P. *The Enforcement of Morals*. Oxford: Oxford University Press, 1965.
Douglas, M. *Purity and Danger*. London: Routledge, 1966.
Hart, H. L. A. *Law, Liberty and Morality*. Oxford: Oxford University Press, 1963.
Stephen, J. F. *Liberty, Equality, Fraternity* (2nd Edn). London: Smith, Elder and Co., 1874.

3

Pornography and free speech

Antony Grey

That virtue . . . which is but a youngling in the contemplation of evil, and knows not the utmost that vice promises to her followers, and rejects it, is but a blank virtue, not a pure; her whiteness is but an excremental whiteness. (John Milton, 1644)

The Unloved Censor

Censorship has a bad name. It is associated – and rightly – with totalitarian regimes and the circumscribing of individual freedom. It is curious how even its enthusiastic advocates seek more palatable euphemisms (e.g. "quality control") with which to commend it.

This chapter is concerned primarily with the censorship of obscenity and pornography: although, as will be seen, I regard this as being just as political as other forms of censorship. I start from the premise that *all* censorship is evil, because it diminishes human freedom and interferes with the spontaneity of communication. In an ideal world there would be no censorship, but the world we live in is far from ideal; and for the foreseeable future there will be some censorship. What there is should be as limited as possible, and should be kept under constant and vigilant scrutiny. The burden of proving that censorship is the lesser evil in any given instance should always lie upon those (be they the representatives of the State or private bodies or persons) who seek to impose it. And such proof should include solid evidence of demonstrable harm, greater than the harm wrought by the proposed censorship, to an individual, to a group, or to society as a whole, if the article or information in question remained uncensored.

Such harm can usually be proved in cases of legitimate restriction of information on grounds of State security or libel upon an individual (even though the law on these matters is currently widely acknowledged to be defective and awaits legislative improvement). In matters of public taste and morals, however, to which censorship of obscenity and pornography relates, tangible evidence of harm or damage is much more elusive. These questions are essentially subjective – and it is for this reason above all that I believe the less the law intrudes into the realm of public and private morality, the better.

What is Pornography?

The 1959 *Obscene Publications Act,* which is the main plank of the existing law of England relating to obscene material, is entitled "An Act to amend the law relating to the publication of obscene matter; to provide for the protection of literature; and to strengthen the law concerning pornography". It is thus clear that the Act – while it is designed to permit something which is obscene to be published legally if it is found by a court to be for the public good because it is "in the interests of science, literature, art or learning, or of other objects of general concern" – is intended to give no quarter to pornographic matter devoid of redeeming qualities.

And of course, we all know what smut is when we see it. Or do we? Like the traveller who, when asked by the customs officer "is that book pornographic?" growled, "How do I know? I haven't got a pornograph!", one may well think at times that dirt lies in the eye of the beholder. Courts and juries have grappled inconclusively with this problem for over 200 years.

The *Oxford Concise Dictionary* unhelpfully sends us round in circles:

Pornography – description of manners etc. of harlots;
          treatment of obscene subjects in literature.
Obscene – repulsive, filthy, loathsome, indecent, lewd.
Lewd – lascivious, unchaste, indecent.
Lascivious – lustful, wanton, inciting to lust.
Indecent – unbecoming, immodest, obscene.

D. H. Lawrence – himself a prime sufferer from the obscenity laws – is more explicit. In his essay *Pornography and Obscenity* (Lawrence, 1929) he writes:

> Genuine pornography . . . is almost always underworld, it doesn't come out into the open . . . you can recognise it by the insult it offers, invariably, to sex, and to the human spirit. Pornography is the attempt to insult sex, to do dirt on it. This is unpardonable.

Yet pornography, he goes on to claim, is itself created by our society's prudish sexual furtiveness. "Without secrecy there would be no pornography. . . . No other civilisation has driven sex into the underworld, and nudity to the W.C." Poor Lawrence! What would he have said about Soho today, I wonder? There are, it would seem, ways of doing dirt on sex quite openly.

A number of more recent definitions of pornography, cited by Francis Bennion (unpublished),* collectively indicate that pornographic material has one or more of the following characteristics:

It causes offence or outrage (usually, but not necessarily, sexual).

It stimulates sexual excitement without engaging the emotions (i.e. promotes lust but not love).

It dehumanizes sex.

It exploits sex for commercial gain.

It harms those who read, see or hear it or who participate in its production.

Most people would agree that debasing or doing dirt on sex is not desirable, either for individuals or for society as a whole. Lasting harm to individuals or to society is even less desirable – if it can be proved. Is censorship, then, the answer, or does it simply make forbidden fruit seem sweeter? One of the most immediately apparent drawbacks to censorship as it has been operated by prosecuting counsel and judges in our courts, even in recent years, is its assumption that *all* sex – and not just pornographic sex – is dirty: surely a most unhealthy attitude. Indeed, one might almost conclude that prurience appears to be a characteristic sexual stance of lawyers. In the mid-1960s, for instance, a former Lord Chief Justice (Lord Parker) made it quite clear that the naked human body was, so far as the law was concerned, "indecent" in judicial eyes:

'Indecent' means unbecoming and immodest . . . something that offends the ordinary modesty of the average man. . . . If you are on the beach with your children and a woman takes off her clothes, that is indecent. We just don't do that sort of thing in this country. Or let us say you were attending an athletic or sporting event and the athletes, beautiful physiques though they may have, have not got clothing which fits properly, and as they perform you see their private parts. This is indecent. (R. v. *Stanley*, 1965)

What would Lawrence have thought of that? And in 1981, when the *Indecent Displays (Control) Act* was enacted by Parliament, its sponsors – and the Government – resisted the inclusion of a statutory definition of "indecency" on the ground that any definition which could be devised would prove unworkable. We are therefore saddled with Lord Parker's views, quoted above, until such time as the House of Lords is asked by the courts to redefine and clarify what "indecency" means in law.

Such legal attitudes may well contribute to the trivialization of sexual feelings and to their becoming imbued with unhealthy guilt on the one hand, and to their commercial exploitation by bootleg purveyors of pornography

---

* I am indebted to Mr Francis Bennion for his kindness in allowing me to see and utilize the material from his unpublished manuscript.

and prostitution on the other. It is notable that the more censorious a society's prevailing attitudes towards the acting out of mutually desired sexual contacts, the more furtive, sordid, drab and corrupt is its sexual underworld – and the more widespread and acute are its psychological, moral and emotional disorders.

Capricious Law

It is not the task of this chapter to describe all the complexities of the laws relating to obscenity, indecency and pornography. I do wish, however, to point out that these laws are almost certainly the most subjective and capricious area of the entire criminal law, because the matters with which they deal are so much ones of taste and opinion. As the Arts Council's Working Party on the Obscenity Laws (1969) succinctly put it, no-one who publishes a book or other material can know for certain in advance whether he has committed a criminal offence by doing so, because the only issue at his trial will be whether the jury or the court agrees that what he has produced is not indecent or obscene. Furthermore, to punish someone for producing something which, in the court's opinion, has a tendency to deprave and corrupt is to punish them for being an unwitting accessory before the fact to a crime that may never be committed: "A man can at least know in his heart whether he is guilty of embezzling; he cannot possibly know whether he is guilty of depraving or corrupting."

It is fallaciously assumed, by those who wish to ban pornography, that no well-intentioned person would disagree with them once it has been demonstrated, or even shown as likely, that some pornography causes harm to individuals or to society. Consequently, much of the banners' energy is spent on quoting researches which have been carried out in various parts of the world with results tending to show that a positive relationship exists between exposure to pornographic material and the commission of crimes of sex and violence. No such studies, however, have yet established, so far as I am aware, a clear correlation between the availability of pornography and the incidence of sexual crimes or of violence. But far from it being the case that opposition to censorship depends upon an erroneous belief that all pornography is harmless, such opposition can be more convincingly grounded upon the contention that the operation of censorship is at least as harmful to society as the ready availability of pornography; and indeed that it is almost certainly more harmful.*

* Although the report of the *Committee on Obscenity and Film Censorship* (1979) accepts the 'harm condition' as the basis for justifying suppression or restriction of some publications and films, I see no reason to modify the views expressed in the above passage.

Censorship Distorts Communication

For all censorship is a hindrance to the free flow of facts, of opinions and of ideas; and therefore, regardless of the motive with which it is imposed, censorship constitutes a distortion of spontaneous communication between human beings. I would not wish to argue that communication should never be restricted by convention or even sometimes by law; but I do maintain that every instance of such restriction ought to be scrutinized vigilantly in a democratic society, and that the onus of justifying it should be upon those authorities or individuals seeking to impose it. The only possible guiding principle for a society that is tolerably free in fact as well as in name has to be that enunciated by John Stuart Mill in his famous essay *On Liberty* that

> if all mankind minus one were of the opinion, and only one person were of the contrary opinion, mankind would be no more justified in silencing that one person than he, if he had the power, would be justified in silencing mankind. (Mill, 1859)

Censorship is the intervention of a third mind between the communicator and those to whom the communication is addressed. The censor says: "For a reason which seems good to me, I must stop this information reaching you." ("You" may be either a specific individual, a class of individuals, or the public at large.)

What is censored may be a *fact*, an *opinion* or a *scene*. A censored fact may be true or untrue. A censored opinion may be well-founded or ill-founded. A censored scene may be real or imaginary. As Mill points out, society can be harmed just as much by the censoring of falsehoods and errors as by the suppression of truth – not least because the truth or falsehood of information and opinions can only be established by free discussion and full examination of all the available evidence.

The censor's "good reason" for censoring a *fact* is usually that a person learning it would be harmed (this argument is frequently advanced as a "reason" for not giving sex education to adolescents); or that a third party would be damaged by it (the basis on which the laws of libel are founded and on which legal measures to protect privacy are advocated by some people); or that the community or the State would be harmed (the *raison d'être* of the *Official Secrets Acts*). The "good reason" for censoring an *opinion about society* is usually that it would undermine the established order (i.e. it is seditious) or that it is highly offensive to the feelings of certain groups in society (e.g. the Race Relations Acts, blasphemy). The "good reason" for censoring an *opinion about an individual or a group* is usually that the person or the group would be harmed or offended by its publication. The censor's "good reason" for censoring a *scene* is usually that it will harm the people seeing it or that some of them are outraged by it: this is the common justification for censorship of pornography. In other situations, censorship may simply be used as a repressive weapon by the State or other authority without being directly related to the content of the material which is censored.

Are the censor's "good reasons" really good? The answers must depend not only on whether the harm he fears is real, but also on whether it outweighs the counter-harm which censorship does to freedom of speech. *Any* act of censorship, whatever its pretext, is by its very nature a *political* action: it is the exercise of power by one group over another. In a democratic society the presumption must always be in favour of free speech. If any other presumption prevails, the society is no longer free and open, but will – albeit gradually – become closed and authoritarian.

Pornography and Politics

Where pornography is concerned, its would-be prohibitors strenuously seek to demonstrate its individual and social harmfulness. David Holbrook (1972a, b) asserts that all pornography is a manifestation of hate. Hard pornography, says the *Longford Report* (1972), appeals "quite unashamedly to various groups of inadequate or sexually maladjusted people". Mary Whitehouse (1977) comments, somewhat evasively, "One is frequently challenged to define pornography, though why one should, when it is so obviously what it is, I sometimes wonder!" She contents herself by endorsing Lawrence's statement that "pornography does dirt on sex", adding: "it does violence to it, too".

John Court (1975), National Chairman of the Australian Festival of Light, accepts the Kronhausens' definition of pornography as material that is erotically stimulating in a context which lacks "reality constraints" (Kronhausen and Kronhausen, 1959; see also Ellis and Abarbanel, 1967). He also cites with approval Francis Schaeffer's (1968) view that some contemporary pornography achieves the sophisticated status of "a philosophy of life which closely associates pornography with atheism". And he links it with perversion, drug-taking, extreme radicalism and moral anarchy. Here, he is clearly advocating its suppression for blatantly political reasons.

Of course, all censorship is inevitably conservative with a small "c", in the sense of upholding a *status quo*, whether it is practised in the Soviet Union, South Africa, Sydney or Soho. The distinction between "moral" and "political" censorship is ultimately spurious.

Pornography itself may also be deliberately political, and its use as a weapon against traditional values has been a recurrent feature of recent years.

Typically, the things attacked are established, conservative and elderly while the things promoted are underprivileged, radical and young. . . . Since suppression of sexuality forms a central feature of establishment attitudes the sexual attack liberates explosive forces. (Bennion, unpublished)

The trials of *Oz* in 1971 and of *International Times* in 1972 were outstanding examples of the use of "morals" offences to strike at politico-social attitudes. Ostensibly accused of conspiring to corrupt public morals by publishing obscene material, it was in reality the defendants' "alternative" lifestyle (associated with anarchistically-flavoured left-wing politics) which was in the dock. These were effectively "show trials" which did much to end the prevalence of the carefree "flower power" era of the 1960s, with its emphasis on rock music, drug-taking and sexual freedom. After *Oz* and *IT* bit the dust, freaks and hippies remained but increasingly as a hangover. An ironical consequence was that the student generations of the mid- and later 1970s became much more directly political in their radicalism. According to one's point of view this may or may not be a good thing. What is indubitably neither good nor healthy is the use of obscenity laws as a political weapon, even against "political" pornography. As John Trevelyan, the former Film Censor, has said:

In a free society we must defend the freedom to express ideas, even if they are minority ideas, and we should therefore closely watch for any possibility of their being an 'unrevealed purpose' behind the use of the chaotic and confused obscenity laws. (Trevelyan, 1973)

Just as some pornography may be deliberately and overtly political, and opposition to it is frequently based on attitudes which are as much political as moral, so my opposition to censorship is grounded in an explicitly political viewpoint – namely, that it is in the end safer to run the risks involved in a free and open society where views, attitudes and opinions are expressed which one does not necessarily approve of, than to live under a regime where free enquiry and expression is stifled and suppressed. Censorship is a habit of mind which, once it gains a foothold, spreads like a cancer. Whatever its starting point, the end of the censor's road is likely to be the same: repression of "dangerous" ideas, not only about sex but about morals, politics, art and life.

What the Law's Role should Be

It is because this danger is a very real one – in Britain, now – and not because I am especially enamoured of pornography (much of which strikes me as crude, tasteless and boring) that I am vehemently opposed to the use of the criminal law to enforce standards of morality in sexual behaviour or attitudes. Sex is a peculiarly personal area of life, and I agree that there should be some protection, for those who wish it, from having what they regard as distasteful aspects of sexuality thrust upon them or flaunted in the streets. But that is an entirely separate issue from the right of all citizens – at any rate adult ones – to behave as they wish sexually, provided that they do not infringe others' rights and freedoms, and to have unrestricted access to pornographic or erotic material if they wish.

As the Sexual Law Reform Society (SLRS) stated in its evidence to the Criminal Law Revision Committee, which has recently studied the law relating to sexual offences, there are only three sets of circumstances in which the law should intervene to limit the citizen's sexual freedom. These are: where there is not true consent; where there is not full responsibility (by reason of age or other circumstances) on the part of all those engaging in the behaviour in question; and where offence is caused to others who are unwillingly involved in or unintentional witnesses to the behaviour. Where pornography is concerned, similar principles should apply and the SLRS report recommended that there should be freedom legitimately to obtain, in circumstances which are not obtrusive upon the public at large, pornographic material of an explicitly sexual nature for private use by consenting persons. Also, the law should protect those who, by reason of age or other incapacity, are incapable of giving fully responsible consent, from involvement in the production of pornography, and should control the display of sexually explicit material. Beyond this, I agree with the SLRS, the law has no legitimate role in this area of conduct in a free society: "victimless crimes" should be decriminalized.

This standpoint will, I am aware, be vigorously contested by the advocates of censorship. Using the spurious argument that, when liberty is allowed to degenerate into license, true freedom is lost, they aspire to control the tastes, to shape the thoughts, and to dictate the values of other adults. Their own values may possibly be superior to those of the millions who purchase *Playboy, Penthouse, Forum* and the rest – but they should nevertheless not be permitted to impose them by invoking the heavy artillery of the criminal law: education and persuasion are the only proper means for them to use. Otherwise they become potential tyrants, albeit virtuous ones. Voltaire's famous declaration: "I disapprove of what you say but will defend to the death your right to say it" carries more hope for the future of mankind than the grotesque attempts by puritans down the ages to suppress a catalogue of works which range from high art to tawdry vulgarity – almost always with the result of increasing the popular awareness of, and demand for, the item in question. As a former chairman of the Defence of Literature and the Arts Society, the late William Hamling, MP, once said: "A piece of low-grade rubbish must be as important to us as *Ulysses,* even though that principle may lose us both sympathy and battles".

The Harm Censors Do

I detest censorship and would-be censors because they attack *my* freedom – and *yours* – to read, see, hear and do what I – and you – choose. While not having the slightest desire to read most of the books and magazines, or to see most of the films, which the bluenose brigade seek to suppress, I feel personally violated by their insidious activities – "Never send to know for whom the bell tolls; it tolls for thee" (Donne, 1624).

The attempt to preserve people from harm by keeping them in ignorance of whatever may "morally pollute" them strikes me as not only misconceived and futile, but as positively evil in its consequences. Because it treats grown adults as if they were children. Living is, by its very nature, a dangerous process; and it is only by being conscious of the depths, as well as of the heights, of human imagination that we can make meaningful choices and accept full moral responsibility for ourselves. As Walker and Fletcher (1955) point out:

> Sooner or later then, willingly or perforce, we must meet life face to face and take the inescapable risk of being what we are, doing what we do in our own freedom and on our own responsibility. Sooner or later we must make the discovery that the only security is the acceptance of insecurity, the only strength the acknowledgment of weakness. What must be done had better be done now. Until it is done we shall not enter into possession of ourselves.

It was not licentiousness, but Government licensing (i.e. censorship) of the press, that John Milton (1644) saw as the negation of liberty. Would I, then, defend the availability (to those who wish to have access to it) of smut? Of the portrayal of sexual violence and torture (as in Pasolini's film *Salo*)? Yes, I would – because these things happen in the world whether we are allowed to know it or not: and because we shall never overcome evil by being kept in ignorance of its existence.

Notwithstanding the oft-cited "Moors murders", it would seem incontrovertible that a great many more people find the graphic description or depiction of torture and violence sickeningly aversive than are attracted by it, and that those few who are impelled to imitate it are psychopaths. Are we seriously being asked to limit what *everybody* is allowed to read or see because something or other might trigger off a psychopath? Although it is monotonously reiterated by the advocates of censorship that aficionados of pornography progress inevitably from "soft" to "hard" and then on to the perpetration of violent sex crimes, it is much more likely that "hard core" pornography is far more aversive to people with a reasonably healthy psyche than it is addictive. When juries find that an allegedly obscene item has a tendency to deprave and corrupt, what they usually seem to mean is that they are disgusted by it – not that they find it dangerously attractive.

Irrational Opponents

And this, surely, is what a few minutes' reflection would lead us to expect. Former President Nixon's celebrated riposte to the U.S. Commission on Obscenity and Pornography (1970) which reported that pornography had no lasting harmful effect: "Centuries of civilisation and ten minutes of common sense will tell us otherwise", merely demonstrates that one man's common sense is another's *non-sequitur*.

That pornography does have a disturbing effect upon the rationality of at any rate some of its opponents is clear from the extreme claims of those who, like Ronald Butt (1976) and David Holbrook (1976), maintain that it is so dangerous that it is likely to incite its participants and consumers to acts of brutal viciousness, rape and even murder. (It is, incidentally, noteworthy that those, such as Lord Longford and Mary Whitehouse, who because they are its enemies must surely be numbered among the most continuous and assiduous students of pornography, find it highly aversive and a potent stimulus to extreme and sustained moral indignation.)

Books in the dock – even hard-core pornographic books – are ideas in the dock. And ideas in the dock – even ideas which may deprave and corrupt – are the hallmark of the totalitarian State. I make no apology for returning to this point. There is a fundamental difference between merely stating a point of view and exhorting your audience to violate the legitimate freedoms of others. This, of course, is as crucial a distinction in the political sphere (and one which is not always clearly enough perceived) as it is in the sexual sphere. There is all the difference in the world between depicting a ritualistic sado-masochistic scene involving consenting partners and inciting someone to go out and commit a brutal rape: such incitement would itself be a serious criminal offence, anyway.

Sexuality is fundamental to our lives, and, because of its central place in our physical and psychical make-up, exerts a perennial fascination. By rights it should be a prime source of human liberation, inspiration and happiness: yet so often, it tragically becomes the opposite. In my experience, inhibitions and hang-ups concerning sex are far more damaging and disabling than an accepting attitude to one's own and others' sexuality. As Haynes and Pasle-Green (1974) have written:

Making love is one way to bridge language, cultural, racial, religious, political, and class barriers. In this violent, divided, confused, and intolerant world of ours it is one common denominator. Making love brings people together. Anything that increases our prurient interest, anything that encourages us to touch one another is a step forward. At least when we are making love, when we are reading about it, when we are watching it, when we are thinking about it, we are not killing or hurting one another.

Misguided Concerns

While I am implacably opposed to the philosophy and the activities of the would-be sexual censors and suppressors, I yet recognize that their concern, however misguided, springs – at any rate in some instances – from a desire to increase human happiness. Yet I hold that because their ideas are mistaken they constitute – whether intentionally or not – a serious threat to the freedom, health, and happiness of humanity. It will indeed be a black day if they are enabled to enforce their views through the extended machinery of the law.

Their attitude to sex is, I believe, fallacious; and they draw a number of erroneous deductions from false premises. These, so far as I understand them, are:

(1) Because sex is God-given, and at its best can impart emotions and sensations that are as near to the Divine as anything that human beings are capable of experiencing, therefore it should be treated as "sacramental" and only approved of when it is hallowed by love and a lasting – preferably life-long – relationship between the partners concerned.

Leaving aside theology, and the debatable question of whether sex is any more "God-given" than Mount Everest, baked beans or washing machines, the "sacramental" attitude to sex falls into the classic pit of making the best the enemy of the good. While it may well be that some sexual episodes are the purest and most blissful experiences that we shall know on this earth, that is no reason for writing off the second-best, either in relationships or orgasms. While we can all aspire to the peaks, and hope to avoid sinking too deep into the troughs, most of us are very content to remain in the foothills for most of the time – and to obtain a great deal of worthwhile pleasure and fulfilment there.

(2) To be morally and socially acceptable, sexual activity should only take place when the parties concerned are (a) married, (b) in love, (c) of opposite sexes.

It is doubtful if as many as 10% of all the human orgasms which occur conform with all of these criteria. Sometimes, it would appear, the formal correctness of a relationship is regarded as rendering it valid even though there is not mutual love between the partners (a view which was pushed to its sexist extreme by Galsworthy's Soames Forsyte in *The Man of Property* – the "property" in question being his sexually alienated wife, Irene, over whom he forcibly asserted his marital rights). In all other cases, however, love is obligatory – whatever is meant by "love". In traditionally "romantic" terms, it implies an exclusive possessiveness between the couple who are "in love", with an inevitable overinvestment of excessive emotional expectations in their relationship and a corresponding disillusionment when their "love" falls short of idealized requirements or even turns sour. While pair-bonding and the nuclear family will probably remain the chosen path of the majority for the foreseeable future (I see no necessity to brainwash most people in that direction), love – including sexual love – can take other, less constricting, forms. There are those who believe that the essence of love is sharing: that love is an attitude, how you feel about yourself and others. The fact that people who are not monogamous talk about "making love" can be more than a euphemism for their sexual encounters.

Love can also exist, of course, in homosexual relationships as well as in heterosexual ones: but this simple and obvious fact is usually denied by puritanical people (especially evangelically religious ones, many of whom seem to be both excessively obsessed by homosexuality and exceptionally ignorant about it). The idea that homosexuality is "unnatural" still persists, although it is self-evidently meaningless. Indeed, in a prize example of censorious megalomania, the Nationwide Festival of Light is reported (Gay News, 1977a) to have considered the possibility of calling for legislation making it an offence to maintain that homosexuality is natural! With commendable prudence, this zany proposal was shelved as being "unrealistic" (Gay News, 1977b). The notion that people of the same sex can actually experience deep emotional feelings of love for one another in the same way that heterosexuals do appears to be profoundly shocking to some folk. They react with incredulity and disdain, preferring to view all manifestations of homosexuality as lustful depravity which must always be immoral and, in the legal phrase, "grossly indecent". No doubt it is a simpler world when you can manage to avoid having to come to terms with the reality of how other people, who are differently constituted from you, actually feel – but the importance of having to do so is a prime reason why such ill-informed and narrow-minded censors must not be permitted to enforce their bigoted and ignorant views of sexuality upon the rest of us. Public education, and a more balanced appreciation of the real-life complexity of homosexuality and many other facets of sexuality, will only come about if there is the fullest possible freedom for different viewpoints to be expressed and exchanged.

Threat to Free Discussion

The next proposition of the censorious crew is a direct threat to free discussion which follows inevitably from points (1) and (2):

(3) It is not in the best interests of society to permit free discussion of all aspects of sexuality, and especially not of viewpoints or categories of behaviour which do not conform with (1) and (2) above.

This constitutes a challenge to the whole concept of a democratic and tolerant open society. If one subject (sex) is to be excepted from the general rule that all matters of public interest are freely debatable within the broad boundaries set by the libel laws, what will follow next? Religious beliefs? Politics? Science? To quote from Mill's (1859) *On Liberty* once more:

The peculiar evil of silencing the expression of an opinion is that it is robbing the human race; posterity as well as the existing generation; those who dissent from the opinion still more than those who hold it. If the opinion is right, they are deprived of the opportunity of exchanging error for truth; if wrong, they lose, what is almost as great a benefit, the clearer perception and livelier impression of truth, produced by its collision with error.

If it is the whole concept of "sexual politics" which frightens the upholders of conventional morality into wanting to restrict or ban the expression of unorthodox sexual attitudes, whether or not these are expressed pornographically, this is surely a striking exhibition of fear and moral weakness. In any event, sexual politics is here to stay; and those of us who find its jargon unfamiliar and sometimes distasteful must perforce come to terms with the fact that its proponents are saying things which have an intense meaning for them and have a message for us.

Sex Education Controversy

(4) Sex education should be postponed as long as possible, and when given should be designed to encourage young people to conform to the ideals of virginity before marriage and lifelong mutual faithfulness within it, rather than to encourage awareness that there is a variety of possible sexual attitudes and lifestyles to choose from.

At first sight it may be thought that there is at least a plausible case for censoring, or at least filtering, the sexual information that is made available to adolescents and children; but on closer examination this argument too is seen to be highly questionable and indeed I would say positively specious.

Pro-censorship bodies such as the Responsible Society and the Order of Christian Unity are currently mounting a sustained and vociferous campaign, not only to put forward their own views on sex education in various pamphlets and articles, as they are of course perfectly entitled to do, but also to attack and denigrate the sex education and teacher/youth worker training activities of bodies such as the Family Planning Association and the Albany Trust whose approach to the topic is too "liberal" for their taste. What they apparently object to is the philosophy that *all* aspects of sexuality should be openly talked about and calmly discussed at some stage of the sex education process; and still more that it should be intimated to young people that it is possible, and perhaps reasonable, that more than one point of view is held on these matters.

But surely what is needed, here even more than elsewhere, is a clear grasp of the fundamental distinction between education and indoctrination. As the great *Manchester Guardian* editor, C. P. Scott, once said: "Comment is free — facts are sacred". At least they should be. And as regards sex, just as in any other area of knowledge, there are facts and there are opinions. Opinions may be either true or fallacious: facts can only be correct — otherwise they are not facts but fallacies. There are bound to be clashes of opinions. But it is possible, by the usual processes of investigation, to ascertain what the correct facts are, in sexual matters as in others; and everybody — including children — should be entitled to know the correct facts when they wish to do so. To maintain otherwise is a gross infringement of human rights. Whenever it is sought to restrict access to factual information, it is incumbent upon those doing so to make out a cast-iron case. Where sex education is concerned, this has not been done.

The thorny question of what sort of education should be given, where, when, and by whom, will not easily be resolved. The principle that there is a body of factually correct information about sexuality which young people have the right to know before their educational process is adequately completed is, however, not negotiable. And some of this information may be pornographic. As Dallas (1972) wrote in her book *Sex Education in School and Society*:*

> A variety of teachers, young and old, mature and immature, demonstrating a variety of attitudes, methods and roles, both communicative, informative and authoritative, provides the ideal situation for sex education in its widest sense rather than searching for any one ideal teacher.

I believe that it is vital for the future health of our society that the channels of communication for imparting to young people the widest spectrum of facts, ideas and opinions about sex and its vital role in all our lives should be

* See Dallas, this volume.

kept open, free and unfettered. Sexual innocence can no more be equated with ignorance than sexual knowledge necessarily implies guilt. It is only those who morbidly regard sex as a "dirty secret" who can possibly hold such perverse views as to the wholly dire effects of sound sex education.

Dangers of Lust

(5) Any idea, book, magazine, film or other article which incites lust is self-evidently harmful and dangerous and should be severely restricted if not totally prohibited.

Here, we are back to the "pornography is harmful" thesis which, as I have already shown, is unproven. Far from being self-evident, it is an assertion for which surprisingly little solid supporting evidence has been adduced – despite all the ideologically committed work which has been put into the search for conclusive data. All Mary Whitehouse can produce is a reference to some research carried out for the *U.S. Commission on Obscenity and Pornography* (1970). Yet the Commission itself reported that:

> Empirical research designed to clarify the question has found no reliable evidence to date that exposure to explicit sexual materials plays a significant role in the causation of delinquent or criminal sexual behaviour among youth and adults. The Commission cannot conclude that exposure to erotic materials is a factor in the causation of sex crime or sexual delinquency [and that] in general, established patterns of sexual behaviour were found to be very stable and not altered substantially by exposure to erotica.

And John Court, the pro-censorship psychologist so favoured by Mary Whitehouse, admits that such studies as have been undertaken are "painfully inconclusive"; simply reiterates that "pornography is hate" and that it "brings perversion"; and takes refuge in the not very scientific assertion that *because* there is no such thing as objective impartiality, even in scientific investigation, "when the question of possible harm is involved, there is a strong ethical case for taking more note of those (studies) which indicate harm than those which fail to find it". Court (1975) also asserts that

> The harmful effects of salacious material, suggestive advertising, and the like, are therefore best defined in moral terms of incitement to lust. . . . We must conclude that the Christian will take a distinctive position about the significance of erotica; *without in any way prejudging the scientific evidence*, [my italics] he or she can come to a resolute condemnation of its inherent harm and to firm opposition to its indiscriminate availability.

Any reader who did not accept Court's value-systems to start with, but was willing to be convinced, will probably smell a fairly large rat at this point. And it emerges into full view when Court attempts to dispose of the "censorship is undemocratic" and "free speech is valuable to democracy" arguments. He does so by calmly asserting that the committed Christian, because of his superior system of moral values derived from God's revelation, has a responsibility to prevent what he considers to be harmful; and that this is not paternalism, or busybodying in the affairs of others, but "a high sense of social responsibility"! After this, it seems scarcely necessary to afford Court the courtesy of treating the remainder of his "arguments" as calling for reasoned refutation.*

Principle at Stake

Not the least interesting and remarkable aspect of the influence of pornography on behaviour is the effect that it has on the behaviour of would-be censors. In their anxiety to suppress the transmission of unwelcome sexual facts and fantasies, they lose sight altogether, or dismiss as irrelevant, the fundamental issues of human liberty which are involved.

In this chapter, I have attempted to state the case for freedom of expression, and against censorship, on general grounds, and have not confined my exposition to the censorship of pornography, because the case for free speech must stand or fall on principle: once the thin end of the wedge is inserted at any particular point, all freedom is obviously in jeopardy.

The impossibility of defining pornography in a way which would command general assent, and the difficulties attached to producing a workable legal definition of what is obscene, simply demonstrate the unwisdom of attempting to exercise censorship which lays any claim to be impartial over what are essentially matters of subjective taste. Few people nowadays would be happy with a censorship law explicitly grounded in feelings of disgust or revulsion, although these are the implicit criteria of our existing law. The test of "tending to deprave and corrupt" is, as has been seen, extremely difficult to prove to the satisfaction of present-day juries (although magistrates seem readier to contemplate the possibility); while scientific evidence that pornography has harmful effects upon the morals or the behaviour of most of those who use it is still inconclusive.†

Influential groups in this country and in the United States have concluded that the laws on this subject should either be liberalized or dismantled altogether. Most of those who press for them to be extended or strengthened do so from a standpoint of religious commitment which precludes rational

---

* *The Committee on Obscenity and Film Censorship* (1979), in their comprehensive critique of his work, reached a similar conclusion.
† Compare Roth and Nelson, this volume.

argument. In the end, the crucial questions are not "Is pornography harmful?" or "Should pornography be banned?", but "How much moral responsibility should each citizen carry for her- or himself?" and "Do we want the Nanny State?"

References

Butt, R. *The Times*, 5 February 1976.
Committee on Obscenity and Film Censorship. In *The Report of the Committee on Obscenity and Film Censorship*. (Chairman: B. Williams.) London: Her Majesty's Stationery Office, 1979.
Court, J. *Law, Light and Liberty*. Adelaide: Lutheran Publishing House, 1975.
Dallas, D. *Sex Education in Schools and Society*. Windsor: National Foundation for Educational Research. 1972.
Donne, J. *Devotions Upon Emergent Occasions,* No. XVII (1624). J. Sparrow (Ed.). Cambridge: Cambridge University Press, 1923.
Ellis, A. and Arbarbanel, M. (Eds). The psychology of pornography. In *The Encyclopaedia of Sexual Behaviour*. New York: Hawthorn Books, 1967.
Gay News No. 129, 1977a.
Gay News No. 131, 1977b.
Haynes, J. and Pasle-Green, J. (Eds). *Hello I Love You*! Paris: Almonde Press, 1974.
Holbrook, D. *Sex and Dehumanization*. London: Pitman, 1972a.
Holbrook, D. *The Case Against Pornography*. London: Tom Stacey, 1972b.
Holbrook, D. *The Times*, 6 February 1976.
Kronhausen, E. and Kronhausen, P. *Pornography and the Law*. New York: Ballantine, 1959.
Lawrence, D. H. Pornography and Obscenity, 1929. Reprinted in *A Propos Lady Chatterley's Lover and Other Essays*. Harmondsworth: Penguin, 1961.
Lord Longford. *Pornography*. London: Coronet, 1972.
Mill, J. S. *On Liberty* (1859). Reprinted Harmondsworth: Penguin, 1974.
Milton, J. *Areopagitica* (1644). Reprinted Cambridge: Deighton-Bell, 1973.
R. v. Stanley (1965). 1 *All E.R.* 1035.
Schaeffer, F. *Escape from Reason*. London: IVP Pocketbooks, 1968.
The Obscenity Laws. A Report by the Working Party set up by a conference convened by the Chairman of the Arts Council of Great Britain. London: André Deutsch, 1969.
Trevelyan, J. *What the Censor Saw*. London: Michael Joseph, 1973.
U.S. National Commission on Obscenity and Pornography. In *The Report of the Commission on Obscenity and Pornography*. New York: Bantam, 1970.
Walker, K. and Fletcher, P. *Sex and Society*. London: Pelican, 1955.
Whitehouse, M. *Whatever Happened to Sex*? Hove: Wayland, 1977.

4

The use of visual materials in sex education

Dorothy M. Dallas

Who is it who has a vested interest in flashers? Simplistically interpreted statistics would imply that it is the headmasters of British schools: under the convenient strategy of protecting those in *status pupillari*, numbers of them tear out pages of school textbooks showing the adult penis (especially if surrounded by full pubic hair), and send them back to the publishers with indignant letters. The letters usually use the words "disgusting" or "filthy" with the occasional cry "Is nothing sacred?" Plenty of things are sacred, but I had thought that lingam worship was long dead in this country – apparently not. As a result, flashers are usually assured of a good shock effect whenever they feel disposed to display; and I must admit, that my own daughter (and her mother a sex educationalist!) in her mixed school with first class inter-disciplinary sex education, and well aware of the shape and size of the penis of small lavatory-minded boys, was herself enlightened by a specimen copy of Reid and Booth (1971) – *How Life Begins*. She was rather bored by constantly being asked her opinion of new books on sex education, but picked this one up as it had a rather attractive baby on the cover, took it off to bed and emerged an hour later with "Hey, *this* one is good!" I asked why, feeling somewhat undervalued – surely I had provided everything the school had missed out on? She was, after all, only fifteen at the time! "I've never seen an adult penis" she said, and far from being disgusted or revolted "It's very different from little boys', isn't it?"*

There also seems to be quite a lobby concerned with keeping females

---

* How life begins, I might add, is head of the list in evoking cries of disgust, and the pages which informed my daughter and immunized her to the flashers are those most frequently torn out, and often returned to the *wrong* publishers!

ignorant of their own anatomy; yet, in Britain, physicians, nurses, midwives, and family planning clinics all expect women to know:

(a) where their primary orifices are;
(b) that anything placed in the vagina or uterus cannot wander about the body. This is not frivolity or humour, at one time there really was a section of the community in London which believed that a condom could choke a woman, entering at Dan and proceeding to Beersheba;
(c) where the clitoris is located. And if one checks the school textbooks, true enough, there are few diagrams which show it;
(d) that the clitoris is not a cancer. The women's agony columns still get letters about this.

In India, by way of contrast, family planning teachers have a model available which shows:

(a) where the uterus lies within the body;
(b) where an IUD fits into the uterus; and
(c) through which primary orifice it is inserted.

This shows an excellent appreciation of perceptual difficulties in educating women about their anatomy – location is catered for as well as the basic structure. There is hardly anything like this in Britain – not because it is not needed, but because anyone seeking to learn about the reproductive organs from diagrams is expected to be able to interpret the two-dimensional drawings, often consisting of what appears to the uninitiated as sets of parallel tramlines, so familiar to students of *Gray's Anatomy,* but puzzle pictures to the majority of the general public and the average school child. Another factor is that such drawings should not, if possible, look as if they have anything to do with human bodies.* This seems to be due to the inability of artists to find a happy medium between realistic drawings, reminiscent of the butcher's slab, and thick-lined simplistics. Symbolism rears its confusing head the more the artist tries to simplify – the human ovum appears to be a golf ball, the uterus (in one *still* recommended film, and a loop film made from it) tied together with what appears to be bootlaces (à la skating boots), and finally the use of colour to distinguish between the various sets of tramlines confounds all the other confusion! As a general rule therefore, pictures in sex education books designed for schools should rarely be left alone in a classroom; the pupils need the protection of a teacher, not from depravity and corruption but from the absorption of totally wrong and anxiety-making ideas about almost everything to do with sexual anatomy.

* A welcome exception to this rule are the imaginative and artistic drawings in Demarest and Sciarra's (1969) *Conception and Birth.*

But why should anyone be interested in keeping females in ignorance about their own anatomy? Usually, the defence quotes (euphemistically, of course), how dangerous life could be for young and innocent females if the males all knew exactly where to put a penis, and exactly how to use a clitoris; alas, they totally discount the misinformation grapevine current among most young people – this is one of the few sets of information about sexuality which seem to be transmitted accurately – it is often the conformist boy, who accepts that these are things he should not enquire into, who suffers from this lack of information usually, if the case histories of pyschosexual problems are to be taken in evidence, to a marked degree. And if evidence from all kinds of surveys, notably one on the effects of the original Grampian television series entitled *Living and Growing* is to be believed, the more information that boys have on female anatomy, the fewer their voyages of discovery – with a resultant embarrassing effect on the discovered girls. If those in authority over sex education refuse the required information, it will be obtained somehow, and now that girlie magazines have long been showing female pubic hair, its odds on that the clitoris will be next and the Devil will then have *all* the best tunes.

I must confess to edited authorship of the section on human sexuality, including menstruation, intercourse and birth in Monger and Tilstone's (1974) *Introducing Living Things,* and also confess, for reasons stated above, that there is not a pubic hair nor a clitoris to be found in it. Nevertheless, some schools have refused to buy it on the grounds that at least one illustration is unsuitable for adolescents. I suspect it is either the Leonardo da Vinci cartoon of human intercourse (which does not appear to have corrupted or depraved its Owner by Whose Gracious Permission it is reprinted) or the diagrammatic drawing of intercourse included by request from the teachers, because the Leonardo was not clear enough.

Unless of course, it was the part on menstruation, which is still found unsuitable for boys eyes to gaze upon in certain British subcultures – and so leads to prurient curiosity on the subject, which irritates girls intensely! And so the adolescent is left to acquire anatomical knowledge of both sexes from the graffiti merchants – often inaccurate, often shocking, or simply not to acquire it at all,

> teaching, in fact, what would interest only a child with the temperament of a cold hearted rake but not an average adolescent surprised by the intensity of new feelings and sensations (Fox, 1971).

And so the necessary facts are often enshrined in hallowed words (with their own perception problems) only; with total lack of concern for that section of the population which learns more, more quickly by good pictures than by verbal means. For this section however, there has been a recent increase in the use of printed visual material in sex education, particularly in the field of human behaviour with the use of cartoons in strip form, discussion cards posing a girl–boy problem, but still the profit-making sector leads the field over the purely educational, as it does in the field of models. The most common model found in schools is Renwall's Visible Woman – within, and I quote, "The Miracle of Life as an Optional Extra" – would you guess that this is a baby? Your Visible Lady can be pregnant or non-pregnant simply by the replacement of a straight set of viscera with one bunched up so that you can pop the baby in! It is too small to show a clitoris and plastic pubic hair is not available.

Diagrams in films, film loops and slides show all the above defects, of course, but these media have their own particular problems in addition. Teachers have been accused of using film as a cloak of darkness for their own embarrassment about sex education; as a general rule, teachers are advised to avoid any or all of the work which causes them embarrassment, as their attitude can only be transmitted to their pupils, with dire results. It may seem negative to advise avoidance, but unless one is to resort to soul-searching and the unearthing of painful hang-ups, which will take time and expertise as well as money, it is perhaps best to leave this problem to gradual decay.

Nor has the day passed when teachers themselves are using film to learn about the sex education they are teaching; a common and sensible strategy is for a teacher to see a film first and then teach it to a class, rather than stagger through a large book on the subject. Perhaps it is for this reason that there are large numbers of sex education films relying on the factual expertise of physicians, as teachers have so often been told that they should not poach on medical preserves. This is true, but it is equally true that physicians should not consider that they know all about education simply because they themselves were once at school. But of course many do and too many sex education films are full of talking heads, physicians' heads, and large quantities of didactic exhortation, rather than good visuals; more of a filmed lecture with visual distractors, than a use of visual material to educate.

In 1974, with a working party of London teachers and a grant from the Health Education Council, I reviewed the available visual material on teaching about sexually transmitted diseases. As any reader who saw the films for the Forces during the last war, on the subject of venereal disease, much of the material was designed to frighten, or at least to show enough syphilitic sores to put people off the idea of intercourse for life. It has, however, been well-researched that fear is soon buried under a mountain of human optimism, and it is also true that viewers often feel no identification either with the ghastly pictures of the people in the film, whereas a reading of Jeremy Seabrook's (1973) description, in his book *Loneliness*, of syphilis before the days of antibiotics, produces a vivid identification with the unfortunate victim. This writing is both simple and intense and gives the feeling that it *could* happen to you, whereas films, statistics, slides happen to other people. One television programme, available on film, was generally thought to be too stark for schools, until one adviser showed it to a group of parents, who thought it was not frightening enough!

Generally, films about microbiology were very explicit on causal organisms, or at any rate, explicit enough to those who were adept at interpreting what is seen under a light microscope, familiar with the use of histological staining techniques etc. There was not a perspex model to be seen anywhere – and would it have meant much if it had been? Probably to satisfy curiosity, but even then assuming a knowledge of the ways of microbiology which it would be illogical to think the audience possessed, the working party decided to produce their own slide strip on micro-organisms passed on by close bodily contact for use in early work in Secondary Schools on microbiology, and the strips were put on trial in schools with a very visual pair of worksheets. Many teachers produce their own well illustrated worksheets on a variety of sex education topics, the educational quality is always high and with the increasing use of Media Resources Offices, at least in schools governed by the Inner London Education Authority (ILEA), the visual aspects of many are now attaining a more professional standard.

It is when the films go onto other factual aspects that their particular philosophy shows through; in 1974 few ever implied that anyone got V.D. unless their reprehensible behaviour deserved it. To some films, reprehensible meant totally immoral, to others, notably the American variety, it was the sadder – but wiser – theme, "Now that we've told you, you won't be so foolish as the people in the film, will you?" Both these philosophies tended to increase the credibility gap; they assume that no-one in the audience has ever known an innocent grannie infected by a syphilitic kiss, or a child unknowingly infected with gonorrhoea by its parents – and even in 1974, if parents had gonorrhoea, their children were automatically given a test. And so symptoms were shown in frightening glory, cure rates rarely mentioned, the idea of a vaccine against gonorrhoea, of which the first news had then been published in the scientific journals, was generally pooh-poohed, and as for treatment, the visuals were meant to show how simple and easy it was, but with little regard for the audience's perception problems. A much used American film ended a sequence on treatment with a close-up of a doctor removing the last air bubbles from a syringe, which, at that focus, looked big enough for a horse; the soothing message which went with the visual was that it often took only one shot to cure. Unfortunately the film never showed into which part of the anatomy the needle finally sank – and almost every boy who saw that film thought that the penis was the target. These boys then told their friends – and another anti-treatment myth was born!

The same film caused problems in the self-diagnosis field, unwittingly, but with some force. A syphilitic rash was shown, but alas for colour film technology (one wonders sometimes if colour blind technicians are deliberately employed by film labs), the copper colour of the rash did not come out well on the copies, which looked all too like your ordinary adolescent acne, and sent many of the audience into agonies of worry, which (having been told that only the reprehensible get such things) they were unable to allay by any appeal to medical authority. The working party were particularly clear on this point in their film strip *and* the accompanying worksheet.

Then there are the social aspects of these very social diseases. Comforting, reassuring visuals were shown of clinics attempting contact tracing and in one, a social worker calling upon a contact at home. Reassuring certainly, for some who know quite well they risk bodily harm by informing their partner that they have passed on a sexually transmitted disease (STD), but often greeted by adolescents with cries of "The V.D. Gestapo". Factual, yet, but unlikely to change behaviour, especially when there was often much talk of "responsibility" which is almost guaranteed to cause a switch-off in those in the audience most at risk. So, unfortunately, most of the film and television seen showed little research into what kinds of audience might see their work, simply assuming that all possessed a certain set of norms of attitude and behaviour. This, unfortunately, is where so many sex education films and television fail to ask the questions:

(1) Is this film to be a simple transfer of information
    (a) to people who know nothing?
    (b) to consolidate previous knowledge, if so what?
    (c) to apply previous knowledge to a human situation?
(2) Is this film attempting to change attitudes and behaviour
    (a) if so, of whom, to what?
    (b) by didactic exhortation?
    (c) by a discussion of a variety of attitudes and behaviour and an indication of their consequences?
    (d) in a completely open-ended way?
(3) What is the age, culture and preferred mode of communication of the audience?
(4) Will there be someone there who can relate the film to local conditions?

Most films and television which were viewed did assume that the audience knew very little – but the ways in which this situation was remedied were extremely varied, too often small pieces of knowledge were visualized, floating in a conceptual void, a terrible temptation for film producers – a lovely picture without a pattern to hang it on. Television producers tend to be worse on the whole – I have heard pundits from both the British Broadcasting

Corporation (BBC) and Independent Television (ITV) say, loud and clear, "It isn't the picture that matters, it's what is said." It would seem obvious that when one is producing video-tape at vast expense, with much hard work and stress, it is only sensible to make the visuals work for you rather than merely constitute the wallpaper on the wall. I might say that both these producers were involved in educational television, whereas a documentary television programme on V.D. did actually use visuals to put over statistics with shots of a number of young people, edited in one film so that the message rapped out like machine-gun fire, "I was 18 when I got V.D." "19", "23". Ho, say those two television men, you have now proved our case! Yes, from the point of view of credibility and involvement; if a physician had said those words, with authority, the *words* would have been more important than the visual, but the audience would largely have discounted them, as happening to other people. In this particular television documentary, most felt that these were Real People, telling the truth, rather than people like themselves, although some identified completely with them. On the whole, the documentaries on sex education topics are better educationally than those of the education sector (with certain notable exceptions), because reporters and journalists do tend to know how to communicate with a larger audience, while the generalizing from one's own experience syndrome is too often encountered among educationalists of *all* types. Documentary producers do seem to have open minds on sex education, and, again with notable exceptions, seem to be less pressurized by the various authoritarian lobbies in the field. One of the notable exceptions was a commercial television series for *adult* sex education which dared to show (you've guessed it!) full details of the female genital anatomy; some nameless overlord judged that the series might be offensive to the British viewing public, but not to the Australians. Whisper it not in Kangaroo Valley, but the implication is that they are made of cruder stuff!

Even when facts and concepts were well organized, visuals were actually communicating with the audience and moralizing was at a minimum, V.D. films still failed by being too long. It seems a simple thing to do to restrict solid content in visual materials to the amount which an average audience can take in, but no, so many films tried to be an encyclopaedia, under the assumption that once through anyone's cerebral cortex is more than enough to assure retention, which is necessary if the whole operation is not to be a complete waste of time. Not one film used, for example, a reinforcement and a consolidation of the learning process, although the BBC *20th Century Focus* film on V.D. did provide some well constructed notes for further education classes to do this themselves, after a film of sensible length. This film also recommended that its situations be related to local conditions; one teacher investigated the local V.D. clinic, before recommending its use, and found it so unpleasant an experience for herself (a State Registered Nurse (SRN) before she trained as a teacher) that she felt unable to recommend it to her pupils! She wrote a report of her experiences which uncovered a conspiracy of silence – no-one would publish it, although she was also a card-carrying professional journalist. Now *here's* a subject for the current affairs programme *Panorama* – leave the comprehensive schools alone for a while and let's have a critical film on some of the worst V.D. Clinics!

From the findings, of which the above is a brief summary, the teachers working party decided:

(a) That there was a need to divide V.D. education into *three* stages, not produce it in one undigestible gulp. First, in the early years of secondary school, there was a need to include causal organisms in the commonly taught work on microorganisms; add STD organisms to the usual list of athletés foot, lice, the common cold, etc. Secondly, there should be some attention to V.D . itself in a depersonalized context, a study of the diseases and their mode of transmission. Finally, the relation of this work to personal situations, and the local facilities, should be emphasized.

(b) That there was a need to provide more *film* for the personal situation stage – as there was already plenty of material on the first two stages, although careful selection was needed and too often the available material was too long.

(c) That there was a need to research the *attitudes* of the target audience – average pupils of late adolescence in London schools.

It was the last decision which found the basic reason why so many films had failed to reach their intended audiences – most of the target population genuinely felt that getting V.D. was unavoidable – *if* your number was on it, then there was nothing to be done to wriggle out of an inescapable destiny. How different from the views of so many physicians who had advised on the current films – to them such an acceptance of fate verged on the irresponsible! Hence when the first film was produced, physicians simply did not understand it – nor did a large number of people involved in the medical aspects of Health Education! Briefly, it is a very short film designed to start adolescents thinking about what they can do about health – anything or nothing? Is a decrepit old age inevitable? Many people think so. Secondly, it brings up the well-known problem, am I ill or only trying to find an excuse for not going to school, work, visiting boring relations? General Practitioners testify that patients mention their ills only with diffidence, often as they are leaving the consulting room rather than entering it. While one section of the population brings every single piece of trivia to the surgery, quite a sizeable chunk exhibits the Walter Mitty syndrome – "Only a broken arm!" The first film also indicates that women may have gonorrhoea without symptoms – but is, in fact, so generalized that it has been used for work on unwanted pregnancy and alcoholism. So, as one may well imagine, it puzzles those who need health education to be didactic and authoritarian; this is not a film to teach a teacher facts unknown, it is for an expert health educator to use as a flexible instrument.

It seems amazing that little of this kind of film work has been done before. Examples nearest to this usage are Dennis Laughton's work for the ITV series *What's it All About?* – a very effective application to a personal and localized situation on subjects such as unwanted pregnancy, with resultant audience identification with the characters in the series. Unfortunately it was seen by relatively few schools and descended into limbo, probably because it was long before its time and the social climate was such that its usage was primarily restricted to the ILEA television series *You in the Seventies*; although crude and unprofessional in parts, this series is still remembered with gratitude in ILEA schools. Perhaps the earliest of all were the Eothen film loop series *Points of Departure* which showed a four-minute stereotyped situation for discussion. Although these were technically open-ended, they were so didactic that there was obviously one conclusion only to be reached in most of them, and seen with the dust of a dozen years on them, they mostly excite hilarity these days. One or two however, stand the test of time, in particular *The Meeting,* where an older man seems to be helping a student who is showing signs of educational despair in a library; they are seen walking off together. Apart from a few heavy dramatic shots which simply invite the insertion of a balloon with the word "THINKS!?!?" above them, there is a neat delineation of the problem, is he just being friendly or is he an importuning homosexual? Which leads on to do I want to be importuned, should I feel guilty if I do, or is it just a father figure which is needed or even a magic spell to get me through those exams? It is a genuinely open-ended film, and so like the first film of the teacher working party, puzzled a lot of people, who simply had no idea of how to use it.

The working party films were researched and produced by a non-profit making organization which gave them the title of *Trigger* films, as their purpose is basically to relate information to the audience's own situation and hopefully to help them make decisions before the crisis actually arrives. In the second film, a boy thinks he has gonorrhoea and is shown trying various people for help and information – his friends, his teacher, his father, a doctor's surgery and finally he pauses with his hand on the door of a V.D. clinic. Every single adolescent who has seen this film is quite sure he does *not* go in! And this easily triggers off a discussion about what *you* would do. The last film shows the boy, having braved the clinic and described his reactions to the treatment ("So many people give false names, its ridiculous, you just get a number") going in search of the girl who gave it to him. He fails to find her, then meets her by accident; the happiness on both faces at this meeting was puzzling to many physicians! "Why is he so happy to see her? She's given him gonorrhoea!" The instant reaction to this meeting which closes the film is "*Aaw*. I wanted him to tell her and then they get married!" Audiences want happy endings!

What is interesting however is that a week later, the audience has absorbed the second two films – where to go if worried and you really ought to tell your contact – and, in a well-organized course where the microbiology and the natural history of STDs has already been understood, have very few questions on them. Not so with the first film – it is so non-didactic that they are almost all provoked to go on thinking about it, and discussing it for some time – can I really do anything to avoid ill health? Few audiences switch off to this film, and happy ending, few of those in authority over Health Education reject it now.

Here, then, is at least one set of films where thought has been taken as to what they are intended to do, namely:

(1) To apply previous knowledge to a personal situation.
(2) To change attitudes and behaviour in an open-ended way – always, however, dependent on the open-mindedness of the teacher using them.
(3) To use characters with which a large spectrum of audiences will identify, and with simple non-technical language.
(4) To facilitate the relation of learned knowledge to the local situation.

But why bother to use expensive film to do such things? Surely much of the above can be achieved by a good teacher? Quite true, but there are relatively few of them about, and one other happy ending of these *Trigger* films is that they have certainly educated the educators, if only that there are aspects of STD transmission which have been totally neglected, and a whole set of sub-cultural attitudes which have formerly been ignored.

Can any of these findings be applied to the other members of the Trinity of so-called sex education in British schools today? *Contraception, birth* and *V.D.* are the favourite end of the summer term topics for mass teaching with film, while the happily freed teachers get on with the form filling, etc. Birth certainly is largely taught by means of film, but there has been a notable advance in the kinds of film shown. Like V.D., birth was once (and according to some information from a couple of girls' boarding schools, still is) used as a means of frightening girls into chastity before marriage, and for some, forever. Gruesome films, with very blue babies and lots of blood, or even, in one case a caesarian in full colour have been cited; a black and white film or television presentation on birth does definitely produce less emotion, especially for those who cannot stand the sight of blood. Birth has, however, attracted a full range of visual material, and a full colour film is, in most schools, worked up to gradually. Monger and Tilstone's (1974) text has X-rays of babies about to be born for teaching about the mechanics of birth in the most unemotional way after work on gestation. Some teachers use the magnificently three-dimensional *Birth Atlas* (1968), and one excellent National Childbirth Trust teacher has demonstrated a highly realistic birth using a plastic doll emerging from a plastic vent in the bottom of a shoe box! Sounds ridiculous, but the performance is first class.

Teachers can even get a pattern for a *knitted* uterus! This, too, is not quite so strange as it sounds and gives a better idea of uterine muscle movement than do the skating boot-laces quoted previously in a much-used film. Of the symbolic representations of birth, perhaps the best is the Grampian television production entitled *Living and Growing*, a series which lives up to its name and refuses to become fossilized. There *were* times in days of not very yore, when headmasters refused pupils to view the birth of rats, and the BBC's first birth film was inundated with letters of protest. This flood has gradually subsided until when recently a full frontal birth sequence in colour was inserted into a school's programme viewed by many nine-year-olds, without a previous warning, only two letters of protest were received. It must be admitted however, that these were probably only the tip of the protest iceberg, but they also indicated that teachers are aware of the need for a more gradual introduction to ideas of birth in an industrial community.

And the films themselves have evolved. When I first showed that magnificent old classic *To Janet, a Son?* some years ago, I was inspected by the distributors to see if I was a "right and proper" person to use it – I am not quite sure whether they expected scenes of mass hysteria, due to my insensitive attitudes or what. At first the film was available for hire only to those showing it to *women*, but the impact *Janet* had on men has, I think, not been equalled, although the French film *The First Days of Life* comes close. With *Janet,* the birth of the child provided a vicarious experience of birth for many men in the audience; indeed, the minute after the film had ended one student with shining eyes stated "God! It must be marvellous to be a woman having a baby!" In the French film, it is the treatment of gestation which tends to turn the men on, rather than the birth, which is a somewhat calmer affair, where the mother has few stars in her eyes, but here a very dishy French father weeps happliy; this, however, tends to affect the women more than the men! *Janet* was produced in the protest era of the 1960s, and when I first introduced it at a training college for biology teachers in training only, the news spread, and I showed it 17 times in one week – finally to the Principal, a most excellent lady who thoroughly enjoyed it with tears, and the Senior Woman Tutor, a character who could only just stand the sight of blood. This was the era of teaching about natural child birth, where so many girls were made to feel that they had let down the hockey team if they could not enjoy every single contraction; in *Janet*, the mother, seen in genuine labour, is admonished by the commentator as being a naughty girl who obviously had not done her exercises properly! The French film on the other hand, merely shows how a well-trained woman with the right pelvic measurements can deliver her own child, without any sententious value judgements. Connoisseurs of labour wards in different cultures might like to compare the false British brightness of *Janet* ("Now there's no need to feel alone – we're all with you" when it is quite obvious to all who precisely is at the receiving end) with the genuine *joie de vivre* of the French. I am told, however, that on the whole the British experience is more comfortable unless you are lucky enough to get into a *naissance sans violence* clinic using the methods of Leboyer.

The distributors of *Janet* used to supply its actual birth film as a separate reel – the introduction being a symbolic birth, one of the best of its kind, plus a number of gestation pictures linked with ante-natal care. *The First Days of Life* has a similar device in that the actual birth is first shown from the mother's point of view – then at the very end of the film it is shown from the doctor's and midwife's viewpoint, plus a tear as the head comes through, so that teachers have the option to stop the film without showing this, if the emotions of the class are considered friable.

Relatively few films on birth, however, indicate anything about its effect on the family. *Brother for Susan* made a superficial attempt at it, many years ago, with an overbright Mum and a somewhat anxious and embarrassed Dad shown being perfectly normal, i.e. going to the flicks, with a suitable accompaniment of what I can only call Merry Music. Jane Madders' amateur film, made by her students at Birmingham College of Education in the 1960s was certainly the first treatment of sibling rivalry accompanying birth as well as the nature of the movements and early learning of a new-born child. This is again an example of a very narrow selection of aspects of, in this case, birth, which are an inevitable result of medically-orientated sex education films. The Pro-Europa film *The Heart of Life* is perhaps the best in portrayal of the effect the new-born has on the parents, and boldly states that the parents are more enraptured with themselves at the birth, rather than considering the effect of their behaviour on their new family member. Although arguably Freudian in interpretation, this film has some of the best visuals on child development including a superb sequence on the experimental kindergarten in Münich, where children are uninhibited by social taboos about wearing clothes, daubing themselves with paint, or even happily using a set of communal toilets together. It is a delightful reminder of the biblical text "Except ye be as little children" nothing is dirty or disgusting, and then we see in further sequences how social taboos are put on natural acts. Unfortunately this film is far too long, and at least one attempt at an edited version was met with refusal; a pity since, all who have seen it agree that there is much excellent material in it, for example, the results of an early abortion, which several 17- and 18-year olds said they were glad to have seen. One viewer said she could not distinguish fact from fantasy in the film, to which the producer replied "Who can, in sexual matters?" But truly it falls between two stools, sometimes being very didactic, and at other times visualizing sexual fantasy; sometimes successfully, sometimes not. It is, in fact, one of those *Omnibus* sex education films, which could generate a whole series of 10-min discussion pieces and several 20-min factual sequences; all human life is there. *Omnibus* films have on the whole, died out, as there is a general realization that treatment in depth is needed and that aspect, other than the purely physiological and anatomical, should be included.

Perhaps it is fortunate that schools are not the only agents of sex education in Britain. The howls of outraged decency which accompanied Martin Cole's various film efforts were accompanied by less emotional criticism from, for example, a student's union – "If he thinks that's what sexual intercourse is, he's the one who needs the sex education." Such comments were provoked by Cole's simplistic and medical approach to the problem, for one thing such films cannot do is to answer the 64 000 dollar question of all adolescents and not a few adults, "What is intercourse really like?" How can this portrayal of the external appearance of intercourse even done with drama by Zeffirelli explain why fathers leave families, why Abelard left the cloister, why Helen launched those thousand ships? This can only be done by those expert in portraying inner emotions, and to my knowledge this has only once been done in a way which would not upset the most insecure watch committee (local review boards), by a Swedish ballet company, in a production called *"Red Wine in Green Glasses"* shown many years ago on *Aquarius,* a television programme on the arts, and never seen since. As it seemed to me to be the best expression ever on the innermost emotions of good intercourse, I checked around a variety of sub-cultures to see whether others agreed – the vast majority did, but any attempt to make the film generally available has so far failed. We need not only education about the emotions, such as the physical basis of human behaviour and its modification by cultural and social effects but also education *through* the emotions, and not only using the emotion of fear.

Perhaps teachers, too, need to be educated in ways other than those of academia; as a sweeping generalization I feel that no-one should pontificate on sex education, especially the House of Lords, until they have seen Joan Littlewood's *Sparrers can't Sing* which neatly demonstrates the mores and value judgements of a sizeable part of the population on sexual mores. Moreover, it is that part of the population which really needs sex education in school, as it is unlikely to get any anywhere else; it is high time that the middle classes acknowledge that there are other cultures in our society, many of whose value judgements are sensible and commendable. Films like *Sparrers can't Sing* (not to mention *Gone with the Wind* although it is too long), are to sex education what *Gale is Dead* has become to education about drugs – far removed from medical aspects and didactic thou shalt nots, and very much to do with the way real people act, behave and think about sexuality.

Contrast with such films, the general run of porn movies, unbelievably unnatural, but worrying to many kids, and providing very low norms of sexual behaviour for all. Most seem to be made with what I can only call the "knothole in the floor" philosophy, harping on relief for the bursting male while the female is relegated to "tossing off" duties, with the occasional pig for variety. School teachers in one part of London are seriously worried about the number of these films seen by some of their pupils, but more worried about the lurid accounts of them told to their fellows. I would think, however, that pornographic books are a greater cause of anxiety, judging from those I have seen circulating round our better boarding schools; nevertheless I would agree with one of the London teachers who felt he would like to show a porn film in school with his own commentary. A quicker way to lose his job cannot be imagined, so he is left to battle on with relatively few weapons against the powerful forces of guilt and anxiety, harnessed by commercialism. To quote Keith Waterhouse "O is for *Oh! Calcutta*!" a film so disgusting that anyone wishing to see it must either join a cinema club or a watch committee.

Fortunately the paradigm of sexual education is slowly changing from a concentration on the plumbing aspects – treated with a severe moral tone – to a validation of norms with respect to behaviour, in terms of attitudes, interests, experience, and arousal patterns, and an emphasis on human relationships in a multi-cultural society. The use of visual material is declining as the central method for sex education unless it is actually dealing with individual decision making – what is taking its place now is the use of education through the emotions, whether by book or film. The use of simulation exercises and role playing enable education through the emotions, and these emotions relate to the whole of human life, to child care and parent-craft, male–female roles, apart from sexual situations, together with work on what the criteria for morality can be, as opposed to a reliance on one set of criteria which are observed by so few. As these aspects of sex education become more widespread, the visual material will need to change, if indeed it can be appropriate, but I suspect there will always be the schools of the Blessed Trinity who will keep on asking for "A good film on V.D.". Medical schools all over the country, however, are awakening to the fact that they ought to do something about sex education; one shudders in anticipation.

References

Demarest, R. J., and Sciarra, J. J. *Conception, Birth, Contraception*. London: Hodder, 1969.

Family Planning Association. *Sex Education Resources List*. London: Family Planning Association, 1977.

Fox, D. Nuffield Secondary Science (Theme 3), *The Biology of Man*. London: Longmans, 1971.

Masters, W. H., and Johnson, V. E. *Human Sexual Inadequacy*. London: Churchill, 1970.

McPhail, P. *Lifeline*. London: Longmans, 1972.

Miller, D. *The Age Between: Adolescents in a Disturbed Society*. London: Cornmarket Hutchinson, 1969.

Monger, G., and Tilstone, E. (Eds). *Introducing Living Things*. (Text 1), Revised Nuffield Biology. (Nuffield Foundation Science Teaching Project.) London: Longmans, 1974.

Reid, D., and Booth, P. Biology for the individual. *How Life Begins* (Human Reproduction). London: Heinemann, 1971.

Seabrook, J. *Loneliness*. London: Maurice Temple Smith and New Society, 1973.

The Maternity Center Association. *British Atlas* (6th Edn). New York: Maternity Center Association, 1968.

5

Erotic art and pornography

Peter Webb

"Erotic" means "pertaining to the passion of love", and it is natural that the passion of love should have inspired some of the world's greatest art. But artists concerned with eroticism are often branded as pornographers, an appellation which does them a great disservice as well as making appreciation of their works more difficult. This confusion betrays a prejudice against sexual material in general which is particularly characteristic of our Judao-Christian civilization. Prejudice against pornography is understandable although unenlightened: far from being dangerous pornography can have a positive value to many. But to confuse eroticism with pornography vitiates against our ability to appreciate some of art's most rewarding experiences.

Pornography has been defined in many different ways, from the eighteenth century Maréchale de Luxembourg's "books you read with one hand" to the *Oxford Dictionary's* "expression or suggestion of obscene or unchaste subjects in literature or art". For the purpose of this discussion I will take pornography to be any material whose *sole* purpose is to excite sexual appetite with no concern for aesthetic response. It seems to me that pornography is related to obscenity rather than eroticism: most people associate eroticism with love, and love has little or no part to play in pornography. That love is at the basis of eroticism the etymology makes clear. Pornography originally meant "the writing of harlots", and is derived from *porne*, Greek for harlot. On the other hand eroticism is derived from *eros*, Greek for love. Eroticism, therefore, has none of the pejorative associations of pornography; it concerns something vital to us all, the passion of love. Images of erotic art have often been sexually explicit to the point where they could be confused with pornography by those who consider only subject matter and ignore intention and execution. But there is a clear dividing line between erotic art and pornography which it is the purpose of this discussion to illuminate. There is today no excuse for describing as pornographic the

Roman frescoes at Pompeii, the Greek Phallic idols at Delos, the Indian temple sculptures of Bhubaneswar, the ceramics of ancient Peru, or the *Shunga* prints of Japan, any more than it would be reasonable to judge as pornographic Michelangelo's *David*, Giulio Romano's frescoes at Mantua, Boucher's *Mlle O'Murphy*, Beardsley's *Lysistrata* illustrations, or Brancusi's *Princess X*. A comparison between two images will suffice to demonstrate the essential differences.

Plate I is a piece of sculpture showing a couple having intercourse. It comes from the Brahrnesvara Temple at Bhubaneswar in India and dates from 1060 A.D. Plate II is a photograph from a Danish sex magazine of about 1967. The initial effect is totally different. The sculpture does not have the shock stimulus of the photograph, which is the immediate image of a real event which is for most people a very private part of their lives. The photograph only exists to stimulate sexual appetite, to cater for a sexual fantasy. If the viewer is not in the mood, or not that way inclined, the chances are that once the initial impact has worn off, the image will have very little of interest to offer.

The sculpture depicts exactly the same activity as the photograph, but has been created rather than mechanically reproduced. It has been carved with great care out of a block of stone, and inspite of the ravages of time we can see that it has involved an enormous amount of skill. Investigation tells us that it forms part of the decoration of a temple in Northern India where the loving ritual of sex was seen as a religious activity leading to a state of *enlightened* ecstasy. Our interest in the sculpture is therefore wide-ranging. It has a deliberate sexual appeal as well as reaching a high level of aesthetic achievement. And it holds an important historical position in relation both to the tradition of erotic art and to the sociology of religion (Anaud, 1963).

The photograph can be taken in immediately, whereas the sculpture requires, and repays, more leisurely consideration. The photograph has nothing of lasting interest to offer after the initial impact; the sculpture can be appreciated in aesthetic terms as well as admired for its historical implications. In the long run, the sculpture will have a more lasting appeal and a more tangible value than the photograph.

Works of art have the power to affect people deeply, and so it is not difficult to understand why opponents of sexual freedom should so often make erotic art works their targets. An example is Brancusi's sculpture *Princess X* of 1916 (Plate III) which was barred from exhibition in Paris soon after its completion and then denied entry into America. The image of the woman's head, neck and breasts has very deliberate phallic connotations in the beautifully harmonious forms of the bronze which seem to invite the spectator's caresses. Most people who would feel offended by this explicitly sexual form would have no objections to an image such as Plate IV, which shows an English seaside post-card of about 1960. The lighthouse depicted here is a similar phallic metaphor, but is used in a much less sophisticated and more titillating manner. The resulting innuendo has no artistic pretensions and gains acceptance through the safety-valve of laughter. Such phallic images are especially common in advertising. Sexual innuendo is quite blatant in the Gala lipstick advertisement (Plate V) which shows an excited girl happily caressing a giant lipstick which rises majestically between her legs.

It would be absurd to label any of these three images pornographic. Each has a role to play, but if any is dangerous, it is the last one, which demonstrates how easily our sexual appetites can be manipulated for commercial gain. This however is no justification for censorship, that preoccupation of the self-proclaimed guardians of public morality who are continually seeking the curtailment of artistic freedom whether it is that of Brancusi, or D. H. Lawrence, or Pasolini.

The degree of freedom achieved by the artist in recent years is fairly large when compared with that of the previous 150 years, but in wider terms it is less impressive. Primitive societies have always concentrated on depicting sexual themes, and still do today. For example, female statuettes such as the *Venus of Willendorf* of about 30 000 B.C. were cult figures with enlarged sexual organs relating, we can presume, to magic fertility rites. Similarly, male images were created with enlarged penises, a custom that remains common in Africa and Polynesia (Rawson, 1973a). In the Classical world, this concern appeared in the many deities who personified aspects of fertility, and who were frequently depicted in a sexual form. Examples include the Hellenistic monuments at Delos showing giant erect phalluses in honour of Dionysus, and the fresco at Pompeii showing Priapus weighing his enormous penis in the scales against a basket of fruit and crops. Sexual themes were not however confined to religious art; also at Pompeii are many frescoes depicting couples in intercourse (see Plate VI), sensitive philosophies of human love in a society where love-making was a vital part of life to be celebrated openly and erotically (Marcadé, 1965).

Erotic art of the Classical world shows no sense of shame in its treatment of sexual themes, for the artists did not associate sex with guilt in the manner of our Judao-Christian civilization. Similarly, the Hindu, Islamic and Taoist philosophies all accept basic human sexual relations as natural, admirable and beautiful, and therefore make no provision for the repression of sexual instincts (Rawson, 1973b). We have already seen how Indian temple sculptures often depict ritualized sexual activities leading to enlightenment. Many Hindu and Islamic miniatures and album illustrations portray the excitements of sex in brightly coloured images of a very high quality, and Chinese watercolour artists painted similar work in the eighteenth and nineteenth centuries (Beurdeley, 1969). Perhaps the finest examples of Oriental erotic art are the *Shunga* created by print-makers in Japan in the seventeenth to nineteenth centuries (Grosbois, 1966). Great masters like Utamaro and Hokusai produced superb colour prints depicting scenes of intercourse between couples elegantly clothed in the latest elaborate fashions, giving tantalizing glimpses of excited sexual organs among the finery. For example, Harunobu's *Fantasy* of the late 1760s (Plate VII) shows a lady masturbating as she day-dreams about her lover who appears with her in a "thought-bubble" at the top of the print.

The carefree eroticism of Classical and Oriental art finds far rarer expression in the Western world, where for many centuries the Christian Church was the main patron of the arts. Since the Christian doctrine taught that everyone was born sinful as a result of the original sin of Adam and Eve, sexual practices were associated with guilt and shame, and the whole concept of eroticism in Western art is coloured by this background of sexual taboos (Bataille, 1966). In the mediaeval period, churches throughout Europe were occasionally provided with erotic images, but unlike in the Indian temples, these were hidden away on capitals, bosses and misericords, proof not so much of the Church's liberality as of the wily artfulness of the craftsmen it employed (Lo Duca, 1966).

The new humanism of the Renaissance in Italy during the fifteenth century, with its renewal of interest in the world of Classical Antiquity, brought about certain changes in the progress of the arts. The shameful connotations associated with nudity *per se* began to lessen in intensity, and with the rise of enlightened secular patronage, the hold of the Church over the arts began to weaken. Venus became a favourite subject with Renaissance artists from Botticelli to Giorgione and Titian, providing the perfect excuse for painting the female nude. But modesty was required, and so Botticelli's *Birth of Venus* (1484–90), Giorgione's *Sleeping Venus* (1505–10) and Titian's *Venus of Urbino* (*c.* 1538) all hide their sex with a hand, a motif which in fact enhances rather than detracts from their erotic effect. The prudery behind this approach also required that Michelangelo's *David* (1504) be provided with a figleaf, and the same fate befell many male nude sculptures of the Classical era as soon as they were excavated. A later indignity was the systematic castration of such sculptures whose penises were knocked off by means of special little hammers distributed to archaeologists. Certain major museums have trays of these pathetic clues to prudery (Webb, 1978).

It is the museums who must be held largely to blame for our lack of knowledge about the important role that explicit eroticism came to play in later Western art. The fact is that most major artists have seen fit to express their sexual natures in their works, but such works are rarely exhibited, just as collections of Classical and Oriental art usually omit the more erotic examples. During the Renaissance period almost all great artists used mythological stories as the excuse for erotic subjects: Jupiter's sexual encounters with mortals such as Leda, Danae and Antiope were depicted in major paintings by Leonardo, Michelangelo and Raphael as well as by many others. But more common was the easily circulated etching, and many great masters produced sets of erotic images euphemistically called *Loves of the Gods*. While researching in the Secret Collection of the British Museum for my book *The Erotic Arts*, I discovered magnificent prints of this nature by Giulio Romano, Marcantonio Raimondi, Parmigianino and others, including *Satyr Copulating with a Nymph* (1584–87) (Plate VIII), one of a series of superb quality by Agostino Carracci which show a great variety of sexual couplings (Webb, 1978).

Mythology provided the basis for one of the finest scenes of erotic frescoes of the Renaissance period, those by Raphael's pupil Giulio Romano in the Palazzo del Te in Mantua (1525–35). Most powerful is the scene showing Jupiter as a sea-serpent with a large erection about to have intercourse with Olympia; opposite this wall, Giulio painted another highly charged scene entitled "Parsiphae concealing herself in the statue of a cow made by Daedalus in order to receive the love of the bull." Raphael himself, with the help of his pupils, had earlier painted frescoes of an erotic nature for the bathroom of Cardinal Bibbiena in the Vatican (after 1515). These scenes from the *History of Venus* are in poor condition today owing to the unfortunate actions of a zealous Vatican official who whitewashed the walls during the nineteenth century. Giulio had been involved in the most celebrated artistic scandal of the period, the publication in the early 1520s of Aretino's *Sonnets*, a book consisting of superb engravings by Marcantonio Raimondi after drawings by Giulio with accompanying sonnets in bawdy language by Pietro Aretino. Each picture showed a man and a woman in a different position of sexual intercourse. All copies of the original publication seem to have been destroyed, as have Giulio's drawings, but the Secret Collection of the British Museum contains a single print from the series and some mutilated fragments (Webb, 1978).

The Bible was the second great store-house of erotic possibilities, although artists found rather less scope here than in the tales of mythology. Michelangelo's *Pièta* sculptures and Leonardo's *Holy Family* paintings often contain barely concealed erotic connotations (Bowie and Christenson, 1970). Martyrdoms provided many subjects for artists concerned in giving expression to erotic interests; Saints Barbara, Catherine, Margaret and Agatha were all the subjects of such works, and St Sebastian was often used as the vehicle for homosexual fantasies. But the most obvious figures for erotic portrayal in the Bible are Judith and Mary Magdalene. The bloody exploit of the former is often depicted as she cuts through the neck of the naked Holofernes, perhaps most revealingly by the female artist Artemisia Gentileschi with a motivation which can clearly be interpreted in Freudian terms (Melville, 1973). The reformed adulteress Mary Magdalene was depicted by Francesco Furini as a full-length frontal nude in a state of excitement, while Titian painted her in 1554 gazing rapturously up to heaven as she clutches her long silky tresses to her body, leaving her breasts provocatively exposed. Similarly erotic depictions were later painted by Van Dyck and Rubens, and perhaps the ultimate version is Rodin's sculpture of 1894 (Plate IX) which shows her in the nude embracing the body of Christ on the cross.

Religious eroticism continued to be a theme of art works during the seventeenth century. Bernini's *St Theresa in Ecstasy* (1645–52) is a life-sized coloured marble sculpture in the Church of Santa Mona della Vittoria in Rome, in which the saint appears to be in the throes of orgasm with an angel standing over her wielding a phallic arrow. Caravaggio's paintings of nude male saints suggest a strong degree of homosexual involvement, and an atmosphere of humanism is already in evidence. Rembrandt and Rubens felt free to celebrate love in its open enjoyment with no pretentions to religious significance. Rembrandt produced many engravings of an explicitly erotic nature: the finest is *Ledakant* of 1646 (Plate X) which shows the couple having intercourse on a large bed, and is believed to represent the artist and his mistress Hendrickje Stöffels; the private, unfinished nature of the work is shown by the experimentation in the treatment of the female figure whose left arm is drawn in two positions. And Rubens was probably the first artist who dared to paint an erotic portrayal of the woman he loved, without concealing it behind a biblical or mythological story: *Helène Fourment in a Fur Cloak* of 1630–31 shows his amply endowed wife in the nude, clutching a fur cloak around her shoulders, perhaps having just got out of bed.

French painting of the eighteenth century reflects the amoral, fun-loving atmosphere of the court of Louis XV and his mistresses, one of whom, the Irish girl, Louise O'Murphy, was the subject of one of Boucher's most erotic works. The canvas of 1755 shows her lying provocatively nude on her stomach: there is no coyness in the blatant titillation of her superb body as she sinks into the silks and satins that cover the beautifully upholstered chaise-longue, her enticing buttocks demanding to be fondled and caressed. For the most famous of the King's mistresses, the beautiful and intelligent Madame de Pompadour, Boucher painted six rustic scenes of erotic engagements between shepherds and shepherdesses surrounded by doves and sheep (Plate XI). Unfortunately, like many such erotic works, this whole series was later destroyed (Webb, 1978).

Later in the eighteenth century two artists in England produced erotic works of a high standard, works that contrasted sharply with those of Boucher and indeed with each other. Rowlandson's erotic prints were issued in small, hand-coloured editions, and most of them are today in the Secret

Collections of the British Museum and Victoria and Albert Museum and in the Queen's Collection at Windsor Castle (Schiff, 1969). They are mainly humorous scenes of contemporary life viewed with the artist's usual sharp eye for telling detail: an example (Plate XII) shows a scene in a tavern where a woman having intercourse with a sailor is waving a handkerchief out of the window to a ship on which her husband is sailing away. Contemporary with Rowlandson was Fuseli whose erotic works were certainly not for publication. Fuseli was an ugly little man who was fascinated by the idea of being masochistically overpowered by dominant women with exotic hairstyles, and two extraordinary drawings in the Victoria and Albert Museum Secret Collection bear witness to this fantasy (Webb, 1978). Other equally private drawings show elegantly coiffeured but fearsome courtesans, and one beautiful example (see Plate XIII) depicts a lesbian scene involving a couple with a mirror on a dressing-table. Unfortunately few such works escaped Mrs Fuseli's kitchen stove after the artist's death. Another artist to suffer such a fate was Turner, many of whose erotic works were burnt by his executor, Ruskin, although a few drawings on sexual themes can be found in his sketchbooks at the British Museum (Webb, 1978).

During the nineteenth century many artists chose to explore the "forbidden" facets of human nature. Ingres, Géricault, Millet and Daumier produced beautiful erotic works, and later, both Toulouse-Lautrec and Degas found inspiration for drawings and paintings in the brothels of Paris. Courbet caused at least two scandals: his *Sleeping Women* of 1866 showed two entwined nude women relaxing on a bed after making love, and is one of the few major works of western art on the theme of lesbianism, and *The Origin of the World* (c. 1867) depicted the torso of a nude woman with her legs apart, concentrating attention on her genitals. The quality of this work was much admired when it was first exhibited, but the painting has since disappeared. Towards the end of the century, Moreau and Beardsley produced startlingly erotic portrayals of Salomé and John the Baptist from the New Testament: a drawing by Beardsley shows her kissing his severed head (Brophy, 1968). Such biblical figures fascinated artists during this period: the Belgian engraver Rops portrayed Mary Magdalene masturbating at the foot of a crucified penis in 1885, and we have already noted Rodin's powerful sculpture of 1894 (see Plate IX) which depicts the nude Magdalene holding the body of Christ in a sexual embrace on the cross.

The darker side of sensuality that so fascinated these *fin-de-siècle* artists becomes especially noticeable in twentieth-century erotic art. The gaunt lovers and lonely masturbators of Klimt and Schiele express a compulsive urgency that reflects the overall mood of despair that was so symptomatic of the early years of the century, and the shocking sensual drawings by Grosz and paintings by Beckmann of the 1920s and 1930s similarly capture the horror of life in Germany between the wars. These artists had to flee from the Nazis, as did Hans Bellmer who created some of the most powerful and disturbing erotic images of the century (Peppiatt, 1973). In the 1930s he gave expression to his sexual dreams and secret desires by constructing the articulated figure of a young girl which could be assembled in many different positions. The photographs which he took of this doll expressed a disturbing eroticism in a painfully honest manner, and this obsessive infatuation with the sexual power of young girls was also the inspiration for many superb engravings and drawings made after Bellmer's escape to France (Jelenski, 1972).

In France Bellmer joined the Surrealist Group. These avid explorers of sexuality were aware of the revolutionary nature of unfettered erotic expression, and they often insisted upon excess. Surrealist art has a compulsive tendency which tends to have a deep effect on the viewer, often communicating on a direct subconscious level, which reflects their knowledge of Freud's discovery that sexuality lies at the root of creativity. Their works show, in place of a concentration on genital organs, a transformation of the whole body into an erotic arena for exciting experiences (Webb, 1978). For example, Dali's *Young Virgin Autosodomized by her own Chastity* (1954) is a woman whose body is made up of sexual symbols which she can detach and pass round for people to admire. And Magritte's *Rape* (1934) shows a woman's face where the eyes and mouth are represented by her breasts and vulva, and the image is at the same time symbolic of intercourse with the face becoming the head of a penis disappearing into a mass of pubic hair.

Since the Surrealists, many artists have chosen to explore the rarified atmospheres of sexuality. Stanley Spencer's erotic works pursued his equation of spiritual and sexual ecstasy: he believed that indulgence of sexual appetites brought one closer to God (Collis, 1972). In America, women are figures of menacing sexuality in the works of Richard Lindner, while Tom Wesselman shows them unveiling their mysteries in matter-of-fact bedroom scenes (Gerdts, 1974). In England, Allen Jones portrays women in leather or rubber with stockings and high heels, inviting the viewer to probe his own and the artist's sexual imagination rather than merely seeking to titillate him (Livingstone 1979). David Hockney uses often prosaic imagery to express a fascination with homosexual love, and Graham Ovenden's images of little girls explore his painful conviction that sexuality is an essential ingredient in the seeming innocence of childhood (Webb, 1978). Eroticism was a continual preoccupation of Picasso's work, and his engravings of 1968 on the theme of *Raphael and La Fornarina* (see Plate XIV) show the young Renaissance master having intercourse with his model in the studio while the modern octogenarian watches with an expression that mixes excitement with wistful nostalgia for his own youth (Hess and Nochlin, 1973). There is no prurience here and no desire to shock: the natural, guilt-free pleasures of the sex act are illustrated in a manner than ennobles rather than degrades. The result is a true celebration of love.

I have strong reservations about pornography. [On the aesthetic level it tends to be very limited and boring and there is little evidence of imagination or intelligence or humour. On the pyschological level it tends towards the exploration of much-too-easily-satisfied human needs in a most basic masturbatory sense and in this way it exploits man]at his most vulnerable. On the moral level its effect on young children is uncertain, especially when such children are engaged in its production. But I do not think that pornography is a corrupting influence; it can certainly be of important therapeutic value to some people, quite apart from its ability to sustain and enliven sexual relations. [On the other side of the coin, erotic art can reach a very high aesthetic level indeed. It can afford a very satisfying and also a very disturbing experience of lasting value, which often leads to real enlightenment. On the psychological level it can reveal a fascinating insight into the personal and sometimes painful fantasies of a creative mind which can in itself be encouraging and also exciting. At the same time, it can provide a very useful historical perspective to the true value that sex can have as a mutual activity. To sum up, I would suggest that pornography can tend to lead towards exploitation whereas erotic art I consider presents a celebration.

References

Anaud, M. R. *Kama Kala, Some Notes on the Philosophical Basis of Hindu Erotic Sculpture.* Hamburg, Geneva and Paris: Nagel, 1963.
Bataille, G. *Eroticism.* London: Calder and Boyars, 1966.
Beurdeley, M. *The Clouds and the Rain: The Art of Love in China.* Fribourg and London: Hammond, 1969.
Bowie, T. and Christenson, C. V. (Eds). *Studies in Erotic Art.* London: Basic Books, 1970.
Brophy, B. *Black and White: A Portrait of Aubrey Beardsley.* London: Jonathan Cape, 1968.
Collis, L. A. *Private View of Stanley Spencer.* London: Heinemann, 1972.
Gerdts, W. H. *The Great American Nude.* London: Phaidon Press, 1974.
Grosbois, C. *Shunga, Images of Spring: Essay on Erotic Elements in Japanese Art.* Geneva, Paris and Munich: Nagel, 1966.
Hess, T. B. and Nochlin, L. (Eds). *Woman as Sex Object: Studies in Erotic Art (1730–1970).* London: Allen Lane, 1973.
Jelenski, C. *Drawings of Hans Bellmer.* London: Academy, 1972.
Livingstone, M. *Allen Jones: Sheer Magic.* London: Thames and Hudson, 1979.
Lo Duca, G. *Erotique de l'Art.* Paris: La Jeune Parque, 1966.
Marcadé, J. *Roma Amor: Essay on Erotic Elements in Etruscan and Roman Art.* Geneva, Paris and Munich: Nagel, 1965.
Melville, R. *Erotic Art of the West.* London: Weidenfeld and Nicholson, 1973.

Peppiatt, M. Balthus, Klossowski, Bellmer: Three approaches to the flesh. *Art International* October 1973.

Rawson, P. (Ed.). *Primitive Erotic Art.* London: Weidenfeld and Nicholson, 1973a.

Rawson, P. *Erotic Art of the East.* London: Weidenfeld and Nicholson, 1973b.

Schiff, G. *The Amorous Illustrations of Thomas Rowlandson.* New York: Cythera Press, 1969.

Webb, P. *The Erotic Arts.* London: Secker and Warburg, 1978.

Captions to Plates

PLATE I.   Mithuna couple, Brahrnesvara Temple, Bhubaneswar, India (*c.* tenth century A.D.).
PLATE II.   Danish pornographic photograph (*c.* 1967).
PLATE III.   Brancusi's "Princess X" (1916).
PLATE IV.   English seaside post-card (*c.* 1960).
PLATE V.   Gala lipstick advertisement (*c.* 1967).
PLATE VI.   Brothel scene, Pompeii (*c.* first century A.D.).
PLATE VII.   Harunobu, a "Fantasy" (*c.* late 1760s).
PLATE VIII.   Agostino Carracci's "Satyr Copulating with a Nymph" (1584–1587).
PLATE IX.   Rodin's "Le Christ et la Madeleine" (1894).
PLATE X.   Rembrandt's "Ledakant" (1646).
PLATE XI.   Boucher, Pastoral scene (*c.* 1750s).
PLATE XII.   Rowlandson's "Departure of the Husband" (*c.* 1815).
PLATE XIII.   Fuseli, Lesbian couple (*c.* 1815–1820).
PLATE XIV.   Picasso's "Raphael and La Fornarina" (1968).

PLATE II

PLATE I

PLATE III

PLATE IV

PLATE V

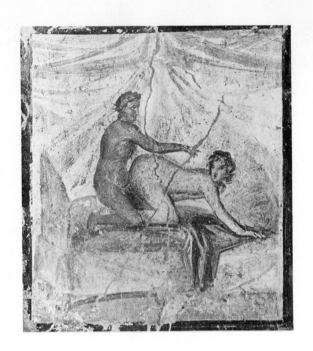

PLATE VI

PLATE VII

PLATE IX

PLATE VIII

PLATE X

PLATE XI

PLATE XII

PLATE XIII

PLATE XIV

6

A perspective on female responses to sexual material

Christine Pickard

Introduction

It was probably inevitable that certain pre-conceptions, because of their general acceptance as eternal truths, would arise in the field of human sexuality. After all, most of these pre-conceptions have existed for a long period of time, receiving constant reinforcement from cultural and social factors: attitudes regarding the differences in male and female sexual behaviour tend to fall into this category. In our Western culture, it has been generally accepted that women are less sexual than men, i.e. have less sexual drive, and their minimal interest in viewing explicit sexual materials has been considered part of the overall proof – when women's orgasmic difficulties and the prolonged time often required for females to become aroused are added to the equation, the scales appear to weigh heavily on the side of their presumed hyposexuality.

However, evidence is now beginning to show that the approach to the question of female sexuality has been somewhat one-sided. Intelligence tests have fallen into a certain amount of disfavour because the questions have a cultural bias, thereby automatically discriminating against those individuals with a different cultural background. Similarly, until very recently, all the research investigating female sexual responses fell into the same trap, and some of the research studies have not yet adapted to correct for this type of bias; questionnaires about sexuality were, of course, all devised by men based upon their own understanding of sexual realities, and women were, generally speaking, asked the same questions as men. There can be no doubt, culturally speaking, that females are exposed to different influences, different mores, and different expectations than men, and arguments suggesting that intelligence tests are more an examination of environmental forces than inherited abilities can be brought to bear even more strongly in the case of research investigating female responses to sexual material.

Historical Aspects

Kinsey's (1953) research on female sexuality was considered for many years the definitive study concerning the female's ability to respond to sexual stimuli, and his team provided evidence of considerable differences in the readiness of the average man and woman to respond to erotic material. For example, with regard to viewing portrayals of sexual activity, 42% of the males reported a *very strong* and definite response as opposed to 14% of the females in the sample. However, a smaller proportion of the females had had the opportunity to see, or had taken the opportunity to see, such portrayals. In contrast, Kinsey reported that practically all of the males in his sample had had the opportunity to observe depictions of sexual activity, and had taken the opportunity to do so. Indeed, 77% of the males who had seen such material indicated that they had been at least *somewhat aroused* by viewing it, whereas only 32% of the females reported such arousal from observing sexual activities. Apparently Kinsey's team could find no reason for this difference, although they remarked that

> many females . . . report that they are offended by portrayals of sexual action, and denounce them on moral, social, and aesthetic grounds. This is ordinarily taken as evidence of the female's greater sense of propriety; but . . . it seems more likely that females are indifferent or antagonistic to the existence of such materials because it means nothing to them erotically (p. 662).

Looking back with the clarity of hindsight, it is easy to provide one suggestion for the obtained results, namely, the questions were primarily designed with men in mind and were angled from the point of view of the male cultural bias. Kinsey's results, therefore, probably reflected differential experiences with sexual materials, rather than sex differences in psychosexual arousability. Not only have women not often experienced these types of stimuli, but the lack of sexual material designed specifically to suit female tastes has rarely been considered because women were not supposed to respond to it.

Steele and Walker (1976) have recently shown that females generally prefer depictions of heterosexual petting and coital activity, the "ideal" film from a feminine perspective being described by most women interviewed as follows:

> the cast of the film would consist of one attractive male and one attractive female, displaying affection, 'romance', and prolonged foreplay in a bedroom setting. The film would involve a *gradual* process leading to coitus involving a variety of positions, and the emotional tone of the film would emphasize the 'total' relationship, and not merely genital sexual behaviour (p. 272).

How unlikely, then, that any sexual material in general circulation several decades ago would have appealed to women, since the most frequently seen examples of explicit sex consisted of the female body in various stages of undress – which was as far as the mores of the time allowed the standard material to go – and erotica, that could be expected to excite both sexes, must have been generally unavailable, especially in America which was not known for its erotic tradition. Kinsey's female respondents must have been primarily visualizing erotica aimed at male audiences when the questions were asked, so that a lack of response is hardly surprising; unfortunately, the final report does not make this point completely clear. Males, however, generally report being more highly aroused by portrayals of nude females that do females (Byrne and Lamberth, 1971; Steele and Walker, 1974). If Kinsey's female respondents were, in fact, visualizing the nude female body, then perhaps the results are not too surprising after all. Exposure to sexual material for most women probably consisted of nude or semi-nude females depicted on calendars, famous art drawings or paintings reproduced for the mass media, and possibly a glance at some explicit sexual depictions which could have been available. In these circumstances, considering the social pressure to avoid anything explicit, it is surprising that Kinsey had any response at all to visual material, particularly to nude females. Perhaps more surprising, however, was the fact that Kinsey found only 12% of the females in his sample had ever been aroused by seeing male nudes – exactly the same percentage that reported arousal to observing portrayals of female nudes! In contrast, 54% of the males were aroused upon observing female nudes. Since a lack of response to observing nude figures and portrayals of sexual activity – plus less opportunity for or interest in viewing such material – characterizes the results for women in Kinsey's study, the proportion of males reporting arousal to sexual materials appears unusually elevated in comparison. Commenting on this issue, Stauffer and Frost (1976) have indicated that "until recently, sexually oriented magazines and pornography have been produced exclusively for men. The purveyors of this material simply assumed that women were not in the market for their products. This presumption runs through much of the early literature on female sexuality. For instance, in the Kinsey studies

> 88 per cent of the females compared to 46 per cent of the males reported that they were *never* aroused by observing portrayals of nude figures. More recent research, however, casts doubts on these conclusions . . . (and) suggests that sexually-oriented magazines and pornography may have an appeal to women (p. 25).

In comparison, literary materials – such as romantic novels – have always been available to women, and because of the wide range available and the considerable numbers of books and stories written by the women themselves, most of them have usually been able to find something to suit their tastes. Many books written with a female cultural bias exist; women recognize these as socially appropriate for themselves and, as a result, sexual response can be triggered. A slow moving story of a love affair between a young man and woman culminating in passionate kisses covering the face, ears and neck used to be as far as the story in an average woman's magazine – great arbiters of what is socially acceptable – would go. This is also as far as the activities of socially well-trained teenage girls of yesteryear were supposed to proceed; even though her private fantasies would run the whole gamut of sexual experience as far as she could perceive it, these kissing scenes could, if effectively written, be intensely moving to the young girl, and she might well have felt a general overall excitement and butterflies in her stomach; genital sensations may well be absent (because she had not learnt to expect them) until the time when actual genital pleasure is felt during sexual play or intercourse. Thus, not surprisingly, Kinsey found that males and females responded similarly to literature concerning sexuality, with about 60% of each sex indicating at least some response to these materials. However, although he obtained better results in regard to female response to written materials, Kinsey's figures were quite likely still too low. For example, the supposedly innocent stories in women's magazines may not have been re-garded by the respondent as anything explicitly sexual, and even though she experienced a strong response at the time, she may have, years later, forgotten their previous power to move her; moreover, she may not have thought it relevant to the type of questions being asked.

Gebhard (1973) offers several possible explanations as to why the female statistics generally lagged behind the male equivalents. In his view, the retrospective design may have mitigated against the accuracy of the results *if* one assumes that females are more likely than males to minimize or forget the strength of their sexual response to stimuli some months or years removed. Finding this argument insufficient on its own, however, he offers two addi-tional and, perhaps, more important explanations. First, the wording of the questions themselves made it likely that many positive female responses were missed; for example, for the poorly educated or less intelligent the question was often phrased "Does it get you hot and bothered to . . .?" This implies a very strong reaction and suggests that the subjects would ignore mild titilla-tions and flutters that were so relevant to the enquiry. Even the standard wording "Does it arouse you sexually to (see or read various stimulus items)" suggests a response of major significance; in either case, Gebhard indicates that "the response threshold was thereby set too high for mild, or even moderate, responses – particularly from female respondents. . . . Only those who grasped the idea that we were seeking any degree of response would reply appropriately" (p. 201). Apparently, any answer in the affirmative tended to be recorded as a strong yes; if the men were only slightly more inclined to report arousal to explicit sexual material (and after all, the male sub-culture encourages the male to express an interest, even if simulated) this would emerge as a significant difference. Presumably, when an individual felt doubtful about what his or her response should be, the male would tend to say yes (and thereby be recorded as providing an emphatic positive reply), whereas the female would tend to provide a denial; as Gebhard expresses it, "the high threshold probably had more effect on females than on males since the former are culturally less conditioned to expressing sexual impulses, especially in such stark terms" (p. 202). Secondly, Gebhard believes that the speed with which a sexual stimulus is presented accounts for some of the differences Kinsey found. Indeed, he states that when sexual stimuli are presented suddenly, females are more inclined to react negatively since in our culture they are trained to be cautious about sex and act with initial restraint. Therefore, when females are shown pictures of sexual activity – presented instantaneously and in their blatant totality – they are likely to react negatively; in contrast, males do not receive this defensive conditioning. In his view, then, this largely explains the fact that written stories, motion pictures, and even music are effective, as far as women are concerned, in producing a sexual response. And, he believes that if culturally produced variables can be identified and analytically partialed out, males and females will eventually prove to be very similar, if not identical, in their inherent capacity to respond sexually to visual stimuli.

Cultural Influences

Attitudes towards sexuality are obviously influenced by cultural differences in the socialization of male and female children. Can we determine what these are and how pervasive their influence may be? Undoubtedly innate biological differences between male and female exist; this is apparent in all animal species. But as we move up the phylogenetic scale, hormonal influences and other predictable sexual parameters seem to play a smaller part in the sexual response of the individual. Individual differences and learned responses seem to be of ever expanding significance, and limitations on sexual behaviour at the human level are universal, both culturally determined and amazingly diverse. Mead (1935) comments on her observations of the Arapesh culture, in which

> we found no idea that sex was a powerful driving force for men or women. In marked contrast to these attitudes, we found among the Mundugumor that both men and women developed as ruthless, aggressive, positively-sexed individuals, with the maternal cherishing aspects of personality at a minimum. Both men and women approximated to a personality type that we in our culture

would find only in an undisciplined and very violent male. . . . In the third tribe, the Tchambuli, we found a genuine reversal of the sex attitudes of our own culture, with the women the dominant, impersonal managing partner, the man the less responsible and the emotionally dependent person (p. 190).

These observations add weight to the view that cultural factors are of crucial importance in determining the finer details of sexual behaviour.

The instinct which drives the male to seek pleasure from the female and vice-versa is very strong, despite all society's restraints, as the persistence of a high level of sexual activity, such as pre-marital intercourse, during the Victorian years shows. But the way the individual approaches sex and his or her attitude to related issues are very much conditioned by society's values – such as the official role of the passive female. In my experience women admit to taking much of the initiative for sexual activity, but the moves must be made in a subtle, roundabout, or underhand way; because of their enforced status of "underdog" in the sexual stakes they have learnt a great deal of subterfuge which is variously described as the "wisdom of Eve", "knowing how to give a man what he wants", "boosting his ego", etc.

For many women, avoiding explicit sexual material is, or at least was, part of the subterfuge, and for most of them, whether they actually liked the stuff or not was irrelevant. The taboo was tacitly assumed and for the majority not really important enough to bother to break, apart from a secret look out of curiosity or a desire for titillation – normally it was just simply easier to avoid the issue. Of course, the occasional nude female would be encountered but that was indulgently tolerated by women who tended to view their men as overgrown boys, and the woman who is subjected to truly explicit sexual material as we perceive it today, depicting sexual acts, is still relatively rare. There is no female equivalent of the male "stag party" to introduce her to it, so that she has been largely dependent on what the men close to her have wished to share. It is hardly surprising that the first response to something so new, which early training has implied is wrong, tends to be viewed negatively – unless the girl's upbringing has been exceptionally liberal. Even if she is actually turned on by the material in a sexual sense, her pre-conditioned mind is likely to be sending out alarm signals which suppress any excitement; only when she has had time to become familiar with sexual material and her mental processes have ceased to rebel can the conscious process of excitation express itself to the full. Of course, the degree of negative feelings in some women is so great that the anxiety generated by contact with this material never disappears – those who perceive sexual material as morally degrading and socially disruptive fall into this group. However, even the average girl who is apparently well-adjusted sexually, initially senses that some type of negative response is appropriate, although there is some evidence that the need for this instinctive protective reaction is diminishing.

However, in a society which still teaches girls to be sexually cautious and places the blame firmly on them for any transgressions and accidents, such as an unwanted pregnancy, it behoves the female to react with caution in any unfamiliar sexual situation, a matter of survival in a world where sex used to be considered a male prerogative. She is, therefore, conditioned to respond slowly, as Gebhard points out, and these factors operate all the time, even when she views a situation favourably; they are, of course, compounded on the not infrequent occasions when something undesirable does occur. For every approach from a man whose attentions are welcome, an attractive woman might be at the receiving end of a score of annoying attempts at seduction – some of them downright threatening. However, exhortations from family, school, etc., to reject men as a whole are quickly seen to be unrealistic through the influence of the peer group, but the negative associations of sexual material have little chance of being rejected as the group tends to see them – if they are considered at all – merely as covert objects which can bring a little naughty pleasure. But these objects of secret mirth are, or were, rarely explicit material as we know it. These generalizations, of course, cannot be applied with equal weight in all social strata, the middle classes seeming to have a more rigid conception of how a "nice" girl should behave.

It is generally accepted that girls develop a social sense at an earlier age than boys although contemporary research tries to exclude cultural differences as far as possible. However, this exaggerated socialization of the female sex appears to represent a genuine and lasting divergence, girls being more concerned with languages, communication and with socialization. Of course, these variations have been culturally encouraged so that women emerge, probably by a combination of genetic and environmental factors, as more concerned with relationships, more concerned with the established status quo and with perpetuating the social mores extant. They are in the social and sexual sense, labile, or as women themselves probably prefer to term it, more flexible. Bernard (1966) suggests that women are assigned the task of supporting the existing sexual norms because of greater sexual plasticity, and draws attention to the importance of the greater cultural susceptibility of the female than the male to whatever sexual restraints are necessary. Staples (1973) believes that the increasing relaxation of societal restraints on the expression of female sexuality predicts a greater symmetry in heterosexual behaviour and relationships. Thus, he comments that

in the past when her status depended on sexual repression the female abstained from any overt expression of sexual satisfaction and sought to employ the enticement of sex relations with a man for whatever emotional or material gains she could obtain. To a greater extent today her sexual activity may be enjoyed more nearly for its own sake without provoking a label of promiscuity and loss of status. Women do not have to see themselves any longer as sex objects, as commodities governed by market relations. Sexual relations are no longer something to withhold for exchange purposes but an act to be mutually enjoyed (p. 18).

Moreover, most observers would probably agree that contraception has provided women with the means to evade society's wrath if "things" go wrong, thus facilitating a readjustment of sexual mores.

For all these reasons, the female's ability, encouraged by external forces, to bend her desires to accommodate the prevailing wind, plus her economic and social need to remain a suitable candidate for marriage (to the extent in some parts of the world of having an operation prior to the ceremony to ensure that she satisfies the virginity rules by bleeding when "deflowering" takes place), made her control her sexual behaviour and attitudes. The fact that so many women "fell by the wayside" bears testimony to the presence of strong sexual urges that could not always be submerged despite strong forces inducing her to do so. Reiss (1960) points out that there is little factual basis in the widespread belief that men need sex more than women. The basis for the difference, he contends, lies almost certainly in the fact that men do not try so hard as women to *control* their sexual behaviour. Yet, in the past, market forces seemed to push women to a point where this became necessary; as a result, open appreciation of sexual materials was considered to be inappropriate for them. Therefore, any study which shows a lower interest for this kind of material among females compared with males should not be surprising; not, of course, that results of this kind prove anything about innate capacity to respond sexually to erotic stimuli. But what of present day studies? If any of them demonstrates a clear capacity on the part of the fair sex to respond equally, or almost equally, with their opposite numbers when shown erotic material, then the hypothesis that women have an innately lower arousability to sexual stimuli and consequent hyposexuality flounders, if it does not collapse altogether.

Contemporary Research

In part, not much has changed since Kinsey's time as males still report much more exposure to, interest in, and reaction to erotic material than do females in sex *surveys* (Abelson *et al.*, 1971). But on the other hand, a great deal has changed. Baron and Byrne (1977) have recently observed that *experimental* research in human sexuality has shown males and females to be remarkably similar in their responsiveness to sexual stimuli. Schmidt and Sigusch (1973) note that these recent findings refute Kinsey's evidence for a lesser capacity of women to become sexually aroused by erotic material, and suggest that Kinsey's data reflects, more accurately, the cultural desexualization of women in Western societies which was more prevalent in his day than now. The authors conducted a number of experimental studies comparing the responses of young men and women to sexually explicit stimuli, and found that the pattern and intensity of reactions were generally the same for men and women. Thus, on the average, brief exposure to sexual materials led to subjectively described "moderate" sexual excitation, and physiological correlates of arousal. When significant sex differences were found, women reported somewhat lower subjective arousal and stronger emotional avoidance reactions than men; on the other hand, when erotic stories were used as stimuli, women reported greater sexual activity over the next 24-hour period than men. Overall, the authors concluded that these variations do not detract from the evidence showing that women can react to the same extent and in the same direction as men do to pictures, films, and stories with an explicitly sexual content (cf. Schmidt and Sigusch, 1970; Schmidt et al., 1973). Thus, not surprisingly, Fisher and Byrne (1978) point out that it seems inappropriate to generalize from survey data concerning whether or not women have been aroused by erotica to assumptions that they are unable to respond in such a way.

These results differ considerably from Kinsey's findings about the marked sex differences in the area of psychosexual arousability. Schmidt and Sigusch (1973) attribute the discrepancy between studies to cultural factors which have facilitated the divergence of sexual behaviour and attitudes among men and women. They note that although the stereotype of the less libidinous, less initiative-taking woman whose sexuality can be realized only within emotional and personal relations is still important, tremendous inroads have been made into the concept of the double standard; accordingly, the incidence of premarital coitus for men and women is equally high in north-west European societies although inequalities still exist. Women, however, can now take some of the initiative and can indulge in sex, more or less, when they want to and for its own sake. No longer is sex a bargaining point whereby the female achieves the desired position in society, but a pleasure for the woman as well as the man. The old theory that women can only enjoy sex when love is an accompaniment has been questioned, and whereas the combination may be necessary for some, it is apparent that relatively liberated women are capable of enjoying sex without love. Christensen and Gregg (1970) have argued that in a heterosexually-oriented society there is no significant sexual liberalization without giving up the double standard and culturally conditioned sexual inequality because male and female sexual behaviour are mutually dependent. They believe that the sexual liberalization process has been a major factor in the convergence of male and female sexual behaviour patterns, and that the greater ability of young women today to be stimulated by sexually explicit stimuli is only one outcome of a long and still incompleted process of the resexualization of women. Schmidt (1975) speculates on the changing economic circumstances in our industrialized Western societies which have altered the perceptions of traditional sexuality; hard work and the need for material success coincided in the past with rather puritan values, and sexual energy had to be diverted as much as possible into physical effort – society made sexuality take a back seat. Now, however, there is a certain "peacock' effect – a desire to buy things and show them off – that is the result of the liberalization of adolescent sexuality accompanied by the development of a special market with an extremely sexualized advertising. The need to work has been reduced and market forces now are using sex as a means of increasing consumption – society is now coaxing sexuality back into the limelight. Gagnon and Simon (1973) agree that sexual norms are becoming more and more influenced by consumption values as opposed to production values, and as a result our culture is now pushing women towards a more direct expression of their sexuality, which allows them to be more explicit in their interests. Yet, on the surface, women are still reticent about their reactions toward sexual material. Today, although a few admit readily, and often with a smile, that they have always had a capacity to be "turned on" by sexual stimuli (a characteristic they sometimes kept secret because of the fear of being in some way abnormal), large numbers of women, when questioned, still report a low reaction, presumably because of what they believe to be appropriate. However, these *self-reports* do not accord well with the results of experimental research in which women are confronted with real life visual images. In the latter case, protected by the atmosphere of scientific enquiry, a woman is apparently more likely to admit that she is stimulated psychologically and that, to a greater or lesser degree, her physiology is responsive.

Social desirability is still an important factor in determining the outcome of the *surveys* attempting to evaluate response to sexual materials. This is true for men, but as we have seen, the rules and conditions laid down for females as to what is appropriate are much more tightly defined, and considering the stringent training females get as to what is acceptable, the extra resistance they register as to what is "not nice" or "obscene" is readily understood. Thus, it is not surprising that the *reported* response to sexual material often depends upon whether the material is seen as socially good or bad. Schmidt and Sigusch (1969), for example, found a negative correlation between what was sexually arousing and its favourableness; i.e. anything stimulating was viewed as bad if the material was considered against society's norms, irrespective of whether the person *admitted* to feeling aroused or not. Thus, even if the person was titillated by the material, if he or she basically disapproved of it, then overall, a negative evaluative response was given. Byrne, Fisher, Lamberth and Mitchell (1974), in their study of evaluative responses to erotica, hypothesized that judgements about the attractiveness of erotic stimuli are a function of the *affect* elicited by such material. Furthermore, they thought it should be possible to identify those individuals for whom particular kinds of erotic stimuli elicit positive or negative affect, and to investigate both the antecedents and the consequences of such responses. The authors initially asked subjects to complete a scale that required self-ratings of affect on 11 dimensions: sexually aroused, disgusted, entertained, anxious, bored, angry, afraid, curious, nauseated, depressed, and excited. The subjects were then exposed to 19 themes of heterosexual, homosexual, and autosexual acts in either pictorial or verbal form, and asked to rate how arousing they found each theme to be. The original affect scale was then readministered to assess each subject's emotional responses to the stimuli. Byrne's team factor analysed the responses to this scale and instead of finding a single affective dimension ranging from positive to negative, they found two independent affective dimensions, accounting for 90% of the total variance; the first factor was labelled *Positive Affect* and consisted of items such as excited, entertained, sexually aroused, anxious, and curious; the second factor was labelled *Negative Affect* and consisted of items like angry, depressed, and disgusted. This procedure divided and categorized the responses of the individuals into four groups irrespective of sex:

(1) those subjects who are easily aroused by sexual stimuli and experience very little, if any, anxiety or conflict about it (the *affectively pro-sex group*);

(2) those who are barely aroused by the material but feel a very strong aversion to it (the *anti-sex group*);

(3) those subjects who experience a great deal of conflict over the material, but are none the less very aroused by viewing it (the *ambivalent group*); and

(4) whose who are relatively bored with erotica, feel low arousal to it, and yet feel no distaste for it either (the *indifferent group*).

These researchers believe that the affect an individual experiences when exposed to sexual material is the result of various rewards and punishments that were associated with sexual matters during their socialization. It is, then, this previously conditioned affect that determines how sexual material is evaluated. Other variables such as religious preference, liberalism–conservatism, and frequency of church attendance also help to predict how an individual will judge sexual material because they, too, are associated with differential sexual rewards and punishments which have come from parents, peers, religious sources and the mass media.

Interestingly, there are specific sex differences in the way in which affect influences evaluations of sexual stimuli. For example, for females, the degree of negative affect was the only predictor of evaluative responses towards erotica, the number of sexual themes judged "pornographic" being significantly related to the degree of negative affect, regardless of the level of positive affect. However, for males, it is the interaction of positive and negative affect that determines evaluative responses; for example, the anti-sex males, those subjects *high* in negative affect and *low* in positive affect, gave significantly more negative evaluative judgements. Byrne and his colleagues suggest that for females there may be a basic association of varying degrees of negative affect towards explicitly presented sexual material, while for males both positive and negative affect become associated with erotica, probably because of the differential conditioning that males and females experience during socialization. Males, for example, learn that it is acceptable to obtain sexual material, share it with same-sex members of their peer group, and use it as a stimulus for masturbation fantasies, whereas females rarely participate in such experiences; females generally have only negative experiences with sexual material while growing up, whereas males have various positive experiences as well as some negative ones invoked by cultural propriety. Thus, as a result, the authors believe that attempts to alter judgements and perceptions toward sexual material in women will only succeed when it is possible to alter the underlying emotional responses from which they derive; in effect, a resocialization experience in which women can learn to view sexual material in a more positive way.

The Byrne *et al.* (1974) research points out that the traditional emphasis upon male and female differences in response to sexual material tends in part to make one overlook the issue of *individual differences*. Obviously, as we have seen, sex differences are very important, but it is necessary to look at other variables which may partially account for the differences in response to viewing erotica, since the Byrne *et al.* findings clearly indicate that males and females are both represented within the four groupings of affective response to sexual material; thus, males and females who are classified as "anti-sex" may be more *similar* to each other than traditional socialization experiences would predict. Such findings tend to reinforce the idea that responsiveness to sexual material is influenced by variables other than gender. *Sex guilt*, for example – conceived as a generalized expectancy for self-mediated punishment or censure for violating (or anticipating violating) internalized standards of proper sexual conduct – is another variable that has been found to influence responsiveness to sexual stimuli. Mosher (1973) reports that high sex guilt subjects say that they are less likely to purchase or expose themselves to sexual material, especially "hard-core" material. Similarly, Schill and Chapin (1972) found that high sex guilt subjects were less likely to look through *Playboy* or *Penthouse* magazines while waiting for an appointment than low guilt subjects. Love *et al.* (1976) also found that high sex guilt subjects tended to minimize their exposure to sexual stimuli and to rate them as more obscene and disgusting than low scorers; interestingly, the moderate sex guilt subjects rated the slides as relatively obscene and disgusting and yet spent an increasing amount of time viewing them, a pattern that may conform to the Byrne *et al.* formulation of the "ambivalent" group in which individuals experience a great deal of aversion and conflict over the sexual material, but are none the less very aroused by viewing it – perhaps, as the authors suggest, it is from the ranks of this group that the stereotype of the film censor emerges! Not surprisingly, sex guilt influences actual sexual behaviour as well as responsiveness to sexual material. Indeed, numerous research studies continue to show that there is a highly significant inverse correlation between sexual guilt and sexual behaviour in both males and females (DiVasto *et al.*, 1981; Langston, 1973; Mosher and Cross, 1971). Apparently, simply living in a more liberal society does *not* significantly alter the factors which predispose a person to have sexual guilt, factors which increase the probability that an individual will respond negatively toward explicit sexual material. Fisher and Byrne (1978) indicate that in comparison with those individuals whose responses to sex stimuli are positive, those who respond negatively to erotica report negative experiences of sexual socialization that include fear, guilt, and religious proscriptions against sexual expression. Consequently, it seems reasonable to suspect that sexually explicit stimuli can function as either rewards or punishments because of their ability to evoke conditioned emotional responses; indeed, for those individuals whose affective responses are primarily positive, sexual stimuli should be rewarding and, as a result, approached, whereas such stimuli should act as punishments for and be avoided by those whose affective responses are negative.

Griffitt and Kaiser (1978), in a study designed to test this implication, attempted to demonstrate the reinforcing and aversive properties of sexual stimuli by using a relatively simple discrimination learning task in which experimental subjects were shown slides of sexually explicit acts following "correct" choices and non-sexual slides following "incorrect" choices; control subjects, of course, were shown non-sexual slides following all choices in the task. Both male and female subjects participated in the experiment and were classified as either high or low on the variable of sex guilt according to Mosher's (1966, 1968) forced-choice measure of sex guilt. Since research has shown that high sex guilt individuals respond with negative affect to erotica, it was expected that such stimuli would function as a punishment for them; in contrast, erotic stimuli were expected to be rewarding for low sex guilt subjects. Gender, however, was also expected to influence the outcome of the task; specifically, it was predicted that males would make more correct choices since research has shown that their affective responses to sexual material are generally more positive than those of females (Griffitt, 1973; Schmidt and Sigusch, 1970). Of course, such gender differences are, as

Griffitt (1973) points out, highly dependent upon the specific erotic themes portrayed; for example, Fisher and Byrne (1978) reported only marginal gender differences in response to a film showing an attractive couple engaging in various sexual acts. The present investigation included depictions of acts (e.g. group sex) that have been shown to elicit considerably more positive affect in males than in females (Griffitt *et al.*, 1974).

The idea that sexual stimuli can function as rewards or punishment due to their affect-eliciting properties was strongly supported by the results; thus, subjects whose affective responses to sexual stimuli were highly positive learned and performed responses that increased or at least maintained their opportunities to view sexual stimuli, whereas those whose affective responses were negative or minimally positive engaged in behaviour to reduce their exposure to this material. Moreover, both sex guilt and gender differences were predictive of affective reactions to erotica as well as of behaviour in the learning task. Consistent with previous findings (Love *et al.*, 1976), the emotional reactions of high sex guilt subjects during exposure to sexual stimuli were more negative than those of low sex guilt subjects. And, not surprisingly, males reported more positive affect than did females, which also supports previous findings (Schmidt and Sigusch, 1970). Perhaps more important, however, the results showed that for *females* generally and for high sex guilt males and females alike, sexual stimuli served as punishment by decreasing the probability of choice responses resulting in further exposure, whereas for *males* generally and for low sex guilt subjects of both genders, sexual stimuli served as rewards. Further analyses, however, indicated that the sex guilt and gender differences resulted from variations in the intensity of *positive* affect alone. Griffitt and Kaiser conclude that, for males and females, it appears that whether sexual material will be rewarding and subsequently approached and desired or punishing and therefore avoided is dependent upon the positivity of affect evoked by such stimuli, reactions which are determined primarily by conditioning processes operating during socialization.

One of the more important differences in the socialization of men and women derives from the psychological context of initial sexual experiences; yet, whereas most males are introduced to sexuality via solitary masturbation that precedes their introduction to heterosexuality and subsequent social contact with women, females often bypass early experience with masturbation and are introduced to heterosexuality directly. Masturbation has been described as a complex and important event in socialization, and the differential experiences of men and women in this regard have led to some interesting theoretical speculation about male and female differences. Gagnon and Simon (1973), for example, suggest that men and women create or invent a capacity for sexual behaviour through various learning procedures such as modelling or the cognitive rehearsal of how to be aroused and responsive. If masturbation represents one of the primary sources of learning how to be sexual, then sex differences in the frequency of masturbation suggest that females have relatively *less* experience in producing and identifying states of sexual arousal than males (cf. Rook and Hammen, 1977); recent research suggests that female masturbation *rates* continue to be lower than those of males although there is some evidence to suggest an increase in masturbation experience among females (Mosher and Abramson, 1977). The importance of masturbation for the female is evident in the fact that it is the one method by which she most frequently reaches orgasm (Kinsey *et al.*, 1953). In fact, the direct teaching of masturbation is being used increasingly in the treatment of primary orgasmic dysfunction in women, with masturbation to orgasm being highly predictive of the ability to reach coital orgasm (cf. LoPiccolo and Lobitz, 1972). Perhaps it is not too surprising, therefore, to find that masturbation has received increasing attention within the last few years (e.g. Abramson, 1973; Abramson and Mosher, 1975, 1979; Abramson, Perry, Rothblatt, Seeley and Seeley, 1981; Arafat and Cotton, 1974; Heiby and Becker, 1980; Mosher and Abramson, 1977; Mosher and O'Grady, 1979).

Abramson and Mosher (1975) originally proposed the idea that a measure of *negative attitudes toward masturbation* might prove to be more helpful than the construct of *sex guilt* in predicting individual differences in the frequency of masturbation, and they have recently developed and provided validational evidence for such a measure. In line with expectations, their research showed that sex guilt was more highly correlated with sex experience than with frequency of masturbation. In contrast, the measure of *negative attitudes toward masturbation* was more highly correlated with frequency of masturbation than sex experience for females; for males, it was *only* correlated with frequency of masturbation – not sex experience. Thus, negative attitudes toward masturbation appears to be related to a lower frequency of masturbation and to less sex experience in females, but only to low masturbation in males. Sex guilt, of course, was related to less sex experience and less masturbation in both sexes; not surprisingly, perhaps, sex guilt was highly correlated with negative attitudes toward masturbation in both males and females ($r = 0.47$ and 0.61, respectively). However, frequency of masturbation and sex experience were not correlated, which supports the differential predictiveness of the two measures. The major advantage of using such measures is that they yield psychologically meaningful dimensions of behaviour rather than simply statistical frequencies of masturbation which often tell us little; moreover, they seem likely candidates for helping to predict differences in responsiveness to sexual material. Interestingly, if masturbation does represent one of the primary sources of learning how to be both sexual and orgasmic (and the matter is complicated because women tend to define arousal and orgasm in different ways, from gentle tingling to bells clanging) negative attitudes toward masturbation, as well as sex guilt, may well serve to inhibit both sex experience and orgasmic success in women. Men, of course, do not have quite the same problem. They have a convenient feedback system that announces that they are aroused, and orgasm is easily defined by ejaculation. Such considerations suggest that the male experience of sexual arousal is more specifically *genital* as a result of socialization via masturbation, whereas women experience their sexual arousal in more global terms, including feelings like sensuousness, passion, and excitement in addition to genital sensations. And yet, curiously, Kinsey *et al.* (1953) contended that frequency of masturbation was superior to frequency of heterosexual activity as a predictor of sexual interest or responsiveness in females as compared to males.

Recently Griffitt (1975), defining sexual responsiveness in terms of erotic reactions to visual depictions of sexual activities, designed a study in an attempt to test Kinsey's idea of an *experience–responsiveness* relationship. In general, his findings supported the notion that differential types of sexual experience are significantly related to the degree of responsiveness to depictions of those same types of experience; thus, subjects with the greatest amount of sexual experience were the most responsive to the depictions of sexual activities. Unfortunately, the findings were not consistent with the Kinsey hypothesis. For example, among females, both heterosexual and masturbatory experience were found to be related to sexual and emotional responsiveness to the erotic stimuli used; indeed, three out of five categories of heterosexual experience were found to be superior to masturbation experience as predictors of sexual responsiveness. Among male subjects, *only* frequency of masturbation consistently related to both sexual responsiveness and positive affective responses, suggesting that masturbation is a better predictor of male responsiveness to sexual material than heterosexual experience. As tempting as it may be to conclude that greater sexual experience leads to greater responsiveness to erotic material, Griffitt stresses that his correlational study equally supports the idea that subjects who are highly responsive to sexual stimuli are also more inclined to engage in frequent sexual activities. Moreover, some third variable such as subjects' affective responses to sexual activities might determine responsivity to depictions of such activities, as well as decisions to engage in or not engage in such behaviour. Adding to the confusion, it is also possible that one's sexual experiences determine affective evaluations of such activities, and these affective responses in turn influence sexual reactivity to erotic materials; according to this interpretation, emotional responses to sexual experiences mediate the experience–responsiveness relationship. However, although the relationship between various measures of sexual experience and sexual responsiveness to erotic stimuli is obviously unclear, these findings tend to support the idea that the female experience of sexual arousal is not specifically genital, as a function of masturbation, as it seems to be in the male.

In an effort to shed more light on the experience–responsiveness issue, Mosher and Abramson (1977) studied the reactions of males and females to films of masturbation. Interestingly, although contemporary research has shown that there are no significant gender differences in sexual arousability to erotic visual stimuli, the authors found that some women – those who masturbated more frequently per month – reported higher levels of subjective arousal than men after viewing films of masturbation. In contrast, women who masturbated less frequently, if at all, reported the lowest level of sexual arousal. Here we have one of the few reports of the *greater* sexual arousability of women to erotic stimuli. However, the use of three measures of subjective sexual arousal indicated that women reported a higher level of sexual arousal than males only on an affect adjective measure of sexual arousal; the other two measures – ratings of sexual arousal, and self-reported genital sensations – did not show significant differences in this respect. Yet, importantly, the data made it clear that these results were not a function of a response set of women to endorse more affect adjectives. Such findings again suggest that women experience their sexual arousal in not only genital but in more global terms (cf. Gagnon and Simon, 1973). Indeed, as Mosher and Abramson point out, such an explanation is compatible with most women's desire for more non-genital, sensuous stimulation in foreplay (and with their concern for the total interpersonal relationship) than is true for more genitally focused men (cf. Steele and Walker, 1976).

Ordinarily, males report few negative affective reactions to films of explicit sexual stimuli in comparison to women. However, one of the most interesting findings of this study was that males who watched a film of a male masturbating reported the lowest level of sexual arousal and the highest levels of disgust, depression, guilt, and shame, but when they watched a film of a female masturbating, the findings were reversed. Females, in contrast, were about equally responsive to both masturbation films in terms of all three measures of subjective sexual arousal; moreover, females reported slightly, but not significantly, less negative affect to the male than to the female film. These findings parallel those of Schmidt (1975) who discussed his results in terms of the Money and Erhardt (1972) hypothesis of *projection* versus *objectification*. According to them, men are aroused by female nudes in a completely understandable way by a simple process of attraction to a sexual object confronting them, whereas women do not see the male body as a sex object at all and are thereby not excited by glimpses of attractive men. Thus,

when he reacts to a sexy pin-up picture of a female, a man sees the figure as a sexual object. In imagery, he takes her out of the picture and has a sexual relationship. . . . The very same picture may be sexually appealing to a woman, but that would not mean that she is a lesbian. Far from it. She is not in imagery bringing the figure towards herself as a sexual object, as does the man. She is projecting herself into the picture and identifying herself with the female to whom men respond. She herself becomes the sexual object. What if the picture portrays a sexy male? The basic sex-specific difference still manifests itself. Men . . . do not project themselves into the picture and identify with the man there represented. Women, unable to identify with the male figure, also do not respond to it as a sexual object (p. 252).

If this description of the sequence of events in female arousal to erotic stimuli were correct, then women should report significantly more sexual arousal to seeing another woman masturbate than to viewing a man doing the same thing. However, this proves to be untrue: basically women respond like men – they are turned on by the sight of the opposite sex masturbating, a result which is unlikely to surprise women themselves. Mosher and Abramson, like Schmidt, found that males objectify the female stimulus and, in turn, females objectify the male stimulus. Thus, both sexes can be aroused by opposite-sex erotic stimuli; however, it remains unclear whether this arousal is due to an erotic fantasy of having sex with the stimulus person, through a fantasy in which the person is sexually exploited, or from an erotic–aesthetic appreciation of the person's sexuality (or perhaps some combination of these). In contrast, there are real differences in regard to observing same-sex erotic stimuli: women do have the capacity to enjoy watching other women indulging in masturbation, whereas men tend to be relatively unmoved by sexual depictions of their brethren – except to reject them.

The fact that males generally respond with much less sexual arousal and more negative affect to same-sex stimuli raises the possibility that differences inherent in male–female socialization may account for this; in particular, early experiences which create anxiety and fears about homosexuality in males. Schmidt (1975), for example, points out that homosexual threat or anxieties may be more quickly stimulated in the male because the taboo against homosexual activities is much more stressed in the upbringing of boys; hence males may have a greater inclination to avoid same-sex arousal as such a response may be indicative of homosexual attraction, and this could affect their basic sexual identity more than it would affect a female's identity (cf. Morin and Garfinkle, 1978). Alternatively, Mosher and Abramson (1977) suggest that males' negative reactions to the same-sex masturbation film may be linked to socialization experiences which instil guilt over masturbation. In their study, for example, males with negative attitudes toward masturbation reported the lowest level of affective sexual arousal and the most disgust after watching the film of the man masturbating which suggested that the film might be inducing guilt over masturbation, through negative projective identification. Unfortunately, their data could not distinguish between the possibilities that males are disgusted with a male "object" whom they watch masturbate or that they negatively identify with the male and experience self-disgust, since, although they disapprove of masturbation, they nevertheless are highly likely to masturbate anyway. Women, on the other hand, are not taught to reject images of their own sex; indeed, the authors found that women were better able to identify positively with same-sex stimuli, in the sense of reporting moderate sexual arousal to the film of the female masturbating. Lacking a strong taboo regarding involvement with her own sex, a woman can enjoy looking at beautiful women and can find the experience a genuinely erotic one without it threatening her own femininity She also has some capacity to be stimulated by burlesque and night club shows even though these occasions almost exclusively involve the sexual gyrations of her own sex. In this connection it is relevant to draw attention to the general aesthetic standards of our Western culture. The female form fits in with the highest aesthetic values – reflecting exquisite perfection and lines that satisfy our desire for harmony. An attractive breast, indeed all the other feminine features have a roundness, fineness, and softness that seem to be universally admired. Small wonder that women also find it easy to appreciate the pleasing female form. In this case, there are no sanctions against enjoyment and women are "allowed" to appreciate the beauty they see. Women, as a result, undoubtedly gain considerable experience in identifying positively with sexually attractive females portrayed in the mass media, whereas men find it more difficult to form such an identification as they continue to experience cultural sanctions against appreciating the beauty of male bodies. Supporting this pattern of differential ability to identify with same-sex erotic stimuli, Abramson and Mosher (1979) report further evidence which strongly suggests that women identify positively with female protagonists in films of masturbation in contrast to men who are unable to form such identification with male protagonists. Such findings help to bring the cultural parallel full circle by emphasizing that gender differences in sexual arousability to erotic visual stimuli are highly influenced by the nature of the sexual stimulus and by the particular sexual background of the observer.

These differences indicate that socialization experiences still have a considerable effect on the responsiveness of both males and females to sexual materials. And, despite the apparent convergence of male–female sexuality, in terms of decreased differences in the capacity to respond to pictorial and narrative stimuli, significant sex differences do persist. Indeed, though women are not very different from men in their *capacity* to be aroused by sexual material, they are still very different from men in their *interest* in such material. British women remain relatively indifferent to the full frontal male nude – sales figures for the American imported *Playgirl* are very poor – much like their American counterparts. Stauffer and Frost (1976), for example, report on an American survey designed to compare the reactions of men to *Playboy* and women to *Playgirl*, reasonably equivalent magazines in terms of expressed sexuality available in the mass media. The sample was evenly distributed by sex, and the ages of the respondents ranged between 15 and 23. Subjects rated their interest in 11 features which were closely parallel in terms of sexual content in two different issues of the magazines, with *The Saturday Evening Post* serving as a sexually neutral control. The results indicated that the women were much less interested in nude photographs of males than the men were in female nudes; ratings of parallel features in *Playboy* and *Playgirl* produced significant sex differences, with 88% of the men compared to 46% of the women giving the nude photographs a high rating; moreover, none of the men gave these colour photographs of frontal nudity a low rating, but 14% of the women did. In contrast, men and women did not differ significantly in their interest in features in *The Saturday Evening Post*. Women's ambivalence about male nudity, the authors conclude, "may reflect their reaction to social meanings, rather than only to sexual content, and to still powerful traditional social pressures" (p. 30).

Brownrigg (1975) cites various sources which indicate that the British female public is not that interested in erotica either. For example, she points out that 81% of *Mayfair's* 1·75 million readers are men (National Readership Survey, July 1973 to June 1974); the current survey figures (July 1980 to June 1981) indicate that 89% are men, and a similar male audience can be found in the readership figures of the other leading British sex magazines. In contrast, five times more women from the 15 to 34 age group read *True Romances* than *Mayfair*, which is the equivalent of about two million readers, and over six million women read *Woman's Own*. Acknowledging that these figures mask the socio-economic differences that undoubtedly exist between the readerships, Brownrigg asserts that it is still romance that pulls in the numbers and sales figures. When women do go for explicit sex, according to *Mayfair* magazine, they like female descriptions of erotic female experiences and fantasies. Interestingly, *Mayfair* sees little difference between such features in their magazine and a Barbara Cartland novel: the fantasy is the same, the sensations are the same, the enjoyment too; moreover, the sexual implications, however implicit, are recognizable. Yet as Brownrigg points out, "implication is the point: they are both about sex, but Cartland's novels throb with what is not minutely described, and are therefore romantic and not erotic. There, along with the sales figures, is the difference" (p. 59). However, by today's standards, the distinction between romantic and erotic stories is often obscured in a stroke of creative advertising; indeed, in both magazines and books, writers and publishers are aware that many women are interested and turned on by erotica when it is in a romantic context and capitalize on this by marketing their products to fit this image.

Interested in the theory that women go for romance while men go for sex, Heiman (1977) specifically designed a study to test the assumption that women prefer romantic descriptions, or at least that they prefer eroticism tempered with romance to straight sex. Divided into four groups, male and female subjects heard a series of four tape recordings of either erotic, romantic–erotic, pure romantic, or control content, each 6–8 min long:

(1) erotic tapes described sexual intercourse between a man and a woman occasionally preceded by masturbation and the enjoyment of the other person as a good sexual partner;

(2) romantic-erotic tapes included a description of the couple's loving relationship and emphasized the expression of affection in a context in which events culminated in sexual intercourse;

(3) romantic tapes contained the expurgated version of the same scene, that is, without any explicit sex. Instead, the couple expressed tenderness and affection for each other verbally but not physically;

(4) control tapes included a couple sharing conversation, dinner, or wine, but not in any sense each other.

In addition, the erotic and romantic–erotic stories were modified according to whether the man or the woman initiated the sexual encounter and also according to whether the description concentrated upon the female's body and pleasure, or the male's. The findings showed that explicit sex, not romance, is what turns people on – women as well as men; erotic and romantic–erotic themes were equally effective in producing sexual arousal in both sexes. The romantic elements, however, did not facilitate arousal to the erotic content, which suggested that romance is not crucial for sexual arousal. Pure romantic tapes, in fact, did not differ significantly from the control tapes – both were equally non-arousing. Heiman concludes that the assumptions that women would react only to the romantic tapes, or at least that they would prefer a combination of romance and eroticism to explicit sex, were simply wrong – at least for sexually experienced American college students. Interestingly, the female-initiated, female-centred story was especially arousing to women; their response to that tape was significantly greater than to the others, and the same tended to be true for males. The second most popular tape, again for both sexes, was the one which was male-initiated and female-centred. Such findings suggest that descriptions of a woman's body and her sexual response play an important part in facilitating arousal for both men and women; more important, perhaps, these results again suggest that women identify positively with female protagonists in depictions of sexual activity.

Heiman also tested the cultural assumption that women are less easily aroused than men. Predicting that women would have more difficulty than men in detecting when they were sexually aroused, she asked her subjects to describe their reactions after each tape by indicating whether they felt any physical arousal. Measures of physiological arousal and self-report corre-lated highly for both sexes, indicating that a majority of the subjects could label their arousal accurately (cf. Rook and Hammen 1977). Women, how-ever, did make more mistakes than men, although this appeared to be partially due to measurement problems (see Hoon, 1979 for a review).* For example, it was remarkable that 42% of the females, compared to none of the males, claimed to experience no physical arousal during their largest genital blood volume responses; the women's self-appraisal did not improve much over time either, as large percentages continued to be unaware of the extreme changes in their vaginal blood volume (VBV). In contrast, women did about as well as men in identifying changes in the genital pulse amplitude measure of arousal; this measure also yielded better female physiological-subjective agreements than did the VBV measure. These findings suggested that VBV may be a slower and more generalized arousal response which, because of its gradual increase and decrease, is subjectively easier to adapt to but more difficult to discriminate than pulse amplitude changes. Indeed, women who showed a very strong arousal response to the tapes, as measured by pressure pulse, were much more likely to report subjectively that they were excited. Heiman believes that the discrepancy between body arousal and verbal report may be partially attributable to women's acquired ability to suppress, ignore, or reinterpret signs of sexual excitement rather than to just differences in measurement alone. Thus, since most of the women who underestimated their arousal were those responding to the *non-erotic tapes*, she reasoned that their minds ignored their bodies because they did not have a socially valid reason – in the form of external erotic cues – to account for their physiologi-cal responses. In contrast, women who were excited by the erotic tapes may have relied on contextual cues to interpret any physical change as sexual since they would, logically, have found it difficult to ignore their arousal – espe-cially in this situation in which it was legitimate for them to be aroused. Such findings suggest that women are not necessarily more slowly aroused than men; more likely it appears that they are merely slower to – or less likely to – *admit* arousal since they rarely receive social reinforcement for identifying or expressing their sexual interests.†

Heiman's (1977) results which indicate that males and females are not

* It is important to note that although it is valid to directly compare subjective estimates of sexual arousal between males and females, this is *not* the case in regard to physiological arousal; measures of vaginal vasocongestion and penile volume or circumference are not equivalent estimates of arousal.

† Males may also find it easier than females to discriminate sexual arousal since erections generally provide them with a unique form of feedback regarding their level of arousal.

differentially responsive to erotic or romantic–erotic themes are consistent
with those from other research studies investigating sex differences in response to erotica (Fisher and Byrne, 1978; Mosher and White, 1980). Apparently, romantic or affectional emphasis is not a pre-requisite for women to
respond to erotica. Such findings, however, contrast sharply with females'
expressions of *disinterest* in erotica and suggest that social desirability considerations may account for much of the discrepancy – a difference which is
perhaps best reflected by the poor sales figures of explicit erotica to women.
Indeed, research has documented the fact that women rarely frequent adult
sex shops or pornographic movies, and they are not large-scale consumers of
erotica (Nawy, 1971; Winick, 1971). In contrast, romance continues to sell
very well among women; the sales of Mills and Boon – traditional purveyors
of pure romance since 1908, and currently pulling in 25% of the
women's market – still top a million a month. Packaging romance a bit
differently, top selling romantic novelists such as Harold Robbins and Janet
Dailey combine it with erotica in a way which capitalizes on the selling power
of pure romance plus the arousing power of erotica. In effect, this clever
manoeuvre takes advantage of the traditionally acceptable romantic format
to market the traditionally unacceptable erotic one – and the sales figures are
extremely impressive. So much so, in fact, that the British publishers of
Silhouette Romances, a division of Coronet Books, are hoping to edge Mills
and Boon off the bookshelf. And, since women appear to be much more
willing to buy erotica in this form than in any other, they may well succeed if
the 80 000 000 books Janet Dailey has sold in America are any indication of
what she will do for Silhouette in Britain. Of course, the marketability of this
type of romance seems to depend upon appropriate labelling. Thus, striving
to be free of the "Wham Bam, Thank You Ma'am" approach, the contents of
Dailey's books are described as sensual – not erotic or explicit – as this is
thought to be so much more feminine, and to promise so much more in the
way of relationships which offer touching, caring, love and romance, as well
as sexuality. Lots of foreplay characterizes these stories, both psychologically
and physically – not merely genital sexual behaviour. And what other format
could successfully capture the interests of women better than this? As
Steele and Walker (1976) found out, most women prefer exactly what these
novels deliver – a bit more naked Barbara Cartland than Erica Jong.
Indeed, women seem to respond well to stories and fantasy material which
involves both a gradual process of arousal and aspects of love and romance
(cf. Byrne and Lamberth, 1971; Gebhard, 1973; Gillan and Frith, 1979).
Such stories closely approximate the masturbatory fantasies of most women in
which they make love to someone they love (Hunt, 1974). However Mosher
and White (1980), like Heiman (1977), found that females respond just as
strongly, if not more so, to erotic themes – such as a chance sexual encounter

in which the man and woman feel an immediate sexual attraction – as to erotic themes with an affectional or romantic emphasis. These findings again suggest that social desirability accounts for much of the discrepancy between women's inherent capability to respond to sexual material and their basic disinterest in acquiring erotica. But as sex goes up-market – in the guise of romantic novels that have a traditionally acceptable cover and can be sold anywhere – more women are willing to buy this form of stimulation which, according to research, is just as arousing as straight erotica and its social content (in terms of the sex roles portrayed, the nature of the sexuality, and the relationship between the sexes) is much more acceptable than that found in the traditional "adults only" paperbacks (cf. Smith, 1976). The belief that males and females differ in their responsiveness to erotica has a long history. And, indeed, research supports, in part, the hypothesis of gender-specific differences in terms of preferences for and responsivity to various types of erotic stimuli (e.g. Steinman et al., 1981). However, despite the fact that *patterns* of sexual arousal can vary as a function of gender, both men and women clearly demonstrate the capacity to respond sexually to erotica. Social proscription of female interest in sexually explicit depictions appears to account for women's greater indifference to this material – an indifference that rejects the form and content of what is normally seen as pornography, not erotica, by most women, and one which will probably always remain.

References

Abelson, H., Cohen, R., Heaton, E., and Suder, C. National survey of public attitudes toward and experience with erotic materials. In *Technical Report of the Commission on Obscenity and Pornography* (Vol. 6). Washington, D.C.: U.S. Government Printing Office, 1971.

Abramson, P. R. The relationship of the frequency of masturbation to several aspects of behavior. *Journal of Sex Research*, 1973, 9, 132–142.

Abramson, P. R., and Mosher, D. L. Development of a measure of negative attitudes toward masturbation. *Journal of Consulting and Clinical Psychology*, 1975, 43, 485–490.

Abramson, P. R., and Mosher, D. L. An empirical investigation of experimentally induced masturbatory fantasies. *Archives of Sexual Behavior*, 1979, 8, 27–39.

Abramson, P. R., Perry, L. B., Rothblatt, A., Seeley, T. T. and Seeley, D. M. Negative attitudes toward masturbation and pelvic vasocongestion: A thermographic analysis. *Journal of Research in Personality*, 1981, 15, 497–509.

Arafat, I. S., and Cotton, W. L. Masturbation practices of males and females. *Journal of Sex Research*, 1974, 10, 293–307.

Baron, R. A., and Byrne, D. *Social Psychology: Understanding Human Interaction*. Boston: Allyn and Bacon, 1977.

Bernard, J. The fourth revolution. *Journal of Social Issues*, 1966, 22, 76–87.

Brownrigg, M. Still very different. *Psychology Today* (U.K. Ed), 1975, **1**, 59.

Byrne, D., Fisher, J. D., Lamberth, J., and Mitchell, H. E. Evaluations of erotica: Facts or feelings? *Journal of Personality and Social Psychology*, 1974, **29**, 111–116.

Byrne, D., and Lamberth, J. The effect of erotic stimuli on sex arousal, evaluative responses, and subsequent behaviour. In *Technical Report of the Commission on Obscenity and Pornography* (Vol. 8). Washington, D.C.: U.S. Government Printing Office, 1971.

Christensen, H. T., and Gregg, C. F. Changing sex norms in America and Scandinavia. *Journal of Marriage and the Family*, 1970, **32**, 616–627.

DiVasto, P. V., Pathak, D., and Fishburn, W. R. The interrelationship of sex guilt, sex behavior, and age in an adult sample. *Archives of Sexual Behavior*, 1981, **10**, 119–122.

Fisher, W. A., and Byrne, D. Sex differences in response to erotica? Love versus lust. *Journal of Personality and Social Psychology*, 1978, **36**, 117–125.

Gagnon, J. H., and Simon, W. *Sexual Conduct*. Chicago: Aldine, 1973.

Gebhard, P. H. Sex differences in sexual responses. *Archives of Sexual Behavior*, 1973, **2**, 201–203.

Gillan, P., and Frith, C. Male-female differences in responses to erotica. In M. Cook and G. D. Wilson (Eds). *Love and Attraction: An International Conference*. Oxford: Pergamon, 1979.

Griffitt, W. Response to erotica and the projection of response to erotica in the opposite sex. *Journal of Experimental Research in Personality*, 1973, **6**, 330–338.

Griffitt, W. Sexual experience and sexual responsiveness: Sex differences. *Archives of Sexual Behavior*, 1975, **4**, 529–540.

Griffitt, W., and Kaiser, D. L. Affect, sex guilt, gender, and the rewarding-punishing effects of erotic stimuli. *Journal of Personality and Social Psychology*, 1978, **36**, 850–858.

Griffitt, W., May, J., and Veitch, R. Sexual stimulation and interpersonal behavior: Heterosexual evaluative responses, visual behavior, and physical proximity. *Journal of Personality and Social Psychology*, 1974, **30**, 367–377.

Heiby, E., and Becker, J. D. Effect of filmed modeling on the self-reported frequency of masturbation. *Archives of Sexual Behavior*, 1980, **9**, 115–121.

Heiman, J. R. A psychophysiological exploration of sexual arousal patterns in females and males. *Psychophysiology*, 1977, **14**, 266–274.

Hoon, P. W. The assessment of sexual arousal in women. In M. Hersen, R. M. Eisler, and P. M. Miller (Eds) *Progress in Behavior Modification* (Vol. 7). London and New York: Academic Press, 1979.

Hunt, M. *Sexual Behavior in the 1970's*. Chicago: Playboy, 1974.

Kinsey, A., Pomeroy, W., Martin, C., and Gebhard, P. *Sexual Behavior in the Human Female*. Philadelphia: Saunders, 1953.

Langston, R. D. Sex guilt and sex behavior in college students. *Journal of Personality Assessment*, 1973, **37**, 467–472.

LoPiccolo, J., and Lobitz, W. C. The role of masturbation in the treatment of orgasmic dysfunction. *Archives of Sexual Behavior*, 1972, **2**, 163–171.

Love. R. E., Sloan, L. R., and Schmidt, M. J. Viewing pornography and sex guilt: The priggish, the prudent, and the profligate. *Journal of Consulting and Clinical Psychology*, 1976, **44**, 624–629.

Mead, M. *Sex and Temperament in Three Primitive Societies*. New York: William Marrow, 1935.

Money, J., and Ehrhardt, A. A. *Man and Woman, Boy and Girl: Differentiation and dimorphism of gender identity from conception to maturity*. Baltimore: Johns Hopkins University Press, 1972.

Morin, S. F., and Garfinkle, E. M. Male homophobia. *Journal of Social Issues*, 1978, **34**, 29–47.

Mosher, D. L. The development and multitrait-multidimensional matrix analysis of three measures of three aspects of guilt. *Journal of Consulting and Clinical Psychology*, 1966, **30**, 25–29.

Mosher, D. L. Measurement of guilt in females by self-report inventories. *Journal of Consulting and Clinical Psychology*, 1968, **32**, 690–695.

Mosher, D. L. Sex differences, sex experiences, sex guilt, and explicitly sexual films. *Journal of Social Issues*, 1973, **29**, 95–112.

Mosher, D. L., and Abramson, P. R. Subjective sexual arousal to films of masturbation. *Journal of Consulting and Clinical Psychology*, 1977, **45**, 796–807.

Mosher, D. L., and Cross, H. J. Sex guilt and premarital sexual experiences of college students. *Journal of Consulting and Clinical psychology*, 1971, **36**, 27–32.

Mosher, D. L., and O'Grady, K. E. Homosexual threat, negative attitudes towards masturbation, sex guilt, and males' sexual and affective reactions to explicit sexual films. *Journal of Consulting and Clinical Psychology*, 1979, **47**, 860–873.

Mosher, D. L., and White, B. B. Effects of committed or casual erotic guided imagery on females' subjective sexual arousal and emotional response. *Journal of Sex Research*, 1980, **16**, 273–299.

Nawy, H. The San Francisco erotic marketplace. In *Technical Report of the Commission on Obscenity and Pornography* (Vol. 4). Washington, D. C.: U.S. Government Printing Office, 1971.

Reiss, I. *Premarital Sexual Standards in America*. New York: Free Press, 1960.

Rook, K. S., and Hammen, C. L. A cognitive perspective on the experience of sexual arousal. *Journal of Social Issues*, 1977, **33**, 7–29.

Schill, T., and Chapin, J. Sex guilt and males' preference for reading erotic magazines. *Journal of Consulting and Clinical Psychology*, 1972, **39**, 516.

Schmidt, G. Male–female differences in sexual arousal and behavior during and after exposure to sexually explicit stimuli. *Archives of Sexual Behavior*, 1975, **4**, 353–365.

Schmidt, G., and Sigusch, V. Sex differences in responses to psychosexual stimulation by films and slides. *Journal of Sex Research*, 1970, **6**, 268–283.

Schmidt, G., and Sigusch, V. Women's sexual arousal. In J. Zubin and J. Money (Eds). *Contemporary Sexual Behavior*. Baltimore: Johns Hopkins University Press, 1973.

Schmidt, G., Sigusch, V., and Meyberg, U. Psychosexual stimulation in men: Emotional reactions, changes of sex behavior, and measures of conservative attitudes. *Journal of Sex Research*, 1969, **5**, 199–217.

Schmidt, G., Sigusch, V., and Schafer, S. Responses to reading erotic stories: Male–female differences. *Archives of Sexual Behavior*, 1973, **2**, 181–199.

Smith, D. D. The social content of pornography. *Journal of Communication*, 1976, **26**, 16–24.

Staples, R. Male-female sexual variations: Functions of biology or culture? *Journal of Sex Research*, 1973, **9**, 11–20.

Stauffer, J., and Frost, R. Male and female interest in sexually-oriented magazines. *Journal of Communication*, 1976, **26**, 25–30.

Steele, D., and Walker, E. Male and female differences in reaction to erotic stimuli as related to sexual adjustment. *Archives of Sexual Behavior*, 1974, **3**, 459–470.

Steele, D., and Walker, E. Female responsiveness to erotic films and the "ideal" erotic film from a feminine perspective. *Journal of Nervous and Mental Disease*, 1976, **162**, 266–273.

Steinman, D. L., Wincze, J. P., Sakheim, B. A., Barlow, D. H. and Mavissakalian, M. A comparison of male and female patterns of sexual arousal. *Archives of Sexual Behavior*, 1981, **10**, 529–547.

Winick, C. A study of consumers of explicitly sexual materials. In *Technical Reports of the Commission on Obscenity and Pornography* (Vol. 4). Washington D. C.: U.S. Government Printing Office, 1971.

7

Therapeutic uses of sexually explicit material

Maurice Yaffé

Introduction

The publication of *Human Sexual Inadequacy* by Masters and Johnson (1970) heralded the start of a new era in the rapid and effective treatment of sexual dysfunction, but since then there have been important developments (e.g. Hawton, 1980, 1982; Marks, 1981; Wright, Perreault and Matthieu, 1977; Yaffé, 1981b) including the use of sexually explicit material as an adjunct to therapy (Yaffé, 1980a, b, 1981b). A similar involvement of such materials has also occurred in the assessment and treatment of sexual deviations (e.g. Adams, Tollison and Carson, 1981), and in workshops designed specifically for sexual enrichment (Glide Foundation, 1971). This chapter will be concerned with an account of specific applications involving materials which comprise depictions or representations of sexual objects and situations (rather than the objects and situations themselves), and these can be classified into erotic art, sex education material, and material relating to both hetero-sexual and non-heterosexual arousal. (The chapter by Peter Webb – this volume – deals with the interface between erotic art and other explicit sexual depictions.) In the therapeutic context, materials are available that have been specifically prepared for education/therapy purposes (e.g. National Sex Forum films), compared with commercially available "pornography".

There are very few studies reporting the incidence/prevalence of sexual problems (Yaffé, 1980a), but it is clear that the numbers are substantial (e.g. Frank, Anderson and Rubenstein, 1978; Nettelbladt and Uddenberg, 1979). Regarding the kinds of problems seen in psycho-sexual problems clinics, they tend to be more complex than they were in the past, mainly on account of two developments: physicians identifying problems early and making appro-priate recommendations which are generally effective, and the increased availability to the general public of self-help books (e.g. Brown and Faulder, 1978; Kaplan, 1976). As a result, there has been an emphasis in clinical research to tease out active ingredients of sex therapy (e.g. Crowe, Gillan and Golombok, 1981), and a drive to streamline therapy procedures, including the rapid and accurate transmission of sexual information that explicit materials can provide.

Two major reviews of the therapeutic applications of sexually explicit material have been published (Björksten, 1976; Gillan, 1978) and both report its positive contribution when used with specific populations in specific ways as an adjunct to other procedures; these are detailed later. Björksten (1976) highlights the unique features of sexually explicit material that sets it apart from non-sexual depictions, related to the way sex is viewed in our society. Accurate information exchange about sex is limited due to moral restraints, and when people do discuss their sexual attitudes, feelings and knowledge, they often do so with anxiety, indignation, embarrassment, or avoidance; and health professionals are no exception in this respect. As the materials under consideration are explicit, the opportunity for therapists and sex educators to gain information about sexual practices outside their own frame of reference or preference can be of much therapeutic value.

The therapeutic use of sexually explicit material began as part of desensitization treatment programmes for reducing anxiety in specific sexual dysfunctional cases (Wolpe, 1958) and relevant material was soon adopted by therapists interested in *de-conditioning* (aversive) and *re-conditioning* (positive training) procedures for sexual deviance. However, even today, only a small proportion of therapists use such materials, principally due to lack of availability, but this is also a function of the therapist's theoretical orientation – more behavioural therapists than traditional psychotherapists, however, are likely to incorporate them into their regimes. Before discussing the details of these procedures, it is necessary to review briefly the behaviour changes which occur in normal, i.e. sexually functional, adults as a consequence of viewing sexually explicit material.

Effects of Sexually Explicit Material on Normals

Yaffé (1972, 1979a, b) has provided comprehensive accounts of the effects on normals of exposure to sexually explicit material and Annon and Robinson (1978) have summarized the principal conclusions as follows:

(i) No study has convincingly shown any long-term effects of pornography on the sexual behaviour and attitudes.

(ii) Attitudes regarding various sexual behaviours appear to be quite stable, despite exposure to erotic visual materials.

(iii) Many males and females exposed to erotic films frequently report various degrees of short-term arousal.

(iv) There tend to be increases in the frequency of coital activity (if the activity already exists in the individual's behaviour repertoire) within 24 hours after viewing pornography. However, there is still no significant increase to the overall rates of intercourse.

(v) It is relatively rare that novel sexual activities are tried, or that low frequency sexual behaviours are increased, following exposure to erotica. The most reliable behavioural effect is an increase in masturbation during 24 hours following exposure.

(vi) The majority of individuals who increase masturbation following exposure tend to be individuals with already established masturbatory patterns.

(vii) Viewing pornography often results in a temporary increase in sexual fantasy, dreams, and conversation about sex during the first 24 hour period following exposure. (p. 37)

These conclusions have been arrived at in spite of various factors which make evaluation problematic; they include: the fact that the content of sexual stimuli varies from study to study, is often complex, and unspecified; subjects are often unrepresentative of the general population; and there are few longitudinal and virtually no long-term follow-up studies. Moreover, individual responses are coloured by several factors, such as the context of viewing, the nature of the material, level of consciousness, and the sexual need state of the observer. Nevertheless, Pearsall (cited by Björksten, 1976) devised a self-explanatory list of the reactions of 300 U.S. mental health professionals to "erotic" films; he split them into those where the orientation was "subjective" and others where it was "objective"; the results do seem to have face validity:

A. *Subjective Orientation toward Erotic Films*
  (1) Neutraliser "I've seen it all before; that was not very impressive".
  (2) Isolator: "I don't get the point; what are the films trying to prove?"
  (3) Teacher: tends to use big words: "Did you notice this or that?"
  (4) Primary voyeur: watches the films, but doesn't get involved himself.
  (5) Secondary voyeur: watches everyone else watching (doesn't really see the films himself).
  (6) Tertiary voyeur: watches himself watching: "I think that I felt excited by that last film" (doesn't really see the films himself).
  (7) Accelerator: tends to make the first comment in the group: "Okay, when do we see the real stuff?"
  (8) Shocker: "Did you ever see 50 horses doing it together?"
  (9) Panicker: "Oh my God . . .!" That is all they can express.
 (10) Innocent: "I can't imagine anyone ever seeing that stuff."

B. *Objective Orientation toward Erotic Films*
 (11) Film critic: comments on the quality of the sound track, story line, etc.
 (12) Artist: sees a symbolic message in every action in the film.
 (13) Competitor: "I can make films much better than that."
 (14) Validifier: "It's not what I do, so it cannot be real."

(15) Actor: tries on many different reactions, but does not consistently have one of his own (like the "as if" person).
(16) Withdrawer: doesn't talk at all (these people never seem to desensitise).
(17) Executive: talks about his career, schedule, etc.
(18) Diagnostician: labels everything that he sees in the films.
(19) Parent: tries to protect other group members from the horrible things they are seeing.
(20) "Gone": this person does not come to the group meeting after seeing the films (pp. 190–191).

Stoller (1976) has argued that a person's choice of "pornography", when combined with masturbation, is one effective way of increasing sexual excitement, but recent studies have shown that sexual arousal can be brought under voluntary control (enhancement *and* suppression), given visual or auditory feedback of genital responses, in both normal men (e.g. Rosen, Shapiro and Schwartz, 1975) and women (Cerny, 1978; Hoon, Wincze and Hoon, 1977). These findings have led to clinical applications for increasing sexual arousal to formerly non-arousing stimuli, but these investigations have not been as successful as teaching reduction of deviant arousal (self-control) to those males with sexual variation problems (Blanchard and Epstein, 1977). Furthermore, sexual arousal and arousability appear to be a function of endogenous testosterone levels in both healthy men (Rubin *et al.*, 1979) and women with reduced sex drive (Carney, Bancroft and Mathews, 1978), and so need to be taken account of as relevant variables in studies involving exposure to sexual material.

Sex Education in Sex Therapy

The essential difference between sex education and sex therapy is that in the former, the persons concerned do not present with a specific sexual problem: they have an implied deficit of knowledge which is provided by information-giving on the part of the instructor, whereas in sex therapy the person involved has a problem with respect to sexual function; often there is attendant anxiety, and poor information or mis-information about sexual facts. The population for whom formal sex education has been evaluated and applied using sexually explicit materials are: school-age children (Money, 1970; Rosenberg and Rosenberg, 1976; also see Chapter 4, this volume); late adolescence (Sarrel and Sarrel, 1979); normal adults (Glide Foundation, 1971); health professionals (Rosenzweig and Pearsall, 1978; Price *et al.*, 1978; W.H.O., 1975); medical students (e.g. Money, 1972; Stanley, 1977); the mentally handicapped (Craft, 1980; Craft and Craft, 1981, 1982); and those with sexual problems (Björksten, 1976; Gillan, 1979).

In a study to compare the influence of formal sex education, that is sex education taught within school classrooms, and informal sex education (all other sources of sex information to which an individual might be exposed), in pre-marital sexual behaviour in U.S. college students, Spanier (1976) used face-to-face interviews with 1177 male and female respondents. Questions were asked about past and current involvement and other attitudinal, behavioural and background variables, and results indicated that there was no support for the belief that exposure to sexuality through *formal* sex education influences pre-marital sexual behaviour; *informal* sex education,* however, has significantly more impact on pre-marital sexual behaviour, though pressures and experiences which confront young people in a given dating or peer group situation appear to take precedence over all past socialization influences of a sexual kind.

Effects of Sex Education using Sexual Materials

Marcotte and Logan (1977) conducted a questionnaire study prior to, and upon completion of, a medical sex education course in the U.S. in order to examine its effects on both students' sexual attitudes towards self and others and students' attitudes towards women. They found that the course led to an increased tolerance of others' sexual behaviour and fantasy, as well as influencing their tolerance of their own sexual fantasies; furthermore, students were less dogmatic in non-sexual opinion – an unexpected, but positive outcome. Moreover, Garrard et al. (1976) described the follow-up effects after 12 months of a medical school course in sexuality, where sexually explicit material was also used, and found that participants virtually without exception reported personal benefit, with a significant number claiming greater satisfaction in their own sexual behaviour. Kilmann et al. (1981), in one of the most thorough reviews of the effectiveness of sex education, looked at the courses offered to college students, educators and counsellors and medical school populations, among others, and although only a few studies indicated a follow-up, the general conclusion was that "the subjects reported gains in sexual knowledge and shifts toward more tolerant and liberal sexual attitudes". Thus, it can be concluded that sex education programmes using sexually explicit material have a generally positive effect on those who are exposed to them. However, it is difficult, as Szasz (1981) argues, to divorce morals and politics from sex education, especially in schools, which will inevitably affect the dissemination of information.

* Regarding informal sex education, two of the most comprehensive illustrated texts available are The Sex Atlas (Haeberle, 1978) and The Visual Dictionary of Sex (Trimmer, 1977); they are to be recommended, for compared to many other books of similar content, the facts presented are accurate and are not contaminated with prejudicial bias.

Nevertheless, it is helpful to quantify the extent of such knowledge; fortunately, a questionnaire is available, The Sex Knowledge and Attitude Test (SKAT), designed expressly to measure knowledge, attitudes, and degree of experience, in a variety of sexual behaviours (Miller and Lief, 1979) enabling an objective account of change in these parameters after a course or programme in human sexuality. It has been administered to over 40 000 undergraduates, graduates and medical students in the USA and is also used to aid patients with sexual problems.

Sexual attitude re-evaluation/enrichment programmes

Sex-negative attitudes are prevalent in our society; the realities of sex are rarely mentioned or discussed between adults, and even less so with younger members of the community, yet, as Francoeur (1977) points out, "at the same time, with an indulgent smile we adjust to the demands for breathing space from the monster in our groins with the socially redeeming values of sex for marital sanity and procreation". The mystification of sex, he says, makes it easier for parents and teachers and adults generally to deal with their own lack of comfort with respect to it, and this distancing emphasizes, to some extent, the contemporary phenomena of graffiti, "dirty jokes", men's magazines and X-rated films. Effective sex education involves dealing with such sex-negative attitudes and values; traditional classroom lectures on sex are, Francoeur maintains, the best way to leave these barriers intact, for the younger generation usually do not adopt recommendations by their lecturers that readily.

Although Alfred Kinsey had suggested 30 years ago the use of explicit films for sex education, it was not until 1968 that an innovative method called *Sex Attitude Re-structuring* (SAR) was devised by a group of Methodist ministers in San Francisco. SAR involves an exploration of sexual behaviours and attitudes through exposure to basic information about human sexuality, a wide range of explicit, sex-related media, and discussion of individual reactions and feelings in small groups. The sessions are held in comfortable settings and an informal and relaxed atmosphere is encouraged; participants are given permission to recognize, feel and accept their own sexuality and that of others present, and can see that others respond similarly in terms of being turned-on, embarrassed, bored, or upset. This makes for greater acceptance of one's own sexuality, *vis-à-vis* others and provides a valid starting point for pragmatic discussions involving sexual self-disclosure – an effective platform for learning about sexuality and establishing future goals.

In the first 10 years of SAR workshops over 40 000 people have gone through the weekend programme and according to Francoeur (1977), "Six months after the programme 96% of the participants reported that it had been very helpful to them personally and professionally. Three per cent were not sure and 1% had a negative reaction to its results and usefulness." One positive and commonly expressed feeling after such workshops is that people find out that they are, after all, perfectly normal in their behaviour; but if not, a problem will probably have been identified and the person(s) can be referred on appropriately.

Workshop format

There are a variety of different workshop formats in use today and these can be divided into "massed" presentations or those where materials are used only occasionally or with a significant period of time between exposures. The rationale of the former is to bombard the group with considerable visual input in order to extinguish contingent anxiety – a rapid form of desensitization, and thereby facilitate discussion of sexual topics. On the other hand, the rationale of most intermittent presentations is that demonstrating something is superior to talking about it; according to Björksten (1976) the most effective use for materials presented this way is for the education of couples with respect to anatomy and sexual behaviour. Other examples of spaced presentations are: the use of anatomical models with patients who have limited knowledge about sex in order to educate them about genital anatomy; showing films in order to demonstrate specific techniques such as massaging, the "squeeze" (for the control of premature ejaculation), or various sexual behaviours including different positions of intercourse; or showing explicit sexual material to those with sex drive problems in order to provide fantasies necessary for sexual arousal.

Björksten (1976) deals with the two kinds of workshop format in some considerable detail, as do Rosenzweig and Pearsall (1978); these provide essential information for the intending practitioner in this area.

Briggs (1978) points out the significance and values of using films which are sexually explicit; they:

(1) provide information accurately and rapidly about what people actually do sexually;
(2) produce an emotional response, making thoughts, feelings and attitudes more accessible to the participants;
(3) make the group discussions more concrete, more specific, more personal.

After a few years of using such material a need for other kinds of sex-related films has developed particularly in the training of nurses, social workers, ministers, and rehabilitation counsellors; these include explicit films and sex during pregnancy, and of aged or disabled people. To quote from Briggs (1978):

> we knew that watching a film of a quadriplegic having sex would help another quadriplegic learn more about his or her sexuality as well as help the professionals who deal with these persons to give help (p. 133)

though there have not so far been any formal evaluations quantifying the effectiveness of such interventions.

Group process issues

Björksten (1976) has evaluated ingredients considered preferable for the therapeutic effectiveness of group discussions running in conjunction with SAR workshops where explicit sexual material is used. These comprise: group leaders, usually one of each sex, experienced in group therapy, who are prepared to self-disclose to some extent, are more responsive than in traditional psychotherapy groups, and do not necessarily follow psychodynamic leads or make global interpretations to the group. The emphasis is on a shared expression of immediate thoughts and feelings, anxiety reduction, on non-judgemental messages, and acceptance of differing viewpoints.

Björksten has compiled a useful list of appropriate behavioural group rules or expectations he feels are desirable in such meetings:

1. focus on present thoughts, feelings;
2. emphasis on active personal attitude re-evaluation;
3. knowledge that individuals will not be belittled for holding and expressing different points of view;
4. avoidance of using euphemistic phrases in sexual descriptions, thoughts and reactions to material;
5. encouragement of humour;
6. openness and some self-disclosure by group leaders;
7. cohesiveness. (p. 189.)

He also deals with how to manage individuals who stand out in SAR groups: such people include those who show excessive moral indignation or extreme liberal views, and those who constantly avoid issues defensively or the opposite, the extreme discloser.

Use of Sexually Explicit Material with Clinical Populations

Although this chapter is concerned with the therapeutic involvement of specifically *explicit* sexual materials, it is sometimes difficult to know where to draw the line with respect to this dimension; in other words, how overt does the sexual depiction have to be in order to be designated as explicit? For practical purposes materials included in this category are confined to pictures, films and videotapes showing genital details of individuals or sexual activities between partners as well as audio recordings of lovemaking, though these days sound and vision are usually combined. Sex aids, mechanical and chemical adjuncts to therapy, are therefore not discussed in this chapter, but are evaluated critically by Rhodes (1980) and Haslam (1978), who both conclude that their contribution may simply be a placebo one. This might well satisfy the client but not the scientist. Such devices apparently sell well and include the Blakoe ring (for erectile problems), pelvic exercisers (known as "Geisha balls" or "love eggs"), penile attachments (to increase clitoral stimulation in the partner), inflatable life-size dolls, penile anaesthetic creams (to control premature ejaculation), and electrical vibrators. Rhodes (1980) makes the subtle distinction between *sex aids* and *sex toys*, but the latter often involve the same paraphenalia and are used to enhance pleasure and performance in those who are not sexually inadequate.

Assessment of sexual problems

The determinants of human sexual arousal are both complex and multiple, and assessment of preferences for sexually explicit material is probably one of the most relevant. However, Stoller (1976) lists, in addition to "pornography", the following variables of sexual arousal and response which must also be taken into account:

(1) *Physical attributes* the ideals of anatomical configurations which include: genitals, secondary sex characteristics, height, bulk, muscle, fat, hair distribution (amount, colour), voice, skin quality and colour; special idiosyncratic features of the culture (such as bound feet in old China or scarification in Africa); bisexual qualities; needs to push definitions of masculinity and feminity to opposing extremes versus unisex trends.

(2) *Adornments* such as clothes, cosmetics, jewellery, tattooing and other decorations that modify anatomical appearance, both positive (e.g. stockings, codpieces, diaphonous dresses) and negative (e.g. female circumcision, penile infibulation).

(3) *Body styles*: postures (e.g. lying, sitting), walking, dancing, and context of use.

(4) *Taboos to heighten excitement* involves the modulation of pleasure and danger in order to increase *arousability,* i.e. the ease or difficulty of moving from one level of sexual arousal to a higher one. An example might be love-making in a semi-public place such as the bedding department of a large store, but too much danger produces anxiety and erectile problems; too little leads to indifference or boredom.

(5) *Language* and its use to stimulate sexual excitement, during preliminary and pre-coital activities and intercourse itself. Responses include the utterance of sweet nothings, speaking so-called "obscenities", silence.

(6) *Daydreams*: this category relates to pornography, which Stoller sees as formalised daydreaming in which a person can choose in the market place the daydreams he prefers.

(7) *Masturbation* according to Stoller, is the mechanism that puts daydreams to work, and the techniques a person uses or forbids himself or herself gives the clinician a feel of the underlying fantasy; alternatively, the person may not masturbate for lack of interest, or awareness of such possibilities.

(8) *Subliminal communications*: the discreet non-verbal erotic passage of information that indicates shifts in excitement, such as facial expression, voice tone.

(9) *Looking and being looked at* concerns the body parts that excite the viewer, and the specific techniques for exposing or covering the body and circumstances for doing so, which affect arousal level.

(10) *Eroticism of body parts* refers to the body parts which can be stimulated to excitement and a determination of which stimulation techniques are most likely to excite.

(11) *Boredom*: as the opposite of excitement, boredom relates to all the above, and in any assessment procedure it is useful to try and establish how quickly, under what circumstances, and with which people a person becomes bored.

(12) *Other sexually related affects*: the role in erotic situations of disgust, rage, fear, cruelty, pleasure in pain, and eroticised anger, needs to be determined, if present.

(13) *Aberrations* are usually violations of the moral, legal and/or behavioural norms held by the society and/or sub-culture in which the person lives. These also need to be established in order to make full sense of the arousal/behaviour pattern under assessment. (pp. 901–902)

The above points indicate the importance of construing the role of, and response to, explicit sexual materials within a broad assessment framework.

Behavioural assessment

Accurate and systematic behavioural assessment of sexual problems enables the clinician to identify specific areas of concern, analyse the components of the problem behaviour, and determine the necessary and sufficient conditions for its appearance/maintenance. Three channels of data need to be monitored: subjective report, behavioural observation, and physiological measurement (Barlow, 1977).

While there are obvious advantages in collecting such information in the patient's own environment where the problems manifest themselves, the clinician, for obvious reasons, is required to develop analogue or contrived situations in the clinic for both assessment and therapy. The use of sexually explicit material reduces the artificiality of such procedures, and serves to bridge the gap between clinic and community, hospital and home.

Measures. From least to most objective include: direct questioning (verbal report), observational reports from a respondent (partner or surrogate), self-report questionnaires and scales, and psycho-physiological methods.

The direct questioning method enables the clinician to assess from the patient's verbal account whether he or she is anxious, embarrassed, or angry, and the influence of this on arousal responses to the explicit material. If the patient has a partner who also viewed material, then he or she will be an important source of observational data, in the same way that a partner or sexual surrogate can report on how effectively a sexual homework assignment was carried out during therapy.

In order that repeated responses can be recorded within individuals over time and comparisons made between the patient and a similar clinical population, standardized questionnaires (self-report inventories and self-monitoring devices of sexual attitudes and patterns of sexual arousal) have been developed, to assess sexual:

(1) knowledge (SKAT – Lief and Reed, 1972)
(2) experiences (Heterosexual Behaviour Assessment, for males and females – Bentler, 1968a, b)
(3) attitude (Sexual Orientation Method (SOM) – Feldman *et al.,* 1966)
(4) anxiety (Sexual Attitude Scale (SAS) – Obler, 1973)
(5) arousal (Sexual Arousal Inventory (SAI) (for females only) – Hoon *et al.,* 1976)
(6) behaviour (Sexual Behaviour Record Form – Heiman *et al.,* 1976)

A complete issue of the *Journal of Sex and Marital Therapy* (Schiavi, 1979) is devoted to the assessment of arousal and marital function from which further information can be obtained.

Physiological indices of genital sexual arousal are the most objective and accurate and data is available for normals (Geer, 1975, 1976) and those with dysfunctions (Hatch, 1981) and include for the male: volumetric and circumferential measures of penile erection (Rosen and Keefe, 1978), and for the female: vaginal pressure pulse, vaginal blood volume, and labial temperature changes (Geer, Morokoff and Greenwood, 1974; Gillan, 1976; Henson, Rubin and Henson, 1979; Hoon, 1978). But researchers stress the advisability of using multiple, i.e. self-report (cognitive, affective) and physiological measures, in order to link appropriate meaning with objective arousal (Heiman, 1980; Wincze, Venditti, Barlow and Mavissakalian, 1980).

According to Whalen (1966), the capacity to respond genitally and subjectively to sexually explicit material will be affected by a variety of factors including: sexual need state; time since last orgasm; prior sexual and social experience; age; environmental factors (nutrition, disease, season, temperature); stress; state of consciousness (intoxicants, fatigue, medication, general arousal); expectations – all of which are likely to influence conclusions regarding sexual arousal and arousability potential. Nevertheless, such assessment procedures help us to understand better the process of sexual arousal in both men and women.

Quantifiable physiological differences have been found between sexually distressed persons and individuals not complaining of sexual problems; for example, Wincze, Hoon and Hoon (1977) demonstrated significant differences in vaginal vasocongestion during exposure to sexually explicit films between women with sexually dysfunctional problems and those satisfied with their sexual behaviour, though Heiman and Morokoff (1977) and Morokoff and Heiman (1980) detected only reduced *subjective* sexual arousal in their dysfunctional women. Such psycho-physiological measures enable the therapist to identify problem areas not obvious from the patient's verbal report alone, due to unwillingness or inability to provide such information (e.g. Kockott *et al.*, 1980). Some individuals respond by sexual inhibition to specific stimulus elements of explicit material whereas others only become aroused to very specific components of a sexual stimulus complex. Finding out this information enables the therapist to develop a personal and individualized treatment programme, especially when dealing with persons who present with sexual deviation problems (e.g. Adams, Tollison, and Carson 1981; Freund, 1976).

A major goal of assessing a patient with deviant sexual arousal is to determine those specific stimuli that elicit such arousal. Adams *et al.* (1981) suggest that it is useful first to identify stimuli that are likely to elicit inappropriate arousal, from the patient's self-report of situations, objects and people associated with the deviant arousal and behaviour. These stimuli are then presented in sequence to the patient (using explicit pictures, slides, sound tapes, textual material, guided imagery) to ascertain which elicit a physiological arousal response. Adams *et al.* point out that the percentage of arousal produced by various stimuli can be determined by comparing the degree of arousal produced to an individual's full erection. A range of heterosexual stimuli are then used in the same way to identify if any lead to arousal; self-report ratings are monitored throughout both procedures for correlation purposes.

Abel and his colleagues in a series of investigations on sexual aggressives (e.g. Abel, Barlow, Blanchard and Guild, 1977; Abel, Blanchard, Becker and Djenderedjian, 1978), have measured the erections of rapists and non-rapists during audio descriptions of rape and non-rape sexual scenes. In terms of erection measures, rapists were readily separated from non-rapists in that the former developed erections to rape descriptions while the latter did not.

Moreover, their method was successful in discriminating those rapists with the highest frequency of rape, those who had injured their victim, and those who chose pre-pubertal individuals as victims. The response profiles of the rapist group contributed importantly to the classification of the problem, treatment needs, and also response (or failure to respond) to treatment.

Similarly, Kolářský, Madlafousek and Novotná (1978) have exposed exhibitionists and normals to a variety of sexual stimuli and found that what distinguishes offenders from non-offenders are significantly larger erectile responses to scenes containing explicit shots of female genitalia where the woman was *not* erotically active, a condition which inhibited sexual arousal of their normal subjects.

Hinton, O'Neill and Webster (1980) measured subjective sexual arousal and penile diameter increase in a group of male deviants who were committed to a maximum security hospital for abnormal sexual behaviour, mainly involving violence. The sex offenders (against women, girls, boys and men), were compared with non-sexual attackers of women, and typical heterosexuals, on their profiles of response to films showing consenting adult heterosexual, adult homosexual, and boy homosexual activity, girl abduction, and girl rape. Despite the fact that a high proportion of detained patients gave results which could be interpreted as indicating defensiveness or faking, typical heterosexuals and non-sexual attackers of women showed significantly less response to the film of girl abduction ($p < 0.001$) and rape $p < 0.001$) than did groups of sex offenders generally, although sex offender and non-sex offender groups did not differ on the consenting heterosexual activity films.

The issue of defensiveness or faking erection responses so as to give false information regarding arousal patterns or response to treatment is of great concern, especially when dealing with sexual aggressives. Laws and Holman (1978) state that:

 1) it is entirely possible to produce phoney increases in sexual response in the presence of a non-preferred stimulus, and
 2) it is entirely possible to suppress the erection response in the presence of a preferred stimulus known to be effective. (p. 354)

They admit that in spite of the above, measurement of penile erection is the best dependent index of sexual arousal but put forward some recommendations to minimize suppression or feigning of responses; these include a *detection task* to ensure that the subjects are looking at the projection screen or video monitor; a *fake box* to prevent subjects from stimulating their penis manually; and the *surveillance camera* to ensure that the person observes the screen and keeps his hands away from his penis. Barlow (1977) suggests that

using the strongest sexual stimuli available may reduce unwanted responses, and Freund, Chan and Coulthard (1979) have developed a "non-admitter" scale which they claim can separate those paedo- or hebe-philes who deny responding to explicit deviant stimuli when in fact they do.

Legal applications

Psycho-physiological assessment of sexual arousal in sex offenders can play a role in both criminal court proceedings and sex offender rehabilitation pro- grammes (Rosen, 1977) for purposes of differential diagnosis and psychiatric prognosis. As mentioned earlier Abel and his co-workers (Abel *et al.*, 1977, 1978) were able to discriminate rapists with the highest frequency of rape, those who had injured their victims, and those who preferred child victims, on the basis of specially prepared sexually explicit audiotape recordings. Freund and his associates (Freund, Langevin, Laws and Serber, 1974; Freund, Langevin, Weslom and Zajal, 1975) used penile volume changes to differ- entiate males who have an erotic preference for fellow male adults, from those who choose pubescent males and the homosexual paedophile who is attracted to pre-pubescent males.

Penile circumference and volume change measures are employed also in the ongoing evaluation of patients in sex offender therapy programmes, and termination of treatment is to some extent contingent on the objective assess- ment of sexual arousal to critical sexual and non-sexual stimuli. Clearly, prognosis is likely to be more favourable, as Rosen points out, when the offender no longer responds to these critical stimuli, and those who show continuing sexual interest in deviant stimuli should continue treatment before release.

Education

Sexually explicit material, as previously suggested, can provide information both accurately and quickly, e.g. it is simpler to show a man an illustration of a female's genitalia in order to indicate the location of the clitoris than to try to do so verbally. Money (1970) has demonstrated that such material is invaluable in teaching patients about their sexual anatomy whether or not they have anatomical defects; it is particularly useful with individuals and couples who have limited if any sexual experience. Visual material also enables patients to develop an appropriate sexual vocabulary; using explicit material in sessions endorses the view that sexual activity is permissible and can be enjoyable; furthermore, individuals can model their behaviour on that seen and this facilitates the learning process.

Therapy

Sexual dysfunctions

Kaplan (1974) describes the involvement of sexually explicit material, and fantasy, to enhance sexual arousal and to stop patient's from worrying about their sexual performance in the treatment of erectile failure, retarded ejaculation, general sexual dysfunction, and primary orgasmic dysfunction, and even to distract a male from his "painful" thoughts in a case of psychogenic male dyspareunia (Sharpe and Meyer, 1973).

It is disappointing that most reports of studies where explicit materials are used in the treatment of sexual problems are limited to case reports, rather than controlled trials, and so it is often difficult to determine their precise contribution. A selected review of this literature follows covering sexual anxiety, orgasmic difficulty, ejaculation and erectile problems.

Wincze and Caird (1976) made a comparison of the relative effectiveness of imaginal systematic desensitization and "video desensitization" with an untreated control group. Both experimental groups indicated significant decreases in heterosexual anxiety at the end of therapy, but the video-treated group showed greater overall positive changes than the group exposed to standard desensitization procedures.

Wishnoff (1978) randomly placed 45 anxious, coitally-experienced women in one of three treatment groups: explicit and non-explicit sexual stimuli and control, and found that the ones exposed to sexually explicit stimuli in a controlled situation had lower sexual anxiety levels, lower manifest anxiety levels, and were more willing to participate in a greater variety of sexual behaviour subsequently.

Nemetz, Craig and Reith (1978) assessed the effects of individual and group graduated symbolic modelling on 15 secondary orgasmic dysfunctional and seven primary orgasmically dysfunctional females who reported severe anxiety that precluded sexual enjoyment or activity. Therapy involved relaxation training followed by viewing video-taped scenes depicting graduated sexual behaviours; six women acted as non-treatment controls. Both experimental groups compared with the controls demonstrated a reduction in anxiety, with greater improvement for those receiving group treatment.

LoPiccolo and Lobitz (1972) recommended the use of sexually explicit reading material or pictures to enhance arousal as part of their nine-step graduated masturbatory programme for anorgasmic women, designed to lead to heterosexual coital orgasm. But McMullen (1979) reports that it does not matter whether the informational material is provided by video-tape or written text – so long as the informational content is equivalent. Her controlled study involved a group of 60 non-orgasmic women who went through a masturbatory training programme; she was able to conclude that

> data from this study contradict claims made by distributors of audio-visual sex aids. Although such media materials might contribute to treatment of other sexual problems, they do not seem necessary in the treatment of primary orgasmic dysfunction.

In two related studies, Reisinger (1978, 1979) treated married and single women with secondary orgasmic dysfunction by masturbatory training in the clinic with exposure to erotic films; rate of orgasm was monitored by heart rate and verbal report. Treatment resulted in an improved ability to attain orgasm by self-masturbation in the clinic and home; follow-up studies after six months indicated the maintenance of treatment effects concerning masturbation and into existing heterosexual patterns of behaviour. Similarly, Barbach (1974), as part of her approach to the group treatment of pre-orgasmic women, showed a female masturbation film in order to "demystify" the process of orgasm, followed by an assignment to go home to masturbate, but not to the point of orgasm.

Robinson (1974) attempted to assess the effects of a specially developed video-taped treatment programme on the sexual behaviours and attitudes of orgasmically dysfunctional women. He hypothesized that, compared to un-treated control subjects, those exposed to a series of video-tapes would experience: (1) an increase in self-stimulation and other sexual behaviours discussed and/or modelled on the video-tapes; (2) more favourable attitudes towards particular sexual activities presented on the video-tapes; and (3) the occurrence of, or increased frequency in, orgasm. The data strongly supported the first two hypotheses, but orgasm frequency only increased for those who had experienced orgasm previously; one person only who had never experienced orgasm before, was able to do so solely as a result of viewing the video-tape. Of importance is the author's suggestion, on the basis of the experimental findings, that patients with sexual concerns may not, contrary to popular opinion, need to develop more general positive sexual attitudes *before* significantly changing their sexual behaviour – a point absent from many presentations.

As for male dysfunctional problems, there are few studies that have specifically used explicit sexual material as an independent variable. Csillag (1976) used a biofeedback method for modification of penile erections on six patients with psychogenic erectile insufficiency. The investigation attempted to find out whether men with non-organic erectile problems can develop voluntary control over their tumescence. Each patient was instructed to mobilize either his own sexual fantasies or view erotic pictures, each with or without analogue feedback (visual or auditory). All six patients demonstrated improvement in erectile performance during the 16 sessions over eight days; these responses were significantly different from those obtained in six normal subjects. Results obtained are encouraging and suggest that patients with psychogenic erectile problems can learn to initiate and maintain penile erection of a significant quality.

Reynolds (1980) investigated the role of biofeedback and facilitation of erection in 30 men with psychogenic dysfunction. They were instructed to concentrate on cognitions that facilitated erection over four training sessions following a preliminary assessment session. Subjects were divided into three groups (though a no-treatment control group was not included): one received continuous visual and auditory feedback of erection changes plus segments of an explicit film depicting a heterosexual couple's activities which were shown contingent on erection increases; the second group received contingent film segments without continuous feedback; and the third non-contingent film segments. He found that although subjects who received non-contingent film segments initially showed greater erection increase than did subjects in the contingent feedback groups, the groups did not differ by the last session of training. However, when subjects were told to increase their erection without the aid of feedback or film segments during evaluation trials that followed each training session, subjects who had received contingent films without continuous feedback showed greater erectile responsivity than subjects in other groups. But the groups did not differ in the amount of clinical improvements shown on self-report measures concerning erectile functioning over a one month follow-up period. Reynolds concludes that although his results indicate that the provision of erotic film feedback enhances the voluntary improvement of erection in the laboratory, the therapeutic value of erectile feedback was not demonstrated. He suggests combining the erectile facilitation procedures with other sex therapy techniques designed to promote change in sexual knowledge, beliefs and attitudes (see Reynolds (1977) for an account of these).

Cerny (1978) has shown that non-dysfunctional females are able to exercise voluntary control of the physiological measures related to sexual arousal but did not find biofeedback useful in facilitating enhancement and/or suppression of vaginal vasocongestion and self-reported sexual arousal. In fact, Geer (1979) believes that the effectiveness of biofeedback training is not likely to

> be based upon a model that tends to gradually shape or instrumentally condition increases or decreases in genital responses. Rather, the procedures should act to increase the association between cognitive and physiological responses, and should act as a guide for the development of effective erotic cognitions (p. 64).

Rosen (1976) agrees, but points out that sexual problems, erectile or vaginal vasocongestive, are usually related to a specific sexual relationship, and to this extent biofeedback training/treatment "is likely to miss the mark".

Gillan (1979) has developed a technique which she labels "stimulation therapy", i.e. presentation of auditory and visually sexually explicit materials (erotic stories read silently and heterosexual slides) in the treatment of males with erectile problems and females with orgasmic dysfunction. Compared to a control group who were not exposed to the sexual stimuli, the ones who were showed an increase immediately after treatment with respect to sexual intercourse frequency, increase in quality of sexual feeling, and improved relationship with partner. This study bears replication with a wider range of stimuli, preferable on video or film, longer therapy duration, and physiological measures, but nevertheless demonstrates the value of using sexual stimuli in treatment. Kaplan (1979) encourages the sharing of erotic material of her patients with sexual desire problems, but like other programmes (e.g. Ellis, 1980; Hartman and Fithian, 1972) their precise contribution has not been evaluated formally; nevertheless Annon and Robinson (1978) provide a sound overview of the field.

Sexual deviations
Sexual deviations are usually defined as sexual arousal to inappropriate persons, objects, or activities (Adams *et al.,* 1981), but they often also involve deficient sexual responses to appropriate people. Therapy, therefore, is focused upon the establishment of rewarding adult sexual responses and relationships as well as the self-control of unwanted sexual behaviour, but for others that focus may need to be widened to include improving sexual functioning within an existing adult relationship, and teaching some patients to adapt to the deviant role (as in transexualism and homosexuality) (Bancroft, 1979; Crawford, 1979). Sexually explicit materials have been used extensively over the past decade in the modification of deviant sexual orientation in males (see Adams *et al.,* 1981), and in this context appropriate persons as objects of sexual arousal may be men or women, depending upon the goals of therapy; e.g. for a homosexual paedophiliac patient the aims of treatment might well be to change the individual's preference from pre-pubertal boys to adult males (Yaffé, 1981a), rather than develop heterosexual responses. Abel, Blanchard and Becker (1977) provide a global review of the field specifically applied to the rapist.

(i) Increase of heterosexual arousal. According to Adams *et al.* (1981) "successful suppression of deviant sexual arousal requires the development of an alternative mode of gratifying the sexual drive" (p. 330). Several techniques using sexual materials have been developed to this end:

(a) Aversion relief. This procedure involves establishing an association

between heterosexual stimuli and relief from an aversive stimulus; by this means heterosexual stimuli become painful with escape from unpleasant stimulation and acquire properties of positive reinforcement. Feldman and McCulloch (1965) had their homosexual subjects, after determining a level of electric shock as "very unpleasant", view several slides of nude and partially clothed males; they were told that they should turn off the slides whenever they were no longer found sexually arousing. If the subjects did not do so within 8 s of exposure of the slides, they were presented with an electric shock whose strength increased until they did. The electrical impulse was terminated as soon as the patients turned off the male slides, which were replaced with female images. After a pre-determined period of time, the schedule of continuous negative reinforcement was changed to an intermittent one. According to Adams *et al.* (1981): "A number of patients subjected to this procedure have reported increased heterosexual interest and responsiveness following treatment" (p. 331).

(b) Shaping is a procedure designed to induce the performance of new behaviours by the initial reinforcement of behaviours in the individual's repertoire which have some similarity to the desired behaviour. Quinn, Harbison and McAllister (1970) attempted to increase penile response to heterosexual stimuli using such a procedure; they reported a pilot study where a homosexual who had already received conditioning in relation to homosexual stimuli, was deprived of water for 18 h. Drinks were made contingent on increased erection response to heterosexual stimuli, and it was found that the subject was able to increase his erection significantly, measured by strain gauge; Quinn *et al.* also reported increased heterosexual interest, as have Sandford, Tustin and Priest (1975) in a similar study.

Herman and Prewett (1974) investigated the effect of visual feedback concerning the level of penile response on subsequent sexual arousal in a case of bisexual erectile insufficiency. Penile response to slides of nude males and nude females, measured separately without feedback, was significantly increased during a period where treatment sessions contained contingent feedback, decreased when feedback was given non-contingently, and increased once again when contingent feedback was re-introduced. The increase in penile responding was paralleled by achievement of ejaculation during masturbation, changes in masturbatory fantasy and reports of homo- and heterosexual arousal outside the laboratory; thus indicating that the feedback technique is an effective method of modifying penile responsiveness.

(c) Orgasmic reconditioning was developed by Marquis (1970) to increase heterosexual arousal through pairing unarousing but wanted fantasy (heterosexual stimuli) with elicited sexual arousal from deviant fantasy. The effectiveness of the technique has been demonstrated by Van

Deventer and Laws (1978) in the redirection of sexual arousal in a paedophile, and Laws and O'Neil (1981) with four paedophiles, one sadomasochist and one rapist, but less enthusiastic results were obtained by Conrad and Wincze (1976) with four self-referred adult male homosexuals, and Abel *et al.* (1977) in their study of rapists. Keller and Goldstein (1978) point out that these procedures do not conform to learning principles and propose modifications in them involving the introduction of the established sexually arousing (deviant) fantasy before the unarousing but desired one; they also claim that arousal and not orgasm is the crucial unconditioned response, and designate the procedure as *arousal,* not orgasmic, conditioning. This technique, where explicit materials can be used to substantiate fantasy content, has therapeutic promise, but the Keller and Goldstein claims for it remain to be substantiated.

In two further studies using a classical conditioning paradigm, Bebbington (1977) treated a 44-year-old fetishist by pairing erection, elicited by vibrator, with heterosexual photographic material, and who was shown to have maintained an increase in heterosexual erectile responsiveness in follow-up studies after six months; and Herman, Barlow and Agras (1974) found increasing heterosexual arousal in two of three adult homosexual subjects as a result of pairing slides and films with homosexual content with female stimuli.

(d) Fading. This technique involves the introduction of "fading in" of heterosexual stimuli while the patient is sexually aroused in an attempt to change arousal-eliciting stimuli, and was applied successfully in the therapy of three male homosexuals by Barlow and Agras (1973). Laws and Pawlowski (1974) employed an automated stimulus fading procedure in order to strengthen sexual responsiveness to adult stimuli in two paedophiles, which was indicated by changes in penile response. Subjects were shown slides of children and adults which were superimposed. When they produced an erection above a designated criterion, one slide faded out and the other faded in; the fading process was reversed if responding then fell below this criterion. The procedure ensured that when a slide of a child was faded into an adult, subjects produced a high percentage of above-criterion responding; slides of adults and children presented alone, produced a lower response to adults. The authors claim that when a slide of an adult was faded into a child and a covert self-instruction procedure (see next Section for details) was initiated to decrease response to the child, both subjects in test sessions produced high-level responses to adult slides and decreased responding to slides of a child. The findings reinforce the notion that positive rather than negative (aversive) conditioning procedures (see next Section) can be used effectively for the alteration of maladaptive sexual behaviour.

(e) Exposure. This is a technique involving the presentation of explicit heterosexual stimuli in an attempt to specifically produce heterosexual

rousal, and can be used for both sexually dysfunctional and deviant subjects
equiring therapy. (It is possible, however, that the bombardment of patients
with sexually explicit stimuli results in a *decrease* of heterosexual *anxiety*
through extinction/habituation) rather than a direct increase in heterosexual
rousal.) Herman (1971) and Herman, Barlow and Agras (1974) treated two
homosexuals and one paedophile using this procedure, which involved
initially showing the patients a film of a seductive female nude for several
days; this phase was followed by a similar film of a male nude, and in the last
period the first film was shown again. Findings indicated that the men
responded with increased heterosexual arousal to the second showing of the
female film which led to an increase of heterosexual fantasies and behaviours
outside the laboratory. Exposure to the male film resulted in lowered
homosexual arousal.

(f) Systematic desensitization. This procedure is aimed specifically at the
alleviation of maladaptive sexual anxiety; it involves the pairing of relaxation
with specific sexual scenes depicting situations that the patient has indicated
cause him to feel anxious. The assumption is that if the patient is taught to
experience relaxation rather than anxiety in the face of scenes of desirable
sexual activity, the real-life situations will cause much less discomfort.

Caird and Wincze (1977) have applied this technique to the treatment of
sexual problems, both dysfunctional and deviant. Their library of 4-min
video-cassettes contain depictions of a wide variety of sexual interactions,
ranging from a couple simply talking to each other, to straightforward
heterosexual intercourse; these are shown in a graded sequence at which time
the deviant is instructed to identify with the male illustrated in the film. He
proceeds to the next video-tape when some relaxation is achieved. Problems,
however, may occur in homosexual subjects who find it difficult to resist
imagining sexual contact with the male involved in the video action (Tollison,
Adams and Tollison, 1979).

(ii) Elimination of deviant arousal. Punishment and aversion procedures
involve either the withdrawal of reward or the presentation of an aversive
stimulus contingent upon the occurrence of a maladapted sexual response.
The aim is to establish a strong association between inappropriate sexual
arousal or response and aversive reinforcement. As Adams *et al.* (1981) point
out

> Although a sexually deviant individual may regard his sexual activity as repug-
> nant and may actually desire alteration of his sexual orientation, his deviant
> sexual behaviour has acquired reinforcing properties by virtue of its connection
> with orgasmic pleasure. (p. 324)

Techniques designed to specifically decrease inappropriate sexual arousal, for their efficacy, usually require to be used in combination with procedures which provide training for the patient in a satisfactory, acceptable, alternative kind of sexual arousal and behaviour.

(a) Aversion (chemical and olfactory). This technique requires the production of an aversive physical state through administration of certain emetic or nausea-inducing drugs. Sexually implicit material has been used by Maletzky (1977) in the treatment of 12 exhibitionists where the aversive stimulus was a distasteful chemical substance. Subjects utilized imagery and photographs of exhibitionistic behaviour to achieve sexual arousal, at which time they were exposed to a noxious odour; this led to subsequent reduction in deviant arousal.

Laws, Meyer and Holmen (1978) report the eight-week treatment of a sexual sadist by an olfactory aversion procedure using inhalation of a noxious odour (valeric acid). This stimulus was paired with slide presentation of sadistic materials while penile erection was monitored; this led to immediate and permanent suppression of the response for the duration of treatment; erectile response to non-deviant imagery remained at a high level throughout therapy.

One major problem with using chemical and olfactory aversion therapy is that the stimulus conditions are difficult to control; so too are their effects. This is why preference has been shown for electrical or faradic aversion methods.

(b) Electrical aversion. The aversive stimulus here is a mild but unpleasant electrical shock, whose delivery is contingent on the occurrence of specifically unwanted deviant responses. This is usually an internalized deviant fantasy, but several researchers have used sexually explicit material. In an early investigation, Marshall (1973) employed a classical conditioning paradigm with a mixed deviant group who included fetishists, paedophiles and rapists, where relevant fantasies and slides were paired with faradic shock; this shock in turn was preceded immediately by the command "Stop!" The outcome after 27 treatment sessions indicated the elimination of deviant sexual arousal in 11 of 12 subjects, and most maintained improvement at up to 16 months follow-up.

Callahan and Leitenberg (1973) used two different aversion therapy procedures (contingent electric shock and covert sensitization) in the treatment of six subjects with mixed sexual deviation problems (exhibitionism, homosexuality (paedophiliac), and a transvestite/transsexual). The contingent shock group were given an unpleasant electric shock following erection to slides depicting sexually deviant material, whereas those assigned *covert sensitization* were offered an aversive event in imagination (e.g. feeling nauseous, discovery by a friend during deviant sexual activities, or partner develops diarrhoea) following erection. Effects of treatment were monitored by measurement of penile circumference changes during slides of both deviant and heterosexual stimuli presented prior to treatment sessions, and by daily subjective recording of sexual desire and fantasies as well as masturbation and sex acts. Both procedures led to a suppression of penile responses to deviant stimuli, but covert sensitization appeared to be more effective in suppressing subjective measures of sexual arousal than contingent shock.

Forgione (1976) used a novel source of sexually explicit stimuli, the deviant patient himself indulging in his unacceptable practice, but with surrogates; he treated two paedophiles by photographing the interactions they made with life-sized models of children. The resultant images were then used as deviant arousal stimuli in a faradic aversion therapy paradigm, which led to the elimination of paedophiliac behaviour in both subjects.

(c) Shame aversion. This approach uses shame or humiliation as the critical aversive stimulus. As in the Forgione (1976) study, the sexually deviant subject is required to engage in his deviant behaviour, but this time in front of a number of observers. It is important that the performance in front of the audience is as close as possible to the patient's actual deviant sexual activity in his natural environment, and should last for about 30 min. One technique devised by Wickramasekera (1972) requires the patient, usually an exhibitionist, to expose himself genitally in the presence of an increasing number of female observers, selected specifically for their similarity to the patient's typical deviant sexual target. Adams *et al.* (1981) described the procedure as follows:

> While enacting his deviant behaviour, the patient must: verbalise an introspective dialogue between himself and his penis, describe his bodily sensations, tell the observers what his fantasies and assumptions are regarding their reactions to his behaviour, and verbalise what he thinks the female observers are feeling, perceiving, and thinking about him. Observers are trained to stare expressionlessly at the patient. Further, the impact of this procedure has been enhanced by having the female observers ask the patient brief, direct questions during his demonstration and by *videotaping* [my emphasis] the patient during this procedure, for his future viewing. (p. 329)

The treatment appears to be effective in disrupting patient fantasies of secrecy and anonymity, in addition to increasing his anxiety level. Clearly, video-tape recordings of the unwanted sexually explicit behaviour are valuable components of therapy and may be used in follow-up booster sessions to maintain suppression of the negative response.

In a single case study involving a similar procedure with a young transvestite, Serber (1971) reports observation and photography of the patient during cross-dressing, which was sufficient in eliminating the deviant behaviour through feelings of distress and anxiety.

These applications of the shame aversion therapy technique suggest that continued and refined use of video-tape procedures would be fruitful in potentiating the aversive effects of observers.

(d) Satiation. This procedure involves instructing a patient with deviant sexual arousal to verbalize his unwanted fantasies while masturbating. He is required to masturbate continually and to carry on even if ejaculation occurs; throughout he is to constantly elaborate upon his deviant fantasy. Marshall and Barbaree (1978) call the procedure "satiation"; it is aimed deliberately at associating boredom with a patient's deviant fantasies and the authors found it effective with a man with multiple fetishes who attacked young girls by destroying the erotic nature of his deviant fantasies. For those subjects who find it difficult or impossible to either create or sustain deviant fantasies, appropriate sexually explicit material would enable them to avail themselves of this promising procedure.

(e) Biofeedback is used clinically to assist in either enhancement or suppression of the male sexual response, and in the context of the present discussion, the latter has been brought under control in the treatment of a bisexual paedophile (Laws, 1980). The subject's erection response to sexually deviant slides of young boys and girls were displayed on a closed-circuit television monitor. He was told to develop a strategy of self-control using the visual feedback, and his response to young boys and girls was treated sequentially. Laws found that the treatment was successful in suppressing deviant response while maintaining the strength of non-deviant response to adult males. It transpired that the patient had used a self-developed technique of covert sensitization to suppress deviant response and had simply employed the visual biofeedback of his erectile response to confirm and validate his self-control strategy. However, Rosen and Kopel (1977) were not so successful in the use of penile measures and biofeedback in the treatment of a transvestite/exhibitionist who during sessions viewed a video-tape made of his cross-dressing and exposure routine.

Indications/contra-indications for use of explicit sexual material

According to Björksten (1976), the indications for the therapeutic use of sexually explicit materials include: inability to discuss sexual matters using specific terms due to inhibition; anxiety about sexual behaviour and about having sexual fantasies; paucity of sexual fantasies; excessively restrictive or conservative attitudes about one's own sexual behaviour; sexual naïvety and ignorance; unrealistic expectations of sexual performance in self or partner; sexual identity confusion; sexual enrichment of couples with no specific dysfunction, e.g. the "humdrum" marriage; couples with communication difficulties; the increase in heterosexual arousal in deviants with low or no heterosexual arousal, and in the elimination of deviant arousal.

Sexually explicit materials are poorly tolerated by psychotics, especially where paranoid features are in evidence, in severe depression accompanied by feelings of performance inadequacy, and in those with a strong non-defensive, moral indignation, and are therefore contra-indicated in therapy.

Ethical Issues

Ethical issues specifically relating to the clinical use of sexually explicit material are similar to those which have relevance for sex therapy and research in general, i.e. informed consent, and the confidentiality of sex clinic files and correspondence. These topics are dealt with exhaustively in two volumes which contain the proceedings of conferences held at the Masters and Johnson Institute (Masters, Johnson and Kolodny, 1977; Masters, Johnson, Kolodny and Weems, 1980), and the reader is directed to these sources for detailed discussion of the arguments.

Conclusion

It has been demonstrated that sexually explicit materials have a definite place as an adjunct to a wide variety of procedures in sex education and therapy, and Gagnon and Simon (1974) and Wilson (1978) suggest encouragingly that this kind of material also has a positive role to play in the prevention of sexual problems. For the future, research needs to be directed towards the resolution of several central issues; Annon and Richardson (1978) state the problems by asking:

> ... what form of vicarious learning will be most helpful for what specific problem presented by what type of client to which therapist from what orientation? Should the therapist use films, videotapes, audio cassettes, slides, pictures, diagrams, and selected readings for each problem? How often and how many forms of symbolic learning would be most helpful? (p. 40)

They rightly point out that indiscriminate use of a particular film or videotape just because it is available is obviously not therapeutically justified.

As will be apparent from the substance of this chapter, some of the emotional heat generated by this delicate subject in both clinical and non-clinical settings over the past decade has been translated into productive light, enabling attitudes towards, and knowledge about, sex and its explicit depictions to be put into proper perspective. The next ten years will, no doubt, provide further illumination, and thereby increase the efficency and effectiveness of limited but much-needed psycho-sexual services and resources.

References

Abel, G. G., Barlow, D. H., Blanchard, E. B. and Guild, D. The components of rapists' sexual arousal. *Archives of General Psychiatry*, 1977, **34**, 895–903.

Abel, G. G., Blanchard, E. B. and Becker, J. An integrated treatment program for rapists. In R. Rada (Ed.). *Clinical Aspects of the Rapist*. New York: Grune and Stratton, 1977.

Abel, G. G., and Blanchard, E. B., Becker, J. and Djenderedjian, A. Differentiating sexual aggressives with penile measures. *Criminal Justice and Behavior*, 1978, **5**, 315–332.

Adams, H. E., Tollison, C. D. and Carson, T. C. Behavior therapy with sexual deviations. In S. M. Turner, K. S. Calhoun, and H. E. Adams (Eds). *Handbook of Clinical Behaviour Therapy*. New York: Wiley, 1981.

Annon, J. S. and Robinson, C. H. The use of vicarious learning in the treatment of sexual concerns. In J. LoPiccolo and L. LoPiccolo (Eds). *Handbook of Sex Therapy*. New York: Plenum Press, 1978.

Bancroft, J. H. J. Treatment of deviant sexual behaviour. In R. Gaind and B. L. Hudson (Eds). *Current Themes in Psychiatry*, Vol. 2. London: Macmillan, 1979.

Barbach, L. Group treatment of anorgasmic women. In S. R. Leiblum and L. A. Pervin (Eds). *Principles and Practice of Sex Therapy*. London: Tavistock, 1980.

Barlow, D. H. Assessment of sexual behaviour. In R. A. Ciminero, K. S. Calhoun, and H. E. Adams (Eds). *Handbook of Behavioral Assessment*. New York: Wiley, 1977.

Bebbington, P. E. Treatment of male sexual deviation by use of a vibrator: Case report. *Archives of Sexual Behavior*, 1977, **6**, 21–24.

Bentler, P. Heterosexual behaviour assessment I. Males. *Behaviour Research and Therapy*, 1968a, **6**, 21–25.

Bentler, P. Heterosexual behaviour assessment II. Females. *Behaviour Research and Therapy*, 1968b, **6**, 27–30.

Björksten, O. J. W. Sexually graphic material in the treatment of sexual disorders. In J. K. Meyer (Ed.). *Clinical Management of Sexual Disorders*. Baltimore: Williams and Williams, 1976.

Blanchard, E. B. and Epstein, L. H. Clinical applications of biofeedback. In M. Hersen, R. M. Eisler, and P. M. Miller (Eds). *Progress in Behavior Modification* Vol. 4. New York and London: Academic Press, 1977.

Briggs, M. M. The use of audio-visual materials in sexuality programs. In N. Rosenzweig and F. P. Pearsall (Eds). *Sex Education for the Health Professional: A Curriculum Guide*. New York: Grune and Stratton, 1978.

Brown, P. and Faulder, C. *Treat Yourself to Sex*. London: Dent, 1977.

Caird, W. K. and Wincze, J. P. *Sex Therapy: A Behavioral Approach*. Hagerstown, Md.: Harper and Row, 1977.

Callahan, E. J. and Leitenberg, H. Aversion therapy for sexual deviation: Contingent shock and covert sensitization. *Journal of Abnormal Psychology*, 1973, **81**, 60–73.

Carney, A., Bancroft, J. H. J. and Mathews, A. Combination of hormonal and psychological treatment for female sexual unresponsiveness: A comparative study. *British Journal of Psychiatry*, 1978, **133**, 339–346.

Cerny, J. A. Biofeedback and the voluntary control of sexual arousal in women. *Behavior Therapy*, 1978, **9**, 847–855.

Conrad, S. R. and Wincze, J. P. Orgasmic reconditioning: A controlled study of its effects upon the sexual arousal and behavior of adult male homosexuals. *Behavior Therapy*, 1976, **7**, 155–166.

Craft, A. *Health, Hygiene, and Sex Education for Mentally Handicapped Children, Adolescents and Adults: A Review of Audio-visual Resources.* London: Health Education Council, 1980.

Craft, A. and Craft, M. Sexuality and mental handicap: A review. *British Journal of Psychiatry*, 1981, **1391**, 494–505.

Craft, A. and Craft, M. *Sex Education and Counselling for Mentally Handicapped People.* Tunbridge Wells: Costello Press, 1982.

Crawford, D. A. Modification of deviant sexual behavior: The need for a comprehensive approach. *British Journal of Medical Psychology*, 1979, **52**, 151–156.

Crowe, M. J., Gillan, P. and Golombok, S. Form and content in the conjoint treatment of sexual dysfunction: A controlled study. *Behaviour Research and Therapy*, 1981, **19**, 47–54.

Csillag, E. R. Modification of penile erectile response. *Behavior Research and Experimental Psychiatry*, 1976, **7**, 27–29

Ellis, A. Treatment of erectile dysfunction. In S. R. Leilum and L. A. Pervin (Eds). *Principles and Practice of Sex Therapy.* London: Tavistock, 1980.

Feldman, M. P. and MacCulloch, M. J. The application of anticipatory avoidance learning to the treatment of homosexuality: I. Theory, technique, and preliminary results. *Behaviour Research and Therapy*, 1965, **2**, 165–183.

Feldman, M., MacCulloch, M., Mellor, V. and Pinschof, J. The application of anticipatory avoidance learning to the treatment of homosexuality: III: The sexual orientation method. *Behaviour Research and Therapy*, 1966, **4**, 289–299.

Forgione, A. G. The use of mannequins in the behavioural assessment of child molesters: Two case reports. *Behavior Therapy*, 1976, **7**, 678–685.

Francoeur, R. T. Sex films. *Society*, 1977, July/August, 33–37.

Freund, K. Assessment of anomolous erotic preferences in situational impotence. *Journal of Sex and Marital Therapy*, 1976, **2**, 173–182.

Freund, K., Chan, S. and Coulthard, R. Phallometric diagnosis with 'non-admitters.' *Behaviour Research and Therapy*, 1979, **17**, 451–457.

Freund, K., Langevin, R., Laws, D. R. and Serber, M. Femininity and preferred partner age in homosexual and heterosexual males. *British Journal of Psychiatry*, 1974, **125**, 442–446.

Freund, K., Langevin, R., Wescom, T. and Zajac, Y. Heterosexual interest in homosexual males. *Archives of Sexual Behavior*, 1975, **4**, 509–517.

Gagnon, J. H. and Simon, W. *Sexual Conduct: The Social Sources of Human Sexuality.* London: Hutchinson, 1973.

Garrard, J., Vaitkus, A., Held, J. and Chilgren, R. A. Follow-up effects of a medical school course in human sexuality. *Archives of Sexual Behavior*, 1976, **5**, 331–340.

Geer, J. H. Direct measurement of genital responding. *American Psychologist*, 1975, **30**, 415–418.

Geer, J. H. Genital measures: Comments on their role in understanding human sexuality. *Journal of Sex and Marital Therapy*, 1976, **2**, 165–172.

Geer, J. H. Biofeedback and the modification of sexual dysfunctions. In R. J. Gatchell and K. P. Price (Eds). *Clinical Applications of Biofeedback: Appraisal and Status* Elmsford, New York: Pergamon, 1979.

Geer, J. H., Morokoff, P. and Greenwood, P. Sexual arousal in women: The development of a measurement device for vaginal blood volume. *Archives of Sexual Behaviour*, 1974, **3**, 559–564.

Gillan, P. Objective measures of female sexual arousal. *Proceedings of the Physiological Society*, 1976, May, 66–678.

Gillan, P. Therapeutic use of obscenity. In R. Dhavan and C. Davies (Eds). *Censorship and Obscenity*. London: Martin Robertson, 1978.

Glide Foundation. Effect of erotic stimuli used – National Sex Forum training courses in human sexuality. In *Technical Reports of the Commission on Obscenity and Pornography (Vol. 5): Societal Control Mechanism*. Washington, D.C.: U.S. Government Printing Office, 1971.

Haeberle, E. J. *The Sex Atlas: A new illustrated guide*. New York: Seaburg, 1978.

Hartman, W. E. and Fithian, M. A. *Treatment of Sexual Dysfunction: A bio-psycho-social approach*. Long Beach, Califonia: Centre for Marital and Sexual Studies, 1972.

Haslam, M. T. *Sexual Disorders: A practical guide to diagnosis and treatment for the non-specialist*. London: Pitman Medical, 1978.

Hatch, J. P. Psychophysiological aspects of sexual dysfunction. *Archives of Sexual Behaviour*, 1981, 10, 49–64.

Hawton, K. The behavioural treatment of sexual dysfunctions. *British Journal of Psychiatry*, 1982, 140, 94–101.

Heiman, J. Use of the vaginal photoplethysmograph as a diagnostic and treatment aid in female sexual dysfunctions. Paper presented at the annual meeting of the American Psychological Association, Illinois, 1975.

Heiman, J. R. Female sexual response patterns: Interactions of physiological, affective, and contextual cues. *Archives of General Psychiatry*, 1980, 37, 1311–1316.

Heiman, J., LoPiccolo, L. and LoPiccolo, J. *Becoming Orgasmic: A sexual growth programme for women*. Englewood Cliffs, N. J.: Prentice Hall, 1976.

Heiman, J. and Morokoff, P. Female sexual arousal and experience as correlates of sexual malaise. Paper presented at the Annual Conference of American Psychological Association, San Francisco, 1977.

Henson, D. E., Rubin, H. B. and Henson, C. Analysis of the consistency of objective measures of sexual arousal in women. *Journal of Applied Behaviour Analysis*, 1979, 12, 701–711.

Herman, S. H. An experimental analysis of two methods of increasing heterosexual arousal in homosexuals. Unpublished doctoral dissertation. University of Mississippi, 1971.

Herman, S. H., Barlow, D. H. and Agras, W. S. An experimental analysis of classical conditioning as a method of increasing heterosexual arousal in homosexuals. *Behavior Therapy*, 1974, 5, 33–47.

Herman, S. H. and Prewett, M. An experimental analysis of feedback to increase sexual arousal in a case of homo- and heterosexual impotence: A preliminary report. *Journal of Behavior Therapy and Experimental Psychiatry*, 1974, 5, 271–274.

Hinton, J. W., O'Neill, M. T. and Webster, S. Psychophysiological assessment of sex offenders in a security hospital. *Archives of Sexual Behavior*, 1980, 9, 205–216.

Hoon, P. W. The assessment of sexual arousal in women. In M. Hersen, R. M. Eisler, and P. M. Miller (Eds). *Progress in Behavior Modification* Vol. 7. New York and London: Academic Press, 1978.

Hoon, E., Hoon, P. and Wincze, J. The SAI: An inventory for the measurement of female sexual arousal. *Archives of Sexual Behavior*, 1976, 5, 291–300.

Hoon, P. W., Wincze, H. B. and Hoon, E. F. The effects of biofeedback and cognitive mediation upon vaginal blood volume. *Behavior Therapy*, 1977, 8, 694–702.

Kaplan, H. S. *The Illustrated Manual of Sex Therapy*. London: Souvenir, 1976.

Kaplan, H. S. *The New Sex Therapy*. New York: Bruner/Mazel, 1974.

Kaplan, H. S. *The New Sex Therapy Vol. 2: Disorders of Sexual Desire and other new concepts and techniques in Sex Therapy.* New York: Bruner/Mazel, 1979.

Keller, D. J. and Goldstein, A. Orgasmic reconditioning reconsidered. *Behaviour Research and Therapy,* 1978, **16**, 299–300.

Kilmann, P. R., Wanlass, R. L., Sabalis, R. F. and Sullivan, B. Sex education: A review of its effects. *Archives of Sexual Behavior,* 1981, **10**, 177–205.

Kockott, G., Feil, W., Ferstl, R., Aldenhoff, J. and Besinger, U. Psychophysiological aspects of male sexual inadequacy: Results of an experimental study. *Archives of Sexual Behavior,* 1980, **9**, 477–493.

Kolářský, A., Madlfousek, J. and Novotná, V. Stimuli eliciting sexual arousal in males who offend adult women: An experimental study. *Archives of Sexual Behavior,* 1978, **7**, 79–87.

Laws, D. R. Treatment of bisexual pedophiles by a biofeedback assisted self-control procedure. *Behaviour Research and Therapy,* 1980, **18**, 207–211.

Laws, D. R. and Holmen, M. L. Sexual response faking by pedophiles. *Criminal Justice and Behavior,* 1978, **5**, 343–356.

Laws, D. R., Meyers, J. and Holmen, M. L. Reduction of sadistic sexual arousal by olfactory aversion: A case study. *Behaviour Research and Therapy,* 1978, **16**, 281–285.

Laws, D. R. and O'Neil, J. A. Variations on masturbatory conditioning. *Behavioural Psychotherapy,* 1981, **9**, 111–136.

Laws, D. R. and Pawlowski, A. V. An automated fading procedure to alter sexual responsiveness in pedophiles. *Journal of Homosexuality,* 1974, **1**, 149–163.

Lief, H. and Reed, D. *Sexual Knowledge and Attitude Test* (SKAT). Pennsylvania: University of Pennyslvania, School of Medicine, Divisions of Family Study, Department of Psychiatry, 2nd Edition, 1972.

LoPiccolo, J. and Lobitz, W. C. The role of masturbation in the treatment of orgasmic dysfunction. *Archives of Sexual Behaviour,* 1972, **2**, 163–171.

Maletzky, B. M. "Booster" sessions in aversion therapy: the permanency of treatment. *Behaviour Therapy,* 1977, **8**, 460–463.

Marcotte, D. B. and Logan, C. Medical Sex Education: Allowing attitude alterations. *Archives of Sexual Behaviour,* 1977, **6**, 155–162.

Marks, I. M. Review of behavioural psychotherapy, II: Sexual disorders. *American Journal of Psychiatry,* 1981, **138**, 750–756.

Marquis, J. N. Orgasmic reconditioning: changing sexual object choice through controlling masturbation fantasies. *Journal of Behaviour Therapy and Experimental Psychiatry,* 1970, **1**, 263–271.

Marshall, W. L. The modification of sexual fantasies: a combined treatment approach to the reduction of deviant sexual behaviour. *Behaviour Research and Therapy,* 1973, **11**, 557–564.

Marshall, W. L. and Barbaree, H. E. The reduction of deviant arousal: satiation treatment for sexual aggressors. *Criminal Justice and Behaviour,* 1978, **5**, 294–303.

Masters, W. H. Johnson, V. E. and Kolodny R. C. (Eds). *Ethical Issues in Sex Therapy and Research* Vol. 1. Boston; Little, Brown, 1977.

Masters, W. H. Johnson, V. E. Kolodny, R. C. and Weems S. M. (Eds). *Ethical Issues in Sex Therapy and Research* Vol. 2. Boston: Little, Brown, 1980.

McMullen, S. The use of film or manual for anorgasmic women. In M. Cook and G. Wilson (Eds). *Love and Attraction: An international conference.* Oxford: Pergamon, 1979.

Miller, W. R. C. and Leif, H. E. The Sexual Knowledge and Attitude Test (SKAT). *Journal of Sex and Marital Therapy,* 1979, **5**, 282–287.

Money, J. The Positive and constructive approach to pornography. In *The Technical Reports of the Commission on Obscenity and Pornography* Vol. 8. Washington, D.C. U.S. Government Printing Office, 1970.

Money, J. Pornography in the home: A topic in the medical education. In J. Zubin and J. Money (Eds). *Contemporary Sexual Behaviour: Critical Issues in the 1970s.* Baltimore: The Johns Hopkins University Press, 1972.

Morokoff, P. J. and Heiman, J. R. Effects of erotic stimuli on sexually functional and dysfunctional women: Multiple measures before and after sex therapy. *Behaviour Research and Therapy,* 1980, **18**, 127–137.

Nemetz, G. H., Craig, K. D. and Reith, G. Treatment of female sexual dysfunction through symbolic modelling. *Journal of Consulting and Clinical Psychology,* 1978, **46**, 62–73.

Nettlebladt, P. and Uddenberg, N. Sexual dysfunction and sexual satisfaction in 58 married Swedish men. *Journal of Psychosomatic Research,* 1979, **23**, 141–147.

Obler, M. Systematic desensitisation in sexual disorders. *Journal of Behaviour Therapy and Experimental Psychiatry,* 1973, **4**, 93–101.

Price, S. Golden, J. Golden, M. Price, T. Leff, J. Heinrich, A. G. and Munford, P. Training family planning personnel in sex counselling and sex education. *Public Health Reports,* 1978, **93**, 328–334.

Quinn, J. T., Harbison, J. J. M. and McAllister, H. An attempt to shape human penile responses. *Behaviour Research and Therapy,* 1970, **8**, 213–216.

Reisinger, J. J. Effects of erotic stimulation and masturbatory training upon situational orgasmic dysfunction. *Journal of Sex and Marital Therapy,* 1978, **4**, 177–185.

Reisinger, J. J. Generalization of treatment effects following masturbatory training with erotic stimuli. *Journal of Behaviour Therapy and Experimental Psychiatry,* 1979, **10**, 247–250.

Reynolds, B. S. Psychological treatment models and outcome results for erectile dysfunction: A critical review. *Psychological Bulletin,* 1977, **84**, 1218–1238.

Reynolds, B. S. Biofeedback and facilitation of erection in men with erectile dysfunction. *Archives of Sexual Behaviour,* 1980, **9**, 101–113.

Rhodes, P. The use of aids in the management of disorders of sexual function. *Clinics in Obstetrics and Gynaecology,* 1980, **7**, 421–432.

Robinson, C. H. The effects of observational learning on sexual behaviours and attitudes in orgasmic dysfunctional women. Doctoral dissertation, University of Hawaii, 1974. *Dissertation Abstracts International,* 1975, **35**, (9B).

Rosen, R. C. Genital blood flow measurement: Feedback applications in sexual therapy. *Journal of Sex and Marital Therapy,* 1976, **2**, 184–196.

Rosen, R. C. The use of penile plethysmography in a medicolegal evaluation. *Journal of Forensic Sciences,* 1977, **22**, 791–794.

Rosen, R. C. and Keefe, F. J. The measurement of human penile tumescence. *Psychophysiology,* 1978, **15**, 366–376.

Rosen, R. C. and Kopel, S. A. Penile plethysmography and biofeedback in the treatment of a transvestite-exhibitionist. *Journal of Consulting and Clinical Psychology,* 1977, **45**, 908–916.

Rosen, R. C., Shapiro, D. and Schwartz, G. Voluntary control of penile tumescence. *Psychosomatic Medicine,* 1975, **37**, 479–483.

Rosenberg, P. and Rosenberg, L. Sex education for adolescents and their families. *Journal of Sex and Marital Therapy,* 1976, **2**, 53–65.

Rosenzweig, N. and Pearsall, F. P. *Sex Education for the Health Professional: A Curriculum Guide.* New York: Grune and Stratton, 1978.

Rosenberg, P. and Rosenberg, L. Sex education for adolescents and their families. *Journal of Sex and Marital Therapy,* 1976, **2**, 53–65.

Rubin, H. B., Henson, D. E., Falvo, R. E. and High, R. W. The relationship between men's endogenous levels of testosterone and their penile responses to erotic stimuli. *Behaviour Research and Therapy,* 1979, **17**, 305–312.

Sandford, D. A., Tustin, R. D. and Priest, P. N. Increasing heterosexual arousal in two adult male homosexuals using a differential reinforcement procedure. *Behavior Therapy,* 1975, **6**, 689–693.

Sarrel, L. J. and Sarrel, P. M. *Sexual Unfolding: Sexual development and sex therapies in late adolescence.* Boston: Little, Brown, 1979.

Schiavi, R. C. (Ed.). The assessment of sexual and marital function. *Journal of Sex and Marital Therapy,* 1979, **5**.

Serber, M. Shame aversion therapy. *Journal of Behaviour Therapy and Experimental Psychiatry,* 1971, **1**, 213–215.

Sharpe, R. and Meyer, V. Modification of "cognitive sexual pain" by the spouse under supervision. *Behaviour Therapy,* 1973, **4**, 285–287.

Spanier, G. B. Formal and informal sex education as determinants of pre-marital sexual behavior. *Archives of Sexual Behavior,* 1976, **5**, 39–67.

Stanley, E. A course in human sexuality for medical students at St. George's Hospital. *British Journal of Family Planning,* 1977, **3**, 16–17.

Stoller, R. J. Sexual excitement. *Archives of General Psychiatry,* 1976, **33**, 899–909.

Szasz, T. The case against sex education. *British Journal of Sexual Medicine,* 1981, **8**, 5, 8.

Tollison, C. D., Adams, H. E. and Tollison, J. W. Physiological measurement of sexual arousal in homosexual, bisexual and heterosexual males. *Journal of Behavioral Assessment,* 1979, in press.

Trimmer, E. (Ed.). *The Visual Dictionary of Sex.* London: Macmillan, 1978.

Vandervoort, H. E. and McIlvenna, T. Sexually explicit media in medical school curricula. In R. Green (Ed.). *Human Sexuality: A Health Practitioner's Text.* Baltimore: Williams and Wilkins, 1975.

Van Deventer, A. D. and Laws, D. R. Orgasmic reconditioning to redirect sexual arousal in pedophiles. *Behavior Therapy,* 1978, **9**, 748–765.

Whalen, R. E. Sexual motivation. *Psychological Review,* 1966, **73**, 151–163.

Wickramsekera, I. A technique for controlling a certain type of sexual exhibitionism. *Psychotherapy: Theory, Research, and Practice,* 1972, **9**, 207–210.

Wilson, W. C. Can pornography contribute to the prevention of sexual problems? In C. A. Qualls, J. P. Wincze and D. H. Barlow (Eds). *The Prevention of Sexual Disorders.* New York: Plenum, 1978.

Wincze, J. P. Sexual dysfunction (distress and dissatisfaction). In S. M. Turner, K. S. Calhoun and H. E. Adams (Eds). *Handbook of Clinical Behavior Therapy.* New York: Wiley, 1981.

Wincze, J. P. and Caird, W. K. The effects of systematic desensitization and video desensitization in the treatment of essential sexual dysfunction in women. *Behavior Therapy,* 1976, **7**, 335–342.

Wincze, J. P., Hoon, E. F. and Hoon, P. W. Physiological responsivity of normal and sexually dysfunctional women during erotic stimulus exposure. *Journal of Psychosomatic Research,* 1976, **20**, 445–451.

Wincze, J. P., Venditti, E., Barlow, D. and Mavissakalian, M. The effects of a subjective monitoring task in the physiological measure of genital response to erotic stimulation. *Archives of Sexual Behavior,* 1980, 9, 533–545.

Wishnoff, R. Modeling effects of explicit and nonexplicit sexual stimuli on the sexual anxiety and behavior of women. *Archives of Sexual Behavior,* 1978, 7, 455–461.

Wolpe, J. *Psychotherapy by Reciprocal Inhibition.* Stanford: Stanford University Press, 1958.

World Health Organisation. Education and Treatment in Human Sexuality: The training of health professionals. *Technical Report Series* No. 572. Geneva: World Health Organisation, 1975.

Wright, J., Perreault, R. and Matthieu, M. The treatment of sexual dysfunctions: A review. *Archives of General Psychiatry,* 1977, 34, 881–890.

Yaffé, M. Research survey. In Lord Longford (Ed.). *Pornography: The Longford Report.* London: Coronet, 1972.

Yaffé, M. Pornography: An updated review (1972–1977). In B. Williams (Chairman). *Report of the Committee on Obscenity and Film Censorship* (Appendix 5). London: Her Majesty's Stationery Office, 1979a.

Yaffé, M. Pornography and violence. *British Journal of Sexual Medicine,* 1979b, 5, 32–36.

Yaffé, M. Commentary on current trends in sex therapy. In T. G. Tennent (Ed.). *Current Trends in Treatment in Psychiatry.* Tunbridge Wells, Kent: Pitman Medical, 1980a.

Yaffé, M. The law relating to pornography: A psychological overview. *Medicine, Science and the Law,* 1980b, 20, 20–27.

Yaffé, M. The assessment and treatment of paedophilia. In B. Taylor (Ed.). *Perspective on Paedophilia.* London: Batsford, 1981a.

Yaffé, M. Disordered sexual relationships. In R. Gilmour and S. Duck (Eds). *Personal Relationships Vol. 3: Personal Relationships in Disorder.* London and New York: Academic Press, 1981b.

8

Pornography and forensic psychology

Lionel Haward

The Origins of Censorship

One of the primary reasons pornography is an issue today is because of the legal restrictions surrounding it. Before such prohibitions existed, whether secular or ecclesiastical, pornography merely coloured the cultural scene either in private pleasure or public aesthetics. In early times, free from the repressions of Hebrew ideology or the puritanical excesses of later Christianity, civilized man could spice his writing with a sexual variety which at the time was neither remarked upon nor remarkable. For many centuries now, classical scholars have been able to enjoy, free from judicial interference, the unexpurgated tales of early Roman and Greek authors, whilst archaeological translators of cuneiform and hierglyph have come across sexual references which are far from chaste.

Pornography probably came to England with the Roman invaders. Before then its denizens had not developed the skills needed to record their more lascivious ideas, and no doubt many a saucy joke about Boadicea was lost to posterity because of the illiteracy of the ancient Britons. Later, when Christianity reached England, chastity was elevated to a virtue, and sex became an unfortunate atavistic and animal propensity that could be tolerated only because there was no alternative way of perpetuating the race. Yet, despite this sex-degrading climate, sex books themselves were left untouched; even the *Decameron* of Boccaccio, which raised ecclesiastical eyebrows – among other things – when it appeared in the fourteenth century, was not banned until the Reformation. Throughout both the Elizabethan and the Regency periods pornography was unrestricted by law: Merry England was merry indeed. Then came Queen Victoria, a monarch not easily amused, together with an industrial revolution which created a prosperous middle class. This swelling tide of literate intermediaries between peer and peasant had not only the new-found wealth to buy books, but the leisure to read them. Pornography, previously an almost exclusive "benefit of clergy", now fell into the hands of a new social class. Before the end of the century, it could be found anywhere and everywhere, from below stairs in the servants' hall to the upper deck of the Clapham omnibus.

The increasing availability of pornography has been, as Alschuler (1971) has argued, a prime factor in determining society's attitude towards it. Thus, although sexual activity has been illustrated since man first invented pictography, it was the introduction of widespread printing in the eighteenth century and the growth of literacy in the nineteenth century which preceded legislative attempts to contain and control it. The history of English censorship is, as Robertson (1979) puts it, the story of one society's inability to solve a problem posed by the invention of printing; and was it merely coincidence that the first law concerning obscenity in the United States accompanied the introduction of free and universal education? One thing was clear: what was good enough for the upper classes was too good for the lower orders. The elite could remain uncorrupted, but the working classes were vulnerable to the depraving effects which only an unhealthy mind could possibly imagine. King George III set the anti-pornography wagon on its way by expressing his imperial displeasure at the spread of erotic literature, and exhorted his subjects to "suppress books dispensing poison to the minds of the young and unwary, and to punish the venders thereof". The acme of erotica was now past, and there was no dearth of dedicated and zealous individuals, possibly seeking to sublimate their energies on *good works*, to jump on the bandwagon. The Vice Society was founded in 1802 and, during its first half century, initiated 159 prosecutions under common law, only five of which led to an acquittal. Even this 97% success rate failed to satisfy the membership, which pressed Parliament to close existing loopholes in the law by introducing a statute against obscenity. Unfortunately for the Society, sex proved too embarrassing a subject for the Gentlemen of the House to discuss in a common-sense way, and the best they could do was to distort the purpose of the 1824 *Vagrancy Act* by an amendment which made it illegal to exhibit obscene prints in public.

The Victorian era, which regarded even piano legs as immodest unless they were curtained with their own individual "trousers", was accompanied by even more punitive and repressive attitudes towards sexual expression, and stronger penalties were considered a necessary means of taking pornographers' minds off their livelihood. In 1857, therefore, Parliament passed the first of the *Obscene Publications Acts*, which introduced larger fines and longer terms of imprisonment for publishing pornography than were permitted under the *Vagrancy Act*. Despite the draftsman's best endeavours, however, occasional acquittals still occurred, mainly due to the definition of obscenity – a semantic eel which occasionally eluded the Court's clutches when introduced by a verbally adept and etymologically-experienced defence lawyer. In R. v. *Hicklin* (1868), Lord Justice Cockburn went eel-hunting when, in a lengthy summing-up, he interpreted the definition of obscenity to mean "a tendency to deprave and corrupt". This definition, unfortunately, has remained with us to this day and it continues to plague our courts by its lack of objectivity. Actually, the book on which this test of obscenity was formulated, *The Confessional Unmasked*, was written less for any prurient purposes than to discredit the Roman Catholic Church. In essence the trial was really concerned with the conflict between the protection of free speech and the protection of the established church, and this conflict is still implicit in many prosecutions under the Obscenity Acts today. With the choice of common law or statute law as the basis of prosecution, and armed at least with a definition of obscenity from the *Hicklin* decision, Victorian prosecutors found it exceedingly easy to gain convictions and anything with a hint of sex suffered the full weight of the law. *Three Weeks,* a novel by Elinor Glyn in which the only "improper" passage described a lady clad in a voluminous dressing gown – lying on the floor with a flower in her lips, was called in 1916 a "work of grossly immoral tendency" by Mr Justice Younger, and even a painting of *Venus* in the Dulwich Art Gallery was judged obscene.

The Obscene Publications Act 1959

Victoria passed in all her pomp and circumstance, but the Edwardian era provided no respite for the pornographer; even the Gay Twenties were anything but gay to the writer who mentioned sex. The conviction of Marie Stopes for writing a family planning booklet created a public scandal second only to the trial of Oscar Wilde, in which the jury recommended that his letters should be burnt, even though they were less explicit, on any criterion, than Shakespeare's sonnets to Henry Wrothesley (Box, 1967). By the 1950s, public attitudes towards pornography had eased. *The Philanderer*, a book about a young man's obsession with his desire for women, had been acquitted in 1954 and the ban on Boccaccio's *Decameron* was lifted as well. Radclyffe Hall's novel *The Well of Loneliness*, convicted in 1928 as obscene literature because it dealt with lesbianism – despite the fact that Lord Birkett, onetime Lord Chief Justice, had to read it several times before discovering the alleged obscenity (Hyde, 1964) – received the final accolade when it was read over the airwaves as a BBC *Book at Bedtime*. Nevertheless, there was still a vocal minority who were concerned at this trend in what they regarded as moral laxity, and a successful attempt to tighten up the law was made in the 1959 *Obscene Publications Act.**

This Act possesses four main sections, each of which is designed to help regulate the publication of obscene matter, to provide for the protection of literature, and to strengthen the law concerning pornography. Section 1 makes the publication of pornography an "indictable" crime, that is, a more serious offence which carried various legal implications; it also increased the number of people who can be convicted as a "publisher", defined as anyone who distributes, sells, lets or hires, or lends or offers for sale, or in the case of a record or film, anyone who shows, plays or projects the alleged obscene material. Section 2 explicitly prevents prosecution under common law (with its more flexible processes and interpretations) by restricting it to statute law and the rigid hand of Parliament: a jury trial is permitted but at the risk of considerably higher penalties. Section 3 authorizes search, seizure and forfeiture of material which can lead to a fine or an order for destruction or return, usually after a long period of time. The value of such stock to a publisher could be as much as £25 000; add to that the court costs normally imposed on the convicted offender and most are made bankrupt – an effective, if unjust, way of preventing recidivism. Section 4 reflected a change in public attitudes towards sex in that it was recognized that sexually explicit material could have some merit which redeemed it in the eyes of the law. Conviction and forfeiture need not result if it is proved that the publication in question "is justified as being for the public good on the ground that it is in the interests of science, literature, art or learning, or of other objects of general concern". Paragraph 2 of this section also declares "that the opinion of experts as to the literary, artistic, scientific or other merits of an article may be admitted in any proceedings under this Act, either to establish or negate the said ground".

Good use was made of Section 4 during the following decade, when the literary and artistic merit of a number of books brought before the court was established by a succession of expert witnesses consisting of authors, publishers, and university professors. The first and most notable, though perhaps not the most meritorious, of these trials was that of D. H. Lawrence's *Lady Chatterley's Lover (R. v. Penguin,* 1960). The book's defence cost £10 000, only part of which was recouped by a book about the trial itself (which had a lot more to commend it than the original novel). The publishers were acquitted after 35 experts had testified to its artistic and literary merit. The success of *Lady Chatterley's Lover* led to other erstwhile forbidden classics chancing their arm at the Bar, and gaining new literary respect in

* See chapter by Offenbach, this volume, for a more in-depth discussion of obscenity and the law in Britain.

doing so. The importance of these trials, however, was that the nature and criteria of expert evidence were established for the first time, in that a publication should be judged: (1) as a whole and not in part; (2) on its honesty and purpose; and (3) in the climate of contemporary standards, i.e. in comparison with similar books available in publication. Happy news for some, but other publishers were still on the tumbrils, especially when, because of the nature of the indictment, they were deprived of the benefit of a jury trial and convicted by magistrates. John Cleland's *Fanny Hill* suffered twice in this way, and when *Cain's Book* by Trocchi followed suit such a howl of protest arose that the Attorney General had to promise Parliament that any future case involving Section 4 would be given the opportunity of trial by jury.

Parliament was concerned with justice, however, not with defending pornography. Therefore, it attempted to sharpen the teeth of the judiciary by introducing, in 1964, an amending Act which strengthened the law in regard to publishing for "gain". This new legislation allowed for the prosecution of shop assistants, bookbinders, printers, and almost everyone involved in the production of the offending book, many of whom were, by the very nature of their role in the trade, completely unaware of the contents. Additional use was also made of confiscation and proceedings under the 1953 *Post Office Act*, which makes it an offence to send "indecent" materials through the post, indecency being easier to prove than obscenity. The Customs and Excise officers were also effectively brought onto the scene, since most of the pornography originated abroad. To complete the blunderbuss approach to conviction, old offences under Common Law were retrieved from legal obscurity, such as "inciting to corrupt public morals" (*Shaw* v. *Director of Public Prosecutions*, 1962).

Until 1970, the Section 4 *public good* defence was used exclusively to extol a publication's artistic and literary merits. But in the following year, the publishers of an underground magazine called *Oz* brought psychologists into court for the first time as expert witnesses in an obscenity trial (*R.* v. *Anderson*, 1971). Despite its unsavoury content, *Oz* had remained unmolested by the police until the so-called "School kids' issue" appeared, an edition of the magazine which utilized the contributions of teenagers. The most vulnerable minds of those who George III called the "young and unwary" have always been of special concern, and the erroneous belief that this issue of *Oz* was directed specifically at schoolkids led to police action on this occasion. The trial, which took place in the Old Bailey's historic No. 1 Court, not only created legal precedent by its use of psychologists as expert witnesses, but became something of a carnival in itself, complete with strangely garbed *Oz* supporters filling the public gallery and a bizarre procession, which included an elephant, marching down Newgate Street to the court itself (Palmer,

1971). This colourful event became the longest obscenity trial in British legal history, and formed a milestone in the development of forensic psychology in this country (Haward, 1975). Oz itself was defined by a succession of experts on art and literature in the same way as its more illustrious predecessors. The reason psychologists were brought into an obscenity case for the first time lies in the special consideration given by the Director of Public Prosecutions to the fact that the magazine was, in the prosecution view, intended specifically for the juvenile market. The main role of the psychologists was to review for the court the likely effect of this publication on young readers, and to show that the distribution of the magazine could be for the "public good". The defence of public good, as mentioned above, can be raised whenever there is some evidence of artistic, literary or scientific merit, or of some other *object of general concern*. It is the latter clause which provides the statutory authority for the admission of psychological evidence. The evidence of psychologists usually refers to the allegedly beneficial effects of exposure to sexual materials and thus comes within the "public good" category (Haward, 1975). Despite the introduction of psychologists in this capacity, Oz was successfully prosecuted; the decision was reversed on appeal, but only due to a technicality relating to the fact that the trial judge was considered to have mis-directed the jury as to the presumed effects of the material on those likely to see it. Perhaps more importantly this trial created a precedent by allowing psychological evidence to be presented and considered in an obscenity trial in which the question of whether or not an article is deemed to be obscene is one for the court to answer on the basis of their own experience and knowledge; it also offered hope in those cases where the material was, on the face of it, devoid of any literary, artistic or scientific merit whatsoever.

Expert Testimony

Sexually explicit content in any book or magazine is likely to offend the susceptibilities of some people and to arouse the sexual passions of others. What is not always easy to convey to the jury is the idea that the presence of explicit sex does not of itself make a book pornographic within the general meaning of the term. If "pornographic" is defined literally, i.e. "writing about prostitutes" then the New Testament must be so labelled. Indeed, publishers accused of depraving and corrupting society by including details of some explicit practice in their book have not been slow to point out that a few pages of *Genesis* alone provide accounts of a wide range of sexual offences, including indecent exposure, rape, incest, and sexual murder. And what can one say of sexual content when, in 1974, the 22 July edition of *The Sunday Times* included accounts of seduction, adultery, prostitution, an orgy, sex scandals, sex vibrators and whips, transvestites, a brothel keeper, a 16-year old forni-

:ator who had four illegitimate children, strip club performances, queers, wife-beaters, sexual decadence and sado-masochism. And that was just the text: the illustrations included a full length nude photograph in colour of Brigitte Bardot, two nude figures making love, and another nude couple in bed. In comparison, some of the publications brought to court as allegedly obscene take on the character of a Sunday School pamphlet.

Forensic psychologists called to give expert testimony in court cases heard under the *Obscene Publications Acts* have consistently been at pains to point out that in matters of influence it is not the actual content of a book but the way the content is *presented* which is important to consider. For this purpose, sexually explicit materials are usually classified into one of three categories first suggested by Kutchinsky (1973) as follows: (1) *sexual education*, where the content informs; (2) *sexual realism*, where the content describes; and (3) *pornography* proper, where the content is intended to arouse. Sex education refers to that class of literature where sex is discussed or portrayed specifically to educate the reader; medical texts discussing sexual disorders, or illustrating sexual anatomy, would come under this heading.* It is a sad reflection on British puritanism and prejudice that, even in the post-war years, medical authors have felt the need to clothe their discussions of sex in the Latin tongue to avoid the threat of prosecution from the anti-pornography brigade. Marie Stopes' crime was not that she advocated birth control, but that she preached it to the lay public. Throughout the many decades since George III started the witch-hunt on pornographers, there has existed this curious double standard which accepts that upper-class literates, professional men, lawyers and policemen are quite immune from the alleged depravity and corruption which follows exposure to pornography, whereas the rest of the population must be protected from it. Thus, the preface to the first edition of Krafft-Ebing's classical treatise *Psychopathia Sexualis* (1928) states: "technical terms are used throughout the book *in order to exclude the lay reader* [my emphasis]. For the same reason certain portions are written in Latin." To further emphasize this fact the publishers inserted their own preface which said: "The sale of this book is rigidly restricted to members of the medical and legal professions." By the time the twelfth edition had been published, even these safeguards against prosecution were felt to be insufficient, and the preface was therefore changed to read: "The number of technical terms has been increased and the Latin language is more frequently made use of than in former editions." However honest and moralistic the motives of sex educators, goodwill and good intent are not enough, Kant notwithstanding, to prevent sex education literature from receiving the same fate as the most sordid, sleazy and salacious product of the gutter press. *Forum*, for example,

---

* See Dallas, this volume.

is a monthly sex education magazine, of which Clifford Longley (1973) the religious correspondent of the *Times* newspaper wrote: "most adults would be better for two years' exposure to *Forum's* brutally frank, no-holds barred attitude to sex"; interestingly, one of *Forum's* regular contributors is Reverend Chad Varah, founder of the Samaritans and holder of an ecclesiastical office in St Paul's Cathedral. Despite such endorsements by contemporary Christian morality, *Forum* has been brought to court as allegedly obscene on more than one occasion.

Sexual realism, in contrast, refers to literature in which the content is used specifically to provide artistic impact by realistic description. The argument in favour of sexual realism states that if a detailed description of a death-bed scene is accepted as artistically necessary to convey the emotion of the occasion, then it is equally valid and justifiable to graphically detail a consummation of love or rape for the same purpose. It is not always easy, of course, to differentiate sexual realism from pornography proper as the effect upon the reader may be the same in both cases; pornography, however, is defined as sexual content whose *sole* purpose is to arouse the reader or viewer sexually. Sexual realism can perhaps be recognized and set apart from pornography as such by referring to the work of established authors, like D. H. Lawrence; in this case, the nature of the work and the intention of the author are immediately apparent. The courts themselves, however, recognize no distinction between these various categories and have happily convicted textbooks on contraception, manuals on marriage, and serious novels in the same spirit of prejudice and ignorance as they bring to bear upon less noble works. In practice, of course, it is not always possible to place a publication clearly into one single category, for many magazines have a mixed content which includes all three.

The introduction of forensic psychologists as expert witnesses in obscenity trials set an important precedent, but it also led to a rather anomalous situation. Experts testifying to the artistic, literary, or scientific merits of a book under the Section 4 "public good" defence were, in essence, providing evidence of the positive value of the book which the court set in balance against the degree to which it was believed the book tended to deprave and corrupt; if its artistic or other merit was deemed to exceed its power to deprave and corrupt, then it was found to be not obscene. The psychologists evidence, on the other hand, was concerned *not* with the intrinsic merits of a book, but with its beneficial effects upon some or all of its readers. What the psychologists for the defence were asking the jury to accept, on the face of it at least, was that the book was *both* depraving and improving, a paradox of contrasts which managed to escape the notice of the jury and the attention of the prosecution for a number of years. What the psychologists wanted to say on the basis of the scientific evidence available to them at the time, was that nothing was known to support the view that the particular publication, film, or object they were defending could be expected to deprave or corrupt. By one of the many oddities of English law, however, they were not allowed to say this. The question of whether or not an article is deemed to be obscene is *not* one for the psychologists to comment upon, irrespective of their own experience and knowledge. Similarly, the prosecution is *not* permitted to introduce evidence purporting to demonstrate that an article is obscene. The court, without help from either the defence or prosecution, must reach its own verdict about whether or not an article is obscene on the basis of their own experience and knowledge. This procedure evolved from the nature of the law as set forth in the Obscenity Acts of 1959 and 1964, and from the definition of the term obscenity in case law. Indeed, the very existence of these attests to the assumption that an article can have "a tendency to deprave and corrupt". This *presumptio juris et jure* is irrefutable. The figure of justice surmounting England's premier court, erroneously portrayed as blindfolded, might just as well have been on the occasion of obscenity trials. The depraving and corrupting tendency of a book, magazine, film or object (for on some occasions the sinister threat to a nation's morals brought before the court has been nothing more than such fun objects as penis-shaped candles or comic contraceptives) is expected to be judged in complete isolation from any evidence which could contribute scientifically to the judgement. Instead, the magistrates or the jury — sometimes seeing a sex magazine or sex aid for the first time in their lives — are expected to assess its tendency to cause social, moral, psychological or spiritual harm on the basis of their own common sense. Unfortunately, this is often a poor substitute for factual knowledge and scientific inference — in matters pertaining to such an emotionally-charged topic as sex, common sense is no more than a euphemism for ignorance and prejudice. Defence Counsel, thus blocked by legal procedure from presenting relevant psychological evidence in a reasonable way, overcome this impediment by presenting the psychologists' findings as a positive virtue of the book, rather than by the scientifically more acceptable method of showing that the book's alleged "tendency to deprave and corrupt" is unproven.

The outcome of any obscenity trial depends, of course, very much upon the nature of the material brought before the court, and forensic psychologists, acknowledging this, have tended to organize their evidence for presentation according to (1) the sources from which the relevant facts were obtained, or (2) the particular type of "public good" which could be expected to result from the publication of the article. Until recently, the sources of relevant facts at the disposal of the psychologist were as follows: (1) research into the effects of exposure to sexually explicit materials, (2) official statistics of sexual offences, and (3) clinical experience. The result of this sort of evidence has been an increasing tendency for juries to acquit in pornography cases.

The findings of the *U.S. Commission on Obscenity and Pornography* (1970) were our major source of scientific knowledge about the effects of exposure to pornography throughout most of the 1970s. The establishment of the Commission was an attempt to examine the problem of pornography from many perspectives before making recommendations to the Congress and the President. In particular, the Commission was requested to determine whether viewing sexual materials is harmful to the public, and to study its relationship to crime and other antisocial behaviour. The information obtained to answer the questions posed by the Congress was incomplete and imperfect, yet it was a vast improvement over what was available before the Commission began its work. Importantly, most of the research information pointed in the same direction. This information, however, was insufficient to permit a unanimous report, although a majority of the commissioners voted to recommend that all federal, state, and local legislation prohibiting the sale, exhibition and distribution of sexual materials to consenting adults be repealed, based upon considerable research evidence showing that exposure of adults to erotic materials offers no clear and present danger. Pornography may be vulgar, distasteful, irritating, and wasteful, but it did not appear to be a significant evil. Moreover, there was no evidence to support the thesis that there is a meaningful causal relationship between exposure to erotica and immediate or delayed antisocial behaviour among adults. In fact, there was some evidence to suggest just the opposite – that exposure to sexually explicit material leads to a reduction in callous attitudes to sex, an improvement in relationships within marriage, a reduction in sex guilt and an increase in sexual tolerance. By the late 1970s, however, criticisms of the Commission's findings (e.g. Eysenck and Nias, 1978) led several investigators to re-examine the issue. This research has indicated that exposure to *violent pornography* can lead to an increase in aggressive behaviour, especially toward women (cf. Donnerstein, 1982; Donnerstein and Berkowitz, 1981; Malamuth and Donnerstein, 1982).* By and large, however, these investigations have tended to confirm the Commission's majority view regarding the effects of exposure to *non-aggressive sexual material*; indeed, one major criticism of this early work rests upon the fact that the studies relied almost exclusively upon presentations of non-aggressive sexual themes to the exclusion of aggressive and deviant portrayals of sexual relationships.

Another source of defence evidence which has been found to be acceptable and convincing to jurors relies upon criminal statistics of sexual offences. Studies in this area suggest a lack of correlation between the availability of erotica and sex crime, although it is very difficult if not impossible to draw a causal link between these two general social phenomena. The causes of

* See Nelson, this volume.

antisocial sexual acts are usually complex and multiple; it is simplistic to blame pornography for these, and easy, though quite mistaken, to infer causality from an association between the two. Kutchinsky (1978) argues that if the sex crime rate decreases or stays the same when the availability of sexually explicit materials increases, as happened in Denmark in the late 1960s and early 1970s, it is unreasonable to suggest that pornography encourages sex crimes. In general, although there are a number of unanswered questions about the Danish experience (e.g. Bachy, 1976; Cline, 1974), the concern that pornography − pure erotica without any violence added to it, as we have little knowledge about the effects of violent pornography on sexual crimes − induces people to commit sex crimes seems unfounded as statistics suggest that they are unrelated.

The third source of evidence comes from both clinical research and experience. Over the past few years there has been a great deal of research into the therapeutic uses of sexually explicit materials, especially in the treatment of sexual dysfunctions (education, desensitization, and stimulation therapy), and in the treatment of sexual deviations (assessment, aversion therapy, and reconditioning therapy).* Kaplan (1974), for example, describes the involvement of sexually explicit material and fantasy to enhance sexual arousal, and to stop patients from worrying about their sexual performance in the treatment of various sexual dysfunctions; patients with sexual desire problems also seem to respond well to the use of erotic material during therapy programmes, although its precise contribution has yet to be evaluated formally (Yaffé, 1980). Many of the clinical psychologists who have appeared as expert witnesses have reported on the basis of such information, and on their own observations regarding the beneficial effects which such material has had on their patients (and the spouses). Of course, not everyone benefits from exposure to sexually explicit materials as Björksten (1976) points out; there are definite indications and contra-indications regarding the therapeutic use of such material.

An alternative way of presenting defence evidence involves giving testimony on the benefits to the public that may result from exposure to sexually explicit materials. Of course, to cover in any detail the evidence offered by psychologists in defence of pornography would need a book in itself; some experts have been in the witness box for no less than three days presenting and discussing this evidence. This is *not* to say, however, that psychologists have given pornography carte blanche. They have not. The following, however, is intended only to provide a brief overview of the type of psychological evidence presented under the "public good" defence.

Sexually explicit materials have been shown to be of great individual

* See Yaffé, this volume.

benefit due to their ability to impart sexual knowledge. Sexual ignorance is definitely not bliss. But it is definitely prevalent, even in our permissive society today. The World Health Organisation (1976), in one of their publications on human sexuality, stated that "every person has the right to sexual information and to consider accepting sexual relationships for pleasure". The need to accept sexuality as a positive component of health has been stressed by medical and psychological experts for many years, yet narrow sexual attitudes and beliefs may keep many people ignorant about their own sexuality. Unfortunately, sexual ignorance and misinformation tend to foster sexual inadequacy and anxiety. A number of people who consult therapists for the treatment of frigidity or impotence suffer only from misinformation. For example, it is extremely common to find women who consider themselves frigid because they can only reach orgasm manually. Bandura and Walters (1963) point out that many people are uncertain and uninformed about sexual matters because of the traditional inhibitory sex training they receive; this is primarily due to the transmission to children of parental anxiety reactions to the exploratory, manipulative and curiosity behaviour of children in regard to their own sexuality. Dealing with these sex-negative attitudes and values is, of course, the most difficult part of good sex education. Yet even here we find that sexual information, despite the efforts of many enlightened educators, remains confusing and contradictory at times. Hill and Lloyd-Jones (1970), for example, studied a total of 42 different sex education books and found them to be "generally inaccurate, misleading, and in some cases deliberately deceitful". Is it any wonder, then, that even in this supposedly enlightened era, clinicians' caseloads are full with sexually dysfunctional individuals. As Fromme (1966) points out, "although sex is here to stay, there are many people and many forces attempting to drive it underground. In addition to legal censorship, we have religious bans and, probably most pervasive of all, just plain common prudishness." The use of sexually explicit materials openly challenges the sex-negative attitudes and values of our society by providing a platform on which to discuss sex more freely and a perspective with respect to various sexual practices. The fact that a book or magazine is not specifically intended to serve as a sex education manual does not in itself destroy its educational potential (Fader and McNeil, 1966). Unfortunately, those who oppose the availability of sexually explicit materials are also opposed to sex education, despite the lack of evidence to indicate that the latter promotes promiscuity or other undesirable consequences (Kilmann *et al.*, 1981). To date, the issues of whether, when, and how information about sex should be communicated have not been satisfactorily resolved because the benefits of sex education to the public at large are still questioned by people who believe that it fosters sexual curiosity and acting-out. Forensic psychologists have tried to put this controversial issue into some perspective for the courts by showing how sexually explicit materials are of some benefit to both the individual and society, particularly in terms of health.

Limitations upon Psychological Testimony

The result of this type of psychological evidence, as pointed out earlier, has been an increasing tendency of juries to acquit in these cases. In turn, this has led the police to rely more frequently upon forfeiture and destruction orders which prevent the owner of the books from obtaining trial by jury, and so increase the probability of conviction in magistrates courts. The probability of an article being found obscene by the class of people from whom magistrates are drawn is extremely high. As Sir Norwood East (1955) remarked: "Bias is almost inevitable if conduct is viewed solely in the light of narrow personal experience and the distastes of . . . sexually anaesthetic men and women incompetent to pass judgement upon the inter-relationship of the sexes." If the police can confine obscenity cases to the magistrates courts they can, therefore, be reasonably sure of a high conviction rate. Two subsequent decisions, both designed to undermine the defence case, have changed the way in which psychological evidence is handled in court.

The first change occurred at Maidenhead Court in late 1974. Until then, obscenity cases had followed the tradition of criminal court practice, hearing first the case for the prosecution, including the prosecution witnesses, and then similarly the case for the defence, hearing the defence experts. This method not only conformed to normal practice, it also enabled the magistrates to reach a decision on the basis of *all* the evidence available. In the Maidenhead case, however, the prosecutor devised a new way to hedge his bets, by separating the hearing into two parts. First, the justices would consider whether or not the books were obscene. If they decided they were, then they would hear the defence experts on the common good. On the face of it the argument has a certain plausibility, and was certainly put forcibly by the prosecutor. Why waste the court time, the argument runs, by hearing a succession of expert witnesses, when the material before the court may not be judged obscene in the first place? The argument would have greater strength if the acquittal rate in such courts offered reasonable expectations of this occurring. Unfortunately, such an event seemed, at best, a remote possibility. What has become known as the *Maidenhead Rule* puts the defence under two disadvantages psychologically. In the first place, it effectively prevents the court from hearing relevant information about sexual behaviour outside the experience of the magistrates. This means that there is no opportunity for their natural distaste for this type of sexual material to be modified by scientific evidence. Secondly, as numerous social psychological studies have shown, once explicit and public commitment has been made to a point of view, it becomes highly resistent to any argument to the contrary. By using this separated judgement on the matters in hand, the justices are unwittingly augmenting their pre-existing bias, and the probability of an acquittal becomes further reduced. It also affects the way the forensic psychologist presents his evidence. When the case is, on the face of it at least, still an open one, the psychologist will be able to present facts impartially, knowing that the justices will be weighing the merits against the demerits. When a decision has already been made, however, and the material has already been declared obscene, the psychologist's evidence is limited to that supporting a plea of its public good. It must therefore be completely one-sided and inevitably imposes problems of selectivity upon the expert (Haward, 1975). The *Maidenhead Rule* destroyed much of the psychological advantage which the Section 4 defence provided, but it still permitted the defence to bring before the court scientific evidence and expert opinion to supplement the so-called common sense – as well as misconceptions and prejudice which otherwise are left to determine judicial decision in these cases.

The second limitation imposed upon psychological evidence in an obscenity case first occurred at the Northampton Crown Court in 1975 (*R. v. Staniforth*). In his opening address, Mr Mortimer, QC, acting for the defence, explained to the jury that he would be calling experts to testify as to the public benefit which would follow free publication of the books then before the jury. Mr Gorman, representing the Director of Public Prosecutions, asked if the jury could be cleared from court whilst he raised an objection to the defence on a matter of law. After the exodus of the 12 good men and true, Mr Gorman made his point. Psychological evidence should be excluded altogether from the trial, he claimed, on the ground that it did not refer to the *merit* of the books in the same way as merit which the law defined as artistic, literary or scientific. These latter merits were intrinsic; they were there somewhere between the covers of the book which laid claim to them. The psychological merits, in contra-distinction, were extrinsic, for they referred to the effects which the book had on the reader. A second point made by the prosecution counsel was that by attempting to show that sex books could have a beneficial effect upon the reader, psychologists were contradicting the consensus of Parliament that such books could be depraving and corrupting. In a previous case before the Court of Appeal, Lord Wilberforce had taken this view when he ruled that in dealing with obscenity, courts must do without psychological, sociological and medical evidence. In similar circumstances, Lord Denning, too, had criticized the sophistry of a psychological defence which negated the intention of Parliament.

Mr Mortimer, in reply, refuted the validity of these two arguments. He maintained that the distinction between intrinsic and extrinsic merits was a purely philosophical one and was not relevant to the Section 4 public good defence; as far as the latter was concerned, the wording of the 1959 Act clearly and explicitly provided for the calling of psychologists to give expert testimony on the merits of an allegedly obscene book which were related to *matters of general concern* . The mental and physical health of a community and its freedom from sex offenders were, he argued, matters of general concern and evidence on this subject was therefore admissible under the Act. He then referred to a long list of cases in which psychological evidence had been heard, and quoted the judgement given by the Appellate Court in the *Last Exit to Brooklyn* case (*R*. v. *Calder and Boyars Limited*, 1968), where it had been established that the book had an aversive quality which, far from inciting the reader to wallow in homosexuality and drug-taking, was more likely to put him off these practices (cf. Offenbach, this volume).

By now it was dusk, and the jury, who had spent the whole day waiting outside, were getting restive. Judge McGregor, who was trying his first obscenity case, finally decided to reach a decision. Using metaphors drawn from accountancy, he talked about debits and credits, ledgers, and balancing the accounts. In the end he concluded that the demerits of obscenity could not be balanced against its social or psychological merits. Either a book depraved and corrupted, or it did not. It could not both deprave, corrupt and be for the public good at the same time. Judge McGregor said there were no precedents in case law for judgements of this kind, and he would therefore accept Mr Gorman's submission and rule that the expert evidence which the defence wished to present was inadmissible. Judge McGregor clearly thought the two things were incompatible, but there are numerous examples in medicine of things which are both beneficial and detrimental at the same time. The common aspirin, the most widely ingested medication in the Western World, has side-effects which are sometimes dangerous and even fatal. While sexual standards and sexual morality are matters for society itself to decide, the psychologist can materially assist the development of more rational attitudes, both in public and in court, by making explicit the nature of sexuality, and by interpreting the growing – but still inadequate – accumulation of experimental and clinical evidence (Haward, 1975).

The case went to the Court of Appeal, where in early 1976 the Appellate Judges found in favour of the Crown Court verdict by ruling that juries should apply "their own good sense and not be directed from it by the irrelevant opinions of experts". The Court of Appeal refused the appellants leave to appeal to the House of Lords, but they did certify that a point of law of general public importance was involved, namely, that

whether, upon a true construction of Section 4 of the *Obscene Publications Act* 1959, expert evidence is admissible in support of a defence under that Section, to the effect that pornographic material is psychologically beneficial to persons with certain sexual tendencies in that it relieves their sexual tensions and may divert them from anti-social activities.

The Appeal Committee of the House of Lords overruled the Court of Appeal's refusal and gave leave to appeal. Unfortunately, however, in late 1976 the House of Lords upheld the ruling of the lower Appellate Court. Not only did this mean that psychologists could no longer be called to give scientific or clinical evidence regarding the effects of exposure to sexually explicit materials, but neither could they give evidence upon the fact that there is no measurable relationship between the availability of this material and sexual offences. We now have, in essence, a law which is based primarily upon sexual prejudice, and one which prevents any empirical evidence relevant to such prejudice from being taken into account. The House of Lords ruling does not, however, exclude psychologists as expert witnesses from court; what it does in particular is to exclude that part of their evidence which refers to the therapeutic merits of an allegedly obscene article. There is still considerable scope for their evidence relevant to the other merits explicitly included under the Section 4 defence. There is therefore no reason why any book possessing artistic, literary or scientific merit should be forfeited for the want of sound psychological evidence of such merits. What remains surprising is the view of the Appellate Judges that any tendency which a book may possess to deprave and corrupt its readers is acceptable if at the same time the book has some *intrinsic* merit, whereas the therapeutic value which would tend to nullify any depraving and corrupting effect must not be taken into account. One could be forgiven for assuming from this that the preservation of parliamentarians' preconceptions is more important than the psychosexual health of the community. In practice, it means that the better class of erotic publications will be able to defend themselves whilst lesser publications will now have to go undefended, and most people will feel that this is not an unacceptable compromise.

In marked contrast to the *Obscene Publications Act*, one might look at the law's antipodean twin, the *Indecent Publications Act* of New Zealand. Here the government's approach to pornography is balanced and well-defined: *Indecent* includes describing, depicting, expressing or otherwise dealing with matters of sex, horror, crime, cruelty or violence in a manner that is injurious to the public good. In this context sex is given its rightful and non-dominant place among various factors that can be detrimental to society. The court is specifically authorized by the Act to take into consideration the medical and social character or importance of the book, and to determine whether any person is likely to be corrupted by reading the book or whether other persons are likely to benefit therefrom. This Act also recognizes the authors' or publishers' motives in producing the book, reflecting an awareness of the three types of explicit sexual material described earlier; for example, "the court shall take into consideration whether the book displays an honest purpose or honest thread of thought or whether its content is merely camouflage designed to render acceptable any indecent parts of the book". Clearly there will be marginal cases which will cause difficulty to courts and experts alike, but most readers, no less than the forensic experts, will have no difficulty in distinguishing the works of sex educators and authors of merit from those of the gutter press. In England we have a long way to go before we catch up with the enlightened standards and logic of our former colonial cousins. Our present obscenity laws are unjust in that no artist, writer, publisher, or bookseller can decide in advance whether or not he is committing a crime. It is comparable to having a law prohibiting speeding on the highway, but which gives no speed limits for reference, relying instead on only what a prejudiced pedestrian regards as too fast. Worse, it prevents potential offenders from gauging what is, or is not, obscene from case law or from common practice, for books which are sold freely in one country may be seized and forfeited in another, and a publication which is acquitted by the magistrates in one town may be convicted a few miles away.

Well known to an older generation of psychologists, Dr Hastings Rashdall was one of those academicians whose intellectual brilliance was somewhat divorced from the mundane trivia of everyday life. He could ride a bicycle, but could not understand it. On one occasion, a colleague passing by noted that although he appeared to have a puncture in his front tyre, he was vigorously pumping up the rear one. When this was pointed out to him, he exclaimed in some surprise "What! Do they not communicate?" For many decades, law and psychology were like the wheels of Dr Rashdall's bicycle, always pursuing the same course together, but rotating quite independently on their own axes. And certainly not communicating (Haward, 1981). Unfortunately, this is still the case today as far as obscenity is concerned. This is perhaps surprising considering the fact that human behaviour is the *raison d'être* for both law and psychology. Fortunately, their communication is very good indeed in many other ways. Maybe one day soon they will get it right in regard to obscenity and pornography.

References

Alschuler, M. Origins of the law of obscenity. In *Technical Report of the Commission on Obscenity and Pornography*, Vol. 2. Washington, D.C.: U.S. Government Printing Office, 1971.

Bachy, V. Danish "permissiveness" revisited. *Journal of Communication*, 1976, **26**, 40–43.

Bandura, A. and Walters, R. H. *Social Learning and Personality Development*. New York: Holt, 1963.

Björksten, O. J. W. Sexually graphic material in the treatment of sexual disorders. In J. K. Meyer (Ed.) *Clinical Management of Sexual Disorders* Baltimore: Williams and Wilkins, 1976.

Box, M. *Trial of Marie Stopes*. London: Femina, 1967.

Cline, V. B. *Where Do You Draw the Line? An Exploration into Media Violence, Pornography, and Censorship*. Provo, Utah: Brigham Young University Press, 1974.

Donnerstein, E. Pornography and violence: Current research findings. In R. Geen and E. Donnerstein (Eds). *Aggression: Theoretical and Empirical Reviews*. New York and London: Academic Press, 1982.

Donnerstein, E., and Berkowitz, L. Victim reactions in aggressive erotic films as a factor in violence against women. *Journal of Personality and Social Psychology*, 1981, **41**, 710–724.

East, Sir Norwood. *Sexual Offenders*. London: De Lisle, 1955.

Eysenck, H. J. and Nias, D. K. B. *Sex, Violence and the Media*. London: Maurice Temple Smith, 1978.

Fader, R. and McNeil, B. *Hooked on Books*. New York: Berkeley Medallion, 1966.

Fromme, A. *Understanding the Sexual Response in Humans*. New York: Pocket Books, 1966.

Haward, L. R. C. Admissibility of psychological evidence in obscenity cases. *Bulletin of the British Psychological Society*, 1975, **28**, 466–469.

Haward, L. R. C. *Forensic Psychology*. London: Batsford Academic and Educational Ltd., 1981.

Hill, M. and Lloyd-Jones, M. *Sex Education: The Erroneous Zone*. London: National Scenter Society, 1970.

Hyde, H. M. *History of Pornography*. London: Heinemann, 1964.

Kaplan, H. S. *The New Sex Therapy*. New York: Bruner/Mazel, 1974.

Kilmann, P. R., Wanlass, R. L., Sabalis, R. F. and Sullivan, B. Sex education: A review of its effects. *Archives of Sexual Behaviour*, 1981, **10**, 177–205.

Krafft-Ebing, R. von. *Psychopathia Sexualis*. Brooklyn, New York: Physicians and Surgeons Book Co., 1928.

Kutchinsky, B. Eroticism without censorship. *International Journal of Criminology and Penology*, 1973, **1**, 217–225.

Kutchinsky, B. Pornography in Denmark: A general survey. In R. Dhavan and C. Davies (Eds). *Censorship and Obscenity*. London: Martin Robertson, 1978.

Longley, C. Walking the line between sexual plainness and prurience. London: *The Times*, 1973, 20 December.

Malamuth, N., and Donnerstein, E. The effects of aggressive-erotic stimuli. In L. Berkowitz (Ed.) *Advances in Experimental Social Psychology*, Vol. 15. New York and London: Academic Press, 1982.

Palmer, T. *Trials of Oz*. London: Blond and Briggs, 1972.

R. v. Anderson (1971) 3 All E.R. 1152.

R. v. Calder and Boyars Ltd (1968) 3 All E.R. 644.

R. v. Hicklin (1868) L.R. 3 Q.B. 360.

R. v. Penguin Books Ltd (1961) Crim. L.R. 176.

R. v. Staniforth (1975) 2 W.L.R. 849.

Robertson, G. *Obscenity: An Account of Censorship Laws and their Enforcement in England and Wales*. London: Weidenfeld and Nicolson, 1979.

Shaw v. *Director of Public Prosecutions* (1962) A.C. 220.

Sunday Times, 1974, 22 July.

U.S. National Commission on Obscenity and Pornography. In *Report of the Commission on Obscenity and Pornography*. New York: Bantam, 1970.

World Health Organisation. *Human Sexuality: Training of Health Professionals*. World Health Organisation Technical Report (No. 572). Geneva: World Health Organisation, 1976.

Yaffé, M. Commentary on current trends in sex therapy. In T. G. Tennent (Ed.). *Current Trends in Treatment in Psychiatry*. Tunbridge Wells, Kent: Pitman Medical, 1980.

9

Pornography and sexual aggression

Edward C. Nelson

Introduction

In recent years there has been an enormous increase of interest in the effects of the mass media upon social attitudes and behaviour. And, in particular, interest has focused upon the effects of media presentations of sexual and aggressive behaviour. A number of influences seem to account for this trend. One is the publication of five major reports dealing respectively with the effects of sexually explicit material or "pornography", two in this country (*Committee on Obscenity and Film Censorship*, 1979; *Longford Committee*, 1972) and one in the United States (*National Commission on Obscenity and Pornography*, 1970), and the others dealing in part or entirely with the effects of television violence in America (*National Commission on the Causes and Prevention of Violence*, 1969; *Surgeon General's Scientific Advisory Committee on Television and Social Behaviour*, 1972), the latter being especially concerned with the effects of television violence on children. A second and equally important influence has been a change in the orientation of social scientists toward the application of research in dealing with applied human issues. And a third major influence has been the arguments advanced by various writers that portrayals of sexual violence and aggression towards women in the mass media negatively affect both social attitudes and behaviour, increase sexual responsivity to sexually violent fantasies, and create an atmosphere in which acts of sexual violence against women are not only tolerated but ideologically encouraged (Brownmiller, 1975; Dworkin, 1981; Gager and Schurr, 1976; Griffin, 1981; Medea and Thompson, 1974). The purpose of this chapter is to present a summary and discussion of recent research findings regarding the effects of exposure to sexually explicit material upon sexually aggressive attitudes and behaviour. To facilitate this aim, the present chapter is structured into three sections. The first section deals with general research issues and approaches in studies designed to evaluate the effects of pornography. The second section dealing with sex and aggression examines the role of heightened arousal as a facilitator of aggressive behaviour, and focuses in depth upon recent research dealing with the effects of exposure to violent sexuality. And the third section looks at sexual materials and psychopathology, exploring the issues surrounding the viewing of sexual stimuli and sex offences, sex offenders, deviant sexual arousal, and sexual violence. The chapter concludes by examining the evidence linking sexual materials to sexual violence and aggression, and by providing an overview to this area of investigation. The aim, however, is not to discuss the issues specifically relating to censorship and obscenity, nor to examine the broader questions relating to the kind of society in which we want to live or in which we want our children to live (cf. Eysenck, 1978).

ISSUES AND APPROACHES

Problems of Definition

As will be readily evident from even a casual perusal of the scientific literature on pornography, the term has no well-defined and generally acceptable definition and different authors use it with different implications (cf. Eysenck and Nias, 1978; Yaffé, 1972). Some authors have attempted, like Rosen and Turner (1969), to relate it to the culture, though anything which a culture defines to be pornographic assumes that there is an agreed cultural definition of what is or is not pornographic. Others have attempted to delineate unrealistic situations, low percentage of non-sex detail, and absence of antierotic elements (Kronhausen and Kronhausen, 1959). In contrast to these approaches, Stoller (1976a) has recently concluded that no depiction is pornographic until an observer's fantasies are added; nothing is pornographic *per se*. He believes that pornography is essentially a "daydream in which activities, usually but not necessarily overtly sexual, are projected into written, pictorial, or aural material to induce genital excitement in an observer" (p. 63). This definition clearly attempts to account for the tremendous individual differences in labelling anything as pornographic, and also avoids all the usual pitfalls involved in attempting to maintain the term's purely descriptive meaning – defined simply as depictions of sexual behaviour.

The word pornography derives from the Greek *pornographos* and means the depiction of prostitutes, describing the life, manners, and customs of harlots and their patrons. Today the term is used more generally to mean "the expression or suggestion of obscene or unchaste subjects in literature or art" (*Oxford English Dictionary*), which means that the terms pornography and obscene are partially linked by definition; some writers argue that some pornography is obscene but not all, whereas others tend to view anything pornographic as being obscene. Moreover, the definition of pornography tends to vary considerably depending upon the purpose of those who write about it; thus, pornography has been characterized as a liberating and healthful influence and as violence against women. For example, Griffin (1981) states that "for whether or not pornography causes sadistic acts to be performed against women, above all pornography is in itself a sadistic act. . . . The actual images of pornography degrade women. This degradation is the essential experience of pornography" (p. 111). Similarly, Dworkin (1981) indicates that the

> word pornography does not mean 'writing about sex' or 'depictions of the erotic' or 'depictions of sexual acts' or 'depictions of nude bodies' or 'sexual representations' or any other such euphemism. It means the graphic depiction of women as vile whores. . . . The fact that pornography is widely believed to be 'depictions of the erotic' means only that the debasing of women is held to be the real pleasure of sex (pp. 200–201).

For these and many other feminist writers the real question is not: Does pornography cause violent, or aggressive behaviour against women? These writers believe that pornography *is* violence against women, violence which pervades every aspect of our culture and distorts women's sexual integrity.

Unfortunately, the term pornography remains an evaluative one which is often used pejoratively, and the value of such definitions in scientific research remains unclear. Interestingly, Byrne *et al.* (1974) have shown that affect is a general predictor of evaluative responses to erotica and that judgements of the pornographic quality of erotic stimuli are made simply on the basis of how such stimuli make one feel. Presumably the affect an individual experiences when exposed to sexual material is the end product of affect-eliciting rewards and punishments that were associated with sexual matters during the socialization process. The authors believe that it is this previously conditioned positive or negative affect that becomes paired with the otherwise neutral pictures and words presented in the laboratory and that mediates evaluations of those words and pictures (cf. Martin and Levey, 1978). These findings are certainly consistent with available research that indicates age, gender, individual sexual preferences, sexual experience, and educational level are important determinants of affective responses to sexual stimuli; moreover, Zajonc (1968) has shown that merely increasing the frequency of exposure to a stimulus produces a more favourable attitude toward and evaluation of that stimulus which suggests that judgements about what is pornographic can be altered by repeated presentations of the same sexual theme. However, the hypothesis that increasing exposure results in greater positivity has generally been supported in studies that used stimuli for which the subjects did not have well-developed cognitive schemas; that is, stimuli that were relatively novel and affectively neutral (see Harrison, 1977, for a review). Therefore, more germane is what happens with stimuli for which individuals are assumed to have well-developed schemas. Under these conditions, when stimuli are not initially neutral, polarization of attitudes has generally been found to occur with increased exposure. Thus, initially disliked stimuli tend to become even more disliked with greater exposure whereas such exposure produces more positive and favourable attitudes toward stimuli that are initially pleasing. It follows that individuals holding well-developed cognitive schemas toward pornographic stimuli will be divided into two camps, pro- and anti-pornography, and that increased exposure to such stimuli will only further polarize attitudes toward such material; similarly, giving an individual time to think about the issues surrounding pornography on which groups polarize will tend to result in the individual's attitude also polarizing (cf. Lord *et al.*, 1979; Myers and Lamm, 1976).

Social scientists have long recognized the issues existing between the pro- and anti-pornography camps and acknowledge the problems inherently involved in labelling anything as pornographic. For example, Eysenck and Nias (1978) have recently attempted to restrict the term to sexually aggressive stimuli which involve harm, such as those involved in depictions of rape, and to use the term erotic to define non-aggressive sexual stimuli such as depicted in common sexual activities like petting, intercourse, and oral-genital behaviour; this terminology has yet to be adopted and probably never will be in research situations due to methodological imprecision. Research has, however, shown this to be a valid distinction, one that strongly suggests that the effects of exposure to non-aggressive sexual material should be considered separately from the effects of viewing violent sexuality. Eysenck and Nias clearly embrace this contextual separation in describing the former as pro-love, pro-sex, and pro-women – depictions which capture the mutuality of consent and enjoyment in sexual relationships – and the latter as pro-force and violence, anti-women, and anti-love. Unfortunately, although it seems unlikely that any definition of pornography will survive to serve a useful function in scientific research, the term seems destined to remain popular in the media and even among many social scientists.

Research Approaches

Much social concern about explicit sexual materials stems from the fear that people, especially children and adolescents, will be adversely affected by exposure to it; as a result, such concerns give rise to the need to examine the effects of both long- and short-term exposure to these stimuli because of the possible influence they may exert on an individual's sexual identity, attitudes, values, and behaviours. A parallel concern is that exposure to sexual stimuli, especially aggressive or deviant portrayals, may contribute to a breakdown of normal inhibiting mechanisms and result in uncontrolled or deviant sexual arousal and behaviour, or the development of antisocial attitudes and behaviours. Thus, in an attempt to provide some answers to these extremely broad social concerns, the American Congress established an advisory Commission and requested it to determine whether viewing sexual materials is harmful to the public, and particularly to minors, and to study its relationship to crime and other antisocial behaviour. Today the final report of the *U.S. Commission on Obscenity and Pornography* (1970), along with the many technical volumes of research and documentation published later, constitutes much of our early knowledge about the effects of viewing sexual materials, even though the conclusions sometimes go beyond the evidence (cf. Cline, 1974; Eysenck and Nias, 1978; Yaffé, 1972, 1979). In attempting to translate social and moral concern into scientific evidence that could support or refute the hypothesized causal relationship between viewing explicit sexual material and harmful social behaviours, the Commission began by formulating specific research questions and selecting research strategies to investigate them. For example, does exposure to sexual material sexually arouse the viewer and, if so, what are the effects of being stimulated by such material; that is, does such exposure affect subsequent conduct, emotions, attitudes, opinions, and values of the viewer, and who experiences these effects – adults, children, or both – and do disturbed individuals respond to such exposure in the same way as do relatively well-adjusted individuals? These questions seem simple enough until one realizes that one is speaking about measuring the effects of many sexual depictions that differ in many respects and that the individuals who view these stimuli also vary significantly. Therefore, hoping to answer some of these questions satisfactorily, the Commission relied upon three methodological approaches in the hope that these alternative strategies would complement and supplement one another; the research methods consisted of surveys employing various sampling procedures, retrospective personal history studies involving matched comparison groups (e.g. sex offenders *vs* non-sex offenders), and experimental studies using self-report, physiological, or biochemical measures of change in response to viewing sexually explicit materials.

All research approaches are, of course, susceptible to certain limitations. Interview and questionnaire data, for example, may be affected by faulty recall or by dissimulation, particularly since the behaviour being reported is so personal; other limitations include unwillingness to cooperate, or over-willingness to comply on the part of the subject, and the fact that findings cannot always be generalized to other populations. As far as experimental studies are concerned they too face limitations in that the subjects are self-selected volunteers, which restricts generalization especially where relevant variables like amount of sexual experience and extent of previous exposure to sexual materials have not been controlled.

Volunteer Problems

The issue of volunteer bias in sexual research is one area of major concern to behavioural investigators. While volunteer bias remains a general research problem (cf. Rosenthal and Rosnow, 1975), studies of human sexuality in particular are thought to attract volunteers who are different from people who choose not to volunteer; thus, it is not surprising that increasing attention has been paid to this problem in recent years. The initial impetus for this research stems from early detractors of Kinsey's work who argued that volunteers for sex research constitute a small, atypically permissive group, and that use of such subjects tends to inflate the percentage of unconventional or disapproved sexual behaviour being reported. Barker and Perlman (1975) examined this issue of volunteer bias in sex surveys and found that volunteers for questionnaire or interview studies of human sexuality do not differ from non-volunteers or volunteers for other topics of research in terms of general personality measures; similarly, Johnson and DeLamater (1976) found that volunteers are not different from non-volunteers in terms of socio-economic characteristics. Thus, it appears that volunteer bias is a non-significant factor when anonymous questionnaires are being used to study sexual behaviour in college populations.

Recently, however, Higginbotham and Farkas (1977) have reported on the trend away from studying sexual behaviour by means of self-report surveys. In response Farkas et al. (1978) attempted to assess volunteer bias in experimental studies, for which the subjects are thought to be considerably different from those who decline to volunteer for such studies. Their investigation of 108 males between the ages of 18 and 61 (mean 25) yielded no evidence to support the contention that volunteers for laboratory experiences are more maladjusted than non-volunteers as assessed by general personality measures, including the PEN Inventory (Eysenck and Eysenck, 1968) and the Marlow-Crowne Social Desirability Scale (Crowne and Marlowe, 1960). Volunteers were found to have less sex-guilt, but no other index of psychological functioning showed a significant difference. However, volunteers were significantly older, more sexually experienced, and considerably less anxious about sex than those who declined to participate. The authors conclude that future research in human sexuality conducted in laboratory settings should impose strict limits on the generalization of research findings. Interestingly, further research on this issue by Kenrick *et al.* (1980) suggests that there may well be a strong inverse relationship between the tendency to respond with negative affect to sexual stimuli and the likelihood of volunteering for an experimental study involving sexual materials, especially among females. This data is consistent with findings that indicate evaluative responses, including approach and avoidance behaviour, vary with the magnitude of positive and negative affect conditioned to stimuli (Byrne *et al.*, 1974; Martin and Levey, 1978). In another study designed in part to clarify the volunteer issue Zuckerman *et al.* (1976) found that three times as many males as females among single college students would definitely volunteer for an experiment in which they would rate their reactions to an erotic film; moreover, significantly more married than single females reported an interest in seeing sexual films, although there were no differences in the incidence of married and single males with such interest. The investigators concluded that permissive attitudes and greater sexual experience are predictive of greater interest in seeing erotic films among single college females. Zuckerman (1976) points out that volunteers to view erotica can be generally characterized as uninhibited, experience seekers and risk takers, and suggests that "rather than sexual needs driving college students to pornographic material, the students want to go for the experience itself which is somewhat out of the ordinary and mildly socially taboo" (p. 156).

Measures of Sexual Arousal

Research studies in human sexuality have tended to rely on self-report measures for a long time. The fact that researchers continue to use these measures emphasizes the fact that self-report is behaviour, and is therefore just as important as the direct observation of physiological arousal (Barlow, 1977). However, one reason for the increasing reliance upon psychophysiological measures of sexual arousal is the basic assumption that they are less amenable to distortion than verbal behaviour, especially since sexual research is such a sensitive area of investigation and subjects may be more inclined to fake responses (cf. e.g. Farkas, 1978; Geer, 1976; Rosen and Kopel, 1978), particularly if well motivated (Laws and Holmen, 1978). Thus it is not surprising that researchers studying basic and applied problems in

human sexuality have repeatedly attempted to develop quantifiable physiological measures of sexual arousal. In the 1960s several useful instruments for
assessing male sexual arousal by direct penile measurement were introduced
as measurement of erection appears to be the only psychophysiological
method which reliably discriminates sexual arousal from other emotional
states (Bancroft and Mathews, 1971; Zuckerman, 1971), especially during
lower levels of sexual arousal. Most researchers now use either a plethysmograph for measuring penile volume or a mercury-in-rubber strain gauge for
measuring penile circumference, depending on the nature of the study (Abel
and Blanchard, 1976; Farkas *et al.*, 1979; Rosen and Keefe, 1978). Most
importantly, the objective measurement of female sexual arousal has finally
become a reality through the recent development of the vaginal photoplethysmograph (Geer *et al.*, 1974; Hatch, 1979). Unfortunately direct comparison of penile and vaginal responses is not possible and the search continues for objective non-genital measures that will allow indirect comparison
of sex differences during sexual arousal.

Research on Sexual Arousal to Aggressive–Erotic Themes

Experimental studies conducted by the *U.S. Commission on Obscenity and
Pornography* (1970) show that exposure to sexually explicit stimuli produces
arousal in substantial numbers of both males and females, and that this
arousal is dependent on both stimulus and viewer characteristics. For
example, persons who are college educated, religiously inactive, sexually
experienced and younger are more likely to report arousal to sexual depictions. Moreover, portrayals of conventional sexual behaviour are generally
regarded as more stimulating than depictions of less conventional activity;
thus, heterosexual themes tend to elicit more arousal than depictions of
homosexual activity among heterosexually-oriented subjects; similarly,
petting and coitus themes elicit greater arousal than oral-genital sexuality,
which in turn elicits more than aggressive sado-masochistic themes. In fact, in
a recent summary of the literature on the effects of exposure to various sexual
themes, Baron and Byrne (1977) concluded that sexual acts involving aggression and violence are among the least arousing sexual depictions for males
and females. Recent work by Abel *et al.* (1977a) tends to support these
findings. For example, they report clear physiological differences between the
sexual responsiveness of rapists and non-rapists to portrayals of sexual
aggression; the rapists showed high levels of sexual arousal to audio-taped
portrayals of both rape and mutually-consenting sexual acts, whereas the

non-rapist comparison group showed considerable sexual arousal to the mutually-consenting acts only.

Unfortunately, the results of the various studies that report low sexual arousal in normals to sexual aggression are clearly at variance with the results of Schmidt (1975). He reports on research which indicates that films which do not describe sexual aggression as a deviant or strange ritual (as most sado-masochistic films do) can "induce strong sexual arousal in both men and women". Schmidt concludes that strong aggression in films with sexual content (such as rape) does not inhibit either men's or women's ability to react with sexual arousal. A resolution to this particular issue emerges in the work of Malamuth et al. (1977) in their analysis of the relationship between sexual arousal and aggression. They argue that certain elements within rape portrayals may serve to either disinhibit or inhibit sexual responsiveness; the latter might include emphasis on the victim's suffering or the social inappropriateness of the act, whereas the former could depict the rape victim as experiencing sexual arousal. Barbaree et al. (1979) lend support to the idea that the differences between the sexual arousal of rapists and non-rapists are inhibitory elements in rape portrayals that "turn off" arousal in non-rapists.

Briddell et al. (1978) have recently found evidence that supports the Malamuth et al. (1977) inhibition–disinhibition analysis. They discovered that college males who were led to believe that they had consumed alcohol, irrespective of whether they actually had, responded with as much sexual arousal to an audio-tape description of rape as to mutually-desired intercourse. Conversely, subjects who were led to believe that they had not ingested alcohol, irrespective of whether they actually had, revealed sexual arousal differences between rape and mutually desired intercourse that were similar to those reported by Abel et al. (1977a), namely, arousal only to the mutually consenting version. Furthermore, alcohol did not significantly influence levels of sexual arousal. The findings indicate that the subjects' cognitive set regarding the nature of beverage, not its actual content, significantly influenced sexual arousal; the data also show that disinhibiting subjects via a change in their cognitive set results in their becoming sexually aroused to rape depictions that would normally inhibit such arousal.

Malamuth and his colleagues have reported on a number of studies designed to assess sexual arousal in response to portrayals of sexual violence and aggression (Malamuth, 1981; Malamuth and Check, 1980a, b; Malamuth et al., 1980a, b). Experiments were conducted to identify the specific factors in portrayals of sexual violence that inhibit or disinhibit the sexual responsiveness of male and female college students. Whereas the results showed that normals are less sexually aroused by depictions of sexual assault than by themes of mutually-consenting sex, portraying the rape victim as experiencing an involuntary orgasm disinhibited subjects' sexual arousal and resulted in levels of responsiveness comparable to those elicited by themes of mutually-consenting sex (Malamuth *et al.*, 1980b). The authors suggested several possible reasons for their subjects' higher levels of sexual arousal to the involuntary orgasm theme: (1) subjects may re-interpret the events preceding the victim's orgasm so that the assault is no longer seen as coercive; (2) subjects identifying with the woman may respond with greater arousal if she is aroused; (3) the victim's orgasm may serve to justify the assault in the reader's mind and thus minimize guilt feelings; or (4) the perceived power of the rapist to force an orgasm from an unwilling woman may be stimulating to individuals with macho ideals and attitudes. Since female subjects reported higher levels of sexual arousal when the woman victim was portrayed as experiencing no pain and an orgasm, the authors felt that identification with the victim would explain the arousal effect. For males, the possibility of confusion between pain and pleasure cues exists since they reported higher arousal when the victim experienced an orgasm and pain, a finding, however, not inconsistent with the power explanation.

A study designed to replicate and extend the above findings was reported by Malamuth and Check (1980b). This study involved male subjects only and utilized direct genital measures of physiological arousal as well as self-report measures. The rape theme portraying the victim as involuntarily becoming sexually aroused was found to be significantly more exciting to subjects in comparison to a rape theme emphasizing the victim's abhorrence. Inter-estingly, those subjects pre-exposed to the rape-abhorrence theme were sub-sequently inhibited in their sexual arousal to a rape-criterion story not involving arousal. The authors believe that this inhibition effect may be considered the equivalent of an educational inoculation in that exposure to a theme stressing the true horror of a rape victim's experience lessened subjects' excitement to a subsequent rape portrayal. A serious attempt to demonstrate an "enhancement" effect of pre-exposure to rape-arousal depictions upon the rape-criterion depiction was not successful. These findings are consistent with the data of Barbaree *et al.* (1979) which suggests that the sexual arousal of normals may be particularly sensitive to inhibitory cues.

Short-term Exposure to Non-aggressive Themes

Although research provides ample evidence that brief exposure to both aggressive and non-aggressive sexual themes can sexually arouse viewers to a considerable degree, what are the effects of being stimulated by such material? The bulk of early experimental work was conducted by the U.S. Commission, but while these studies generated some very valuable data they were also limited by relying almost exclusively upon presentations of non-aggressive themes to the general exclusion of aggressive and deviant portrayals of sexual relationships (Cline, 1974; Dienstbier, 1977; Eysenck and Nias, 1978; Malamuth et al., 1980a), partially because the prevalence of such themes is a relatively recent phenomenon (Malamuth and Spinner, 1980; Smith, 1976). The Commission did sponsor some research that included sado-masochistic depictions (Mann et al., 1971), but they were not representative of the type of aggressive themes found in contemporary portrayals of violent sexuality. The Commission's experimental work was also limited in that it depended upon college students, that highly educated population which forms such a large part of the subject volunteers for studies in human sexuality. With these considerations in mind, what did the Commission's research tell us about the effects of short-term exposure to non-aggressive sexual depictions?

Brief exposure to these stimuli temporarily increases general sexual arousal in both males and females, and raises the likelihood that already well-established sexual behaviours will be engaged in within the next two days, either alone or with the usual partner; thus, brief exposure seems to raise drive levels but does not change habits. Most interesting of all is that the majority of people report no change in sexual behaviour; it appears that most people's sexual identity and patterns of sexual behaviour are relatively stable and well-established by early adulthood and are therefore not substantially altered by brief exposure to sexual stimuli. Similarly, such exposure appears to have little effect on already established attitudes regarding sexuality or sexual morality. Not surprisingly, Abelson et al. (1971) showed that younger, better educated, and less religious persons tended to have many more sexually liberal views; similarly, Schmidt et al. (1969) found evidence that sexually permissive, politically liberal, and less religious persons are less critical and rejecting of and have had greater experience with sexual materials. Brief exposure to sexual stimuli also produces mild and transient emotional responses in most viewers which appear again to be determined mainly by established response dispositions; responses vary depending upon the expectations of the viewer, his or her personality, and the type of sexual theme presented. Schmidt and Sigusch (1970) reported their subjects experienced a variety of positive and/or negative affective responses, and diffuse emotional activations such as feelings of inner agitation and restlessness, while Mosher (1971) found that persons who are unfamiliar with erotic materials may experience feelings of guilt. Interestingly, exposure to erotica also seems to increase conversation about sex in both young and middle-aged adults and, in fact, increased openness in discussing sex was claimed as a major benefit by a large percentage of the married couples who participated in the research – couples reported more agreeable and enhanced marital communication, and a willingness to discuss sexual matters with each other following exposure.

Long-term Exposure

More important than the effects of brief exposure to sexually explicit stimuli are the effects of long-term exposure. In the only Commission study which looked specifically at this question, Reifler *et al.* (1971) exposed 23 male university students to a variety of sexual material for 90 min a day, five days a week, for three weeks. The authors compared the subjects' penile responses and urinary acid phosphatase excretion (a generalized measure of sexual arousal) to sexual films before and after the three week exposure period with those of a control group of nine subjects who saw only the two control sex films. After 15 days the experimental group showed less interest in sexual material as measured by time spent viewing such material, decreased penile response to the control films, and reported loss of interest in viewing more erotica. The authors noted that the introduction of novel sex stimuli partially rejuvenated satiated interest, but only briefly; however, there was a partial recovery of interest after two months of non-exposure. Generalizations from this study were limited by the age and educational level of subjects used and it is unfortunate that there were no unstable or less educated individuals included since such people are thought to be more likely to experience negative effects from viewing sexual depictions.

The importance of this research stems from the fact that it was the only attempt to evaluate the effects of long-term exposure to sexual material; even though this provides some evidence that points to pornography as being boring and having little effect, there are many individuals and groups, for example, members of the *Longford Committee* (1972), who believe that it is harmful and that repeated exposure to such material results not in satiation and boredom but in an ever growing appetite for it. Thus it is not surprising that a number of objections have been made about the conclusions of the Reifler *et al.* investigation, some based more on ideological and moral considerations while others are based strictly on methodological concerns. For example, Bancroft (1976) has questioned the generality of the findings as regards the concentrated exposure used which *per se* might have had a satiating effect, but if stretched over a long period might not produce satiation of such magnitude. The very fact that interest in viewing sexual material showed strong signs of recovering its initial base level over time emphasizes that permanent satiation rarely occurs in real life. Cline (1970), for example, also suggests that satiation to sexual stimuli probably depends upon conditions of viewing that are not true to life; thus, he points out that the experimental conditions in the Reifler *et al.* study did not approximate a real-life situation or call for the use of viewing the materials in a setting that the subjects would have chosen for themselves. One implication of this is that viewing sexual stimuli is often followed by an increase in sexual behaviour which could reinforce subsequent response to and interest in viewing sexual material. Continual non-reinforcement and massed exposure to similar sexual stimuli would seem to be ideal conditions to foster satiation. Schaefer and Colgan (1977), for example, found a significant decrement in penile response to sexual stimuli presented repeatedly for six trials over a period of two weeks, although novel stimuli continued to elicit a response. Yet responding increased markedly in subjects exposed to the same procedure when immediate sexual reinforcement (ejaculation) followed each trial. Thus, despite the fact that the Reifler *et al.* research shows that repeated exposure to explicit sexual stimuli results in a loss of interest in it and decreased sexual responsiveness to it, this work shows that spaced exposure and reinforcement helps to maintain, if not strengthen, sexual arousal to and interest in sexual materials. Certainly studies on masturbatory conditioning would support this view (Abel and Blanchard, 1974, 1976; Kantorowitz, 1978; Laws and O'Neil, 1981). In general, studies of satiation to sexual materials in young people appear to be of questionable value when they force a level of exposure upon people that deviates significantly from what they would normally choose for themselves, levels of self-exposure that would vary according to a number of variables, such as age, personality, attitudes, and availability of other sexual stimuli. One major concern about long-term exposure to sexual materials is the fear that such exposure will change existing sexual habits and preferences but, as we have seen, the effects of long-term exposure appear to be completely determined by what happens repeatedly in the short-term. Therefore, studies that demonstrate how existing sexual habits and preferences can be changed are of greater interest because mere exposure to explicit sexual stimuli only tends to lead to an increase in sexual drive, and does not, in itself, lead to a change in habits.

Sexual Fantasies and Conditioning

That people can easily learn to become sexually aroused in response to different stimuli that have simply been associated with sexual excitement hardly seems surprising. And certainly the idea that stimuli can acquire the power to elicit sexual arousal and overt sexual behaviour is not a new one. Indeed, there is already considerable evidence that sexual arousal is amenable to the general laws of learning; as a result, the strength and patterns of sexual arousal which have an important effect on sexual preferences and habits can be changed by conditioning procedures. Interestingly, one of the distinctive aspects of human sexuality is that viewing sexual stimuli usually evokes sexual thoughts and fantasies which tend to initiate and accompany sexual excitement and can lead to actual sexual behaviour. In fact, most individuals report that they regularly utilize self-generated erotic fantasies when looking at sexual stimuli, when daydreaming, while masturbating, or during other sexual behaviours (Barclay, 1973; Crepault *et al.,* 1977; Crepault and Couture, 1980; Hariton and Singer, 1974; Hessellund, 1976; Moreault and Follingstad, 1978). Since sexual fantasies can lead to physiological arousal which, in turn, can motivate the preparation for actual sexual behaviour, Byrne (1977) has suggested the possibility that "individual differences in sex drive and behaviour may rest in great part on individual differences in the tendency to think about erotic possibilities" (p. 18). He believes that individuals could strengthen their sexual drive by engaging in erotic fantasies with increased frequency, and that viewing explicit sexual stimuli could facilitate this process, especially in individuals who have trouble visualizing images. This suggestion results from previous research (Byrne and Lamberth, 1971) in which he found that self-induced sexual fantasies were judged to be twice as arousing as erotic pictures, with females being somewhat more aroused than males. Such findings point to the truth of the aphorism "sex is really all in the mind" and suggest that sexual depictions are exciting only to the extent that they match our preferred fantasy images.

Nelson (1973), in an attempt to assess these findings with physiological measures, found that there is a great deal of individual variation in ability to produce arousing sexual fantasies. For example, some males can consistently produce fairly large erectile responses to self-induced sexual fantasies, while some males show little or no ability to do this at all; mean erection response for a group of high fantasy subjects was about 50% of a full erection compared to 6% for low fantasy subjects. Fantasy plus the addition of an external sexual stimulus (slide of a nude female masturbating) increased mean responsiveness in both groups initially, 30% for the high group and 10% for the low, while repetitions with the same stimulus returned both groups to their fantasy base levels of response within eight trials. These findings demonstrate that fantasy alone can produce moderately strong sexual arousal, and suggest that responsiveness to external sexual stimuli is highly influenced by this; external sexual stimuli seems to augment sexual arousal by stimulating fantasy, perhaps by channelling its direction and narrowing its focus toward a specific sequence of erotic actions, or by simply providing an opportunity to realize new possibilities. Individuals who lack the ability to generate arousing sexual fantasies seem to benefit less from viewing sexual stimuli, although it is likely that they respond to stimuli that are more sexually stimulating than slides; moreover, such findings suggest that low fantasy arousal may predict lower drive and interest in sexuality, plus greater dependence upon direct physical contact for sexual arousal and excitement. Overall, these results support the idea that studies designed to measure sexual arousal to various sexual stimuli involve measurements of the interaction between one's ability to produce arousing fantasies and the erotic stimulus, with high fantasy responsiveness predictive of higher sexual arousal to most erotic stimuli; however, non-preferred sexual stimuli could decrease sexual arousal by interfering with self-generated fantasy (cf. Bancroft and Mathews, 1971; Mavissakalian et al., 1975; Mosher and Abramson, 1977; Schmidt, 1975; Tannenbaum, 1971).

Much attention has been devoted to the role conditioning plays in the shaping and strengthening of sexual arousal to different stimuli. For example, Rachman (1966) created a mild boot fetish in heterosexual male students by pairing slides of sexually provocative women with a picture of a pair of black knee-length women's boots. Not only did the boots become somewhat sexually arousing, but there was a slight tendency for this conditioned response to generalize to other footwear as well. The author concluded that there is little question that sexual responsiveness can be conditioned to external stimuli that initially fail to elicit any sexual arousal (cf. Rachman and Hodgson, 1968); Langevin and Martin (1975), however, were unable to classically condition arousal to abstract external stimuli. In contrast, Nelson (1973) attempted to alter the sexual arousal value of internal stimuli in normal heterosexual males who consistently showed only very small, if any, erection responses to their sexual fantasies. Segments of a sexually explicit film were used to reinforce progressively larger increases in penile tumescence in an operant paradigm in which the delivery of reinforcement was contingent upon small erection increases induced solely by concentrating upon sexual thoughts. The same film reinforcers served as unconditioned stimuli in a classical paradigm in which a different group of subjects concentrated upon their self-induced sexual thoughts. The results suggested that cognitively induced sexual stimuli which were initially ineffective could acquire the power to elicit penile responses; the operant paradigm proved to be the most effective procedure in terms of the number of subjects who met the criterion of conditioning, and follow-up sessions showed even further increases in the effectiveness of fantasy to elicit arousal. Reynolds (1980) has recently attempted to evaluate these reinforcement procedures in a clinical population of 30 men with psychogenic erectile dysfunction. The patients were instructed to concentrate upon thoughts that facilitate erection and during this time they received either: (1) segments of erotic film delivered contingent upon erection increases, plus feedback about those changes; (2) contingent film segments without any feedback; or (3) non-contingent film segments. The results showed that the patients who received contingent film reinforcement without feedback produced greater increases in erectile responsivity than patients in the other groups, in terms of mean penile amplitude scores, thus demonstrating the effectiveness of the operant paradigm for enhancing the arousal value of self-induced sexual thoughts in a clinical population.

Overall these studies provide some evidence that sexual arousal can be easily conditioned to neutral stimuli, either external objects or internal thoughts and images (cf. Keller and Goldstein, 1978).

The idea that sexual preferences develop and change partly as a result of conditioning procedures is not new. For example, McGuire et al. (1965) proposed such a theory in which sexual thoughts and images are reinforced by masturbation which culminates in orgasm. McGuire's team based their theory on an investigation of the sexual fantasies of 45 sexual deviants; apparently the first real sexual experience that they had actually been involved in, as opposed to an experience they had read about or heard from others, supplied deviant fantasy material for later masturbation in 75% of the cases. The authors hypothesize that the repeated pairing of these deviant fantasy images and thoughts with direct sexual stimulation and orgasm results in their acquiring sexually arousing properties which help to sustain the sexual excitement and arousal so necessary to maintain interest in the sexual deviation. In this analysis, then, which is certainly consistent with the evidence from conditioning studies, reinforced sexual imagery and thoughts are viewed as an important link in the acquisition, maintenance, and altera-tion of deviant sexual arousal and behaviour. Obviously this analysis in regard to the formation of sexual deviation is just as applicable to the acquisition of non-deviant preferences, and indeed such an approach forms the basis of many treatment programmes for sexual deviation (cf. Abel et al., 1976, 1977; Adams et al., 1981; Brownell and Barlow, 1980; Laws and O'Neil, 1981). Although McGuire's team do not consider the role of explicit sexual depictions in their theory, such portrayals may facilitate conditioning by providing new fantasy material as well as by increasing motivation for masturbatory experiences; irrespective of the nature of the depictions – deviant, violent, normal, or whatever – these sexually reinforced thoughts and images should gain a foothold in an individual's repertoire of sexual attitudes and behaviour.

Today there are many behavioural techniques for the treatment of sexual deviations. All of these approaches imply, directly, or indirectly, that there is a link between the maintenance of deviant fantasy and the maintenance of deviant behaviour – change the nature of the fantasy and a change in behaviour should follow. The major goals of treatment are suppression or elimination of inappropriate arousal patterns and enhancement of appro-priate sexual arousal; while suppression of deviant arousal patterns per se can facilitate or increase appropriate sexual arousal, investigators realize that specific techniques are often required to accomplish this goal and that the treatment of sexual deviations requires a broader approach (cf. Barlow, 1973, 1977; Brownell et al., 1977). One technique for increasing sexual arousal that is relevant to the current discussion is called exposure. This is a

echnique whereby an individual is exposed to explicit heterosexual stimuli in
n effort to directly elicit heterosexual arousal. Herman *et al.* (1974), for
xample, repeatedly exposed patients with deviant arousal patterns to
eterosexual stimuli and instructed them to "imagine engaging in heterosexual
ehaviour" while watching a film of a nude female in various sexual poses.
heir results showed that there were increases in arousal to the heterosexual
timuli in all sessions used to measure generalization; moreover, patients
eported changes in masturbatory fantasies coincident with the measured
rousal patterns. Although an experimental analysis of the results attributed
he patients' enhanced heterosexual arousal to mere exposure and reinforced
antasy, the mechanism of change is in doubt. Barlow (1974) suggests that
xposure may be similar to flooding or desensitization, resulting in a decrease
n heterosexual anxiety rather than directly increasing heterosexual arousal.
A similar analysis might suggest that such exposure to aggressive sexual
lepictions on a repeated basis would decrease an individual's normal inhibi-
ions against the use of force in sexual relationships.

SEX AND AGGRESSION

o far our discussion suggests that the effects of exposure to sexual stimuli
an be rather variable. Cline (1974), for example, points out that portrayals
f explicit sex might provide fantasies for later masturbation which, in turn,
ould affect behaviour adversely, whereas Abel and Blanchard (1976) have
hown that these same materials can facilitate increases in appropriate
eterosexual arousal and functioning in the treatment of individuals with
exual deviations. Importantly, McGuire *et al.* (1965) strongly suggest that
eal sexual experiences are commonly used in masturbatory fantasies which
an foster either deviant or non-deviant association, and that explicit sexual
naterial would be chosen by the individual to fit in with pre-existing pre-
erences, rather than determining those preferences. Wilson (1978) suggests
hat exposure to sexual stimuli may have many therapeutic advantages, such
s promoting greater communication and openness in discussing sex among
ouples, and Björksten (1976) and Gillan (1978) suggest that sexually
raphic material is very useful in the treatment of sexual dysfunctions.
Obviously there are many possible effects that may result from exposure to
exual materials, but one hypothesized effect, in particular, has aroused
ontinued interest and can be traced to suggestions in the psychological
iterature regarding a special link between sexual and aggressive motives, and
he idea that sexuality shows an admixture of aggression; namely, the effect
hat sexual arousal will often, if not always, encourage the occurrence of
vert aggressive behaviour.

The idea that sex and aggression are closely related received little empirical investigation until the late 1960s, even though it had been advanced by leading theorists. For example, Freud (1933) posited a biological model in which erotic and aggressive elements function interdependently, and suggested that desires to hurt or to be hurt by one's lover form a normal part of heterosexual relations and should be viewed as pathological only when they become extreme. Similarly, Berne (1964) asserted that the arousal of aggressive motives or feelings often serves to heighten sexual pleasure for both men and women. Moreover, Meyer (1972) states that while sexual behaviour and aggressive behaviour may appear at first glance to be distinctly different types of behaviour, comparisons of physiological characteristics of the organism in both states of arousal show a great deal of similarity. Certainly the work of Schmidt and Sigusch (1970) and Schmidt et al. (1973) tends to support the idea that exposure to sexually stimulating material produces aggressive feelings. Specifically, they found changes in mood in the direction of increased aggressiveness and decreased friendliness after viewing explicit sexual stimuli. And Schmidt (1975) reported much aggressiveness in both males and females after viewing sexually aggressive stimuli (viz., a rape scene). Findings similar to these have prompted some writers to suggest that public concern over the harmful effects of media violence and aggression should also be extended to the closely allied effects of exposure to sexually arousing material. Moreover, these studies emphasize that the literature on viewing aggression *per se* is directly relevant to an understanding of the relationship between sex and aggression.

Definition and Measures of Aggression

Confusion and disagreement over the definition of pornography is, perhaps, paralleled and reflected in the definition of aggression and in the multiple measures used to assess it. Geen (1976) indicates that the term aggression is often used in a broadly descriptive sense and in reference to a variety of functionally different behaviours. He believes that the confusion over the meaning can be attributed to the fact that psychologists have taken the word from everyday language and tried to invest it with scientific precision. Unfortunately, attempts to formulate a precise definition have not succeeded. Similarly, the search for valid dependent measures of aggression has proved unrewarding; in fact, little research seems to have been devoted to this problem. Green reports that "the common practice is to adopt an operational definition of aggression and to attempt to show that such measures are systematically related to antecedent variables; the dependent measures themselves most often have face validity and little else" (p. 2).

Despite the considerable amount of disagreement among social scientists, Baron (1977) suggests that a partial resolution of the controversy over definitions of aggression has recently yielded one definition which most – although by no means all – researchers would find acceptable: *Aggression* is any form of behaviour directed toward the goal of harming or injuring another living being who is motivated to avoid such treatment. Importantly, Baron points out that physical damage to the recipient is not essential as long as the person has experienced some type of aversive consequence. Thus, in addition to direct physical assaults, actions which cause others to "lose face" or experience public embarrassment, deprive them of needed objects, and even withhold love or affection can, under certain circumstances, be described as aggressive in nature. Buss (1961) suggests that aggression can be categorized along three dimensions: *physical–verbal, active–passive* and *direct–indirect*. These dimensions yield eight possible categories into which most aggressive actions can be divided. Thus, for example, actions such as spreading malicious rumours about other people, or disparaging them to others would be described as verbal, active and indirect.

The most commonly used assessment technique for the laboratory study of aggression involves direct physical assaults against a live victim. Such procedures rest upon an important deception, in which research subjects are led to believe that they can physically harm another person in some manner, when in fact they cannot; thus intentions or desires to hurt the victim can be assessed without any risk to the individual. Normally, a subject is given the opportunity to deliver electric shock via a device called an "aggression machine" (see Buss, 1961) to a confederate of the experimenter in the context of either a learning experiment, study of stress upon problem-solving, bogus ESP investigation, game, or some other variation in which the subject is led to believe that he is assisting in a separate experiment (Baron, 1977). For example, within the general framework of an experiment concerning the effects of punishment on learning, the subject is asked to administer electric shocks to another subject (actually the confederate) whenever a mistake is made on a learning task. The strength of subjects' tendencies to aggress against the confederate is assessed by recording the number, intensity, or duration of shocks he or she chooses to deliver; only shocks of an intensity above the minimum needed to inform the learner of his errors are considered aggressive in nature. Weiss (1969) has pointed out, however, that subjects may employ high levels of shock not out of a desire to inflict pain and suffering on the victim but rather out of a desire to help the victim master the task rapidly and so avoid any future punishment for errors; attempts to reduce this source of confusion consist of altering the instructions to the subjects.

Because these techniques offer an ingenious method for the indiret investigation of physical aggression and assault – under safe, laboratory conditions – such procedures have been widely adopted in recent years, and indeed these techniques have been employed in hundreds of different experiments during the last 20 years. In view of this fact, it is surprising that there has been so little research specifically conducted to determine whether they actually yield valid measures of overt physical aggression. However, despite the very real problems in demonstrating that the findings discovered in laboratory studies of aggression are directly applicable to the occurrence of such behaviour in other settings, researchers believe that there are several grounds for assuming that these methods do yield valid and useful measures of physical aggression (cf. Baron, 1977; Baron and Eggleston, 1972; Hartmann, 1969; Shemberg *et al.*, 1968; Weiss, 1969; Wolfe and Baron, 1971). For example, Hartmann (1969) found that male adolescents with a history of violent behaviour selected stronger shocks on the aggression machine that those without such a history. Similarly, factors that would be expected to influence overt aggression, such as strong provocation, have been found to alter subjects' behaviour in the expected direction. However, the issue remains open despite the encouragement of these findings and researchers caution that it would be inappropriate to suggest any simple or direct relationship between aggression machine performance and actual assaultive or antisocial behaviour.

Aggression and the Mass Media

There is little argument that there has been a marked increase in the amount of violence portrayed on television and in the level of exposure of both adults and children to it, and yet data from several early studies dealing with the effects of television viewing on children generally contended that televised violence had neither harmful nor beneficial effects except possibly on emotionally disturbed or otherwise susceptible children (see Himmelweit *et al.*, 1958). Underprivileged and delinquent groups were found to be exposed to television more than other groups and this suggested to the authors that viewing may be used as a compensation for unsatisfactory peer group relationships. They concluded that it is only in those individuals with existing emotional problems and behavioural difficulties (the maladjusted, the frustrated, and the isolated) that problems are likely to be intensified and already existing deviant patterns likely to be reinforced (cf. Bailyn, 1959; Larsen, 1968). Importantly, although they indicate they did not prove any causal relationship between viewing violence and undesirable behaviour they did find evidence that such viewing may retard children's awareness of the serious consequences of violence in real life and that these portrayals may teach a greater acceptance of aggression as the normal, manly solution of conflict. Overall these early studies emphasize the very complex interplay of factors that operate at the same time, either potentiating or reducing the effect of mass media impact; viewing violence is seen, therefore, as a contributing or reinforcing agent and not as a sole agent. Additional research, motivated by different theoretical considerations, has led to more partisan positions.

Feshbach (1961, 1971) and Feshbach and Singer (1971) proposed a *catharsis theory* of media violence, particularly through fantasy material. They argued that hostility in the viewer could be reduced or eliminated through vicarious participation in violent actions presented by the media; catharsis was seen as being obtained with the perception of the results of aggression, that is, pain and suffering – elements that may be absent from many presentations of violence. Most of the subsequent research, however, has rejected the cathartic model and suggests just the opposite interpretation: increased pre-disposition towards aggressiveness after exposure to violent portrayals. For example, Bandura (1973) has emphasized a social learning approach in which children and, to a lesser extent, adults repeatedly exposed to aggression will tend to adopt such behaviour patterns and adapt them to their own environmental circumstances. Berkowitz (1971) argues more for a cue model of aggression in which media depictions of aggressive behaviour serve as cues and thereby raise the probability of an aggressive response in the individual's hierarchy of possible response. Both theoretical positions tend to agree that the more the media depictions resemble the circumstances of the individual's particular environment, the greater the likelihood of the observed aggressive behaviours being approximated in real-life.

In the late 1960s mounting social concern in America regarding the possible harmful effects of violence in the media, particularly its presumed effects on children who are thought to be extremely vulnerable to such presentations, led to a concerted effort to obtain more definitive evidence upon which to base some possible governmental action (*National Commission on Causes and Prevention of Violence,* 1969; *Surgeon General's Scientific Advisory Committee on Television and Social Behaviour,* 1972). In general, the research findings supported an *instigational theory* for the effects of televised violence, and although the evidence was not conclusive, the Surgeon General's Committee was impressed with the extensive array of different studies by different investigators, working in different research settings, and using different research methodologies and assessment procedures that pointed towards increasing levels of aggressive behaviour and antisocial tendencies as a result of viewing violent media presentations (cf. Cater and Strickland, 1975); a number of social scientists, however, disagree with these findings (Howitt and Cumberbatch, 1975). Importantly, Eysenck (1972) points out how paradoxical it is that controllers of television programmes who argue that the portrayal of sex and violence on the screen has no effect on people also argue that advertisements showing certain types of cars, or drinks, or chocolates have a tremendous effect in making people use that type of car, or drink, or chocolate; why the difference? He reasons that "if television advertising is effective (and there is little doubt that it is), then why should television be less effective when it advertises lax morals, cruelty and violence, and permissive behaviour generally?" (p. 256) (cf. Donnerstein, in press; Eisenberg, 1980; Eron and Huesmann, 1980; Singer and Singer, 1980).

Heightened Arousal and Aggression

One of the findings linking sex and aggression in the early experimental literature comes from the work of Barclay (1971) which shows that exposure to sexual stimuli increases aggressive as well as sexual fantasy elicited in response to Thematic Apperception Test (TAT) pictures. Barclay compared the effects of different types of heightened arousal on aggressive fantasy and found a significant increase only for sexually aroused subjects, which offered some support for the specificity of the relationship between sexual arousal and aggressive fantasy. Moreover, Barclay (1969) provided some evidence that the sex and aggression relationship may be reciprocal in that anger arousal led to an increase in sexual fantasy responses to TAT pictures, and an increase in urinary acid phosphatase – thought to be a specific biochemical indicator of sexual arousal but is actually a non-specific measure. Generalizations from this type of research are, of course, limited, but research using behavioural measures also provides support for the idea that sex and aggression are linked since studies have shown that exposure to erotic depictions can, under certain conditions, facilitate subsequent aggressive behaviour.

In 1970 the *U.S. Commission on Obscenity and Pornography*, after reviewing the various research studies that they had sponsored, finally reached the conclusion that there is no substantial evidence to suggest that exposure to explicit sexual materials results in adverse consequences. Unfortunately, aggression was one variable that was not adequately investigated, although the Commission did report some evidence linking sex and aggression. For example, Tannenbaum (1971) provided some evidence that sexual arousal can facilitate subsequent aggression. In this study previously angered subjects were exposed to either a neutral, erotic, or aggressive film. Subjects then played a game with the experimenter's confederate who had angered them; if he gave a wrong answer, subjects were to administer electric shocks to him by selecting one of several buttons which ostensibly delivered increasingly higher intensities of shock. Tannenbaum found that the subjects administered higher levels of shock in revenge against the confederate after viewing the erotic film than after the aggressive film, the neutral film resulting in the lowest degree of aggression. Moreover, the mean blood pressure index was very high for the erotic group which suggested that a general heightening of arousal might also have had an impact on aggressive behaviour. Importantly, when both the aggressive and erotic films were shown to the subjects, an even higher level of aggressive response was elicited. The author concluded that arousing erotica tends to increase aggressive behaviour although the Commission generally ignored this evidence in its final report (cf. Cline, 1974; Eysenck and Nias, 1978).

In another Commission study, Mosher and Katz (1971) attempted to study male verbal aggression against women. After establishing a base level of verbal aggression, male undergraduate volunteers viewed either a sex film or a neutral film; half the subjects were then told they had to obtain a high level of verbal aggression to see a second sex film or a neutral film, and the other half were told they would see the appropriate film regardless of their aggression level. The authors found that heightened sexual arousal did not lead to increased aggression, but when aggression was instrumental to seeing a sex film the amount of verbal abuse increased. Interestingly, high sex-guilt subjects (men with severe conscience systems) were more aggressive than those with low sex-guilt, suggesting that the need for sexual stimulation can overrule conscience and guilt in permitting aggressive behaviour toward women, although perhaps the low sex-guilt subjects were less motivated to see another sex film. However, in order to establish base levels of verbal aggression, it should be emphasized that the subjects were initially shown examples of aggressive and derogatory comments before being asked to be as verbally aggressive as possible to a female assistant; essentially they were taught to be aggressive before being given the incentive condition. Needless to say, aggression increased. Serious reservations about the meaning and generalization of these findings to real-life situations are raised because the specific training and demand characteristics of this study may have served as direct cues informing the subjects differentially that normally inhibited responses are not only acceptable but are actually desired in this context.

During the past two decades, social scientists have identified a number of influences on human aggression (cf. Geen and O'Neal, 1976; Rule and Nesdale, 1976a; Zillmann, 1979). Although the focus has been on other issues, recent theories of aggression have suggested that general emotional arousal can facilitate aggression, especially in the presence of aggressive cues (Berkowitz, 1971), or other response activators such as modelling cues (Bandura, 1973); interestingly, in spite of differences in their theoretical positions, both authors have suggested that general arousal and aggressive cues combine to increase aggression. Recent research has examined these propositions in a number of studies designed to test the assumption that exposure to a variety of stimuli such as erotic material, physical exercise, white noise or extreme temperature can activate a general state of arousal which may subsequently affect aggression in *non-angered* individuals (Barclay, 1971; Baron and Bell, 1975; Donnerstein, 1980; Donnerstein and Berkowitz, 1981; Geen and O'Neal, 1969; Jaffe *et al.*, 1974; Konecni, 1975; Zillmann *et al.*, 1972; Zillmann and Sapolsky, 1977). For example, Jaffe *et al.* (1974) have shown that sexual arousal induced by the reading of erotic literature elicits greater aggressiveness than does the reading of science fiction (devoid of aggressive content). The aggressive effect of sexual arousal was evidenced by both males and females, irrespective of whether they aggressed against a male or a female victim, or whether the experimenter was male or female. These findings are consistent with the notion that aggressive responses can be energized by general arousal. In an attempt to test the proposition that general arousal facilitates aggression in the presence of aggressive cues, Geen and O'Neal (1969) found that observing a fight compared to a sports film increased intensity and number of electric shocks delivered to subjects when white noise was presented during the shocking phase of the experiment. The authors conclude that the aggressive cues in the fight film apparently elicited greater aggression by subjects who were presumably aroused by the white noise they experienced.

In addition to studies that have examined the effects of exposure to erotic material on aggression in the absence of anger, several studies have investigated the impact of sexual arousal on angered subjects' behaviour. For example, Zillmann (1971) found that male subjects exposed to an explicit non-aggressive erotic film directed stronger shocks against a male confederate who had previously annoyed them than did subjects who were also angered by this person but who viewed only a neutral travel film, or a violent prizefight film. If the aggressive content was the principal factor – Zillmann's boxing sequence was significantly less arousing but significantly more aggressive than the erotic film – in facilitating subsequent aggression, one would expect the boxing film to produce more aggressive behaviour; if the arousal factor predominated, the reverse should be true. The results clearly supported the *arousal model,* now often referred to as the *excitation transfer model* (see Tannenbaum and Zillmann, 1975; Zillmann, 1979). This model points to the arousal properties of the presentations as one causal factor in film-facilitated aggression. Later research led to the realization that aggressive behaviour was dependent upon some sort of prior instigation, some sort of cognitive disposition to engage in aggressive behaviour against a specific target. Thus, the model recognizes that the interaction between cognitive and arousal factors plays an important role, both in the initial encounter phase and in the reinstatement of the anger disposition during the response phase. Thus, when provoked to aggress, a subject's response will be a function of the amount of anger arousal felt toward the object of aggression and of the amount of arousal generated from other sources which apparently summate to yield the total amount of anger arousal; cognitive direction through the reinstatement of the earlier anger motivation seems important for the facilitation of subsequent aggressive responding (cf. Donnerstein *et al.*, 1976; Meyer, 1972; Zillmann *et al.*, 1974).

Facilitation or Inhibition

In contrast to such findings, however, Baron (1974) indicates that heightened sexual arousal induced through exposure to erotic materials may actually reduce later aggression; aggressiveness after exposure to erotic stimuli was found to be lower in provoked subjects than after exposure to neutral stimuli, leading Baron to posit the aggression-inhibiting influence of sexual arousal. This apparent contradiction led to experiments that eventually provided evidence for a curvilinear relationship between sexual arousal and aggression; specifically, the findings indicated that mildly arousing sexual stimuli tend to inhibit aggression while more arousing materials facilitate such behaviour (cf. Baron and Bell, 1977; Donnerstein *et al.*, 1975; Zillmann and Sapolsky, 1977); in fact, Donnerstein's team found that relative to neutral pictures, pin-ups and similar pictures serve to actually inhibit aggression, a finding that has relevance for much of the world's mass media, especially advertising, since they use a similar class of material in their presentations. The authors have proposed a model to explain this effect: while sexual arousal may facilitate aggression, especially high arousal, stimuli that are absorbing can shift attention away from any prior anger provocation, thus allowing for the dissipation of anger arousal and a reduction of aggressive responses. Zillmann and Sapolsky (1977) also report that exposure to mild erotica, as compared to exposure to non-erotica, appears to reduce annoyance in provoked individuals, but does not affect the behaviour of unprovoked individuals. However, they find no evidence for the *attentional shift hypothesis* of Donnerstein *et al.*, and instead present evidence that is consistent with the proposal that the effect of mild erotica is mediated by the hedonic properties of the response to these stimuli.

Aggression or Pro-social Behaviour

While the research described above is very informative and increases our understanding of the complex link between sexual arousal and aggression, it fails to point out that the facilitative effects of arousal should not be limited to aggressive behaviour. For example, Tannenbaum (1971) reports an experiment in which subjects were treated in either a positive, negative, or neutral manner by a confederate and then shown either an arousing erotic film or a non-arousing travel film. The results showed that the arousing film facilitated subsequent reward behaviour toward the confederate, the effect being particularly strong following the positive treatment by the confederate. Mueller and Donnerstein (1981) indicate that if the initial encounter between the subject and confederate is positive, rather than insulting, the subject should feel attraction toward the person and these feelings should lead to a pro-social dominant response in the same way that anger leads to an aggressive response; as a result, when the subject is further aroused by other means, such as by an arousing erotic film, pro-social behaviour should be increased. The authors have recently conducted two experiments to verify this and, in line with prediction, they found that subjects treated in a positive manner and shown an arousing erotic film were significantly more rewarding toward the confederate than were similarly treated subjects shown a non-arousing film. Thus, aggressive behaviour is not invariably the result of exposure to strongly arousing sexual material: whether exposure to sexual stimuli that generate high arousal facilitates aggression or not depends, to an important degree, upon the type of affect the person is experiencing toward others at the time. This position is consistent with a *general arousal model* (Bandura, 1973) which suggests that a state of increased general arousal, when it occurs, is not response-specific but may activate behaviours other than aggression if they happen to be relatively dominant for the individual.

Aggression Against Women

In recent years there has been a great deal of social concern about the factors that promote aggressive attacks against women and, in particular, sexually violent attacks such as rape. That viewing sexually arousing depictions might contribute to this hardly seems surprising because research shows that it can facilitate aggression in individuals predisposed to act aggressively, and because depictions of sexual violence toward women have become increasingly popular in the mass media. Yet most research which has examined the effects of viewing erotica on aggression has not found any evidence to support the idea that women are differentially harmed by such depictions. For example, Mosher (1971) initially thought that viewing erotic films would strengthen attitudes approving of sexual exploitation generally and, in particular, reinforce attitudes concerned with treating women as sex objects for the pleasure of men; however, he found no increase in callous or insensitive attitudes towards females, nor an increase in aggressive verbal comments, which provided some evidence that viewing *non-aggressive* sexual stimuli does not lead to or promote aggressive attitudes toward women. Jaffe *et al.* (1974) also indicate that exposure to non-aggressive erotic material does not differentially affect aggressive behaviour toward women. Donnerstein and Barrett (1978), however, point out a problem with the Jaffe *et al.* study that needs to be considered. Specifically, the problem concerns the fact that a facilitative effect on aggression following exposure to arousing erotica is dependent upon prior or subsequent anger instigation; thus, since subjects were not instigated by the aggressive target, it seems unlikely that Jaffe's team would have found any aggression effect, although they report they did. Interestingly, this study continues to occupy an ambiguous position in the literature because it shows that *non-angered* subjects given strong forms of sexually arousing stimuli deliver significantly more intense shocks to targets than do subjects who are not sexually aroused; although research indicates that some form of anger instigation is required, in addition to high levels of sexual arousal, for such an effect, the Jaffe team seem to refute this. A possible resolution to this apparent contradiction comes from Baron and Eggleston (1972) who point out that in the context of the standard Buss (1961) procedure, performance on the aggression machine may reflect desires on the part of subjects to help the other person and to make the experiment a success as well as to harm this person. Jaffe *et al.* used such a procedure in the context of a bogus ESP experiment in which subjects believed they were participating in a study dealing with the effects of punishment upon learning to receive ESP messages; specifically, subjects were told

> you are probably wondering which is the most effective level to use as punishment in this type of task. This is another thing that we hope to find out, when this study is finished, by comparing the shock levels used to the number of correct responses obtained. At this point, though, there is no information available to guide us in this respect, and you should use your own judgment in choosing the shock levels (p. 761).

Overall, the combination of high sexual arousal plus the probable confounding of helpful and harmful motives may provide an explanation for their atypical findings. Donnerstein and Barrett (1978) believe that an appropriate test of the effects of erotic stimuli on aggression toward females by males would require both high levels of sexual arousal and some form of anger instigation, a particular combination of factors which has not been adequately investigated using both male and female confederates.

In a recent series of investigations, Donnerstein and his colleagues have been investigating whether exposure to sexually explicit films, aggressive or non-aggressive, can differentially affect subsequent aggressive behaviour toward women by men (Donnerstein, 1980a, b, 1982; Donnerstein and Barrett, 1978; Donnerstein and Berkowitz, 1981; Donnerstein and Hallam,

1978). In the first study, Donnerstein and Barrett (1978) exposed male subjects to either a neutral or highly arousing non-aggressive sexual film, the type of stimuli being similar to those used in previous studies that showed facilitative effects on aggression (cf. Zillmann, 1971). Prior to stimulus exposure, subjects were either angered or treated in a neutral manner by a male or female confederate. Following the viewing of erotica, angered subjects showed an increase in aggression, whereas no such effect was observed for non-angered invididuals, thus confirming the results of past research. These results support the excitation transfer model in that only under a state of anger arousal do such effects occur (Tannenbaum and Zillmann, 1975). However, the authors failed to find any evidence of differential aggression toward women by men; in fact, the men were *less* aggressive to the female targets than to the male. They suggest that one possible reason for this might be that since aggression toward females is generally disapproved of, fear of disapproval could act to inhibit its occurrence. In an attempt to clarify this issue, Donnerstein and Hallam (1978) tried to create a condition in which male subjects would be less inhibited or restrained against aggression in general in order to examine the effects that erotic exposure would have upon aggression toward women in particular. The investigators adopted a procedure used mainly in studies of aggression *per se* that deliberately lowers restraints against aggression, a procedure that allows subjects two opportunities to aggress against the confederate who provoked them initially; studies have shown that subjects are more aggressive the second time around – a finding that suggests that the activity may be disinhibiting in itself. Donnerstein and Hallam found that there was no differential aggression toward males or females during the initial aggression opportunity – evidence which supports their earlier research – but when subjects were given a second opportunity to aggress against the target, ten minutes later, aggressive responses were increased against females – the first demonstration that this effect can occur – although they point out that the exact process operating when individuals are given two opportunities to aggress is not understood; however, the primary question is why the effects of exposure to non-aggressive sexual stimuli would influence aggression against females more than against males. The authors suggest that one possibility is that the film contained some specific form of aggressive cue value for female targets; interestingly, male subjects rated the erotic film as somewhat aggressive, even though it was chosen so as not to contain such cues. Overall, this research clearly supports the idea that when aggressive inhibitions are lowered in male subjects there is a tendency to increase aggression against women, but without lowered inhibitions there is no evidence for this phenomenon, at least among well-socialized college students; needless to say, the search for factors that might be influential in lowering aggressive inhibitions has intensified.

Recently investigators have been looking for specific factors within sexual depictions that might play a crucial role in affecting an individual's inhibitions against aggression toward women, although there is ample reason to believe that factors such as personality characteristics are among the many that need to be examined. So far, in the search for disinhibiting cues, the fact that not only objects but individuals can take on aggressive cue value if they have been associated with observed violence has aroused the most interest among researchers (cf. Berkowitz, 1971); for example, in a typical paradigm which demonstrates this, subjects were angered by a confederate of the experimenter and then observed an aggressive film or an exciting non-aggressive film. The subjects were then given the opportunity to deliver electric shocks to a confederate whose name was the same as, or different from, the name of the loser in the fight film. It was found that the greatest aggression was displayed toward the confederate whose name was the same as that of the losing boxer in the fight-film condition (Geen and Berkowitz, 1966); Berkowitz's conceptualization, while not denying the possibility of specific cue effects, tends to emphasize the general arousing properties of anger that need aggression-eliciting cues to direct the response. Thus, given research indicating that arousing erotic films paired with aggressive content can summate to increase aggressive behaviour (Tannenbaum, 1971), and the evidence suggesting that individuals associated with observed violence can acquire aggression-eliciting cue properties (Berkowitz and Turner, 1974), Donnerstein reasons that exposure to aggressive sexual stimuli may have a specific facilitating effect upon subsequent aggressive behaviour toward women.

Donnerstein (1980a) attempted to evaluate this hypothesis regarding the effects of viewing aggressive sexual stimuli on subsequent male aggression toward women. In his study male subjects were angered or treated in a neutral manner by a male or female confederate and were given the opportunity to view one of three types of film: a neutral, erotic, or aggressive–erotic depiction. Subjects were then given the opportunity to aggress against the male or female target via the delivery of electric shock. Since it is possible to explain any increase in aggression in terms of differential levels of physiological arousal (cf. Tannenbaum and Zillmann, 1975), the erotic and aggressive–erotic films were chosen to be equal in arousal value, but different in aggressive content. Donnerstein predicted that angered subjects would display more aggression than non-angered subjects following exposure to either of the erotic films, a safe prediction since it has received consistent research support, and that exposure to the aggressive–erotic film would result in higher levels of aggression than exposure to the erotic films, particularly towards women due to the assumed cue value of female victims in the aggressive–erotic depiction.

In line with expectations, Donnerstein found that exposure to an aggressive–erotic film increased aggressive behaviour to a level significantly higher than that found for the erotic film in subjects who had previously been angered. Importantly, the differential impact of the aggressive–erotic film on aggression against females was fully supported; when angered subjects were paired with a *male target,* the aggressive–erotic film had no more effect on aggressive behaviour than the erotic film, but when paired with a *female target,* the highest level of aggressive behaviour followed exposure to the sexually violent film. Of greater importance in some respects was the finding that even *non-angered subjects* showed a significant increase in aggression against female targets following exposure to the aggressive–erotic film compared to the neutral and erotic films, although the absolute level of aggression was considerably below the level for angered subjects. Why would aggression against females increase following exposure to an aggressive–erotic depiction? Since the amount of *arousal* from the anger instigation and the sexual films was apparently equal, it seems reasonable to assume that some specific aspect of the aggressive sexual film accounts for the increased aggression. Donnerstein believes that the female's association with the victim in the film may be the critical variable in accounting for the results. One other interesting possibility is that male subjects viewing other males being sexually aggressive toward a female may simply become disinhibited against subsequent aggression toward women via *desensitization* or *modelling* effects; in fact, there is no apparent reason why modelling cannot occur in conjunction with aggressive cue effects or desensitization effects.

Donnerstein's results from these investigations show that *violent pornography* can be, under certain conditions, a mediator of aggression toward women. In the light of this, the concern over whether such depictions can be related to actual sexual attacks and other forms of aggression toward women seems particularly warranted. Donnerstein and Berkowitz (1981) analyse the following factors that might determine an audience's reactions to depictions of violent sexuality: (1) the amount of violence observed, (2) the outcome of the observed violence (whether the woman victim is shown to be enjoying the sexual assault or not), (3) the viewer's affective state at the time (angry or not), (4) the arousal level of the person, (5) lowered inhibitions, (6) the available target's association with the victim of the assault in the film, and (7) pain cues from the victim being associated with the predisposition to hurt someone. In their study they report on two experiments designed to investigate whether the behavioural characteristics of the people in sexually explicit films, aggressive and non-aggressive, and the nature of the targets available for aggression afterwards can affect subsequent aggression. In the first experiment male subjects were first angered by either a male or a female confederate. They were then shown a neutral film or one of three different sexual films; one was non-aggressive, and two were aggressive. The two aggressive sexual films differed in terms of the scene's outcome, i.e. whether the female victim enjoyed the sexual assault or not. Although the films were different in aggressive content, they were chosen to be equal in arousal value to rule out any increases in aggression being accounted for in terms of differential levels of physiological arousal. Blood pressure was taken on four different occasions to monitor arousal. Finally, immediately after the subjects saw their respective films, each of them had an opportunity to aggress against the confederate who had previously angered them.

Several specific predictions were made. First, they expected that the non-aggressive film would make them more aggressive toward the male confederate than the female, a prediction that has received considerable research support from earlier investigations (e.g. Donnerstein, 1980a). The assumption is that men are reluctant to aggress toward women in general even when provoked. However, conditions that lower men's inhibitions or that raise the capacity of women to evoke aggressive responses from them should alter this situation. Thus, the second prediction was the exposure to the film of sexual assault with a positive outcome (where the victim eventually enjoys and is a willing participant in the sexual activity) would lead to a high level of aggression against the female target in particular. In this situation, typical of much violent pornography, the authors reasoned that (a) the aggressive content of the film would evoke strong aggressive reactions from the angry viewers, (b) the positive outcome would lower their inhibitions against attacking women, and (c) the female confederate's sex-linked association with the victim in the film would facilitate attacks on her. Thirdly, they thought that the negative outcome of the film of sexual assault (in which the woman victim was shown to be suffering) would also lead to a high level of aggression to the female confederate, but less than in the positive outcome situation. Here they reasoned that seeing the woman victim being hurt by the assault on her might be very stimulating for them since they were already angry at the female confederate and, presumably, wanted to retaliate against her; thus, the victim's pain cues would theoretically stimulate fairly strong aggressive reactions within the male viewers despite the fact that the observed violence in the film was not portrayed as justified. Indeed, the latter aspect in the film was expected to have some inhibitory effect on aggression. Finally, the female confederate's association with the film victim was expected to promote greater aggressive responding toward her than toward the male confederate.

The first prediction was that the men would be more aggressive to the male confederate, not the female, following exposure to the non-aggressive erotic film. This proved to be true and confirmed the results of previous studies (Donnerstein and Hallam, 1978). The authors indicate that "these results tend to suggest, once again, that unless aggressive restraints are reduced and/or the stimulus value of the target is enhanced, exposure to highly arousing but non-aggressive erotica will not significantly increase violence toward women relative to men" (p. 717). In fact, viewing non-aggressive erotica did *not* increase violence toward women any more than viewing the neutral control film. The second prediction was that exposure to a typical theme in violent pornography, one in which the victim eventually becomes aroused after much initial resistance, would heighten the angry viewers' attacks on a female target. Not only did this positive-outcome condition increase attacks against women, but the level of aggression was much higher than that received by male confederates. This finding strengthens the authors' contention that the female confederate's association with the victim in the aggressive–erotic film is responsible for this effect. The final prediction, of course, was also strongly supported. The previously angered men increased their aggressive behaviour toward their female target after exposure to a film of sexual violence in which the victim was portrayed as suffering. Since the male subjects were angry at the time and thus predisposed to hurt someone, the authors suggest that the pain cues from the victim in association with this particular predisposition might have evoked a heightened aggressive desire in them even though the aggression portrayed in the film was unjustified (Berkowitz, 1974; Berkowitz *et al.*, 1981; Berkowitz and Geen, 1966; Swart and Berkowitz, 1976). Logic-ally, although the two aggressive–erotic films did not seem to produce sub-stantial differences in aggression, the film of sexual assault with a positive outcome should have generated more aggression since justified violence normally evokes greater subsequent aggression in the observer (cf. Geen, 1981).

   The second experiment was designed to test whether the suffering dis-played by the victim in the negative outcome film could serve as an aggres-sion-eliciting cue under both anger and non-anger conditions. They tested this by promoting the belief in half of the male subjects that the female confederate had deliberately insulted them, whereas the remaining partici-pants were treated in a neutral fashion by her so as not to promote any anger. Angry people want to inflict injury, and according to their reasoning, observ-ing a woman being hurt should be particularly rewarding for and theoretic-ally facilitate heightened aggression by the angered males. In contrast, no such effect would be predicted in the absence of provocation, and pain cues should help to suppress aggression. The positive outcome film, however, was predicted to produce heightened attacks on the female confederate irrespec-tive of anger. In this case they thought that the aggressive content of the film, the portrayal of the woman victim as gaining pleasure from the attack and her sex-linked association to the confederate would all tend to lower the men's restraints against subsequent aggression; indeed, other research (Donnerstein, 1980a) has shown that non-angered males increase aggression against female targets following exposure to films of sexual violence with typical assault themes.

In line with their predictions, the results indicated that viewers must be disposed to hurt someone before the victim's suffering can serve as an aggression-eliciting cue; non-angered males showed no increases in aggression toward women following exposure to the negative outcome aggressive–erotic film. The same was not true, however, for those non-angered males who viewed the positive outcome film. They increased their aggressive actions toward the female confederate following the film. Angered subjects, in contrast, were very aggressive following both the positive and negative outcome films in comparison to the neutral and non-aggressive erotic film.

The results of these two experiments help us to understand how films in the mass media affect the subsequent responses to various individuals. These responses are, for most people, probably weak and short-lived, but at times they can be translated into strong and aggressive behaviour. Donnerstein and Berkowitz believe that certain factors within mass media depictions of sex and violence tend to heighten the viewer's aggressive tendencies and increase the probability of aggression, at least for a brief period of time. One commonly held interpretation of film mediated aggression emphasizes disinhibitory processes which affect an individual's normal inhibitions against aggression. The authors believe that the heightened aggression exhibited by the males toward the female targets in the positive outcome films above is probably due to this kind of disinhibition. The indication that the female victim had enjoyed being raped apparently reinforced the idea that aggression is justified for just that reason! The message to the viewer is that aggression pays off and, for that reason, may deserve to be imitated. In accounting for the effects of film violence, Berkowitz (1970) argues that the sight of aggression *per se* can elicit transient, aggression-facilitating responses in the same way that observing sexual stimuli can evoke brief sexual responses and increase the probability that actual sexual behaviour will be engaged in. Aggressive content in films of sexual violence is, therefore, thought to stimulate the viewers aggressively. When males who are already angry with women observe violent sexuality in which women are physically and psychologically abused, it apparently arouses them even further and acts to increase their subsequent aggressive behaviour. Arousal, however, is *not* a sufficient explanation for the increase in aggression by itself. In the first experiment, for example, the non-aggressive erotic film was just as arousing as the aggressive erotic films, according to both the subjects' ratings and their mean blood pressure, yet the purely erotic portrayal evoked no more aggression than the neutral film. Rejecting arousal as the primary mechanism by which film violence leads to increased aggression does not mean, however, that it has no effect on the behaviour. Indeed, Donnerstein and Berkowitz believe that a viewer's behaviour is influenced by the interaction of arousal with the film's explicit and implicit communications about people and behaviour. Specific stimulus–response associations are also seen to influence a viewer's behaviour. For example, the woman confederate's sex-linked association with the victim who is sexually assaulted in the film apparently strengthened her aggressive cue value so that she became a more salient target for increased aggression by the angry men. Obviously, such processes do not exist in isolation. Communications which stress that women only pretend not to enjoy sexual assaults can also serve to justify and reduce inhibitions against aggression toward women. Such messages also tend to reinforce certain beliefs and attitudes toward women who are sexually assaulted. In both experiments, for example, subjects exposed to the positive outcome film found it less aggressive and the victim more responsible for her plight than those exposed to the negative version. Unfortunately, the authors believe, this shifting of responsibility to the victims of sexual assault may be one factor that accounts for many men's callous attitudes toward rape and rape victims (cf. Malamuth and Check, 1980b). Reactions to portrayals of sex and violence on the screen today are undoubtedly influenced to some extent by the processes described above; indeed, Donnerstein and Berkowitz draw attention to the multiplicity of factors that can determine the impact of mass media depictions on an audience. They are, however, not the only relevant factors; individual differences in personality and attitudes toward aggression also play some part (cf. Malamuth et al., 1980b; see below).

In a parallel series of investigations, Malamuth and his colleagues have also been actively studying the hypothesized relationship between viewing sexual materials and sexual aggression (Malamuth, 1981; Malamuth and Check, 1980a, b, 1981; Malamuth et al., 1977, 1980a, b). Some of this work on sexual arousal to sexually aggressive depictions has already been discussed earlier, but a brief overview may be helpful. The initial impetus for much of Malamuth's recent work came in part from research showing that rapists evidence high sexual arousal to portrayals of both rape and consenting sexual acts, whereas non-rapists show substantial sexual arousal only to mutually-consenting depictions (Abel et al., 1977a). Such data is inconsistent with work by Schmidt (1975) showing that males and females can be highly aroused sexually in response to viewing sexually aggressive stimuli, such as rape depictions. Therefore, based upon a theoretical analysis of the relationship between sexual arousal and aggression (Malamuth et al., 1977), experiments were initiated to identify the specific dimensions in portrayals of sexual violence that either inhibit or disinhibit sexual responsiveness. Whereas the results showed that normals are less sexually aroused by depictions of sexual assault than by themes of mutually-consenting sex, portraying the rape victim as experiencing an involuntary orgasm disinhibited subjects' sexual arousal and resulted in high levels of responsiveness (Malamuth *et al.*, 1980b). The relevance of Malamuth's research to Donnerstein's recent investigations on aggression against women should be fairly obvious, since both researchers are concerned with the role of the victim's behaviour and reactions within sexually aggressive and deviant portrayals, and with factors that contribute to inhibition or disinhibition of sexual responsiveness and/or aggression (see Malamuth and Donnerstein, 1982).

Several writers have recently pointed to the increase in violent and deviant themes in sexual materials, especially aggression against women in erotica, as cause for concern because such material may negatively affect both attitudes and behaviour toward women, and may cause and/or perpetuate undesirable perceptions of rape and aggressive behaviour generally (Brownmiller, 1975; Eysenck and Nias, 1978; Gager and Schurr, 1976; Malamuth and Spinner, 1980; Smith, 1976); such concerns appear justified since research has documented the strong effect attitudes can have upon future behaviour (see Bentler and Speckart, 1981). Malamuth and his colleagues have attempted to evaluate experimentally these possible relationships in their recent work, citing past research on exposure to explicit sexual stimuli, desensitization of inhibitory or avoidance tendencies, and conditioning studies which utilize fantasy to alter the arousal value of stimuli as possible factors which may mediate attitudinal and behavioural changes (Malamuth, 1981; Malamuth and Check, 1980b; Malamuth *et al.*, 1980a). In particular, Malamuth's team is concerned about exposure to the *fusion* of sexuality and violence, especially when relatively high levels of sexual arousal are stimulated. For example, they are concerned that the elicitation of sexual arousal within a violent context may result in a conditioning process whereby violent acts become associated with sexual pleasure, possibly as a result of later masturbatory conditioning to fantasies or depictions of sexual aggression; as we have previously discussed, research has shown that similar procedures also form the basis for the behavioural treatment of sexual deviations (Adams *et al.*, 1981; Brownell and Barlow, 1980). Moreover, Malamuth is concerned about attitudes and beliefs that may be altered by the information conveyed in contemporary mass media depictions of sexual aggression or violence; namely, that even if women seem to be disinterested or repulsed by a pursuer, the basic need to be dominated will eventually emerge in their becoming sexually *aroused* by the attacker – a major myth about rape and rape victims that is continually reinforced in such depictions, and apparently the most significant variable in disinhibiting sexual arousal to rape portrayals in both males and females (Malamuth and Check, 1980a). For example, Malamuth and Check (1980b) found that prior exposure to a typical rape myth story in which the victim becomes sexually aroused results in significantly less perception of victim trauma in subsequent rape portrayals in which victims do not become aroused. Conversely, prior exposure to a rape-abhorrence depiction in which the victim's plight and disgust are emphasized results in reduced or inhibited sexual arousal and greater perception of the victim's pain in subsequent rape presentations that depict the victim as clearly opposing the assault. These findings suggest that exposure to depictions that portray rape in a relatively positive or negative manner affect perceptions and attitudes toward the victims of sexual violence, and that these perceptions mediate the inhibition or disinhibition of sexual arousal to such portrayals in normal subjects.

Similarly, Malamuth *et al.* (1980a) found that exposure to sexual violence influences perceptions of the rape victim. Low aggression-anxious males seemed to view the effects of the rape on the victim in a less negative light following earlier exposure to sexual violence, while high aggression-anxious males tended to become more conscious of the plight of the rape victim and the pain she experienced as a function of their earlier exposure to sexual violence; degree of anxiety about aggression was considered a potentially important variable mediating the effects of exposure to sexual violence, and its inclusion in this study is the first attempt to examine individual differences in susceptibility to aggress against women in this area of research (cf. Dengerink, 1976). The authors speculate that males who have low aggression-anxiety to begin with are likely to become further desensitized to the effects of aggression upon being exposed to a positive depiction of violence, whereas individuals with high aggression-anxiety may become more sensitized to the effects upon exposure to any act of violence. Importantly, Malamuth's team found consistent gender differences in reaction to the portrayal of rape, females identifying more with the victim's plight, being more aware of her pain, and being less inclined to believe that the victim derives pleasure from being raped, although surprisingly, female subjects believed that over 25% of the female population would derive some pleasure from being victimized, but not themselves, which suggested that females may believe myths about rape as well. Moreover, the authors obtained an amazing result when they questioned males about whether they would participate in a rape "if they were assured they would not be caught"; over half the sample suggested that they would do so. Males' self-reported tendency to rape was significantly correlated with identification with the rapist, with relatively positive attitudes towards his behaviour, and with the perception that other men are inclined to rape; moreover, women would enjoy the victimization. The authors interpret these findings as providing some support for the belief that rape is an extension of normal male attitudes and socialization practices in our society, and that people generally do not view rape as potentially committed by deviants only. Although this generalization may be questionable, apparently many college students (presumably low aggression-anxiety males in particular) believe the rape myth that women enjoy victimization and find such portrayals sexually exciting; moreover, these individuals would be inclined to engage in rape if reality were not a factor.

Obviously the discrimination of fantasy from reality is an extremely important issue because many individuals in society are poorly socialized, lack adequate impulse control in various situations, and have trouble maintaining appropriate contact with reality. However, the tendency to confuse fantasy with reality may not be limited to such individuals, since Malamuth's team suggests that normal male socialization practices may actually promote, directly or indirectly, poor discrimination of real sexual aggression toward women. Indeed, confusion between fantasy and reality among their well-educated and well-socialized college student population is suggested by the correlational data, even among some females. For example, women who believed that they might enjoy being raped reported more sexual arousal to the rape passage, believed that the victim enjoyed being raped, and that the victim could have stopped the rape if she had wanted to ($r = 0.44, 0.47$, and 0.57 respectively); these correlations strongly suggest that these women perceived the situation more in terms of being raped by a "friendly" assailant rather than a real one, and thought they could actually control the circumstances to fit their erotic desire. Interestingly, Hariton and Singer (1974) point out that 65% of their sample of 141 married women reported moderate to high levels of sexual fantasy during intercourse, with "imaginary lover" and "submission" representing the most common themes used to increase sexual arousal and pleasure. Obviously individual differences play an important role here since Malamuth's team reports that sexual arousal to the rape depiction was very low for women who strongly fear rape; it seems unlikely that submission fantasies would be popular with this group. However, it would hardly be surprising to find that many males use well-established fantasies of rape, similar to the typical rape myth in which the woman eventually becomes aroused and excited, to further their own sexual arousal and excitement (and certainly the publishers of sexual material believe they do). It might be predicted that those individuals who respond strongly to rape fantasies, and who also tend to confuse fantasy with reality or who tend to ignore reality generally, will also be more negatively influenced by viewing depictions of sexually aggressive behaviours.

Malamuth (1981), in order to further explore these issues, designed a study to examine whether exposure to rape depictions specifically affects sexual fantasies. Twenty-nine male college students classified as sexually force oriented (liking the idea of force in sexual relations or indicating that they might engage in coercive sexual acts) or non-force oriented, were randomly assigned to exposure to rape-arousal (a depiction in which the woman eventually becomes aroused) or mutually-consenting versions of a slide-audio show. All subjects were then exposed to the same rape-abhorrence audio tape, an audio description of a rape read by a female. In general, moderately high arousal was stimulated by both versions of the slide-show, according to self-report measures (subjective mean ratings of 43%), and by the rape audio tape (mean rating of 42%). The results tended to be consistent with earlier findings that show certain rape portrayals can stimulate relatively high sexual arousal in normals; moreover, the levels of sexual arousal generated by the rape audio tape read by a female suggests that even a rape that emphasizes the victim's abhorrence may under certain conditions stimulate sexual arousal.

After exposure to the rape audio tape, all subjects were instructed to try and reach as high a level of sexual arousal as possible by fantasizing about whatever they would like, but without any direct stimulation of the penis. The findings show that exposure to the rape-arousal version of the slide show, plus further exposure to the rape-abhorrence audio show, stimulated more arousing sexual fantasies in subjects classified as force-oriented compared to non-force oriented subjects (subjective mean ratings of 62 and 25% respectively); in contrast, exposure to the mutually-consenting version of the slide show, plus further exposure to the rape-abhorrence audio show, suppressed most arousal to sexual fantasies in force-oriented subjects, whereas non-force oriented subjects produced relatively arousing sexual fantasies (mean ratings of 15 and 43%). Apparently the repetitive presentation of rape stimuli was responsible for the observed increase in sexually arousing fantasies in the force-oriented subjects, and the suppression of arousal in non-force oriented subjects; unfortunately, Malamuth offers no explanation for the paradoxical effect that the rape-abhorrence portrayal presumably had on suppressing sexual arousal in force-oriented subjects who first viewed the mutually-consenting version of the slide show. The actual content of the subjects' fantasies was rated for themes of sexual violence by two judges, blind to experimental conditions; five out of 14 subjects exposed to repetitive rape depictions were judged to have produced sexually violent fantasies, whereas the other nine subjects' fantasies did not contain such material – sexual arousal levels reported in response to the five violent fantasies were moderately high for the three force-oriented subjects and the two non-force oriented subjects who produced these violent fantasies (mean rating of 51 and 47·5%, respectively).

It is unfortunate that Malamuth's important attempt to look at the effects of exposure to aggressive and non-aggressive sexual portrayals upon subsequent fantasy productions failed to consider the possibility of assessing the subjects' pre-existing abilities to generate sexually stimulating fantasies and, moreover, the content of those fantasies; taken together, the arousal and content data during the fantasy period fail to provide convincing evidence that rape depictions foster sexually violent fantasies in subjects despite the suggestion that they do. Indeed, more subjects reported arousing non-aggressive sexual fantasies to the double rape presentation than sexually violent fantasies, and the force orientation appeared to be completely unrelated to violent fantasy production. Furthermore, it is disappointing that penile tumescence data is not reported anywhere in the study since Malamuth goes to some length to describe the instrumentation he used to measure erections; as a substitute he suggests that the physiological responses he recorded yielded information equivalent to the self-report measures of arousal. Unfortunately fantasies are not simple phenomena for researchers to investigate since they are totally subject-induced and controlled, and reliance upon self-report as the only measure of the effect of sexual fantasies would seem, at best, an unwise procedure. Similarly, the assessment of only one fantasy following exposure to the sexually violent depictions contributes to the overall impression of this research, namely, that the limitations of the study make any conclusions very uncertain.

In an experimental field study designed to examine the effects of viewing violent sexuality upon attitudes and beliefs, Malamuth and Check (1981) have recently addressed several critical issues that relate to the generalization and implications of the research findings derived from their experimental studies. Specifically, their research findings have raised some important questions about whether the undesirable effects of exposure to sexually violent depictions last for more than just a short period of time, and whether the various demand characteristics generated in these experiments conducted in artificial laboratory situations permit reasonable generalization to real-life. Therefore, in an effort to partially circumvent these criticisms, Malamuth and Check attempted to examine the effects of viewing sexual violence on dependent variables assessed several days after exposure in a non-laboratory setting. In particular, the authors were interested in evaluating the contention that mass media presentations portraying violence against women as having positive consequences contribute to greater acceptance of sexual and non-sexual violence against women. Drawing upon their previous research that showed that males are more accepting of rape myths and violence against women than females (Malamuth et al., 1980a), the authors expected that males would be negatively affected by exposure to violent sexual depictions. One hundred and fifteen male and female college students were randomly assigned to view either two sexually-violent or control feature-length films in theatres located on the college campus. Importantly, the films were not sexually explicit violent movies but ones that have been shown on television, and moreover, the primary theme of the films was not violent sexuality; specifically, the two experimental films (*The Getaway* and *Swept Away*) were chosen because they portray violence against women as being justified and as having positive consequences, whereas the two control films (*A Man and A*

Woman and *Hooper*) do not portray any such acts of violence. The results indicated that exposure to films portraying violence against women as having positive consequences increased males' acceptance of interpersonal violence against women and non-significantly increased acceptance of rape myths, whereas for females there were non-significant tendencies in the opposite direction. These results resemble attitude polarization phenomena in which people with differing views on a particular topic tend to focus only on information which supports their own views (Myers and Lamm, 1976). Since the undesirable effects on males' attitudes were observed several days after exposure to the films, Malamuth and Check suggest that further research be conducted to assess the immediate effects of such exposure to see if they dissipate with time; however, the authors speculate that a "sleeper effect" may occur in which the information conveyed in the films may be initially discounted by being associated with a fictional presentation, but with the passage of time disassociation may occur so that the information is retained, but its source forgotten (cf. Gruder *et al.*, 1978); if so, such a mechanism may partially explain the effects of long-term exposure to violent sexuality, with each exposure serving to reinforce aggressive attitudes. Indeed, Tieger (1981) has recently shown that a population of males with favourable attitudes toward rape does exist, individuals who exhibit a pattern of beliefs which tend to defuse and minimize the violent and negative impact of rape on a victim. Malamuth and Check suggest that violent sexuality in films may reinforce such belief systems in individuals who have these attitudes by strengthening cognitive structures which may assist in disinhibiting actual aggressive behaviour toward women (cf. Bandura *et al.*, 1975). Moreover, they imply that the effects of viewing mass media depictions of violent sexuality may be more important to examine than just simply explicit depictions of such activities because of the massive audience they influence through repetitious presentations of similar themes reflecting aggression toward women.

SEXUAL MATERIALS AND PSYCHOPATHOLOGY

Sex Offences

A major question that is always asked, but as yet not satisfactorily answered, is whether there exists a relationship between exposure to sexual materials and delinquency in general and sex offences in particular. Sexual offences are a relatively uncommon form of antisocial behaviour if court proceedings are any guide to the volume of crime in a society;* according to the English Home Office publication *Sexual Offences, Consent and Sentencing,* there has been little increase in the frequency of occurrence of such offences in the period from 1946 to 1976 (Walmsley and White, 1979). In England and Wales in 1946, there were just over 9300 indictable sexual offences known to the police; in 1976 the total was 22 203, nearly half of them being for indecent exposure or assault on a female.† Thus the current figure is about 2·5 times that of 1946, which compares with a figure of just over 77 700 for offences of violence against the person which is 19 times that of 1946; sexual offences rose from being 2% of all offences known in 1946 to almost 4% in 1955, and since then the figure has dropped to only 1%. In contrast the rape total has risen four times the 1946 figures, from 251 to about 1100; since rape is generally considered to be the most violent of sexual offences, it seems likely that it reflects on a very much smaller scale the great increase in recorded violence against the person. Unfortunately, although rape and attempted rapes comprise only 4–5% of the annual total of recorded sexual offences, the relationship between the *recorded* incidence of these offences and the *actual* incidence is unknown since we have no figures for this country. However, the most reliable estimate of the reporting of rapes in the United States, a country in which the incidence of reported rapes is over 27 times the figure for England and Wales, suggests that less than 30% of these crimes are reported (FBI Uniform Crime Reports, 1979); obviously, in some countries, sexual offences like rape are not as uncommon as they tend to be in this country.

Much has been made in recent years of the changes in criminal statistics for sex offences in countries where a more liberal attitude to sexually explicit material has been adopted (Cline, 1974; Cochrane, 1978; Court, 1976, 1980). Criminal statistics have been used by both those adopting a pro- or anti-liberalizing attitude to sexual materials, although there are so many pitfalls in the collection and interpretation of criminal statistics that it is unlikely that this alone will greatly assist in identifying the role sexual material plays in the problem of sexual offences. Interestingly, the *U.S. Commission on Obscenity and Pornography* (1970) reached the conclusion that, for America, the relationship between the availability of erotica and changes in sex crime rates neither proves nor disproves the possibility that availability of erotica leads to crime, but the massive overall increases in sex offences that have been alleged do not seem to have occurred. The Com-

---

* Definitions of sexual crime are highly culture bound. Ideas of what is harmful or offensive to society or to individuals change remarkably over time and, for this reason, it is difficult to compare results from country to country (Gibbens *et al.,* 1977; West, 1982).

† See Gayford (1981) for a review.

mission based its conclusion, in part, on an assessment of the criminal statistics in Denmark following the liberalization of the laws on explicit sexual material in the late 1960s which suggested that there had been a decline in major sex offences, or at least that there had not been a sudden increase in such crime. More recently, Court (1976) has stated that there is statistical evidence indicating that the free availability of sexual material can be linked to an increase in sexual offences. Obviously the issue of whether people are more likely to be sexually assaulted as a result of the circulation of certain kinds of publication, or the showing of certain kinds of film, is a very important one. The issues involved in the statistical argument concerning the hypothesized relationship between the free availability of sexual materials and increases in sexual offences have recently been re-examined by the *Committee on Obscenity and Film Censorship* (1979).

A special feature of the statistical argument is that it is possible to measure the effects of increased availability of sexual material on sexual offences, despite the well-known difficulties of proving or even plausibly arguing for causal relationships between general or diffuse social phenomena on a purely statistical basis; even if it is possible to provide an accurate measure of two variables, the existence of a correlation between them is certainly no proof that one is influenced by the other. However, the major drawback to the statistical argument is that the two major variables cannot easily be measured, despite claims that they can be (Court, 1980). For example, attempts to obtain accurate information about the number of sexual offences has been very difficult; certainly we have detailed information about the number of cases reported to the police over a long period, but this is not the same as knowing how many offences occurred, since there is no means of telling how many victims decided not to go to the police to report what happened. Moreover, victims may at different times be more or less ready to report sex offences, possibly due to changing social attitudes and/or practices, or to changes in legal or police practices. However, in comparison, the imperfections in the data concerning the incidence of sexual offences are relatively insignificant compared with the lack of information regarding the availability of sexual materials, both in terms of the quantity and essential character of the material; the issue is whether the differences between various types of "strengths" of sexual materials are likely to have different effects on sexual offences. These difficulties are very real, and severely limit the conclusions that are drawn from the existing data; if no measures exist for what is supposed to be the causal factor, it seems unlikely that any progress will be made to relate the two variables, even on a correlational basis.

The Committee, acknowledging the above issues, came to the following conclusions in their attempt to assess the available information linking sexual materials and sexual offences in England and Wales:

1) There is no accurate information about the availability of sexual materials over the years, despite claims that it became increasingly available at particular times, 2) the rising trend in sexual offences generally, and in rape and sexual assaults, started long before it is alleged that sexual materials began to be widely available, 3) increases in sexual offences generally, including rape and sexual assault, have been significantly slower (although the figures for rape alone indicate the difference is less significant) in the last twenty years than that in crime generally, and 4) the contrast between the upward trend in crime generally and the greater stability in the numbers of rapes and sexual assaults has been very significant for the years from 1973 to 1977 (except for rape alone reported in London, where the increase is consistent with that in other forms of crime), when this period appears to have been the one when explicit sexual materials were most available (p. 78).

The Committee, while not denying the possibility that sexual material may be linked to the commission of sexual offences, came to the conclusion that

> it is not possible, in our view, to reach well-based conclusions about what in this country has been the influence of pornography on sexual crime. But we unhesitatingly reject the suggestion that the available statistical information for England and Wales lends any support at all to the argument that pornography acts as a stimulus to the commission of sexual violence (p. 80).

Sex Offenders

Many questions have been asked about the relationship between sexual offenders and sexual materials. For example, do sex offenders respond to explicit sexual material like others, do they use it differently, and does exposure to sexual stimuli prompt them to commit sexual crimes? Simple though the questions may seem, the answers are generally complex and hedged with caveats. Much of the difficulty lies in the types of studies used to investigate the questions, and the fact that retrospective self-report data and correlational methods have often been extended beyond reason. However, some information has been generated with these techniques and it seems useful, as background data, to provide an overview of this work.

Gebhard and his colleagues (1965), in a retrospectively designed study, investigated the experiences of sex offenders and non-offenders with sexual materials in order to find out whether sex offenders were characterized by greater exposure or responsiveness to explicit sexual material. Personal interviews were carried out among 1356 imprisoned sex offenders, using both an offender group not convicted of any sexual offence, and men from the general population as controls. In response to questions regarding the degree of sexual arousal experienced as a result of viewing sexual materials, on the whole, sex offenders reported the least arousal except for heterosexual aggressors against minors, and homosexual offenders against adults; interestingly, when asked whether stories of rape, torture, or violence arouse them sexually, over 90% of the control and prison groups denied being aroused by such themes, with the exception of the heterosexual aggressors against children, minors, and adults who indicated at least a moderate degree of sexual arousal in about 16% of the individuals. However, in light of recent research findings, questions about sexual arousal appear irrelevant to actual sexual arousal; for example, Malamuth *et al.* (1980b), previously discussed, have shown that contemporary depictions of rape can produce strong sexual arousal in normal college males and females; if asked initially about whether stories of rape, torture, or violence arouse them sexually, it seems very likely that these individuals would have similarly denied being aroused by such themes. Similarly, Abel *et al.* (1975) have shown that very little reliance can be placed on the verbal reports of sex offenders because they are very often unaware of what arouses them sexually. Overall, Gebhard's team failed to find greater interest in explicit sexual material for sex offenders and they concluded that there is no observable relationship between sexual materials and sexual offenders, although no systematic attempt was made to link particular types of sexual material with specific offences. Obviously, the issue of arousal to aggressive or violent sexual materials is important since deviant sexual arousal is often thought to account for deviant sexual behaviour; however, research suggests that this issue is complicated, and that strong arousal to deviant sexual material does not, by itself, necessarily predict deviant sexual behaviour any more than strong arousal to heterosexual sexual material predicts appropriate sexual behaviour (cf. Abel *et al.*, 1981; Malamuth and Check, in press a).

In another retrospective study, Propper (1971) classified 476 reformatory inmates, aged 16–21, according to whether they had experienced a high or low degree of exposure to explicit sexual materials, and found a positive relationship between high exposure and sexually promiscuous and deviant behaviour at very early ages, as well as affiliation with groups high in antisocial and criminal activity. However, it is not possible to say which came first, the deviant behaviour or interest in sexual materials as the correlational data equally supports the hypothesis that persons who come to engage in sexually deviant behaviour also tend to make use of sexual material and to expose themselves to it. Moreover, the inmates' deviant friends may have adversely influenced them by encouraging an interest in sexual material and by promoting deviant behaviours. Since it is quite possible that peer group influences or some other third variable like socialization affect experience with sexual materials, Davis and Braucht (1971) attempted to evaluate this in their study of moral and interpersonal character as it relates to experience with sexual materials and deviant sexuality. Character is, of course, rather a vague global concept, and they concerned themselves with three aspects: moral blindness, quality of moral reasoning, and defective interpersonal character such as that exhibited in exploitative and shallow interpersonal relationships. The authors investigated seven different populations of subjects comprising 365 individuals and found that there was indeed a positive relationship between poor character scores and amount of exposure to sexual materials, and moreover, exposure was not related to having deviant friends which helps to rule out peer influence as a significant factor in the obtained positive relationship. Yet, they clearly state that

> while these data may be interpreted as supporting the hypothesis that exposure to pornography plays a role in the development of sexual deviance and in precocious heterosexual behaviour, limitations of the research design do not permit a definite conclusion in favour of such an interpretation. It should be emphasized that these same data are also interpretable as supporting the hypothesis that persons who come to engage in sexually deviant behaviour also tend to make use of pornography and to expose themselves voluntarily to it (p. 173).

Thus, the possibility exists that interest in and use of sexual materials is simply a correlate of high sexual drive and interest, reflecting a generally uninhibited sexual life style rather than playing some causal role in the development of sexual deviance. Interestingly, the authors suggest that a more refined analysis might well show that it is not the mere presentation of naked bodies or intercourse that has any detrimental effects, but rather that it is the attitude toward the body, toward sexual relations, and toward persons that is critical.

In contrast to the above studies, Goldstein et al. (1971) found that sex offenders have been exposed to less sexually explicit material than normals during adolescence, thus suggesting a negative relationship with sexual deviance. The authors based their findings upon a 267-item interview concerning experience with sexual materials, attitudes to sex, and a sexual case history which was administered to sex offenders comprising rapists, male- and female-object paedophiles, homosexuals, transsexuals, heavy users of sexual materials, and two non-deviant contrast groups. However, the authors admit that the matching of their various groups was only fair, with control subjects being significantly younger, better educated, and of a higher socio-economic status – factors which have previously been associated with individuals who have had greater exposure to sexual materials – than any of the sex offender groups (cf. Abelson et al., 1971). This limitation and the fact that the size of the offender groups was fairly small make conclusions based upon this data somewhat uncertain. Even if the sex offenders did receive more exposure to erotic materials at an earlier age would not prove it was harmful. But in this case, Goldstein's team suggests that the reverse may be true: lack of early experience with sexual material may be positively associated with later emergence of sexual pathology. To support this conclusion, the authors cite clinical studies of the early family history of sex offenders which suggests that they come from repressive homes where sexual matters are rarely discussed openly, if ever, and where sexual curiosity and interest are ignored or punished; inexperience with sexual material is considered a reflection of their generally deprived sexual environment. Cook *et al.* (1971) also found that sex offenders generally experienced less frequent and milder exposure to sexual material than did other offenders; similarly, Walker (1971) reported that rapists have somewhat less experience with sexual material than controls. Overall, retrospective studies have yielded results indicative of both a positive and a negative relationship between experience with sexual materials and deviant behaviour or antisocial acts. Such studies tend to be much less popular today due in part to the problems of relying exclusively upon verbal reports. Basically, however, retrospective comparison studies are unable to evaluate the sexual responses of sex offenders and normals in a meaningful way; of greater interest, therefore, are the more recent experimental studies which attempt to assess the extent to which specific sex offenders, compared to normal adults in the general population, are affected in terms of immediate responses to various types of sexual material, including those related to the nature of the offender's conviction.

Deviant Sexual Arousal

According to the Diagnostic and Statistical Manual of the American Psychiatric Association (DSM-III), the term *paraphilia* refers to psychosexual disorders which are characterized by arousal in response to sexual objects or situations that are not part of normative arousal-activity patterns, and that in varying degrees may interfere with the capacity for reciprocal affectionate sexual activity. Originally the term was coined by Money (1980) who defined it as "an heterosexual condition of being recurrently responsive to, and obsessively dependent on, an unusual or unacceptable stimulus, perceptual or in fantasy, in order to have a state of erotic arousal initiated or maintained, and in order to achieve or facilitate orgasm" (p. 220). The essential feature of these disorders is that deviant fantasy or behaviour are necessary for sexual excitement and arousal; moreover, the fantasy and behaviour tend to be repetitive and involve either: (1) a preference for a non-human object to stimulate sexual arousal, (2) repetitive sexual activity with humans involving real or simulated suffering or humiliation, or (3) repetitive sexual behaviour with non-consenting partners (individuals under the age of consent are, by definition, non-consenting partners). The paraphilias include the following disorders: fetishism, transvestism, zoophilia, paedophilia, exhibitionism, voyeurism, sexual masochism, and sexual sadism (including some forms of rape); such a list emphasizes that it is the persistent and compulsive substitution of some other act for heterosexual genital intercourse which chiefly characterizes the behaviours more commonly referred to as sexual deviations in this country; paraphilias represent, in fact, a restricted number of sexual deviations. Although sexual deviations are usually separated into categories according to the predominant sexual behaviour, there is often considerable overlap between them in that more than one deviation may be present in an individual; moreover, individuals with a wide range of deviant behaviour will be represented within each category, differing in terms of personality, strength of deviant behaviour patterns, attitudes to deviant behaviour, and so on. Typically, individuals with these disorders do not regard themselves as ill, and only come to the attention of professionals in mental health when their behaviour has resulted in their being convicted of a sexual offence; of course, not all sexual deviations are considered sexual offences, including tranvestism and fetishism, any more than all sexual offences are sexual deviations.

Of all behaviour which arouses marked social concern, rape is the one which currently excites the most interest world-wide and the literature is voluminous (see Chappell et al., 1977 for a review). Rape has become a rallying point for various feminist groups and they have not only made the world increasingly aware of the plight of the rape victim, but have also spoken of the need for treatment of the rapist himself. Thus, it is not surprising that research on the rapist, his sexual arousal patterns, classification, and treatment has increased substantially, whereas research on other types of sexual offenders has not been so active (see Abel et al., 1976, 1977b). A criticism common to many of the early studies investigating how exposure to explicit sexual materials affects sex offenders is that type of sexual material was not systematically related to type of sexual offence. Thus, instead of including assessments of interest in and arousal to depictions of rape, sex with children, and other aggressive or deviant themes, the early studies primarily assessed sexual offenders' self-reported interest in and arousal to non-aggressive sexual material such as nudity, petting, intercourse, and oral–genital behaviour. Recently, however, studies with sub-groups of sex offenders, primarily rapists, exhibitionists, and paedophiles, have been designed to evaluate the components of their sexual arousal to a variety of sexual stimuli, including those relevant to their particular offence (Abel et al., 1975, 1977a, 1978, 1981; Barbaree et al., 1979; Hinton et al., 1980; Kolářský et al., 1978; Laws and Holmen, 1978; Quinsey and Carrigan, 1978).

Deviant sexual arousal is often invoked to explain deviant sexual behaviour. For example, it is well known that children can stimulate sexual arousal in paedophiles. Similarly, Abel et al. (1977a) suggest that violence can evoke sexual arousal in some types of rapists, and contend that measures of sexual responsiveness to the depiction of rape can serve as indices of the proclivity to rape; support for this idea comes from their work which showed that portrayals of both rape and mutually-consenting sexual acts can elicit strong sexual arousal in rapists, whereas only mutually-consenting acts can produce such arousal in non-rapists. Abel's team found a highly significant correlation ($r = 0.98$) between descriptions of rape and responses to descriptions of violence alone in their rapist group; they state that "although erection to aggressive cues was 40% to those to rape cues, this relationship was constant, that is, as erection to aggressive cues increased, so did erection to rape cues" (p. 901). Indeed, they also found that in cases of sadism and in cases of sadistic rape, in which the assailant prefers forcing himself on the victim, often injuring her as well, aggression is a necessary component of sexual interaction to produce sexual excitement (cf. Stoller, 1976b). Gebhard et al. (1965) similarly classified a portion of rapists, one-quarter to one-third of their sample, as carrying out rape primarily as an act of aggression; apparently the sexual arousal of these rapists is deviant because force, violence, and non-consent are necessary to generate sufficient sexual excitement, and in these cases sexual arousal to depictions of mutually-consenting sexual activities, devoid of aggression, is minimal. Barbaree et al. (1979) also studied the effects of exposure to depictions of mutually-consenting sex, rape, and violent non-sexual assault upon rapists and non-rapists and reported results that agreed with the earlier study reported by Abel et al. (1977a). Thus, in non-rapists, descriptions of rape and assault evoked considerably less sexual arousal than depictions of mutually-consenting sex, whereas in rapists the different depictions of sexual behaviour did not evoke different levels of sexual excitement. Barbaree's team suggests that "the non-rapists' lower arousal to verbal descriptions of rape is best explained as a suppression or inhibition of erectile responses by the force or violent aspects in the rape episodes" (p. 221). Moreover, they posit that the sexual arousal of the rapists is deviant because force, violence, and non-consent of the female do not inhibit their sexual arousal, perhaps because they are desensitized to the emotional effects of force and violence by greater experience with violence in their peer groups, or perhaps because the rapists are not as well socialized and have not developed appropriate inhibitory mechanisms. These studies emphasize that rapists respond with sexual excitement to a range of stimuli that are very deviant at one extreme and normal at the other. Moreover, they emphasize that not all rapists respond equally to this range of stimuli and how necessary it is to keep in mind that even a single category of sexual offence such as rape can encompass wide variations in arousal and behaviour patterns. Perhaps of greater importance, these studies point out that sexual arousal to normal heterosexual stimuli does not preclude deviant sexual arousal and behaviour, although this is not particularly surprising since some sexual offenders are married or have regular partners and participate in apparently normal sexual activities as well as engage in deviant ones. The issue is complex, however, since recent research has demonstrated that even normal heterosexual males and females can respond with strong sexual arousal to deviant sexual stimuli under certain conditions (cf. Abel *et al.*, 1978; Malamuth and Check, 1980b; Malamuth *et al.*, 1980a, b); the difference, however, is that these individuals do not engage in deviant sexual behaviours, nor are they dependent upon deviant fantasy or deviant stimuli for sexual arousal.

At this point one might begin to wonder what in fact is deviant sexual arousal and how is it related to deviant sexual behaviour? As we have already seen, arousal patterns are highly idiosyncratic and are subject to a number of influences, suggesting that the concept of a qualitative difference between deviant and normal sexual arousal may not hold. For example, Abel *et al.* (1981) found no differences in the degree of sexual arousal to deviant and non-deviant stimuli in rapists and exhibitionists. Similarly, they report that eight male paedophiles showed equal arousal to deviant and non-deviant stimuli, despite young boys being their deviant object choice and adult women being shown in the non-deviant portrayal. In contrast, homosexuals showed more sexual arousal to deviant stimuli than to non-deviant cues as did fetishists and sado-masochists; Abel *et al.* (1977a) have shown that the real deviant stimulus with sado-masochists is primarily aggression, with women providing a context for the paraphilia. Hinton *et al.* (1980) also found that groups of sexual offenders (against women, girls, boys and men), non-sexual attackers of women, and typical heterosexuals did not differ in physiological response to films of heterosexual activity, thus emphasizing the fact that many sexual offenders respond with strong sexual arousal to non-deviant stimuli. These findings may be understandable in view of the fact that the erotic stimulus remains a female in every case with the exception of the sexual attackers of boys and men, the group that also produced the lowest response to the heterosexual film.

Kolářský *et al.* (1978) have also found that sex offenders, primarily exhibitionists, are capable of responding with strong physiological arousal to film scenes of heterosexual activity, in this instance the seductive behaviour of a nude or semi-nude female (cf. Kolářský and Madlafousek, 1972); this research was primarily concerned with whether exhibitionists avoid their victim's erotic cooperation because appropriate heterosexual stimuli, especially pre-coital erotic cues, may be aversive to them. The results suggest that perhaps all sex offenders who offend adult women can respond to normal female erotic behaviour with strong sexual arousal. This, of couse, raises the question as to why such offenders would desire a sexually uncooperative female when they can respond just as well to a cooperative one; Gebhard *et al.* (1965) also point out that exhibitionists avoid exposure to females who might cooperate sexually, and that they do not expose themselves against their regular sex partner if they have one. Wakeling (1976) indicates that exhibitionism, like other forms of deviant sexual behaviour, is dictated more by neurotic or non-sexual needs rather than by erotic ones, and involves a large element of compulsiveness and risk-taking associated with the behaviour. Moreover, he points out that sexual deviation is also compatible with adaptive social functioning and with elements of relatively normal heterosexual functioning; thus, exhibitionism can co-exist with heterosexual behaviour which emphasizes the tremendous variability of sexual behaviour, and that categories of sexual deviation are not discrete phenomena. Smukler and Schiebel (1975), for example, report that the typical exhibitionist is married, has above average intelligence, has apparently normal heterosexual relations, holds a satisfactory job, and cannot be described as demonstrating severe characterological or psychotic features; clinically and psychometrically he can be described as moderately schizoid, mildly obsessive and passive-dependent, and as having great difficulty in recognizing angry feelings, even under circumstances of extreme provocation. The authors indicate that their data do "not support any definitive character type or evidence of severe pathology and if specific reference to their symptom is omitted, they appear relatively normal" (p. 602). Interestingly, all their patients had "peeped" before they exhibited, and so technically they were exhibitionist–voyeurs; exhibiting was not related to frequency or lack of sexual intercourse and, in fact, each patient agreed that, as often as not, he did not feel sexually aroused when he exhibited, again suggesting that neurotic or non-sexual needs predominate over sexual ones. Indeed, the authors indicate that this personality pattern seems consistent with a fear of recognizing unconscious aggressive wishes, and suggest that exposure probably protects them against committing violence and at the same time guards against their awareness of aggressive desires. Interestingly, Rooth (1973) found a low proportion of sexual offences involving force in his group of 30 persistent exhibitionists. Rosen (1979), commenting upon the link between exhibitionism and violence, indicates that although exhibitionism is one of the most common sexual deviations in this country and constitutes about a third of all sexual offences, the persistent and exclusive exhibitionist is somewhat unusual – most offenders are charged only once – and unlikely to be dangerous, the violent minority probably coming from the ranks of the incidental as opposed to the habitual offender. Overall, the above studies demonstrate that sex offenders respond to various sexual stimuli, both deviant and non-deviant, and emphasize that non-sexual factors contribute much to the commission of sexual offences. Indeed, as Cox (1979) points out,

> such complex phenomena as sex offences are always over-determined, and personality characteristics, organic factors, modified inhibition due to drugs or fatigue, the detailed circumstances of the offence (including the specificity of the

victim), together with the patient's previous life-experience, may all contribute to the . . . particular moment when he assaulted his victim (p. 308).

Ideally, one might have hoped that research studies would show all sex offenders to be more sexually excited by portrayals of deviant sexual activities in contrast to non-deviant ones. So far, however, research has been unable to demonstrate specific stimulus control over most sex offenders' sexual arousal, with the possible exception of sadistic rapists who do seem to be specifically aroused by depictions of violence. In general, as we have seen, it is not so much a case of sex offenders responding differently than normals as one of normals responding differently than sex offenders, especially in response to portrayals of violent sexuality; normals appear to be more responsive to inhibitory cues in such depictions, although their sexual responsiveness can be easily disinhibited by changing the stimulus emphasis in the portrayal. Thus, as we know, rape depictions that focus an individual's attention upon the grim realities of rape by emphasizing the pain and disgust of the victim reduce arousal substantially, whereas emphasis upon the victim's arousal disinhibits arousal in the viewer. Moreover, certain disinhibitory cues can heighten sexual arousal even in depictions where the stimulus emphasis has been shown to effectively inhibit arousal in normal males; for example, listening to an audio-presentation of a rape-abhorrence story, when read by a female, will disinhibit males' sexual responsiveness to the normally inhibiting portrayal; reading a sado-masochistic story prior to a rape-abhorrence story also seems to reduce individuals' sensitivity to the normally inhibiting cues in the rape depiction (Malamuth, 1981; Malamuth and Check, 1980b). Interestingly, research suggests that individuals focus their own perceptions to these depictions; for example, normals were found to respond to a film of heterosexual intercourse with as much objective physiological and subjective arousal as homosexuals, presumably because the heterosexuals' attention and fantasies were focused upon the woman, while the homosexuals' attention was on the man; however, certain depictions of sexual activities may be less amenable to such changes in stimulus emphasis because their meaning is over-determined; thus, depictions of two male homosexuals engaging in explicit sexual behaviour being viewed by heterosexual males results in little arousal, presumably due to homosexual threat and the fact that the viewers lack the opportunity to elaborate on the scene by incorporating their own preferences (Mavissakalian et al., 1975). Overall, these findings indicate that various inhibitory and disinhibitory factors can influence individuals' sexual arousal to depictions of sexual activities by changing their perceptions of the sexual interaction. The problem is that normal individuals, once disinhibited, tend to become less responsive to inhibitory stimulus conditions in subsequent portrayals of violent sexuality, and this lack of sensitivity and responsiveness to important inhibitory cues resembles that displayed by sexual aggressives. Such findings have led some researchers to question whether frequent exposure to violent sexuality will adversely influence normal individuals to the extent that they eventually become less responsive to women's communications – perhaps to the point of ignoring the meaning of disinterested responses – and whether it will also lead to changes in attitudes about the appropriateness of using force in sexual relations, thus increasing the probability that some individuals may commit sexually violent acts (Malamuth *et al.*, 1980b).

Sexual Materials and Sexual Aggression: Proving the Link?

The evidence linking sexually explicit stimuli to harmful sexual and aggressive behaviours is still limited, but none the less suggestive. There are, as we have seen, many and varied effects that result from viewing sexual materials, many pros and cons about the harms or benefits of exposure to such stimuli, and yet despite a great deal of new research information we still do not know as much as we would like to know. Interestingly, the results of recent research on viewing violent and aggressive sexuality seem likely to renew the controversy over the harmfulness of exposure to all sexually explicit material. If so, the lines of battle will probably be drawn somewhat differently this time, with non-aggressive erotic depictions being seen as relatively benign and innocent forms of sexual expression, and the sexually violent and deviant portrayals being viewed as dangerous. Social concern about the effects of long-term exposure to non-aggressive erotica still exists because of the possibility of conditioning arousal to sexual objects or situations that are not part of normative arousal-activity patterns; however, the studies we have suggest that fantasies of actual sexual experiences are probably more relevant to such conditioning than explicit depictions. In general, contemporary research continues to support the conclusion that short-term exposure to erotica is relatively harmless – it raises drive levels but does not change habits; and yet, concern about this still tends to be expressed because research has shown that heightened emotional arousal from erotica can facilitate subsequent aggression in previously angered males and females, especially in the presence of aggressive cues. However, exposure to a variety of highly arousing non-sexual stimuli such as physical exercise and white noise can also increase general emotional arousal and facilitate aggression, suggesting that the aggression-eliciting effect obtained is a direct function of the degree of arousal produced by such stimuli – not simply a function of the specific properties of erotic stimuli; indeed, less arousing forms of explicit sexual stimuli have been shown to reduce anger in provoked individuals, thus inhibiting aggressive behaviour. Moreover, aggression is entirely dependent upon prior or subsequent anger instigation, *mere exposure* to these sexually explicit stimuli being necessary but not sufficient in itself, irrespective of the degree of arousal. Finally, the concern that viewing erotica induces people to commit sex crimes seems unfounded since the sex crime rate appears unrelated to this factor – it may not significantly lower the rate, but it does not seem to put it up either.

Greater social concern is, in fact, currently being expressed about the effects of mass media presentations of violent or aggressive sexuality upon attitudes and behaviour, with many writers contending that sexually violent portrayals encourage violence toward women (Brownmiller, 1975; Clark and Lewis, 1977; Russell, 1975). Supported in their claim by the recent spate of films depicting sexual attacks on women and the increasingly violent content of sexual stimuli in the mass media over the last decade, these writers and others have attempted to arouse public interest in sexual aggression against women and, in particular, rape. For example, Brownmiller (1975) asserts that "the anti-female propaganda that permeates our . . . cultural output promotes a climate in which acts of sexual hostility directed against women are not only tolerated but ideologically encouraged" (p. 444). As a result of the increase in social concern among researchers, numerous studies assessing patterns of attitudes toward rape, its victims, and its perpetrators have begun to appear recently (e.g. Burt, 1980; Feild, 1978; Krulewitz and Payne, 1978; Vinsel, 1977). Unfortunately, the history of psychology shows a curious resistance to the subject of rape, the fusion of violence and sexuality being more difficult to address than sexuality *per se*. Some men apparently still share the belief that there is no such thing as rape, thus reflecting the old male myth that it is impossible to rape an unwilling woman. Even now many men tend to believe that rape is always victim precipitated if, in fact, it occurs at all; for example, as Tieger (1981) points out, males rather consistently blame victims of rape and hold them responsible for their victimization to a greater extent than females, although Amir (1971), in his study of rape in the United States, found that only 19% of the rapes were so precipitated. In England, attention was focused on rape by a House of Lords decision that a man could not be convicted of rape if he honestly believed the woman consented, even if he had no reasonable grounds for so believing. This decision engendered widespread public concern and led to a Home Office enquiry, the *Heilbron Report* (1975), and ultimately to legislation, but the investigation supported the original opinion on the question of rape "in error"; a crime must be a deliberate or reckless intent to do something which society brands as criminal. The Report did suggest that the time had come for the definition of rape to be set out in statutory form in order to emphasize that lack of consent (and not violence) is the crux of the matter, and to bring out the importance of recklessness as a mental element in the crime. And, while acknowledging that there is no requirement of law that a belief concerning the victim's consent be based on reasonable grounds, the members indicated that "the presence or absence of such grounds is a relevant consideration to which the jury should have regard, in conjuction with all other evidence, in considering whether the accused genuinely had such a belief" (p. 36). Obviously, although the Report did stress the need to clarify this aspect of the law, many people still felt that too many rapists would simply be able to plead, "I thought she wanted me to."

Important as it is to acknowledge that rape is characterized and defined by non-consent rather than violence, rape remains an aggressive crime that belongs to a sub-culture of violence, although it is not always accompanied by overt violence. Amir (1971), for example, found that rapists in Philadelphia had a high proportion of previous arrest records; in fact, 49% of the offenders had previously been arrested, and whereas nearly 42% had been arrested for offences against property, 20% for offences against the person, and 23% for public disorder, *only* 9% had been previously arrested for forcible rape. Similarly, Amir reports that the New York Mayor's *Committee for the Study of Sex Offences* in 1940 found that only 14% of rapists had a previous record of sex crimes compared to 86% with records of non-sexual crime exclusively; the Committee concluded that rapists are not abnormal individuals, nor are their crimes abnormalities – rape is frequently just incidental, committed with another type of crime, and is only an offshoot of the rapist's criminal propensity. Again, Ellis and Brancale (1956) maintain that rapists tend to be relatively normal individuals whose offences are related to their general antisocial behaviour patterns; they tend to have more previous non-sexual offences than other sex offenders. Gebhard *et al.* (1965) also report that heterosexual aggressors against adults, basically rapists who have used force or threats, are criminally inclined men and their sex offences are by-products of general criminality.

In England, research studies also point out that rape is associated with a general pattern of criminality. Radzinowicz (1957), for example, reported in the large Cambridge study that 91% of convicted rapists were first sexual offenders, although 46% had a previous non-sexual conviction in their past; the other 9% convicted of rape or attempted rape had previous convictions for sexual offences, compared with 21% of persons convicted of indecent exposure. Interestingly, of the whole group of heterosexual offenders including the rapists, at least 56% had in their past one additional self-admitted, but not recorded, sex offence; 35% had two to four offences and 10% had five or more additional, but not recorded, sexual offences, which emphasizes the fact that criminal statistics generally underestimate the number of actual offences. The study also suggested that less than 2% of convicted sex offenders can be described as persistent and exclusive sex offenders, and many of these were presumably exhibitionists. One conclusion arrived at was that sexual recidivists are unlikely to progress from less serious to more serious sexual offences; Tennent (1971), however, reports some evidence which suggests that offenders who use force in a sexual offence will use greater force in subsequent offences.* Recently, Gibbens et al. (1977) examined the previous and subsequent convictions of all those charged with – rather than just convicted of – rape in 1961 in a 12-year follow-up study which found that the offenders could be divided into three behavioural groups: (1) paedophiliac rapists who at some time attacked girls aged 14 or less; (2) aggressive rapists, for whom the rape seemed only a part of a general cycle of aggression; (3) others, in whom the charge or conviction of rape was either totally isolated or with minimal accompaniment of other minor offences. This group included a wide range of offenders, from the young rapist who alleged the girl consented, to the highly pathological rapist–murderer. Overall, the sample of 259 rapists was found to be a fairly seriously criminal group in most respects, only 22% of the paedophiliacs and aggressives, and 55% of the others having no previous convictions; in a sense, all the offenders were considered to be aggressive, including most of those who were acquitted – no less than 58% of the aggressive offenders acquitted had records as bad or worse than those of the convicted aggressive rapists. Interestingly, rape for the aggressive group was thought to be part of a more general pattern of aggressive behaviour in personalities who react to frustration with indiscriminate aggression against whoever is nearest. Consideration of subsequent convictions over the 12 years showed a high level of further crime, and the aggressives, whether acquitted or convicted, led the way with a higher proportion of three or more offences.†

Why do people rape? Or, perhaps more importantly, why do individuals not commit rape? In attempting to account for sexual assault, researchers have developed various explanatory models, often called *blame models,* which involve a series of assumptions that attribute causality or responsibility to someone or something for the assault. Four blame models may be described: *societal blame, offender blame, victim blame* and *situation blame* (Brodsky and Hobart, 1978); these models are essentially working assumptions about the nature and causation of sexual assault which help determine various treatment and prevention plans. Relevant to our discussion, the *societal blame model* suggests that sexual assault results from the accumulation of cultural and social attitudes and values which legitimizes sexual coercion. Indeed, the increase in research investigating the effects of exposure

---

* For an account of the very persistent and dangerous rapist, see West *et al.* (1978).
† See Wright and West (1981) for a discussion of group rape *vs* individual assaults.

to violent sexuality is due in part to contentions by various writers that rape is basically an extension of normal sexual socialization – that men in general express the same range of identification with sexual aggression as rapists (e.g. Brownmiller, 1975; Clark and Lewis, 1977). Support for this idea is found in the overlap of attitudes and behaviours between sex offenders and other men. For example, Brodsky and Hobart (1978) report on research from the University of Alabama Rape Research Group that shows the marked similarity between offenders and the general norms of male populations on scales that measure attitudes toward women. Similarly, Tieger (1981) reports that some normal males do have favourable attitudinal patterns and perceptions toward the commission of rape, and exhibit beliefs which tend to minimize the violent and negative impact of rape on a victim; these males tend to be characterized as having a low degree of anxiety about the expression of aggression, and as being more masculine and dominant, characteristics which support the contention that sex-role stereotyping is related to rape attitudes (cf. Burt, 1980). Additional support for this perspective results from the substantial overlap in sexual arousal to depictions of violent sexuality between sex offenders and non-offenders (cf. Abel *et al.*, 1978; Malamuth and Check, 1980b). Such evidence fits, of course, with feminist views of society in which sexist socialization practices, pornography – especially violent sexuality – or any mass media depiction of violence toward women, and so on make up the societal blame model. In general terms, however, whether viewing violent sexuality actually leads to sexual assault or not means attempting to assess the behavioural end-product of instigations to and inhibitions against assaultive behaviour; unfortunately, we are still only at the stage of identifying some of the individual components of these factors, factors which are also found among non-assaultive individuals (cf. for example, Scott, 1977).

Interestingly, Mednick (1977) observes:

> when one considers the modern urban center in terms of the temptations and, in fact, incitements it offers to a variety of forms of asocial behaviour, one is impressed with the restraint and forebearance of the 80–90% of the population who apparently manage to avoid committing repetitive . . . crimes (p. 3).

It is just this sort of informal observation that suggests that there may be specific traits or characteristics that predispose individuals toward or away from acts of violence and crime in general. Of course, it is hardly surprising to find that some individuals are more law-abiding than others since we constantly observe individual differences in self-control, differences that obviously mediate the effects of situational provocation on aggressive behaviour. Wolfe and Baron (1971), for example, found that prisoners with a history of violence tended to respond to provocation by administering higher levels of shock than college students, a finding consistent with the notion that some people have lower thresholds for aggression, and are usually more prepared to hurt another person; similarly, Shemberg et al. (1968) showed that children with a previous history of aggression are usually more prepared to administer significantly higher levels of shock than are subjects low in aggression. Such findings typify the *offender blame model* of sexual assault; according to this model, sexual assault takes place when a person with deficits in aggressive or sexual behaviour acts on this pathology by forcible sexual contact. A consideration of individual differences in self-control invariably becomes a matter of practical concern in such a model, particularly to the discussion of whether exposure to violent sexuality increases sexually aggressive and assaultive behaviour. Obviously, however, blame models must not be looked at in isolation since they all contribute to an understanding of *sexual assault*; focusing exclusively on one explanatory model can only result in a biased appraisal of this complex interaction between two (or more) people.

Attempts to assess the probability of assaultive and antisocial behaviour are often based upon an evaluation of factors operating within an individual, the assumption being that such action is a reflection, in part, of broad consistencies underlying the behaviour of individuals; thus, at least a part of the variance will be accounted for by relatively stable attributes of people, whether these be motives, attitudes, beliefs, or other personal traits. Obviously, actual aggressive behaviour reflects some interaction of personality and environmental factors, although at times environmental and situational influences can overwhelm individual factors and mask their effects upon behaviour (cf. Dengerink, 1976). Unfortunately, the fact that we often know very little about the relationship between situational provocation and general traits of personality is a major problem in the prediction of sexually assaultive behaviour. However, in theory, at least, personality factors should be capable of being defined with increasing accuracy and predictions made upon them. The assumption that social behaviour is partly determined by general personality traits has, however, been under attack for some time (e.g. Mischel, 1968, 1977), although recent discussions of conceptual and methodological problems indicate that a rejection of trait approaches to personality is based upon the misleading assumption that there should be consistency at both the level of specific behavioural responses and at the intervening-variable level for trait theories to be viable (cf. Epstein, 1977; Eysenck and Eysenck, 1980). Some researchers, in fact, eschew any general statement regarding the origins of trait consistencies and rarely attempt to define the term trait, agreeing only that traits are stylistic consistencies in interpersonal behaviour (Hogan et al., 1977); although there is no point in going into the subject in detail here, it is important to note that the problem of individual differences continues to exist precisely because it is a matter of practical concern. Consider, for example, the research by Malamuth et al. (1980a) on exposure to violent sexuality. They show that, as pointed out earlier, an individual's degree of anxiety about violence and aggression is an important variable mediating the effects of exposure to depictions of rape; high aggression-anxiety males are more likely to identify with rape victims, and to become sensitized to the victim's plight in contrast to low aggression-anxiety males who tend to minimize the impact of aggressive behaviour directed toward the female victim. At this point, acknowledging that people react differently to portrayals of sexual violence depending upon whether they score high or low on a test of anxiety about aggression, it is difficult not to think in terms of relatively stable response dispositions mediating the effects of exposure to such stimuli. Indeed, as Eysenck and Nias (1978) state:

> any satisfactory experiment into the effects of sex and violence in the media should always incorporate separate measures of the most relevant personality traits of the subjects taking part in the experiment, and should explicitly formulate differential predictions about the reactions of different personality types. To treat everyone alike, and expect all subjects to react similarly to these experimental stimuli, is unreasonable, and out of line with the empirical evidence (p. 247–248).

Researchers have, of course, been aware for a long time that personality plays some role in determining whether or not a person will engage in proscribed behaviour; but what, exactly, are the important characteristics of traits that predispose individuals toward aggressive behaviour? Megargee (1966), in his analysis of assaultive behaviour, suggests that the violence of an aggressive act is proportional to the degree of instigation to aggression, but that the appearance of aggressive behaviour will depend upon the strength of inhibitions against such behaviour. Obviously, instigations to aggression and inhibitions against it are both characteristic of the individual and both are also to some extent dependent upon the environment. The balance between these factors can change, and the fact that they can be experimentally manipulated provides the framework for research which attempts to understand the development of self-control, how personality affects aggression, and why individuals defy or ignore society's sanctions (cf. Baron, 1977; Eysenck, 1977; Milgram, 1974; Mischel, 1974). In general, investigators have attempted to isolate those variables which may predispose people toward aggressive and antisocial behaviour in two different populations: *non-assaultive individuals* – those who aggress only under appropriate circumstances – *and assaultive individuals* – those who regularly engage in aggression and who consider it as a normal part of social interaction, or those who engage in relatively infrequent (even rare) but extreme acts of violence.

Since becoming civilized requires learning to inhibit and redirect some desires, researchers have considered the possibility that some individuals fail to acquire appropriate self-control because of some defect in avoidance learning. Thus, on the one hand, a child normally begins to learn to inhibit aggressive behaviour by a conditioning process in which fear of punishment or disapproval comes to inhibit contemplated aggressive actions, and fear reduction reinforces both cognitive and emotional processes which gradually acquire greater strength to regulate appropriate behaviour. But, as Mosher (1965) points out, expectations of social disapproval or punishment will inhibit aggression only in the presence of environmental cues indicating the existence of such consequences and, moreover, that individuals vary considerably in terms of how anxious or fearful they are of such environmental circumstances; thus, not surprisingly, those who are especially prone to such reactions – that is, those who are high in anxiety – will often demonstrate lower levels of aggression than other individuals. Expectations of social disapproval or punishment generally become internalized during socialization so that individuals begin to feel anxieties regarding their own disapproval of aggressive behaviour; Mosher labels these generalized expectancies for self-disapproval and self-mediated punishment as guilt, and suggests that they are relatively stable inhibitors of aggressive behaviour which should be activated whenever a person harms or even anticipates harming another person, regardless of most situational conditions. Indeed, researchers have found that individuals possessing a strong emotional disposition toward guilt over aggression are less likely to engage in such behaviour than those not possessing such tendencies (Knott et al., 1974); of course, measures of guilt and anxiety are often highly correlated and at times it may be difficult to distinguish between their effects on aggressive behaviour. While much research attention has been devoted to investigating the effects of these personality dispositions on aggressive behaviour, they are not the only, nor necessarily the most important factors to consider; many other variables influence the occurrence of aggression as well (cf. Baron, 1977; Dengerink, 1976; Zillmann, 1979). Nevertheless, the above research findings suggest that aggressive individuals may have failed to acquire a normal ability to modulate their emotional arousal and behavioural responses to provocation and stress because they lack appropriate levels of anxiety and guilt which inhibit overt or contemplated aggression in well-socialized individuals.

If we now shift our attention away from the aggression-inhibiting characteristics of normal individuals who rarely, if ever, engage in violent behaviour, we find a group of individuals who seem to lack internal restraints or inhibitions against aggression; Megargee (1966) describes this group as *undercontrolled* personalities and, although small in relative terms, they are responsible for a large proportion of all violent behaviour. Indeed, such individuals seemingly embrace aggressive behaviour, find it personally satisfying, and use it as a means of attaining various goals. In an important attempt to identify the basic personality characteristics of such undercontrolled aggressors Toch (1969), using a peer-interview procedure, finally reached the conclusion that violent individuals' predisposition toward aggression stems from a number of different sources, and that there are several different characteristics related to such actions, not simply one trait or even a single cluster of traits that produces assaultive behaviour. According to Toch, most assaultive individuals can be described as people who have learned to use and rely upon force as a means of compensating for their immature and undeveloped social skills; for example, he characterizes the largest single group of violent individuals as using aggression to ward off feelings of insecurity and low self-esteem. Overall, Toch's findings suggest that individual traits, characteristics, and dispositions are important determinants of assaultive behaviour in the case of undercontrolled aggressors; thus, in contrast to normal individuals who aggress against others primarily in response to strong environmental or situational factors, assaultive men and women appear to engage in such behaviour more often as a result of their need to defend against real or imagined threats to their psychological integrity; paradoxically, anxiety about their self-esteem and self-image seems to propel them into aggressive behaviour, whereas anxiety over aggression appears to be totally lacking or, at least, is sharply reduced (cf. Yeudall, 1980).

While searching for personality variables which may predispose an individual toward aggressive and antisocial behaviour, or interfere with the acquisition of restraints against such behaviour, investigators have also been aware that the attitudes and values of potential aggressors are important in this regard. For example, some individuals find aggression morally wrong and tend to avoid it at all costs, whereas others perceive it as quite acceptable; most people, however, adopt a middle position depending upon whether or not aggression seems justified in a given situation (cf. Rule and Nesdale, 1976b). Basically these differences result from the fact that individuals possess internal standards and values regarding aggression that influences whether they engage in such behaviour and, for the most part, individuals choose to maintain societal expectations regarding appropriate behaviour; needless to say, not all people choose to do this, and some find it very difficult to bring their behaviour into line with such expectations. Researchers have been attempting for a long time to understand individuals who behave in socially undesirable ways, and great differences of opinion exist regarding how to conceptualize these people and their behaviour (cf. Blackburn 1974, 1978; Eysenck and Eysenck, 1976, 1978; Quay, 1972; Sutker et al., 1981). Despite these problems, there is reasonable agreement among investigators that such people share features such as low anxiety and guilt, a reduced sense of social morality, immaturity, impulsivity, and a reduced ability to profit from experience, form meaningful relationships, and identify with others.

While acknowledging that such behaviour varies in terms of how much it deviates from socio-legal expectations, researchers have questioned the assumption that these individuals represent a relatively homogeneous grouping and have made efforts to describe them in terms of various personality, cognitive, attitudinal, genetic, arousal, and learning factors. For example, Quay (1972) reports on a number of studies that have isolated a trait pattern termed *psychopathy* – defined by items reflecting impulsiveness, rebelliousness, aggressiveness, and rejection of authority and family relationships – which is thought to be found among individuals who exhibit antisocial behaviour. Similarly, Blackburn (1979) identifies two independent personality dimensions termed *psychopathy-conformity* and *sociability-withdrawal* which permit the differentiation of antisocial individuals into different classes or types. Eysenck and Eysenck (1976) report on a personality dimension termed *psychoticism* on which high scorers tend to be aggressive, insensitive to others, egocentric, suspicious, and generally antisocial; moreover, Eysenck (1976) suggests that there is a fairly broad association between high scores on psychoticism, strong aggressive and dominant behaviour patterns, and permissive sexual attitudes, including a liking for pornography and impersonal sex; this trait pattern appears to be far more pronounced in males than in females, and to have a genetic basis which suggests that it is a relatively stable pattern, although obviously influenced by situational and environmental factors. Although other distinctions are too numerous for elaboration, these investigations emphasize that exposure to sexually violent depictions is unlikely to have a uniform effect on individuals who possess widely opposing characteristics; on the one hand such exposure may reinforce an individual's aggressive attitudes and behavioural patterns, while on the other it may strengthen social concern about violence and perhaps induce people to take some appropriate action over what they may view as an incitement to violence against women. Moreover, these studies suggest that individuals who deal with provocation and stress through some form of direct action rather than thought are more likely to be adversely affected by portrayals of sexual violence and to engage in actual assaultive behaviours such as rape.

Fortunately, we do have some research which shows that exposure to violent sexuality does indeed have different effects on individuals who possess different personality characteristics and attitudes. For example, rapists and normal individuals respond differentially to depictions of sexual violence; rapists' sexual arousal is not inhibited or reduced by the inclusion of force and violence into sexual depictions, which accords well with the fact that they lack appropriate internal restraints or inhibitions against actual assaultive behaviour; one might easily predict that other aggressive and antisocial personality types would respond similarly to such depictions and, indeed, there is some evidence to support this although research in this area is still quite limited (cf. Hinton *et al.,* 1980). In contrast, normal individuals *generally* perceive and respond appropriately to the force and violent aspects in rape depictions, showing increasingly less arousal as cues of pain, disgust, and violence become more salient. However, as we have seen, normal males' sexual arousal is highly responsive to changes in stimulus emphasis, and inhibitory cues can easily lose their effectiveness. Thus, a simple change in cognitive set which can result from emphasizing cues that signal a change in the woman's arousal, or that mitigate the seriousness of the inhibiting factors, can lead to high levels of sexual arousal. For example, males who believe that they have consumed alcohol, whether they have or not, fail to respond to inhibitory factors in depictions of sexual violence (Briddell *et al.,* 1978); thus, although many people believe that alcohol *per se* acts directly to reduce sexual and aggressive inhibitions, this research suggests that cognitive expectations and beliefs about having consumed alcohol may be more important in disinhibiting actual sexual and aggressive behaviour, at least in the occasional drinker. According to Amir (1971), it is this type of drinker rather than the habitual or chronic drinker who tends to commit sex offences; yet although it is commonly thought that rape is associated with drinking, he reports that alcohol was a significant factor in only one-third of his cases of rape – still important, but perhaps less than one would predict.

Since many sex offenders, such as heterosexual aggressors, apparently lack appropriate responsiveness to elements of force and violence in depictions of sexual assault, what effect will such portrayals have on their behaviour? Unfortunately, it is difficult to investigate this question directly because many complicating factors are involved. Most experts agree that sexual offences, including sexually assaultive behaviours, are the result of multiple predisposing and precipitating factors, and point out that sex offenders are not confined to any single nosological classification – they may be diagnosed as either neurotic, psychotic, psychopathic, sub-normal, or possibly organic. Attempts to understand sex offences generally reveal that such acts are intimately tied to the regulation of the individual's self-esteem and sense of self, and it is certainly not unusual to find that social and cultural factors also play an important role in determining sexually assaultive behaviour. Against a background of multiple contributing factors, the effects of exposure to depictions of sexually violent behaviour on the actual occurrence of such behaviour in already aggressive individuals seem impossible to assess. However, although such depictions alone seem unlikely to instigate assaultive behaviour, viewing sexual violence must be considered as a possible contributing or reinforcing factor, just as viewing violence and aggression *per se* is considered to influence the probability of actual aggressive and antisocial behaviour. In fact, there seems to be little, if any, reason to believe that the general effects of viewing aggressive and violent depictions will significantly change from one context to another. Fortunately we have some research that suggests this is true. For example, Donnerstein and Berkowitz (1981) have shown that, as pointed out earlier, exposure to a sexually violent film in which a female is raped can specifically increase aggressive behaviour toward females in both angered and non-angered normal males; without prior or subsequent anger instigation, the fact that *mere exposure* to such depictions alone seems to produce aggression toward females by males is an important demonstration which will undoubtedly receive much more research attention. Such findings suggest that viewing aggressive and violent behaviour in a sexual context probably augments the effects of viewing violence and aggression *per se* due to the emotionally arousing contribution of the sexual material. Of course, other characteristics of the context in which violence acquires its meaning have been shown to influence reactions to observed violence (cf. Geen, 1978); for example, violence and aggression that is seen as being justified by the situation evokes greater subsequent aggression in the observer than non-justified violence (Berkowitz and Geen, 1966; Berkowitz and Rawlings, 1963; Geen, 1981). What better justification could there be for the aggressive and violent behaviour displayed by men against women in depictions of rape than to portray the victim as becoming sexually aroused and experiencing an orgasm? Such stimulus cues – signifying justification for ignoring women's expressions of non-consent, no matter how strongly they may be voiced – seem likely to increase subsequent aggressive behaviour against females, whereas stimuli which deny such justification should reduce aggression. But, of course, rape myths depend upon placing sexual violence in a context of meaning which emphasizes justification for the aggressive behaviour (cf. Symonds, 1979). And so rape depictions faithfully reproduce the typical rape myth in which the woman's no, no, no, eventually becomes yes, yes, yes; verbal coercion, intimidation, and physical force all seem to be acceptable behaviour in this repetitive melodrama in which disinhibitory factors generally mitigate the effectiveness of inhibitory cues; as a result, lack of appropriate responsiveness to force and violence in depictions of sexual aggression begins to characterize normals as well as rapists and other heterosexual aggressors.

Although individuals who decide to view sexually explicit portrayals of rape – and people do volunteer to expose themselves to these presentations – already know that the victim will eventually become sexually excited, such typical portrayals vary in terms of how much and what kind of aggressive behaviour will be modelled prior to that moment. This pairing of violent and aggressive behaviour with sexual arousal not only facilitates subsequent aggressive responding toward women under certain conditions, but also provides an opportunity for violent stimuli to lose inhibitory value and acquire arousing properties. Although it seems reasonably clear that violent stimuli are not arousing to most heterosexual aggressors, we at least have some evidence that shows that such cues generally fail to suppress their sexual arousal compared to normals (e.g. Barbaree *et al.*, 1979). And, as we know individuals differ considerably in their sensitivity and responsiveness to aggressive and violent stimuli; some respond with strong anxiety to these situations and others do not. From a learning perspective, viewing presentations of aggression toward women paired with high levels of sexual arousal seems an ideal method for decreasing anxiety surrounding the expression of aggressive impulses; desensitization, then, is one procedure that could change such emotional reactions, although this would probably require more than a single exposure to explicit violent sexuality. Similarly, the direct conditioning of sexual arousal to violent stimuli would also require repeated exposure; such conditioning could take the form of masturbation to fantasies or actual depictions of violent sexuality. Theoretically, masturbatory conditioning techniques could alter the arousal value of violent stimuli in such a manner if individuals were motivated enough to follow these procedures, but this seems a remote possibility. Individuals commonly masturbate to fantasies of rape, or engage in such fantasies during other sexual activities to enhance their arousal, and yet it seems doubtful whether such random pairing of sex and violence significantly increase the arousal value of violent stimuli; conditioning procedures are obviously more effective but require greater consistency to change arousal patterns. Thus, although individuals who are frequently exposed to various portrayals of sexual violence will undoubtedly be strongly influenced by desensitization, most will probably not be affected by the direct conditioning of arousal to violent stimuli; this conclusion is consistent with the fact that most heterosexual aggressors do not show specific sexual arousal to violent and aggressive stimuli *per se*; sado-masochists, of course, do show such specific arousal to aggression, psychological and/or physical, and in these instances conditioning probably does play a more important role.

Desensitization is only one of the many processes which can affect an individual's responsivenes to repeated exposures of sex and violence. What is intentionally or unintentionally communicated affectively about the nature of male–female relationships is obviously of equal or greater importance. Thus, the modelling of attitudes and behaviours which suggest that males are justified in their aggression toward females undoubtedly influences some males to disregard women's communications of non-consent and reinforces their beliefs about the appropriateness of using force or intimidation to make a woman do whatever they want her to do. But here again, as with cognitive and learning factors, the effects of social influences upon the subsequent attitudes and behaviours of the viewers are dependent upon how often they are exposed to depictions of sexual violence and their own personal characteristics. Although most individuals probably avoid exposure to explicit portrayals of sex and violence, some people actively seek out and are willing to pay for the opportunity to view these depictions; presumably these people already share attitudes and beliefs that are hostile to women, and enjoy watching men using women when they are under some kind of pressure to cooperate, irrespective of whether the pressure is physical, psychological, or financial. *Self-selection* alone suggests that people have acquired their negative attitudes and behaviours toward women in other contexts, and that choosing to view sexually explicit violent presentations caters to as many non-sexual needs as sexual ones; as a result, frequent exposure to these depictions should act to reinforce males' existing attitudes and beliefs about forcing women to meet their needs, and increase the probability that they may engage in actual assaultive behaviour against women. Although self-selection separates the serious viewer of explicitly violent sexuality from the one-time viewers – those who observe out of curiosity, by accident, or whatever – there is little need, in a sense, to focus exclusively on such portrayals since everyone is exposed to a sub-explicit level of sex and violence on a fairly regular basis; for example, television presentations – mass media portrayals that reach and affect a viewing audience far greater than any other form of communication – often depict non-explicit sexual scenes in which women experience justified violence and degradation at the hands of men. Recently Malamuth and Check (1981) have shown that such portrayals can also negatively affect males' attitudes by increasing their acceptance of interpersonal violence toward women; this suggests that the degree of explicitness in portrayals of sex and violence probably exerts less influence compared to the creation of a hostile interpersonal context in which the portrayal of aggression and violence toward women is justified and leads to positive consequences for men. Indeed, Eysenck and Nias (1978) suggest that any sexual portrayal should be judged in terms of its context; if it is one of pro-love, pro-sex, and pro-women as many sexual portrayals are, then the tone is one of enjoyment, women are not degraded by the men, and there is no violence to destroy this sense of mutuality. But if the context is hostile to women, then such portrayals constitute a clear case of incitement to maltreat women, a position that coincides with feminist assertations that rape and other themes of sex and violence constitute aggression against women.

Fantasies of rape – the stuff dreams are made of if they are produced in the Hollywood of your mind – generally bear little resemblance to the reality. Indeed, many individuals have fantasies of committing rape, yet relatively *few* actually put them into practice. But what is viewed as important by a society is not always judged by the *frequency* of occurrence. True, rape is a relatively infrequent phenomenon compared to other offences, but the fear of rape appears to be completely unrelated to the actual probability of victimization, probably because the consequences of being raped are viewed with great seriousness; obviously, anything which tends to increase this fear might be considered as a form of indirect aggression toward women. Yet fantasies of rape and submission stimulate pleasure and enhance arousal in many people which alone points out that it is better to direct, produce, and star in your own version of reality than to participate in the original; *control* is the hallmark of these fantasies in which you do it your way. You lose some control when you view another director's version of rape, but the belief that such portrayals will approximate your fantasies still remains. And, since you can generally focus your own attention and perceptions – thereby selecting the stimulus emphasis you wish – while viewing such depictions, the idea that they are simply harmless fantasies tends to be reinforced. In contrast, as we have seen, recent evidence shows that the observation of violent sexuality contributes to aggressive behaviour toward women by men, which accords well with the conclusions drawn from the literature on observing violence in the media (e.g. Geen, 1976, 1978); indeed, this vast literature lends much credibility to the limited research there is on viewing explicitly violent sexuality. This is not to say that it is the most important contributor to sexual aggression against women as other influences upon the person also affect the expression of aggressive impulses; indeed, various personality characteristics, traits, and attitudes strongly affect males' responses to females in interpersonal situations and help determine the probability of aggression. Nevertheless, although observation of explicitly violent sexuality may be only one contributor to aggression, it may be a very powerful one for at least a brief period of time in highly aroused and angered males. Obviously, research is only just beginning to investigate the effects of exposure to mass media portrayals of sex and violence and much remains to be discovered. But even now it is reasonably clear that observing violent sexuality can facilitate aggression in the observer – altering the context in which aggression is viewed does not appear to change anything. Moreover, as Geen (1976) indicates, the common criticism of laboratory studies – that they are unrealistic and that their findings are invalid in the real world – is not justified by the bulk of the data collected so far; it seems unlikely that future research will alter this conclusion. Overall, research continues to emphasize the usefulness of discriminating between the effects of aggressive *vs* non-aggressive sexual materials, and to emphasize the uselessness of the term pornography in science. But even an impotent scientific term can still be a potent political weapon; as Byrne *et al.* (1974) indicate, pornography has been characterized as

> a liberating and healthful influence and as a poison to men's souls, as man's great hope in the fight against tyranny and as a Communist plot to weaken our society . . . it is not surprising that research data which are relevant to such systems tend to

be accepted or rejected not on their own merits but on the basis of the justification or vindication which they provide (p. 115).

In reality, the effects of viewing explicit sexual material are extremely variable and belief in absolutes in this as in most other fields is clearly untenable.

References

Abel, G. G. Barlow, D. H., Blanchard, E. B. and Guild, D. The components of rapists' sexual arousal. *Archives of General Psychiatry*, 1977a, **34**, 895–908.

Abel, G. G. and Blanchard, E. B. The role of fantasy in the treatment of sexual deviation. *Archives of General Psychiatry*, 1974, **30**, 467–475.

Abel, G. G. and Blanchard, E. B. The measurement and generation of sexual arousal in male sexual deviation. In M. Hersen, R. M. Eisler and P. M. Miller (Eds). *Progress in Behavior Modification*, Vol. 2. New York and London: Academic Press, 1976.

Abel, G. G., Blanchard, E. B. and Barlow, D. H. The effects of stimulus modality, instructional set and stimulus content on the objective measurement of sexual arousal in several paraphilias. *Behaviour Research and Therapy*, 1981, **19**, 25–33.

Abel, G. G., Blanchard, E. B., Barlow, D. H. and Mavissakalian, M. Identifying specific erotic cues in sexual deviations by audio taped description. *Journal of Applied Behaviour Analysis*, 1975, **8**, 247–260.

Abel, G. G., Blanchard, E. B. and Becker, J. Psychological treatment for rapists. In M. Walker and S. Brodsky (Eds). *Sexual Assault*. Lexington, Ma.: Lexington Books, 1976.

Abel, G. G., Blanchard, E. B. and Becker, J. An integrated treatment program for rapists. In R. Rada (Ed.). *Clinical Aspects of the Rapist*. New York: Grune and Stratton, 1977b.

Abel, G. G., Blanchard, E. B., Becker, J. V. and Djenderedjian, A. Differentiating sexual aggressives with penile measures. *Criminal Justice and Behavior*, 1978, **5**, 315–332.

Abelson, H., Cohen, R., Heaton, E. and Suder, C. National survey of public attitudes toward and experience with erotic materials. In *Technical Report of the Commission on Obscenity and Pornography*, Vol. 6. Washington, D.C.: U.S. Government Printing Office, 1971.

Adams, H. E., Tollison, C. D. and Carson, T. P. Behavior therapy with sexual deviations. In S. M. Turner, K. S. Calhoun and H. E. Adams (Eds). *Handbook of Clinical Behavior Therapy*. New York: John Wiley, 1981.

Amir, M. *Patterns in Forcible Rape*. Chicago: University of Chicago Press, 1971.

Bailyn, L. Mass media and children: A study of exposure habits and cognitive effects. *Psychological Monographs*, 1959, **73**.

Bancroft, J. H. J. Psychological and physiological responses to sexual stimuli in men and women. In L. Levi (Ed.). *Society, Stress and Diseases*, III. *The Productive and Reproductive Age*. Oxford: Oxford University Press, 1976.

Bancroft, J. H. and Mathews, A. Autonomic correlates of penile erection. *Journal of Psychosomatic Research*, 1971, **15**, 159–167.

Bandura, A. *Aggression: A Social Learning Analysis*. Englewood Cliffs, New Jersey: Prentice Hall, 1973.

Bandura, A., Underwood, B. and Fromson, M. E. Disinhibition of aggression through diffusion of responsibility and dehumanization of victims. *Journal of Research in Personality*, 1975, **9**, 253–269.

Barbaree, H. F., Marshall, W. L. and Lanthier, R. D. Deviant sexual arousal in rapists. *Behaviour Research and Therapy*, 1979, **17**, 215–222.

Barclay, A. M. The effect of hostility on physiological and fantasy responses. *Journal of Personality*, 1969, **37**, 651–667.

Barclay, A. M. Linking sexual and aggressive motives: Contributions of 'irrelevant' arousals. *Journal of Personality*, 1971, **39**, 481–492.

Barclay, A. M. Sexual fantasies in men and women. *Medical Aspects of Human Sexuality*, 1973, **7**, 205–216.

Barker, W. J. and Perlman, D. Volunteer bias and personality traits in sexual standards research. *Archives of Sexual Behavior*, 1975, **4**, 161–171.

Barlow. D. H. Increasing heterosexual responsiveness in the treatment of sexual deviation: A review of the clinical and experimental evidence. *Behavior Therapy*, 1973, **4**, 655–671.

Barlow, D. H. The treatment of sexual deviation: Towards a comprehensive behavioral approach. In K. S. Calhoun, E. E. Adams and K. M. Mitchell (Eds). *Innovative Treatment Methods in Psychopathology*. New York: John Wiley, 1974.

Barlow, D. H. Assessment of sexual behaviour. In A. R. Ciminero, K. S. Calhoun and H. E. Adams (Eds). *Handbook of Behavioral Assessment*. New York: Wiley, 1977.

Baron, R. A. The aggression-inhibiting influence of heightened sexual arousal. *Journal of Personality and Social Psychology*, 1974, **30**, 318–332.

Baron, R. A. *Human Aggression*. New York: Plenum Press, 1977.

Baron, R. A. and Bell, P. A. Aggression and heat: Mediating effects of prior provocation and exposure to an aggressive model. *Journal of Personality and Social Psychology*, 1975, **31**, 825–832.

Baron, R. A. and Bell, P. A. Sexual arousal and aggression by males: Effects of type of erotic stimuli and prior provocation. *Journal of Personality and Social Psychology*, 1977, **35**, 79–87.

Baron, R. A. and Byrne, D. *Social Psychology: Understanding Human Interaction*. Boston: Allyn and Bacon, 1977.

Baron, R. A. and Eggleston, R. J. Performance on the 'aggression machine': Motivation to help or harm? *Psychonomic Science*, 1972, **26**, 321–322.

Bentler, P. M. and Speckart, G. Attitudes 'cause' behaviors: A structural equation analysis. *Journal of Personality and Social Psychology*, 1981, **40**, 226–238.

Berkowitz, L. The contagion of violence: An S-R mediational analysis of some effects of observed aggression. In W. J. Arnold and M. M. Page (Eds). *Nebraska Symposium on Motivation*, Vol. 18. Lincoln: University of Nebraska Press, 1971.

Berkowitz, L. Some determinants of impulsive aggression: The role of mediated associations with reinforcements for aggression. *Psychological Review*, 1974, **81**, 165–176.

Berkowitz, L., Cochran, S. T. and Embree, M. C. Physical pain and the goal of aversively stimulated aggression. *Journal of Personality and Social Psychology*, 1981, **40**, 687–700.

Berkowitz, L. and Geen, R. G. Film violence and the cue properties of available targets. *Journal of Personality and Social Psychology*, 1966, **3**, 525–530.

Berkowitz, L. and Rawlings, E. Effects of film violence on inhibitions against subsequent aggression. *Journal of Abnormal and Social Psychology*, 1963, **66**, 405–12.

Berkowitz, L. and Turner, C. W. Perceived anger level, instigating agent, and aggression. In H. London and R. E. Nisbett (Eds). *Cognitive Alteration of Feeling States.* Chicago: Aldine, 1974.

Berne, E. *Games People Play.* New York: Grove Press, 1964.

Björksten, O. J. W. Sexually graphic material in the treatment of sexual disorders. In J. K. Meyer (Ed.). *Clinical Management of Sexual Disorders.* Batimore: Williams and Wilkins, 1976.

Blackburn, R. Personality and the classification of psychopathic disorders. In *Special Hospitals Research Reports* (No. 12). London: Special Hospitals Research Unit, 1974.

Blackburn, R. Psychopathy, arousal and the need for stimulation. In R. D. Hare and D. Schalling (Eds). *Psychopathic Behaviour: Approaches to Research.* London: Wiley, 1978.

Blackburn, R. Psychopathy and personality: The dimensionality of self-report and behaviour rating data in abnormal offenders. *British Journal of Social and Clinical Psychology,* 1979, **18**, 111–119.

Briddell, D. W., Rimm, D. C., Caddy, G. R., Krawitz, G., Sholis, D. and Wunderlin, R. J. Effects of alcohol and cognitive set on sexual arousal to deviant stimuli. *Journal of Abnormal Psychology,* 1978, **87**, 418–430.

Brodsky, S. L. and Hobart, S. C. Blame Models and Assailant Research. *Criminal Justice and Behavior,* 1978, **5**, 379–388.

Brownell, K. D. and Barlow, D. H. The behaviour treatment of sexual deviation. In A. Goldstein and F. B. Foa (Eds). *Handbook of Behavioral Interventions: A Clinical Guide.* New York: Wiley, 1980.

Brownell, K. D., Hayes, S. C. and Barlow, D. H. Patterns of appropriate and deviant sexual arousal: The behavioral treatment of multiple sexual deviations. *Journal of Consulting and Clinical Psychology,* 1977, **45**, 1144–1155.

Brownmiller, S. *Against Our Will: Men, Women and Rape.* New York: Simon and Schuster, 1975.

Burt, M. R. Cultural myths and supports for rape. *Journal of Personality and Social Psychology,* 1980, **38**, 217–230.

Buss, A. H. *The Psychology of Aggression.* New York: Wiley, 1961.

Byrne, D. Social psychology and the study of sexual behavior. *Personality and Social Psychology Bulletin,* 1977, **3**, 3–30.

Byrne, D., Fisher, J. D., Lamberth, J. and Mitchell, H. E. Evaluations of erotica: Facts or feelings? *Journal of Personality and Social Psychology,* 1974, **29**, 111–116.

Byrne, D. and Lamberth, J. The effect of erotic stimuli on sex arousal, evaluative responses, and subsequent behavior. In *Technical Report of the Commission on Obscenity and Pornography,* Vol. 8. Washington, D.C.: U.S. Government Printing Office, 1971.

Cater, D. and Strickland, S. *TV Violence and the Child: The Evolution and Fate of the Surgeon General's Report.* New York: Russell Sage Foundation, 1975.

Chappell, D., Geis, G. and Geis, G. *Forcible Rape: The Crime, the Victim, and the Offender.* New York: Columbia University Press, 1977.

Clark, L. and Lewis, D. *Rape: The Price of Coercive Sexuality.* Toronto: The Women's Press, 1977.

Cline, V. B. Critique of commission behavioral research. In the *Report of the Commission on Obscenity and Pornography.* New York: Bantam Books, 1970.

Cline, V. B. *Where Do You Draw the Line? An Exploration into Media Violence, Pornography, and Censorship*. Provo, Utah: Brigham Young University Press, 1974.

Cochrane, P. Sex crimes and pornography revisited. *International Journal of Criminology and Penology*, 1978, **6**, 307–317.

Committee on Obscenity and Film Censorship. In the *Report of the Committee on Obscenity and Film Censorship*. (Chairman: B. Williams). London: Her Majesty's Stationery Office, 1979.

Cook, R. F., Fosen, R. H. and Pacht, A. Pornography and the sex offender: Patterns of previous exposure and arrousal effects of pornographic stimuli. *Journal of Applied Psychology*, 1971, **55**, 503–511.

Court, J. H. Pornography and sex-crimes: A re-evaluation in the light of recent trends around the world. *International Journal of Criminology and Penology*, 1976, **5**, 129–157.

Court, J. H. *Pornography and the Harm Condition: A Response to the Report of Obsceniy and Film Censorship*. (Chairman: B. Williams). Adelaide: Flinders University, 1980.

Cox, M. Dynamic psychotherapy with sex-offenders. In I. Rosen (Ed.). *Sexual Deviation*. Oxford: Oxford University Press, 1979.

Crepault, C., Abraham, G., Porto, R. and Couture, M. Erotic imagery in women. In R. Gemme and C. C. Wheeler (Eds). *Progress in Sexology*. New York: Plenum Press, 1977.

Crepault, C. and Couture, M. Men's erotic fantasies. *Archives of Sexual Behavior*, 1980, **9**, 565–581.

Crowne, D. P. and Marlow, D. A new scale of social desirability independent of psychopathology. *Journal of Consulting Psychology*, 1960, **24**, 349–354.

Davis, K. E. and Braucht, G. N. Exposure to pornography, character, and sexual deviance: A retrospective survey. In *Technical Report of the Commission on Obscenity and Pornography*, Vol. 7. Washington, D.C.: U.S. Government Printing Office, 1971.

Dengerink, H. A. Personality variables as mediators of attack-instigated aggression. In R. G. Geen and E. C. O'Neal (Eds). *Perspectives on Aggression*. New York and London: Academic Press, 1976.

Dienstbier, R. A. Sex and violence: Can research have it both ways? *Journal of Communication*, 1977, **27**, 176–188.

Donnerstein, E. Aggressive erotica and violence against women. *Journal of Personality and Social Psychology*, 1980a, **39**, 269–277.

Donnerstein, E. Pornography and violence against women: Experimental studies. *Annals of the New York Academy of Science*, 1980b, **347**, 277–288.

Donnerstein, E. Pornography and violence: Current research findings. In R. Geen and E. Donnerstein (Eds). *Aggression: Theoretical and Empirical Reviews*. New York and London: Academic Press, 1982.

Donnerstein, F. and Barrett, G. The effects of erotic stimuli on male aggression toward females. *Journal of Personality and Social Psychology*, 1978, **36**, 180–188.

Donnerstein, E. and Berkowitz, L. Victim reactions in aggressive erotic films as a factor in violence against women. *Journal of Personality and Social Psychology*, 1981, **41**, 710–724.

Donnerstein, E., Donnerstein, M. and Barrett, G. Where is the facilitation of media violence? The effects of nonexposure and placement of anger arousal. *Journal of Research in Personality*, 1976, **10**, 386–398.

Donnerstein, E., Donnerstein, M. and Evans, R. Erotic stimuli and aggression: Facilitation or inhibition. *Journal of Personality and Social Psychology*, 1975, 32, 237–244.

Donnerstein, E. and Hallam, J. The facilitating effects of erotica on aggression toward females. *Journal of Personality and Social Psychology*, 1978, 36, 1270–1277.

Dworkin, A. Pornography: Men Possessing Women. London: Women's Press, 1981.

Eisenberg, G. J. Children and aggression after observed film aggression with sanctioning adults. *Annals of the New York Academy of Sciences*, 1980, 347, 304–318.

Ellis, A. and Brancale, R. *The Psychology of Sex Offenders*. Springfield, Illinois: Thomas, 1956.

Epstein, S. Traits are alive and well. In D. Magnusson and N. S. Endler (Eds). *Personality at the Crossroads: Current Issues in Interactional Psychology.* Hillsdale, N.J.: Erlbaum, 1977.

Eron, L. D. and Huesmann, L. R. Adolescent aggression and television. *Annals of the New York Academy of Sciences*, 1980, 347, 319–331.

Eysenck, H. J. *Psychology is about People*. London: Allen Lane, 1972.

Eysenck, H. J. *Sex and Personality*. London: Open Books, 1976.

Eysenck, H. J. *Crime and Personality* (3rd Edition). London: Routledge and Kegan Paul, 1977.

Eysenck, H. J. Psychology and obscenity: A factual look at some of the problems. In R. Dhavan and C. Davies (Eds). *Censorship and Obscenity*. London: Martin Robertson, 1978.

Eysenck, H. J. and Eysenck, S. B. G. *Psychoticism as a Dimension of Personality.* London: Hodder and Stoughton, 1976.

Eysenck, H. J. and Eysenck, S. B. G. Psychopathy, personality, and genetics. In R. D. Hare and D. Schalling (Eds). *Psychopathic Behaviour: Approaches to Research*. New York: Wiley, 1978.

Eysenck, H. J. and Nias, D. K. B. *Sex, Violence and the Media*. London: Maurice Temple Smith, 1978.

Eysenck, M. W. and Eysenck, H. J. Michel and the concept of personality. *British Journal of Psychology*, 1980, 71, 191–204.

Eysenck, S. B. G. and Eysenck, H. J. The measurement of psychoticism: A study of factor stability and reliability. *British Journal of Social and Clinical Psychology*, 1968, 7, 286–294.

Eysenck, S. G. B. and Eysenck, H. J. The place of impulsiveness in a dimensional system of personality description. *British Journal of Social and Clinical Psychology*, 1977, 16, 57–68.

Farkas, G. M. Comments on Levin *et al.* and Rosen and Kopel: Internal and external validity issues. *Journal of Consulting and Clinical Psychology*, 1978, 46, 1515–1516.

Farkas, G. M., Evans, I. M., Shine, L. F., Eifert, G., Wittlieb, E. and Vogelmann-Sine, S. Reliability and validity of the mercury-in-rubber strain gauge measure of penile circumference. *Behavior Therapy*, 1979, 10, 555–561.

Farkas, G. M., Sine, L. F and Evans, I. M. Personality, sexuality, and demographic differences between volunteers and non-volunteers for a laboratory study of male sexual behavior. *Archives of Sexual Behavior*, 1978, 7, 513–520.

Federal Bureau of Investigation. *Uniform Crime Reports*. U.S. Department of Justice. Washington, D.C.: U.S. Government Printing Office, 1979.

Field, H. S. Attitudes toward rape: A comparative analysis of police, rapists, crisis counselors, and citizens. *Journal of Personality and Social Psychology*, 1978, **36**, 156–179.

Feshbach, S. The stimulating versus cathartic effects of a vicarious aggressive activity. *Journal of Abnormal and Social Psychology*, 1961, **63**, 381–385.

Feshbach, S. Reality and fantasy in filmed violence. In J. P. Murray, E. A. Rubinstein and G. A. Comstock (Eds). *Television and Social Behavior*, Vol. 2: *Television and Social Learning*. Washington, D.C.: U.S. Government Printing Office, 1971.

Feshbach, S. and Singer, R. *Television and Aggression*. San Francisco: Jossey-Bass, 1971.

Freud, S. *New Introductory Lectures on Psychoanalysis*. New York: Norton, 1933.

Gager, N. and Schurr, C. *Sexual Assault: Confronting Rape in America*. New York: Grosset and Dunlap, 1976.

Gayford, J. J. Indecent exposure: A review of the literature. *Medicine, Science and the Law*, 1981, **21**, 233–242.

Gebhard, P. H., Gagnon, J. H., Pomeroy, W. B. and Christenson, C. V. *Sex Offenders: An Analysis of Types*. London: Heinemann, 1965.

Geen, R. G. The study of aggression. In R. G. Geen and E. C. O'Neal (Eds). *Perspectives on Aggression*. New York and London: Academic Press, 1976a.

Geen, R. G. Observing violence in the mass media: Implication of basic research. In R. G. Geen and E. C. O'Neal (Eds). *Perspectives on Aggression*. New York and London: Academic Press, 1976b.

Geen, R. G. Some effects of observing violence upon the behaviour of the observer. In B. Maher (Ed.). *Progress in Experimental Personality Research*, Vol. 8. New York and London: Academic Press, 1978.

Geen, R. G. Behavioral and physiological reactions to observed violence: Effects of prior exposure to aggressive stimuli. *Journal of Personality and Social Psychology*, 1981, **40**, 868–875.

Geen, R. G. and Berkowitz, L. Name-mediated aggressive cue properties. *Journal of Personality*, 1966, **34**, 456–465.

Geen, R. G. and O'Neal, E. C. Activation of cue-elicited aggression by general arousal. *Journal of Personality and Social Psychology*, 1969, **11**, 289–292.

Geen, R. G. and O'Neal, E. C. (Eds). *Perspectives on Aggression*. New York and London: Academic Press, 1976.

Geer, J. H. Genital measures: Comments on their role in understanding human sexuality. *Journal of Sex and Marital Therapy*, 1976, **2**, 165–172.

Geer, J. H., Morokoff, P. and Greenwood, P. Sexual arousal in women: The development of a measurement device for vaginal blood volume. *Archives of Sexual Behavior*, 1974, **3**, 559–564.

Gibbens, T. C. N., Way, C. and Soothill, K. L. Behavioural Types of Rape. *British Journal of Psychiatry*, 1977, **130**, 32–42.

Gillan, P. Therapeutic uses of obscenity. In R. Dhavan and C. Davis (Eds). *Censorship and Obscenity*. London: Martin Robertson, 1978.

Goldstein, M., Kant, H., Judd, L., Rice, C. and Green, R. Experience with pornography: Rapists, pedophiles, homosexuals, transsexuals, and controls. *Archives of Sexual Behavior*, 1971, **1**, 1–15.

Griffin, S. *Pornography and Silence: Culture's Revenge Against Nature*. London: Women's Press, 1981.

Gruder, C. L., Cook, T. D., Hannigan, K. M., Flay, B. R., Allessis, C. and Halamaj, J. Empirical tests of the absolute sleeper effect predicted from the discounting cue hypothesis. *Journal of Personality and Social Psychology*, 1978, **36**, 1061–1074.

Hariton, E. B. and Singer, J. L. Women's fantasies during sexual intercourse: Normative and theoretical implications. *Journal of Consulting and Clinical Psychology,* 1974, 313–322.

Harrison, A. A. Mere exposure. In L. Berkowitz (Ed.) *Advances in Experimental Social Psychology,* Vol. 10. New York and London: Academic Press, 1977.

Hartmann, D. P. Influence of symbolically modeled instrumental aggression and pain cues on aggressive behaviour. *Journal of Personality and Social Psychology,* 1969, **11,** 280–288.

Hatch, J. P. Vaginal photoplethysmography: Methodological considerations. *Archives of Sexual Behavior,* 1979, **8,** 357–374.

Heilbron Report. In *Report of the Advisory Group on the Law of Rape* (Cmnd. 6352). London: Her Majesty's Stationery Office, 1975.

Herman, S. H., Barlow, D. H. and Agras, W. S. An experimental analysis of exposure to 'explicit' heterosexual stimuli as an effective variable in changing arousal patterns of homosexuals. *Behaviour Research and Therapy,* 1974, **12,** 335–345.

Hessellund, H. Masturbation and sexual fantasies in married couples. *Archives of Sexual Behavior,* 1976, **5,** 133–147.

Higginbotham, H. N. and Farkas, G. M. Basic and applied research in human sexuality: Current limitations and future directions in sex therapy. In J. Fisher and H. Gochros (Eds). *Handbook of Behavior Therapy with Sexual Problems,* Vol. 1. Elmsford, New York: Pergamon Press, 1977.

Himmelweit, H. T., Oppenheim, A. N. and Vince, P. *Television and the Child: An Empirical Study of the Effects of Television on the Young.* London: Oxford University Press, 1958.

Hinton, J. W., O'Neill, M. T. and Webster, S. Psychophysiological assessment of sex offenders in a security hospital. *Archives of Sexual Behavior,* 1980, **9,** 205–216.

Hogan, R., DeSoto, C. B. and Solano, C. Traits, tests, and personality research. *American Psychologist,* 1977, **32,** 255–264.

Howitt, D. and Cumberbatch, G. *Mass Media Violence and Society.* London: Paul Elek, 1975.

Jaffe, Y., Malamuth, N., Feingold, J. and Feshbach, S. Sexual arousal and behavioral aggression. *Journal of Personality and Social Psychology,* 1974, **30,** 759–764.

Johnson, W. T. and DeLamater, J. D. Response effects in sex surveys. *Public Opinion Quarterly,* 1976, **40,** 165–181.

Kantorowitz, D. A. Personality and conditioning of tumescence and detumescence. *Behaviour Research and Therapy,* 1978, **16,** 117–123.

Keller, D. J. and Goldstein, A. Orgasmic reconditioning reconsidered. *Behaviour Research and Therapy,* 1978, **16,** 299–301.

Kenrick, D. T., Stringfield, D. O., Wagenhals, W. L., Dahl, R. H. and Ransdell, H. J. Sex differences, androgyny, and approach responses to erotica: A new variation on the old volunteer problem. *Journal of Personality and Social Psychology,* 1980, **38,** 517–524.

Knott, P. D., Lasater, L. and Shuman, R. Aggression-guilt and conditionability for aggressiveness. *Journal of Personality,* 1974, **42,** 332–344.

Kolářský, A. and Madlafousek, J. Female behaviour and sexual arousal in heterosexual male deviant offenders: An experimental study. *Journal of Nervous and Mental Disease,* 1972, **155,** 110–118.

Kolářský, A., Madlafousek, J. and Novotná, V. Stimuli eliciting sexual arousal in males who offend adult women: An experimental study. *Archives of Sexual Behavior,* 1978, **7,** 79–87.

Konecni, V. J. The mediation of aggressive behavior: Arousal level versus anger and cognitive labeling. *Journal of Personality and Social Psychology*, 1975, **32**, 706–712.

Kronhausen, E. and Kronhausen, P. *Pornography and the Law*. New York: Ballantine, 1959.

Krulewitz, J. E. and Payne, E. J. Attributions about rape: Effects of rapist force, observer sex, and sex role attitudes. *Journal of Applied Social Psychology*, 1978, **8**, 291–305.

Langevin, R. and Martin, M. Can erotic responses be classically conditioned? *Behavior Therapy*, 1975, **6**, 350–355.

Larsen, O. N. *Violence and the Mass Media*. New York: Harper and Row, 1968.

Laws, D. R. and Holmen, M. L. Sexual response faking by pedophiles. *Criminal Justice and Behavior*, 1978, **5**, 343–356.

Laws, D. R. and O'Neil, J. A. Variations on masturbatory conditioning. *Behavioural Psychotherapy*, 1981, **9**, 111–136.

Longford Committee. *Pornography: The Longford Report*. London: Coronet Books. 1972.

Lord, C. G., Ross, L. and Lepper, M. R. Biased assimilation and attitude polarization: The effects of prior theories on subsequently considered evidence. *Journal of Personality and Social Psychology*, 1979, **37**, 2098–2109.

Malamuth, N. M. Rape fantasies as a function of exposure to violent sexual stimuli. *Archives of Sexual Behavior*, 1981, **10**, 33–47.

Malamuth, N. M. and Check, J. V. P. Sexual arousal to rape and consenting depictions: The importance of the woman's arousal. *Journal of Abnormal Psychology*, 1980a, **89**, 763–766.

Malamuth, N. M. and Check, J. V. P. Penile tumescence and perceptual responses to rape as a function of victim's perceived reactions. *Journal of Applied Social Psychology*, 1980b, **10**, 528–547.

Malamuth, N. M. and Check, J. V. P. The effects of mass media exposure on acceptance of violence against women: A field experiment. *Journal of Research in Personality*, 1981, **15**, 436–446.

Malamuth, N. M. and Donnerstein, E. The effects of aggressive-erotic stimuli. In L. Berkowitz (Ed.). *Advances in Experimental Social Psychology*, Vol. 15. New York and London: Academic Press, 1982.

Malamuth, N. M., Feshbach, S. and Jaffe, Y. Sexual arousal and aggression: Recent experiments and theoretical issues. *Journal of Social Issues*, 1977, **33**, 110–133.

Malamuth, N. M., Haber, S. and Feshbach, S. Testing hypotheses regarding rape: Exposure to sexual violence, sex differences, and the 'normality' of rape. *Journal of Research in Personality*, 1980a, **14**, 121–137.

Malamuth, N. M., Heim, M. and Feshbach, S. Sexual responsiveness of college students to rape depictions: Inhibitory and disinhibitory effects. *Journal of Personality and Social Psychology*, 1980b, **38**, 399–408.

Malamuth, N. M. and Spinner, B. A longitudinal content analysis of sexual violence in the best-selling erotic magazines. *Journal of Sex Research*, 1980, **16**, 226–237.

Mann, J., Sidman, J. and Starr, S. Effects of erotic films on sexual behavior of married couples. In *Technical Report of the Commission on Obscenity and Pornography*, Vol. 8. Washington, D.C.: U.S. Government Printing Office, 1971.

Martin, I. and Levey, A. B. Evaluative conditioning. *Advances in Behaviour Research and Therapy*, 1978, **1**, 57–104.

Mavissakalian, M., Blanchard, E. B., Abel, G. G. and Barlow, D. H. Responses to complex erotic stimuli in homosexual and heterosexual males. *British Journal of Psychiatry*, 1975, **126**, 252–257.

McGuire, R. J., Carlisle, J. M. and Young, B. G. Sexual deviation as conditioned behavior: A hypothesis. *Behavior Research and Therapy*, 1965, **2**, 185–190.

Medea, A., and Thompson, K. *Against Rape*. New York: Farrar, Strauss and Giroux, 1974.

Mednick, S. A. A biosocial theory of the learning of law-abiding behavior. In S. A. Mednick and K. O. Christiansen (Eds). *Biosocial Basis of Criminal Behavior*. New York: Gardner, 1977.

Megargee, E. I. Undercontrolled and overcontrolled personality types in extreme antisocial aggression. *Psychological Monographs*, 1966, **80**.

Meyer, T. P. The effects of sexually arousing and violent films on aggressive behavior. *Journal of Sex Research*, 1972, **8**, 324–331.

Milgram, S. *Obedience to Authority*. New York: Harper and Row, 1974.

Mischel, W. *Personality and Assessment*. London: Wiley, 1968.

Mischel, W. Cognitive appraisals and transformations in self-control. In B. Weiner (Ed.). *Cognitive Views of Human Motivation*. New York and London: Academic Press, 1974.

Mischel, W. The interaction of person and situation. In D. Magnusson and N. S. Endler (Eds). *Personality at the Crossroads: Current Issues in Interactional Psychology*. Hillsdale, N.J.: Erlbaum, 1977.

Money, J. *Love and Love Sickness: The Science of Sex, Gender Difference, and Pair-bonding*. London: John Hopkins University Press, 1980.

Moreault, D. and Follingstad, D. R. Sexual fantasies of females as a function of sex guilt and experimental-response cues. *Journal of Consulting and Clinical Psychology*, 1978, **46**, 1385–1393.

Mosher, D. L. Interaction of fear and guilt in inhibiting unacceptable behavior. *Journal of Consulting Psychology*, 1965, **29**, 161–167.

Mosher, D. L. Psychological reactions to pornographic films. In *Technical Report of the Commission on Obscenity and Pornography*, Vol. 8. Washington, D.C.: U.S. Government Printing Office, 1971.

Mosher, D. L. and Abramson, P. R. Subjective sexual arousal to films of masturbation. *Journal of Consulting and Clinical Psychology*, 1977, **45**, 796–807.

Mosher, D. L. and Katz, H. Pornographic films, male verbal aggression against women, and guilt. In *Technical Report of the Commission on Obscenity and Pornography*, Vol. 8. Washington, D.C.: U.S. Government Printing Office, 1971.

Mueller, C. W., and Donnerstein, E. Film-facilitated arousal and prosocial behavior. *Journal of Experimental Social Psychology*, 1981, **17**, 31–41.

Myers, D. G. and Lamm, H. The group polarization phenomenon. *Psychological Bulletin*, 1976, **83**, 602–627.

Nelson, E. C. Attention to Heterosexual Imagery as Eliciting Stimuli for Autonomic Sexual Arousal in Males. Unpublished doctoral dissertation. Los Angeles: University of California, 1973.

Propper, M. M. Exposure to sexually oriented materials among young male prisoners. In *Technical Report of the Commission on Obscenity and Pornography*, Vol. 9. Washington, D.C.: U.S. Government Printing Office, 1971.

Quay, H. C. Patterns of aggression, withdrawal, and immaturity. In H. C. Quay and J. S. Werry (Eds). *Psychopathological Disorders of Childhood*. New York: Wiley, 1972.

Quinsey, V. L. and Carrigan, W. F. Penile responses to visual stimuli. *Criminal Justice and Behavior*, 1978, 5, 333–341.

Rachman, S. Sexual fetishism: An experimental analogue. *Psychological Record*, 1966, 16, 293–296.

Rachman, S. and Hodgson, R. J. Experimentally-induced 'sexual fetishism': Replication and development. *Psychological Record*, 1968, 18, 25–27.

Radzinowicz, L. *Sexual Offences*. London: Macmillan, 1957.

Reifler, C. B., Howard, J., Lipton, . A., Liptzin, M. B. and Widmann, D. E. Pornography: An experimental study of effects. *American Journal of Psychiatry*, 1971, 128, 575–582.

Reynolds, B. S. Biofeedback and facilitation of erection in men with erectile dysfunction. *Archives of Sexual Behavior*, 1980, 9, 101–113.

Rooth, F. G. Exhibitionism, sexual violence and paedophilia. *British Journal of Psychiatry*, 1973, 122, 705–710.

Rosen, I. Exhibitionism, scopophilia, and voyeurism. In I. Rosen (Ed.). *Sexual Deviation*. Oxford: Oxford University Press, 1979.

Rosen, L. and Turner, S. H. Exposure to pornography: An exploratory study. *Journal of Sex Research*, 1969, 5, 235–247.

Rosen, R. C. and Keefe, F. J. The measurement of human penile tumescence. *Psychophysiology*, 1978, 15, 366–376.

Rosen, R. C. and Kopel, S. A. Role of penile tumescence measurement in the behavioral treatment of sexual deviation: Issues of validity. *Journal of Consulting and Clinical Psychology*, 1978, 46, 1519–1521.

Rosenthal, R. and Rosnow, R. L. *The Volunteer Subject*. New York: Wiley, 1975.

Rule, B. G. and Nesdale, A. R. Emotional arousal and aggressive behavior. *Psychological Bulletin*, 1976a, 83, 851–863.

Rule, B. G. and Nesdale, A. R. Moral judgment of aggressive behavior. In R. G. Geen and E. C. O'Neal (Eds). *Perspectives on Aggression*. New York and London: Academic Press, 1976b.

Russell, D. E. H. *The Politics of Rape*. New York: Stein and Day, 1975.

Scheafer, H. H., and Colgan, A. H. The effect of pornography on penile tumescence as a function of reinforcement and novelty. *Behavior Therapy*, 1977, 8, 938–946.

Schmidt, G. Male-female differences in sexual arousal and behaviour during and after exposure to sexually explicit stimuli. *Archives of Sexual Behavior*, 1975, 4, 353–365.

Schmidt, G. and Sigusch, V. Sex differences in responses to psychosexual stimulation by films and slides. *Journal of Sex Research*, 1970, 6, 268–283.

Schmidt, G., Sigusch, V. and Meyberg, U. Psychosexual stimulation in men: Emotional reactions, changes of sex behaviour, and measure of conservative attitudes. *Journal of Sex Research*, 1969, 5, 199–217.

Schmidt, G., Sigusch, V. and Schäfer, S. Responses to reading erotic stories: Male–female differences. *Archives of Sexual Behavior*, 1973, 2, 181–199.

Scott, P. D. Assessing dangerousness in criminals. *The British Journal of Psychiatry*, 1977, 131, 127–142.

Shemberg, K. M., Leventhal, D. B. and Allman, L. Aggression machine performance and rated aggression. *Journal of Experimental Research in Personality*, 1968, 3, 117–119.

Singer, D. G. and Singer, J. L. Television viewing and aggressive behavior in preschool children: A field study. *Annals of the New York Academy of Sciences*, 1980, 347, 289–303.

Smith, D. D. The social content of pornography. *Journal of Communication*, 1976, **26**, 16–23.

Smukler, A. J. and Schiebel, D. Personality characteristics of exhibitionists. *Diseases of the Nervous System*, 1975, **36**, 600–603.

Stoller, R. J. *Perversion: The Erotic Form of Hatred*. Hassocks: Harvester Press, 1976a.

Stoller, R. J. Sexual excitement. *Archives of General Psychiatry*, 1976b, **33**, 899–909.

Surgeon General's Scientific Advisory Committee on Television and Social Behavior. *Television and Growing Up: The Impact of Televised Violence*. Washington, D.C.: U.S. Government Printing Office, 1972.

Sutker, P. B., Archer, R. P. and Kilpatrick, D. G. Sociopathy and antisocial behavior: Theory and treatment. In S. M. Turner, K. S. Calhoun and H. E. Adams (Eds). *Handbook of Clinical Behavior Therapy*. New York: John Wiley, 1981.

Swart, C. and Berkowitz, L. Effects of a simulus associated with a victim's pain on later aggression. *Journal of Personality and Social Psychology*, 1976, **33**, 623–631.

Symonds, A. Violence against women – the myth of masochism. *American Journal of Psychotherapy*, 1979, **33**, 161–173.

Tannenbaum, P. H. Emotional arousal as a mediator of erotic communiction effects. In *Technical Report of the Commission on Obscenity and Pornography*, Vol. 8. Washington, D.C.: U.S. Government Printing Office, 1971.

Tannenbaum, P. H. and Zillmann, D. Emotional arousal in the facilitation of aggression through communication. In L. Berkowitz (Ed.). *Advances in Experimental Social Psychology*, Vol. 8. New York and London: Academic Press, 1975.

Tennent, T. G. The dangerous offender. *British Journal of Hospital Medicine*, 1971, **6**, 269–274.

Tieger, T. Self-rated likelihood of raping and the social perception of rape. *Journal of Research in Personality*, 1981, **15**, 147–158.

Toch, H. *Violent Men*. Chicago: Aldine, 1969.

U.S. National Commission on the Causes and Prevention of Violence. *To Establish Justice, to Insure Domestic Tranquility: Task Force Report* (No. 9). (Chairman: M. S. Eisenhower). Washington, D. C.: U.S. Government Printing Office, 1969.

U.S. National Commission on Obscenity and Pornography. In the *Report of the Commission on Obscenity and Pornography*. New York: Bantam, 1970.

Vinsel, A. Rape: A review essay. *Personality and Social Psychology Bulletin*, 1977, **3**, 183–189.

Wakeling, A. A general psychiatric approach to sexual deviation. In I. Rosen (Ed.). *Sexual Deviation*. Oxford: Oxford University Press, 1979.

Walker, C. E. Erotic stimuli and the aggressive sexual offender. In *Technical Report of the Commission on Obscenity and Pornography*, Vol. 7. Washington, D.C.: U.S. Government Printing Office, 1971.

Walmsley, R. and White, K. *Sexual Offences, Consent and Sentencing*. Home Office Research Study (No. 54). London: Her Majesty's Stationery Office, 1979.

Weiss, W. Effects of the mass media of communication. In G. Lindzey and E. Aronson (Eds). *Handbook of Social Psychology*, Vol. 5. Reading, Ma.: Addison-Wesley, 1969.

West, D. J. Victims of sexual crime. *British Journal of Sexual Medicine*, 1982, **8**, 80, 30–35.

West, D. J., Roy, C. and Nichols, F. L. *Understanding Sexual Attacks*. London: Heinemann, 1978.

Wilson, W. C. Can pornography contribute to the prevention of sexual problems? In C. B. Qualls, J. P. Wincze and D. H. Barlow (Eds). *The Prevention of Sexual Disorders*. London: Plenum Press, 1978.

Wolfe, B. M. and Baron, R. A. Laboratory aggression related to aggression in naturalistic social situations: Effects of an aggressive model on the behaviour of college student and prisoner observers. *Psychonomic Science*, 1971, **24**, 193–194.

Wright, R. and West, D. J. Rape: A comparison of group offences and lone assaults. *Medicine, Science and the Law*, 1981, **21**, 25–30.

Yaffé, M. Research survey. In Lord Longford (Ed.). *Pornography: The Longford Report*. London: Coronet, 1972.

Yaffé, M. Pornography: An updated review (1972–1977). In the *Report of the Committee on Obscenity and Film Censorship*. (Chairman: B. Williams). London: Her Majesty's Stationery Office, 1979.

Yeudall, L. T. A neuropsychosocial perspective of persistent juvenile delinquency and criminal behaviour: Discussion. *Annals of the New York Academy of Sciences*, 1980, **347**, 349–355.

Zajonc, R. B. The attitudinal effects of mere exposure. *Journal of Personality and Social Psychology*, 1968, **9**, 1–27.

Zillmann, D. Excitation transfer in communication-mediated aggressive behavior. *Journal of Experimental and Social Psychology*, 1971, **7**, 419–434.

Zillmann, D. *Hostility and Aggression*. Hillsdale, N.J.: Erlbaum, 1979.

Zillmann, D., Hoyt, J. L. and Day, K. D. Strength and duration of the effect of aggressive, violent, and erotic communications on subsequent aggressive behavior. *Communication Research*, 1974, **1**, 286–306.

Zillman, D., Katcher, A. H. and Milavsky, B. Excitation transfer from physical exercise to subsequent aggressive behaviour. *Journal of Experimental Social Psychology*, 1972, **8**, 247–259.

Zillmann, D. and Sapolsky, B. S. What mediates the effect of mild erotica on annoyance and hostile behavior in males? *Journal of Personality and Social Psychology*, 1977, **35**, 587–596.

Zuckerman, M. Physiological measures of sexual arousal in the human. *Psychological Bulletin*, 1971, **75**, 297–329.

Zuckerman, M. Research on pornography. In W. W. Oaks, G. A. Melchiode and I. Ficher (Eds). *Sex and the Life Cycle*. New York: Grune and Stratton, 1976.

Zuckerman, M., Tushup, R. and Finner, S. Sexual attitudes and experience: Attitude and personality correlates and changes produced by a course in sexuality. *Journal of Consulting and Clinical Psychology*, 1976, **44**, 7–19.

10

Obscenity – law, practice and proposals for reform

David Offenbach

The law in Britain regarding obscenity is in confusion and ripe for reform. The main Act of Parliament concerning this is the 1959 *Obscene Publications Act*, which was a Private Member's measure introduced by Roy Jenkins, MP, following the report of a Select Committee of the House of Commons. The Select Committee was set up in response to a "purge" of books in the 1950s, which resulted in prosecutions against five leading publishing houses. As a result of these prosecutions, two publishers were convicted, two acquitted, and in one case, the prosecution offered no evidence after two juries had failed to agree. It was the pressure for law reform following these trials which led to the establishment of the Select Committee on obscene publications and the subsequent Act of Parliament of 1959.

The deliberation of the Select Committee, the debates in the House of Commons, and early subsequent judicial pronouncements all proceeded on the basis that obscene material was of two entirely distinct and separate kinds. On the one hand there was *pornography*, and on the other, *literature*. As the Home Secretary's memorandum to the Select Committee said, "it is the accepted function of the Government to suppress pornography". However, even literature was to be suppressed unless, in particular cases, its *public good* content was so great as to outweigh its obscenity. The gap between these two apparent extremes was reflected in the title to the 1959 Act:

> An Act to amend the law relating to the publication of obscene matter; to provide for the protection of literature; to strengthen the law against pornography.

This title already causes difficulty because that is the first and last time that the word pornography is mentioned anywhere in this Act. It is never defined or described and never referred to again!

The extent of the limitations of this Act has now become clear, nearly 2. years after it was first enacted into law. This statute without a doubt, ha received more criticism than any other contemporary piece of legislation magistrates cannot agree on what is obscene and the police interpret the law in widely different ways. The post-war publishing boom in popular literature and glossy magazines, as well as the popularity of cinema and television programmes with sexual content, have led to a situation where material involving sexual matters has become the staple diet of millions of readers viewers and listeners. It is estimated that somewhere around three and a half million magazines, involving as many as 90 different titles, are sold in thi country each month and read by upwards of 10 million people. Most retailer state that they do not know what is in the magazines they carry because they simply do not have the time to look into each one on a regular basis. Yet each year there are hundreds of police raids up and down the country which cause great embarrassment to the newsagents. Many of these magazines are caught by the provisions of the *Obscene Publications Act* which authorizes the search and forfeiture of material suspected as being obscene, this in turn can lead to an order for destruction or return of the material. Booksellers, of course, are subject to prosecution, although such magazines and books might even be on sale in local and respectable bookshops such as W. H. Smith, or in supermarkets like Tesco. In any case, we always come back to the same old problem – even if retailers thoroughly examine the publications they stock, how are they to decide what is obscene?

Prison sentences can be and are given for publication of obscene matter, although there is no longer any consensus view about what is and is not obscene. Justice Bridge (*R. v. Staniforth and Jordan*, 1976) put the point cogently in this way:

In *Knuller (Publishing, Printing and Promotions) Ltd.* v. *Director of Public Prosecutions* (1972), Lord Morris . . . said that Parliament, in assigning to the jury the task of deciding whether an article tends to deprave and corrupt, had doubtless done so with the knowledge that there is every likelihood that the collective view of a body of men and women on a jury will reflect the current view of society. The difficulty, which becomes ever increasingly apparent, is to know what is the current view of society. In times past there was probably a general consensus of opinion on the subject, but almost certainly there is none today. Not only in books and magazines, on sale at every bookstall and newsagent's shop, but on stage and screen as well, society appears to tolerate a degree of sexual candour which has already invaded a large area considered until recently to lie within the forbidden territory of the obscene. The jury's formidable task, with no other guidance than section 1 of the 1959 Act gives them (and that is precious little), is to determine where the line should be drawn. However conscientiously juries approach this responsibility, it is doubtful, in the present climate of opinion, whether their verdicts can be expected to maintain any reasonable degree of consistency.

adding to the difficulties faced by injuries in obscenity cases, especially as the demarcation line between what is and is not obscene in law becomes more obscure, the courts have, in a number of major decisions within the last few years, consistently reduced the scope and admissibility of expert evidence both on the primary issue of obscenity itself, and in relation to the *public good* defence set out in Section 4 of the 1959 Act. For example, ever since the case involving the *Director of Public Prosecutions* v. *Jordan* (1976), the courts have chosen to reject evidence which suggests that most sexually explicit material is harmless and that it has some therapeutic value for various individuals; consequently, public good defences are now limited to material with intrinsic merit such as literature or art. Many of these problems regarding the general law of obscenity were apparent to the Government in 1977 when they decided to set up the Home Office *Committee on Obscenity and Film Censorship* to take a broader view of the issue before bringing forth any new legislation. This Committee, under the chairmanship of Bernard Williams, was asked "to review the laws concerning obscenity, indecency and violence in publications, displays and entertainments in England and Wales, except in the field of broadcasting, and to review the arrangements for film censorship." In 1979, the Committee made a number of law reform proposals in its extensive report to the Government. But before looking into law reform proposals, we must examine the law itself and how it is applied. The aim of this chapter is to provide a brief overview of the *Obscene Publications Act* and other laws which attempt to regulate offensive publications in Britain, to discuss how the English experience differs from that of the American, and finally to point out some areas of possible reform.*

The Law Relating to Obscenity

Obscene Publications Act, 1959

1 (i). Test of obscenity
The complete statutory definition of obscenity is contained in Section 1 of this Act.

> For the purposes of this Act an article shall be deemed to be obscene if its effect or (where the article comprises two or more distinct items) the effect of any one of its items is, if taken as a whole, such as to tend to deprave and corrupt persons who are likely, having regard to all relevant circumstances, to read, see or hear the matter contained or embodied in it.

* Dhavan and Davies (1978) and Robertson (1979) provide excellent and in-depth discussions of the laws relating to obscenity and censorship.

This definition is derived from the judgement of Lord Chief Justice Cockburn in *R.* v. *Hicklin* (1868) in these words:

> I think the test of obscenity is this, whether the tendency of the matter charged as obscenity is to deprave and corrupt those whose minds are open to such immoral influences, and into whose hands a publication of this sort may fall.

The import of the *Hicklin* definition was that it could be applied to objectionable passages in great works of literature, science, education, art, or philosophy that might arouse sexual desire or challenge prevailing public morality. The fundamental change between this 1868 common law and the 1959 statutory definition was the inclusion of the concept "taken as a whole". This was specifically inserted in an endeavour to protect published works from being judged on the basis of isolated passages alone. However judicial interpretation of this "item-by-item" approach has contradicted the intention of the 1959 Act and caused great problems. For example, Parliament's intention that a book "taken as a whole" was expressly ignored in the 1971 prosecution of *The Little Red Schoolbook*, a 228-page instruction manual mainly concerned with educational issues. The prosecution's claim, upheld in the conviction of the book, was that one chapter of 23 pages dealing with sex, seriously infected the whole book with obscenity. The prosecution argument that, because the book had an itemized table of contents, readers would tend to select chapters which interested them rather than read the whole book from cover to cover. The words of Justice Stable in a passage from *R.* v. *Martin Secker and Warburg Limited* (1954) were ignored in this case:

> Is it really books that put ideas into young heads, or is it nature?

Despite the problem of context in which a work should be judged, the real issue is that no one knows exactly what "tend to deprave and corrupt" means. It has been interpreted and explained in different ways by different judges in different cases. It therefore fails to fulfil the fundamental principle that should be uppermost in criminal law, namely that the law should be certain; otherwise a publisher or bookseller is in danger of being tried, convicted and sent to prison when he does not know at the time of publication or sale that an offence has been committed. The court is not even permitted to seek guidance from the intention of the publisher, as the House of Lords decided that this is irrelevant and that a court should only look at the publication itself (*Shaw* v. *Director of Public Prosecutions*, 1961). The *Obscene Publications Act* is an exception to the general rule that criminal offences require a specific mental element, such as the intention to corrupt, and in this respect the 1959 Act is actually very precise. In *R.* v. *Calder and Boyars Ltd* (1969), Lord Justice Salmon indicated this as follows:

The intent with which the book was written was irrelevant. However pure or noble the intent may have been, if, in fact, the book taken as a whole tended to deprave and corrupt a significant proportion of those likely to read it, it was obscene within the meaning of that word in the Act of 1959.

This judgement, however, applies only to Section 1 of the Act. Under the *public good* defence of Section 4, the intention of the writer, publisher, or bookseller may be discussed and considered (see below).

The function of the 1959 statutory definition of obscenity was to enable juries to make a clear distinction between literature and pornography, and the House of Commons Select Committee hoped that this definition would help them to do this in the manner set forth by Justice Stable in *R. v. Martin Secker and Warburg Limited* (1954).

> Remember the charge is a charge that the tendency of the book is to corrupt and deprave. The charge is not that the tendency of the book is either to shock or to disgust. That is not a criminal offence. Then you say: 'Well, corrupt or deprave whom?' and again the test: those whose minds are open to such immoral influences and into whose hands a publication of this sort may fall. What exactly does that mean? Are we to take our literary standards as being the level of something that is suitable for a fourteen-year-old schoolgirl? Or do we go even further back than that, and are we to be reduced to the sort of books that one reads as a child in the nursery? The answer to that is: Of course not. A mass of literature, great literature from many angles is wholly unsuitable for reading by the adolescent, but that does not mean that the publisher is guilty of a criminal offence for making those works available to the general public.

In the case of *Lady Chatterley's Lover* (*R. v. Penguin Books Limited*, 1961), Justice Byrne tried to help the jury by emphasizing that the Select Committee wanted "a tendency to deprave and corrupt" to mean more than "a tendency to shock and disgust" by issuing this introduction: "the mere fact that you are shocked or disgusted, the mere fact that you hate the sight of the book when you have read it, does not solve the question as to whether you are satisfied beyond reasonable doubt that the tendency of the book is to deprave or corrupt". He rejected, however, the defence counsel's contention that the definition of obscenity *necessitated* proof of verifiable harm in some behavioural sense. Instead, he sought to clarify the words "deprave and corrupt" so that the jury would understand that the law was primarily concerned with harm, irrespective of its nature. Unfortunately, in adopting the *Oxford English Dictionary's* definitions of deprave and corrupt, Justice Byrne reinforced the tendency of judges to attach their own meanings to these words when instructing the jury in regard to obscenity.

In the *Oz* case (*R. v. Anderson*, 1971), a trial involving a magazine of the underground press, one of the grounds of appeal leading to the quashing of the conviction for obscenity in the Court of Appeal was that the judge had not only misdirected the jury on the meaning of the words "tend to deprave and

corrupt", but that he was in danger of leading the jury to believe that the wo
"obscene", for the purposes of the 1959 Act, included in its meaning "repu
sive, filthy, loathsome, or lewd." Similarly, in the *Last Exit to Brooklyn* ca
(*R. v. Calder and Boyars Limited*, 1968), another conviction was thrown o
by the Court of Appeal because of a misdirection on this definition whi
might have led the jury to mistake revulsion for corruption. The court had
consider Hubert Selby's book which provides a graphic description of th
depths of depravity and degradation of life in Brooklyn, but the description
compassionate and condemnatory in nature. On this basis, the defen
counsel contended that its effects would be limited to horror, revulsion, ar
pity, and that instead of tending to encourage anyone toward homosexuali
or drug-taking, it would have precisely the opposite effect. In the appeal th
court confirmed that the essence of the matter is *moral corruption*, no
aversion, and added the warning that "when, as here, a statute lays down th
definition of a word or phrase in plain English, it is rarely necessary and ofte
unwise for the judge to attempt to improve upon or redefine the definition"
Later courts have not only failed to take this advice, but have studiousl
ignored admitting evidence from experts who would be able to identify an
throw light on difficult words, phrases and concepts.

A further attempt was made to elucidate the meaning of the words "t
deprave and corrupt" in the case of the *DPP v. Whyte* (1972). This cas
involved some booksellers in Southampton who were selling "har
pornography". The Magistrate's Court, where the case was first heard
discovered that the regular customers, principally men of middle-age an
upwards, were average people who engaged in private fantasies, but not i
any overt or harmful sexual activities or behaviour. The defence argued tha
evidence of antisocial behaviour was required to establish the presence o
depravity and corruption under the 1959 Act. But when the case reached th
House of Lords, they rejected this argument and held that the words "deprav
and corrupt" refer to the effect of pornographic articles on the *mind*, includ
ing the emotions, and it was not necessary that any physical or overt sexua
activity should result. In this case the House of Lords did not rule that al
books which stimulate sexual fantasies are obscene; instead they merel
rejected the opinion that depravity and corruption are linked to the commission of antisocial behaviour. Depravity may be all in the mind, without ever
causing such behaviour. Unfortunately, this leaves the jury to determine
whether, in the circumstances of the particular case, sexually explicit materia
may cause social, moral, psychological or spiritual harm.

1(ii). Obscenity not limited to sexual matters

The *Obscene Publications Act* has also been used to prosecute books and
magazines which are very different from those originally contemplated by the

gislature. In addition to books and magazines catering for popular tastes,
x education material, and counter-culture magazines like *Oz* and *Inter-
ational Times*, the Act has been judicially extended to material not involving
xual matters at all. *Last Exit to Brooklyn (R. v. Calder and Boyars Limited,
068)*, described above, and *Cain's Book*, a serious work about drug addic-
on (R. v. *John Calders Publishers Limited*, 1965), were also held to be
ithin the scope of this Act.

(iii). Inadmissability of expert evidence

jury, as mentioned above, must decide whether or not an article is obscene
.e. whether the material tends to deprave and corrupt) without the aid of
xpert evidence. This is one of the greatest defects in the 1959 Act. One
xception to this rule was permitted by the Divisional Court in *DPP v. A. and
.C. Chewing Gum Limited*(1968), where testimony by child psychiatrists
oncerning the effects of violent scenes, depicted on the inside covers of
ubble gum packets, on young children was held to be admissible. The Court
f Appeal said that expert evidence was allowable only in very special
ircumstances, such as in cases where the likely readers are a special class and
here the jury cannot be expected, without assistance, to understand the
kely impact of the material upon its members. Apart from this exception, the
ourt has said on many occasions, with blatant disregard for world-wide
esearch and practice, that the opinion of an expert is inadmissible in cases
here jury members can form their own conclusions without assistance (R. v.
nderson, 1971, above; R. v. *Turner*, 1975).

(iv). The significant proportion test

he *Obscene Publications Act* fails to provide any guidance to the jury on the
ifficult question as to how many persons must be corrupted by reading,
earing, or seeing a particular work before it can be judged obscene. Clearly
he Act cannot mean all persons; nor can it mean any one person, for there are
ndividuals who may be corrupted by almost anything. In the *Last Exit to
Brooklyn* case (R. v. *Calder and Boyars Limited*, 1968, above), the Court of
Appeal established that the issue was whether the book was likely to deprave
nd corrupt a significant proportion of the possible readership. Who are the
ikely readers, and what is a significant proportion is a matter entirely for the
ury to decide. The test has been applied at obscenity trials ever since. It
rotects the defendant in that it prevents the jury from speculating on the
ossible effect of "offensive" material upon an isolated individual or even the
verage person; nor does it require the prosecution to prove that a majority of
eaders would be adversely affected.

2. *Who is prosecuted?*

An offence under the 1959 Act requires some act of publication, such as sale to a customer or giving an obscene book to a friend. Commercial gain irrelevant to the 1959 Act, as it specifically refers to anyone who, *whether for gain or not*, publishes an obscene article. The definition of publication in the 1959 Act was found wanting, and a 1964 Amending Act added the concept of "possession for gain". Gain is a prerequisite for prosecution under the 1964 Act, which widens the extent of the law by penalizing those individuals who *possess* an obscene article and have the intention of publishing it for gain. Not only publishers and booksellers, but even printers, taxi drivers, and transport firms engaged in delivering material without any knowledge of the content have all been prosecuted – even a professional "shrink wrapper" manufacturer. In *R. v. Peter Gregory* (1977), the defendant was in possession of magazines for the sole purpose of wrapping them in cellophane so that they could not accidently be thumbed by unsuspecting purchasers! One would have thought that he would have been congratulated on this venture rather than prosecuted, and fortunately the case was dismissed.

3. *Films*

Film exhibitions were formerly proceeded against under the ancient common law offence of "disorderly house" because the *Obscene Publications Act* provided an exemption for commercial cinema, as well as for television and broadcasting. This exemption was subsequently repealed by the 1977 *Criminal Law Act*. The law regarding films is, however, governed by different procedures for different widths of films. The consent of the Director of Public Prosecutions is required for all prosecution cases involving films of a width of 16 mm or more. The Government was advised that cinema clubs and publicly licensed cinemas normally use such films and, therefore, will enjoy this safeguard, but the 8 mm films, which are available as home movies, will still be vulnerable to private prosecution and police action without the DPP's consent. Broadcasting is still exempt from the new Act.

4. *Prosecution v. Destruction orders*

There is an important difference between the provisions of Sections 2 and 3 of the 1959 *Obscene Publications Act*. Section 2 provides for criminal prosecution by either magistrate or jury. Section 3, however, provides only for the destruction of the obscene material, and consequently the defendant has no right to elect a trial by jury. In addition, as it is not a prosecution which would lead to a criminal record on conviction, no legal aid is available for his defence. Accordingly, a small shopkeeper may be subjected to the injustice of having valuable stock seized and not being able to afford to contest its return. It is totally illogical that prosecuting authorities may make an arbitrary

-cision as to whether to prosecute under Section 2, or seek a destruction rder under Section 3. Under the latter, the defendant may even be tried by ie same magistrates who ordered the issue of the search warrant in the first lace. Unfortunately, Magistrates Courts are usually unable to give such roceedings the full and careful attention that the same case would receive efore a jury. The Attorney General, in fact, made it clear during the passage f the 1964 *Obscene Publications Act* that a reputable publisher should have ie right to have the issue of obscenity determined by a jury rather than by 1agistrates. But it is now clear that the Attorney-General's comments are eing ignored both by the Director of Public Prosecutions and by prosecuting uthorities up and down the country, specifically, it seems, to avoid jury rials.

. Defences

) *The aversion theory.* This theory emerged as a defence in the *Last Exit to 3rooklyn* trial (R. v. *Calder and Boyars Limited*, 1968, above). The defence ounsel argued that some of the graphic descriptions of life "in the raw" in 3rooklyn were so unpleasant that, far from tending to deprave and corrupt, eading the passages would have, in fact, the opposite effect. The Court of \ppeal agreed that the trial judge misdirected the jury so badly on the defence :ontention here that the conviction of the book for obscenity should be Juashed. The aversion argument arose again in the *Oz* case (R. v. *Anderson*, 1971) where a similar misdirection by the trial judge led to the conviction for >bscenity being quashed by the Court of Appeal. The Lord Chief Justice, iccepting that the aversion theory could be a complete defence under Section l of the *Obscene Publications Act*, put the matter this way:

> Many of the illustrations in *Oz* were so grossly lewd and unpleasant that they would shock in the first instance and then would tend to repel. In other words, it was said that they had an aversive effect and that, far from tempting those who had not experienced the acts to take part in them, they would put off those who might be tempted so to conduct themselves . . . the learned trial judge never really got over to the jury this argument of aversion, in other words, never put over to the jury that the proposition central to the defence case was that certain illustrations could be so disgusting and filthy that they would not corrupt and deprave but rather would tend to cause people to revolt from activity of that kind.

(ii) Comparing books and the climate of literature. A serious defect in the law is that a defendant may not argue that he should be acquitted because his publication is less obscene than others which are freely circulated. He is, in essence, denied the privilege of being able to refer to other books, which have not been the subject of charges, in determining whether or not his book is obscene. Similarly juries, in considering the question of obscenity, are not

allowed to hear evidence about other publications, at least when it is intr
duced for the purpose of comparison. In the case of *R.* v. *Reiter* (1954), t
Court of Appeal specifically ruled out the prospect of comparing other book
similar in character, to the publication on trial, thereby adopting the reaso
ing of the High Court of Justiciary in *Galletly* v. *Laird* (1953):

> the character of the offending books or pictures should be ascertained by the
> only method by which such a fact can be ascertained, viz., by reading the books
> or looking at the pictures. The book or picture itself provides the best evidence
> of its own indecency or obscenity or of the absence of such qualities. . . . The
> character of other books is a collateral issue, the exploration of which would be
> endless and futile.

If there are several million readers of fairly similar books and magazines ever
month, for one to be selected as being obscene and subjected to a trial, when
cannot be separated from other books and other influences to which th
public are subjected, is surely ridiculous. However, in the case of *Lad*
Chatterley's Lover (*R.* v. *Penguin Books*, 1961), Justice Byrne permitte
expert witnesses to compare this work to the twentieth-century writers fo
two reasons: first, because the literary merit of the book had been questioned
and secondly, because other books were necessary to help establish "th
climate of literature". This ruling is applicable only where a defence o
"public good" is raised, but there have been times when judges have simpl
dismissed this defence as being irrelevant to the setting of general standards.

(iii) Failure to examine the article. This defence was originally provided b
Section 2 (5) of the 1959 *Obscene Publications Act* and was subsequently
re-enacted in Section 1 (3) of the 1964 Act. It simply reads as follows:

> A person shall not be convicted of an offence . . . if he proves that he had not
> examined the article in respect of which he is charged and had no reasonable
> cause to suspect that it was such that his publication of it would make him liable
> to be convicted of an offence.

This provides some protection for innocent handlers of books and magazines,
but it is not very helpful in practice.

(iv) The public good defence. The *Obscene Publications Act* also provides
for the following defence under Section 4.

> A person shall not be convicted of an offence . . . if it is proved that publication of
> the article in question is justified as being for the public good on the ground that
> it is in the interests of science, literature, art or learning, or of other subjects of
> general concern . . . the opinion of experts as to the literary, artistic, scientific or
> other merits of an article may be admitted in any proceedings under this Act
> either to establish or to negate the said ground.

The public good defence for films, however, created by the amendment of the
Criminal Law Act of 1977, is more narrowly defined than that which applies

books and magazines. The *Criminal Law Act* amends Section 4 of the *Obscene Publications Act* with respect to films; it reads like this:

A person shall not be convicted of an offence . . . if it is proved that publication of the film or sound track is justified as being for the public good on the grounds that it is in the interests of drama, opera, ballet or any other art, or of literature or learning.

The scope of this decision was considered by the House of Lords in *DPP v. Jordan*, 1976. Mrs Jordan was a bookshop proprietor who sold publications that were clearly of the character of hard pornography. The police seized a number of files, books, and magazines from her shop which had been freely available and on sale to the public. There was, of course, no evidence to suggest that these publications had any literary, scientific or artistic merit. The defence sought to call upon the expert evidence of a forensic psychologist, and the object of his evidence was to establish that publication of the relevant material was justified as being for the public good on the grounds that it was in the interests of "other objects of general concern". The statement of what he would have said in evidence was summarized by Lord Justice Bridge in the Court of Appeal as follows:

He would have said, if called, that every variety of pornographic material before the court has some psycho-therapeutic value for various kinds of persons, e.g. for persons of heterosexual taste unable to achieve satisfactory heterosexual relationships, for persons of deviant sexuality, and for homosexuals and other perverts, as providing, according to their several needs, appropriate material to relieve their sexual tensions by way of sexual fantasy and masturbation . . . that such relief was beneficial to such persons and that it would act as a safety valve to save them from psychological disorders and to divert them from anti-social and possible criminal activities against others.

The Trial Judge, the Court of Appeal and the House of Lords were unanimous in rejecting this evidence. The House of Lords' view was, that "or of other objects of general concern" had to come within the same category as the words preceding them in the statute "science, literature, art or learning". The wider view expressed, however, was that if this evidence were accepted, it would make nonsense of the whole Act, because it could be used to negate any allegation of obscenity.

(v) Learning. The word "learning" in Section 4, mentioned above, has been further restricted by the Court of Appeal. In the *Attorney General's Reference* of 1977 (Number 3), the court decided that learning means scholarship. The defence had sought to argue that learning meant education in the broadest sense, and that the section had always been interpreted in a wide sense previously, but this argument was not accepted. This means that popular sexual education books and magazines are still in danger of being prosecuted.

Other Major Statutory Provisions

Theatres Act, 1968

This Private Member's measure repealed the *Theatres Act* of 1843 and abolished the Lord Chamberlain's censorship power over plays. The new Act makes theatrical performances subject instead to criminal law, largely on the pattern of the *Obscene Publications Act*. Obscenity is defined by the expression "tend to deprave and corrupt" and there is a *public good* defence, but additionally, there is provision for proceedings to be brought for incitement to racial hatred, or for provocation of a breach of the peace. Proceedings may only be brought with the consent of the Attorney General.

Children and Young Persons (Harmful Publications) Act, 1955

This Act came into force mainly due to a campaign, conducted primarily by the National Union of Teachers, against the availability of horror comics, particularly those depicting acts of violence or cruelty. The then Home Secretary told Parliament that the reason the Act was necessary was because the law of obscenity (at that time the common law) was restricted only to sexual matters. In fact, subsequent cases have shown that this is not the case and, accordingly, the Act has very rarely been used. Recently, however, it has again been used at the request of the Customs and Excise authorities, in conjunction with the *Customs and Excise Acts*, to seek to exclude horror comics, designed mainly for adults, from import to Britain (see below).

Customs and Excise Legislation

The *Customs Acts* incorporate the provisions of the above *Children's Act*, but do not incorporate the provisions of the *Obscene Publications Acts*. This, unfortunately, causes a regrettable inconsistency in that the test of obscenity for articles sought to be brought into the country is wholly different from that which would apply if they were on sale within the country. The test under the *Customs Acts* are the words "indecent or obscene". These are not defined, but in the case of *R. v. Stanley* (1965) it was suggested that this meant articles which "offended against the recognized standards of propriety, indecency at the lower end of the scale and obscene at the upper end". The prosecution has the right either to request a trial or to seek forfeiture but, as in the *Obscene Publications Acts*, the defendant has no right to claim trial by jury when forfeiture alone is sought.

Post Office Act, 1953

Under this Act it is a criminal offence to send any "indecent or obscene" article through the post. The meaning of indecent or obscene is interpreted in the same way as in the *Customs Acts* above. Again, there is a regrettable difference between the test under the Obscene Publications Acts when the book or article is sold on public sale, and an entirely different test, with no right to jury trial, when that same article is sent through the post. This Act is widely used even when articles have been sent to a willing recipient who has paid for the items in question or similar previous items.

Unsolicited Goods and Services Act, 1971

This Act makes it a criminal offence for a person to "send or cause to be sent to another person any book, magazine or leaflet (or advertising material for any such publications) which he knows or ought reasonably to know is unsolicited and which describes or illustrates human sexual techniques". Prosecutions can only be instituted by or under the authority of The Director of Public Prosecutions.

Protection of Children Act, 1978

This legislation was passed as the result of a general election scare coupled with a campaign against child pornography. Most of the provisions of this Act were already covered by existing legislation, but the one new matter was a statutory provision precluding the use of children, in this Act anyone under the age of 16, in the production of indecent or obscene material.

Indecent Displays (Control) Act, 1981

Under this new Act, the public display of allegedly "indecent material" is controlled. This legislation repeals the *Vagrancy Act* of 1824 and all other subsequent enactments dealing with public displays and advertisements. There is, unfortunately, no new definition of "indecent" and therefore there is still much uncertainty as to what precisely falls within the ambit of the new Act. However, the impact of this legislation has already been acknowledged in that shop window displays and front covers of magazines have become significantly less explicit. To that extent, in relation to public nuisance,

ordinary pedestrians should now be less likely to take offence. The Ac
however, does not cover any "indecent" display that is invisible from th
street, provided of course that there is a warning notice properly positione
(in the statutory form) at the entrance to the interior to the shop. The new A
gives the right of jury trial which was not available under the *Vagrancy Act*. I
addition, at the time of writing this chapter, there is new legislation goin
through which introduces the concept of local licensing for shops specializin
in the sale of sexual material, and a separate Act for private cinema clubs tha
show adult films.

Director of Public Prosecutions

One might easily assume that the Director of Public Prosecutions and th
police share the same basic attitude towards prosecutions involving sexua
material. Unfortunately this does not always appear to be the case. Unde
the *Obscene Publications Act*, the Director of Public Prosecutions mus
authorize all obscenity prosecutions; however, he need not be consulted i
relation to other prosecutions which can be brought in relation to sexua
material. The police have a right to make charges as well and, in some cases, i
is believed that they take action and propose alternative one's when the
cannot gain the consent of the Director of Public Prosecutions for an obscen
ity prosecution. The internal workings of the DPP's office is, of course,
well-kept secret, and it is difficult to find out the manner in which th
discretion to prosecute is exercised. In fact, a substantial amount of th
judicial confusion over obscenity appears to have filtered down into thi
department. One suspects that the decision to prosecute may well depen
upon which particular staff officer handles the request for prosecution. Ther
are a number of people involved in this department who spend a considerabl
amount of time reading allegedly obscene material which is sent in by polic
forces all around the country, by individual citizens, by pressure groups, an
by members of Parliament on behalf of their constituents who object an
complain about sexual materials. A substantial amount of material which i
accompanied by a request for prosecution is rejected; in some cases, differen
members of the department are unable to agree as to whether a prosecutio
should be brought. Indeed, arbitrary decisions often seem to be made regard
ing whether material which has been seized will actually be prosecuted, o
merely destroyed. Bearing in mind that any action under the *Obscene Publications Act* means many months of delay (and many months of stock being
tied up) before a decision is reached, is it any wonder that the industry dealing
with adult publications sometimes suspects that the intention of the DPP's
office is basically to try and put the accused person out of business, rathe
than to seek a ruling on the material that he may be selling. There is,

moreover, an enormous disparity in regard to both the frequency of police action and the manner in which prosecutions are handled in different parts of the country. It is clearly unfair and unjust that the attitude of the police and the likelihood of Court action depend upon which particular part of the country in which you may live or trade.

Proposals for Reform

The emergence of problems of the kind mentioned above led to the establishment of the Home Office *Committee on Obscenity and Film Censorship* in 1977, and also to the creation of the *British Adult Publications Association Limited* by publishers, wholesalers, distributors and retailers of adult magazines in the same year. The aim of the association was to keep publications within acceptable limits and within the law since it took the view that a certain amount of self-regulation was necessary both in the interests of the trade and the public. Accordingly, the organization developed a kind of pre-censorship system in the case of the magazines, similar to that which has existed for the film industry, in the shape of the *British Board of Film Censors.** This system was active for about two years, but now the publishers of adult magazines have reverted to informal self-regulation as they are currently able to reach a consensus on standards within the industry; some, however, think that their current guidelines are far too low.

English obscenity law, as we have seen, is unsatisfactory because of the vagueness and uncertainty of its definitions. Therefore, in their final report, the *Committee on Obscenity and Film Censorship* (1979) attempted to make proposals for reform in this area which could be translated into rational and effective legislation. This is obviously important and I have tried to frame my own proposals (some of which overlap with those of the Committee) in this way. Some of the more important reforms that are urgently necessary are as follows:

(1) There should only be *one* test of obscenity under all Acts of Parliament, and not the variety of criteria that exist today in different statutes.

(2) The concept of "deprave and corrupt" is extremely vague and impracticable and, therefore, should be abandoned as it is liable to lead to injustice.

(3) The law regulating sexual material should be based in part on a definition of *harms* which may be caused by exposure to such matter. This

* Contrary to widespread belief, the *British Board of Film Censors* is not a statutory body, but was set up by the film industry and, although its recommendations are almost universally accepted, it does not have the force of law.

definition should be specific and easily comprehensible to a jury. The prosecution should have to prove that an article had done or would do "substantial harm".

(4) The law should also be based partly on the basis of the public's right not to be offended by the display of sexual materials. Restrictions designed to protect the ordinary citizen from unreasonable offence have, in fact, recently been passed.

(5) Some consistency should be brought into the institution of proceedings by making it a requirement that no obscenity prosecution be brought without the leave of the Director of Public Prosecutions.

(6) All common law offences relating to obscenity should be abolished.

(7) The *item-by-item* test should be abolished in relation to magazines; instead, they should be judged, like books as a whole. The reason is simply that all publications should be evaluated on the same basis.

(8) Although the courts have ruled that the intention of the author or publisher is irrelevant for judging whether or not a publication is obscene, this is *not* in line with criminal law in other areas. It has always been a fundamental principle of English criminal law that a person cannot be guilty of an offence unless he *knows* that he is committing an offence at the time. The law governing obscene publications should be brought into line with other criminal offences.

(9) The distinction between forfeiture proceedings and prosecutions under Section 2 of the *Obscene Publications Act* should be ended, in that there should be a right of jury trial in both cases.

(10) Expert evidence, including research evidence on the effects of exposure to sexual material, should be allowed to be considered in respect to the public good defence.

These and other reforms were considered by the *Committee on Obscenity and Film Censorship* which reported to the Government in November, 1979. Unfortunately, the Government decided to reject the findings of the Committee and its proposals for reform. It is a pity that this very sensible attempt to replace the existing chaos with some rational laws was not more favourably received in Parliament.

Obscenity, Pornography and the Law

Pornography clearly presents a problem for society. Invariably it offends someone who complains to the police or some other representative of society. The police, in turn, investigate the complaint and often apply to the courts for warrant to search for and seize the offensive material. The evidence is then examined by the office of the *Director of Public Prosecutions* which decides whether or not to prosecute according to the criminal law, to simply apply for a civil forfeiture, or to return the material. Whatever the outcome, some action of society is always disappointed. Society is not of one mind in regards to the possession, use, or display of sexually explicit materials and it is never likely to be. To expect a single, clear-cut answer to this problem is unrealistic. And certainly the belief that the criminal process can, in its present form, be relied upon to make appropriate pronouncements on the obscenity of a book, magazine, film or play is not justified. Recent jury decisions have clearly demonstrated that the average man and woman are confused by definitions which involve expressions like "tending to deprave and corrupt" and find it difficult to reach decisions in an area in which even experts disagree. If there are going to be any criminal prohibitions against the publication of "obscene" material, then it is clearly important to make the definition of obscenity more *objective*; at present it is much too subjective to be workable. English obscenity law, as Robertson (1979) points out, may be illogical in theory, uncertain in scope, and unworkable in operation, but very few nations have come up with a better solution. This, of course, is *not* a reason for maintaining our present system. It only emphasizes that we must find our own solution to this problem. Hopefully society's lack of agreement as to whether and to what extent pornography should be proscribed will be acknowledged by the creation of a law which respects both liberal and conservative viewpoints. A legal solution to obscenity is, at best, a compromise which will not satisfy everyone. But, then, no one side is likely to be completely satisfied in any event.

Where should the law draw the line? In the United States the Supreme Court has had no more success with the problem of obscenity and its regulations than we have. In *Miller* v. *California* (1973), for example, the guidelines set down by the court proved to be so confusing that very few obscenity convictions were upheld on appeal. Their test of obscenity rests on the following guidelines: (1) whether "the average person, applying contemporary community standards", would find that the work, taken as a whole, appeals to the prurient interest; (2) whether the work depicts or describes, in a patently offensive way, sexual conduct specifically defined by the applicable State law; and (3) whether the work, taken as a whole, lacks serious literary, artistic, political or scientific value. In this definition we see some new words, some old words, but the same old intractable problems. And the same old problem for the jury. Thus, after deciding that the average person applying average community standards would find that a work appeals to prurient interests in a patently offensive way, the jury must still decide whether or not serious literary or scientific merit balances this out. Indefinite concepts like "prurient interest", "patent offensiveness" and "serious literary value" seem to offer no better resolution to obscenity issues than our own "tendency to deprave and corrupt."

Davies (1979) points out an interesting similarity between the British and American attempts to reform the laws relating to censorship and reform on issues such as abortion and capital punishment; over time both Members of Parliament and Congress have shifted their style of argument from what he terms *moralism* to *causalism*. Moralist grounds, he argues, were used in the past to decide whether to allow or prohibit a particular action. For example, individuals in favour of restricting or prohibiting some activity would argue that it was wrong or wicked in itself and that this was quite sufficient reason for imposing a ban on it. Those in favour of the said activity would, using the same moralistic reasoning, appeal to some equally absolute value such as freedom of expression, etc. Yet today, he argues, such debates are conducted in terms of the relative consequences of allowing or prohibiting particular forms of activity:

> Indeed in order to find the clearest instances of such a change in the case of censorship it is necessary to take an American example. The main evidence that there has been some shift from one kind of attitude to the other in America is the sheer amount of expensive research that has been done there to try to test and measure the effects of, say, pornographic literature or television violence on the behaviour of their consumers. Only people wishing to provide answers to essentially causalist questions would finance research on such issues as 'Does television violence cause viewers to behave aggressively?' or 'Does the wider dissemination of pornography lead to more or fewer sex crimes?' Millions of dollars have been spent in several countries by the American Commission on Obscenity and Pornography and the Surgeon General's Committee on the effects of television violence to try and provide answers to these questions. As a result the causalists have, for the first time, data they can use in argument and we can expect an acceleration of the spiral.

The general shift in the direction of causalism is detectable on both sides of the Atlantic, but the change is much more complete in America. There the crucial question is "What is the effect of exposure to sexually explicit material on behaviour?" This is, in fact, the dominant mode of argument in the behavioural sciences world-wide, and researchers agree to disagree only on causalist grounds. But, whereas the majority report of the *Commission on Obscenity and Pornography* (1970) claimed that pornography had no ill-effects and possibly had some beneficial ones on causal grounds, the minority report of Commissioner Keating argued on moral grounds that pornography is wicked in itself:

> Such presumption! Such an advocacy of moral anarchy! Such a defiance of the mandate of the Congress which created the Commission! Such a bold advocacy of a libertine philosophy! Truly it is difficult to believe that to which the

majority of this Commission has given birth . . . [it] does not reflect the will of Congress, the opinion of law enforcement officials throughout our country and worst of all flouts the underlying opinions and desires of the great mass of the American people.

Other Commissioners disagreed with the majority report on causalist grounds, i.e. they questioned the conclusion that pornography is essentially harmless on the basis of fact and procedure; today, however, one suspects that those in favour of censorship of pornography are aware that causal, not moral, arguments carry greater weight. Moralists, by refusing to publicly endorse statements like pornography is wicked in itself, probably influence opinion more effectively now when they proclaim that it causes its readers to behave in criminal or antisocial ways. And certainly causal assertions are more fashionable today. In 1959, for example, Mr Simon, the Joint Under-Secretary of State for the Home Office stated in the debate on the Obscene Publications Bill that "I do not suppose that anyone would deny that such (pornographic) works are inherently liable to cause mischief." Today we find a slightly different emphasis. Lord Lane, the Lord Chief Justice, indicated the following in his 1982 maiden speech in the House of Lords:

> One would only have to sit a short time in [my] court . . . to realize the *imitative effect* [my emphasis] of the huge increase in the sale of pornography. Because of the rarification and recondite type of sexual behaviour which now accompanied crime, crime was almost inevitable. It is traceable to glossy imports which come into the country, disguised as Danish bacon or Dutch tomatoes, in large quantities which percolate through various shops to find their way into the hands of young people with inevitable serious results which we see increasing every day. (*The Times*, 25 March 1982.)

Ultimately, the dilemmas involved in the legal control of pornography cannot be understood or resolved without consideration of the moral, social, and political philosophy of each country. Such an assertion, of course, raises the question of whether the problems of sex in society can ever be objectively considered. If the circulation of obscenity is to be controlled at all, then framing a law to do this in a clear, consistent and above all workable manner requires serious political judgement in the broadest and deepest sense. Obviously, in making such judgements, there are many ways to disagree and to fall short of expectation. Is it any wonder, then, that obscenity remains the subject of unresolved controversy in this and in other countries?

References

Attorney General Reference (1978) 3 All E.R. 753.
Commission on Obscenity and Pornography. In *Report of the Commission on Obscenity and Pornography*. New York: Bantam Books, 1970.

Committee on Obscenity and Film Censorship. In *Report on the Committee on Obscenity and Film Censorship*. (Chairman: B. Williams). London: Her Majesty's Stationery Office, 1979.

Davies, C. How our rulers argue about censorship. In R. Dhavan and C. Davies (Eds). *Censorship and Obscenity*. London: Martin Robertson, 1978.

Dhavan, R. and Davies, C. (Eds). *Censorship and Obscenity*. London: Martin Robertson, 1978.

Director of Public Prosecutions v. A. and B.C. Chewing Gum Ltd (1968) 1 O.B. 159; (1967) 2 All E.R. 504.

Director of Public Prosecutions v. Jordan (1977) A.C. 699; (1976) 3 All E.R. 775.

Director of Public Prosecutions v. Whyte (1972) 3 All E.R. 12.

Galletly v. Laird (1953) S.L.T. 67.

Knuller (Publishing, Printing and Promotions) Ltd. v. Director of Public Prosecutions (1972) 2 All E.R. 898.

Miller v. California (1973) 413 U.S. 15.

R. v. Anderson (1971) 3 All E.R. 586.

R. v. Calder and Boyars Ltd (1968) 3 All E.R. 644.

R. v. Hicklin (1868) L.R. 3 Q.B. 360.

R. v. John Calders Publishers Ltd (1965) 1 All E.R. 159.

R. v. Martin Secker and Warburg Ltd (1954) 2 All E.R. 683.

R. v. Penguin Books Ltd (1961) Crim. L.R. 176.

R. v. Peter Gregory (1977) Inner London Crown Court – Unreported.

R. v. Reiter (1954) 1 All E.R. 741.

R. v. Staniforth and Jordan (1976) 3 W.L.R. 887.

R. v. Stanley (1965) 1 All E.R. 1035.

R. v. Turner (1975) 1 All E.R. 70.

Robertson, G. *Obscenity: An Account of Censorship Laws and their Enforcement in England and Wales*. London: Weidenfeld and Nicolson, 1979.

Shaw v. Director of Public Prosecutions (1961) 2 All E.R. 446.

Subject index

aggressive behaviour increased by
   violence in, 192–210, 222–237
desensitization to violence in,
   203–210, 218, 234
escalation of violence in, 7, 190–192
   205–206, 223
laws regulating, in Britain, 256
therapeutic uses of, sexually explicit,
   119–143
in sex education, 65–78
First Days of Life, The, 75–76
Flagellation, 3, 7, 10
Flashers, *see* Exhibitionists
Flooding, 187
Forum, 54, 157–158
Freud, Sigmund, 5, 188
Fuseli, H., 87

G
Gale is Dead, 78
Galletly v. Laird, 258
Genesis, 156
Genetic factors
   and aggression, 11–15
   and homosexuality, 11–12
   and personality, 229–232
George III, 152, 157
Getaway, The, 209
Gone with the Wind, 78

H
Harleth, Gwendolen, 40
Harms
   from pornography, 34–44, 174,
   196–210, 222–236
   from smoking, 38
Harunobu, fantasy of, 84
Heart of Life, The, 76
Heilbron Report, The, 223–224
Henry VIII, 13
Heredity, *see* Genetic factors
Hockney, David, 88
Hofstadter, Richard, 45
Holbrook, David, 40, 52, 56, 63
Homosexuality, 3, 9–10
   in Ancient Greece, 3, 13
   exclusive, 10, 12, 16
   facultative, 16
   genetic component in, 11–12
   and pornography, 16

and response to sexual material,
   108–109, 219, 221
Hooper, 210
How Life Begins, 65

I
Imitation, *see* Modelling
Immorality, of certain acts, 33
Impoverishment effect, of pornography,
   37, 40–41
Imprinting effect, of pornography,
   37–39
Incest, 9
Indecent Displays (Control) Act, 261
Indecent Exposure, *see* Exhibitionism
Indecent Publications Act, 166–167
Individual differences, in response to
   sexual material, *see under*
   pornography
Inhibition, *see* Disinhibition
International Times, 53, 225
Introducing Living Things, 67
ITV, 71, 73

J
Jones, Allen, 88

K
Kama Sutra, 2
Kinsey, Alfred
   and female sexuality, research on,
   92–95, 98–99, 105–106
Kissinger, Henry, 13
*Knuller (Publishing, Printing and
   Promotions) Ltd
   v. Director of Public Prosecutions*, 250
Kraft-Ebing, R. von, 157

L
Lady Chatterly's Lover, 154, 253, 258
Last Exit to Brooklyn, 165, 254, 255,
   257
Lawrence, D. H., 39, 48, 52, 63, 83
Ledakant, 86
Lesbianism, 5, 10
Lindner, Richard, 88
Literature, climate of, 257–258
Little Red Schoolbook, The, 252
Living and Growing, 67, 75
Loneliness, 68–69
Longford Committee, 52, 171, 182